DR. JUDD

hawaii's friend

A biography of Gerrit Parmele Judd (1803–1873)

GERRIT P. JUDD IV

UNIVERSITY OF HAWAII PRESS • HONOLULU • 1960

Preface

Dr. Judd was a hard-minded Yankee puritan, thrust by circumstance and his own convictions into a turbulent, semi-tropical frontier. The Calvinist moral standards which he cherished and tried to enforce brought him into sharp conflict with the growing secularism of the age. By temperament resourceful, stubborn, and blunt, he evoked hero worship from his supporters and blind rage from his adversaries. For much of his life he was the central figure in a sea of controversy, at the same time admired and abused. It would serve little purpose for his biographer to enter the still-raging debate whether the missionaries, including Dr. Judd, were helpful or harmful people. Such questions may be left to tractarians and propagandists. This book presents facts, as they survive in available sources, and leaves it to the reader to form his own conclusions.

I am particularly indebted to Professor Ralph S. Kuykendall of the University of Hawaii and to Miss Bernice Judd of the Hawaiian Mission Children's Society, not only for their skilled advice, but also for their help in leading me to important source materials which otherwise I would have missed. Invaluable assistance was also rendered by staff members of the Archives of Hawaii, Library of Congress, New York Historical Society, New York Public Library, University of Hawaii Library, U.S. National Archives, and Yale University Library. A grant from Hofstra College provided stenographic and other assistance in the final stages of the research.

The following persons gave freely of their time and knowledge, and to each I extend my profound thanks: Mr. Kenneth W. Barr, Miss Janet Bell, Miss Agnes Conrad, Mrs. Emma Doyle, Mr. Meiric K. Dutton, Mrs. Willowdean C. Handy, Mr. and Mrs. Gerrit P. Judd III, Mr. Alfons L. Korn, Miss Marion Morse, Dr. Thomas D. Murphy, and Miss Margaret Titcomb, of Honolulu; Dr. Robert Davison, Dr. Myron Luke, and Dr. John Marcus, of Hofstra College; Mr. Lawrence Brice and Dr. Charles Ordman, of Washington, D.C.; Mrs. Dorothy W. Brown, Miss Alice C. Dodge, and Mr. Clifford W. Wells, of Utica, New York; Mrs. Anna Z. Jenks, Mrs. W. A. Pine, and Mr. George H. Smith, of Sauquoit, New York; Mr. David L. Johnston and Mr. Edwin K. Tolan of Clinton, New York; Mr. and Mrs. George P. Cooke of Molokai, Hawaii; Mr. Walter F. Judd of Kaneohe, Hawaii; Mr. Alan Beck of Boston; Mrs. Georgia Judd Carpenter of Royal Oak, Michigan; Mr. Charles H. P. Copeland of Salem, Massachusetts; Mr. William S. Ewing of Ann Arbor, Michigan; Mr. Esty Foster of Port Washington, New York; Mrs. Francis Hastings Gott of Pittsford, New York; Mr. and Mrs. William A. Jackson of Cambridge, Massachusetts; Mrs. Mary H. Marks of Old Forge, New York; Mr. Norman A. McNairn of Philadelphia; Mr. Andrew F. Muir of Houston, Texas; Miss Elizabeth Simpson of Littlewood, New York; Mr. Norwood B. Smith of Menlo Park, California; Miss Helen L. Wallace of Woodbury, Connecticut; the Reverend John H. Westbrook of Watertown, Connecticut; and Mr. Wyllis E. Wright of Williamstown, Massachusetts.

The photograph of Betsey Hastings Judd (page 14) is from a daguerreotype in the possession of my father. The photograph on page 37 was provided by the Park Street Church. The other illustrations are reproduced through the courtesy of the Hawaiian Mission Children's Society Library, the Archives of Hawaii, the Honolulu Academy of Arts, the Hawaiian Historical Society Library, the University of Hawaii Library, and the Bernice P. Bishop Museum.

G.P.J.

To Lamb and Tucker

Contents

Illustrations

DR. JUDD

Dr. Gerrit Parmele Judd

I

The Judd Family in North America

One day in January, 1841, six men entered the volcano of Kilauea on the island of Hawaii. Five were brown-skinned natives. The sixth was Dr. Gerrit Parmele Judd, a heavy-set and strong-limbed physician of Yankee descent. The party carried scientific instruments and moved cautiously over the rocky terrain.

At length Dr. Judd lowered himself into a small crater and began to gather pieces of volcanic rock, which he passed by hand to one of the natives on the ridge above. Intent on his work and believing the crater to be inactive, he crouched under a projecting ledge and continued to pick up specimens.

A fall of stones gave ominous warning of an eruption. He heard a tremendous report. The floor of the crater opened. A vast bubble of crimson lava rose in a pillar only fifty feet away. He turned his back to the searing heat and clawed vainly at the rocks with his strong fingers. He could not climb over the ledge, and the onrushing river of fire cut off all other retreat. Above him the terrified natives ran for their lives. Helplessly trapped and facing a hideous death he offered a prayer to God. At the same time he waved his hand above the ledge and shouted desperately to the fleeing Hawaiians.

A native named Kalama, bolder than the others, paused, turned, and, at the risk of his own life, came back to the brim of the crater. He stretched out his strong arms, but the scorching heat drove him back.

Again the doctor shouted. Kalama then squatted down resolutely, turned his face as far as possible from the oncoming lava, grasped Dr. Judd's hand, and gave a mighty heave. As the doctor's body rose above the ledge, lava splashed against the side of the crater. His feet and ankles were protected by heavy boots, but he felt fire on his wrists and elbows. Both men, although severely burned, managed to run to a safe place.

But for the courage of the heroic Kalama this biography might never have been written, as the most dramatic part of Dr. Judd's fantastic career still lay before him.

In 1843, two years after his escape from the volcano, Dr. Judd found himself in a situation which few soothsayers would have dared to predict. While night winds blew gently through the cocoanut fronds and cloud banks scudded across the star-speckled sky, he locked himself in the tomb of Hawaiian kings and lit a small lantern. The flickering light cast eerie shadows among the coffins, but from the outside no light showed, for the door was solid and the tomb had no windows. Using one of the coffins as a desk, he began to write official letters on behalf of Kamehameha III, sovereign of the Hawaiian Kingdom. Although lacking the formal title, he was in fact the king's prime minister—a post which he held for almost twelve years of storm and crisis. The dispatches which he was writing for the king were designed to free the Islands from British rule, hence the need for secrecy in their preparation. He wrote slowly and with care; the stale smell of dusty air hung heavily in the little room. From time to time he paused to listen, fearful of discovery. Outside in the Honolulu harbor a British man-of-war rocked softly at anchor.

His life was filled with contrast. At a political meeting in 1854, stripped of high office, he stood in Kawaiahao Church, which years before he had labored earnestly to build. Before him he saw row upon row of upturned brown faces. In the Hawaiian tongue he made a persuasive oration, but as he spoke he heard hisses of disapproval from his audience. The Kingdom to which he had dedicated his life now rejected him. He left the meeting a forlorn and defeated man.

Yet on the day of his funeral many years later, in belated and reconsidered gratitude for his services, the Hawaiian government gave him a splendid tribute.

This book is his story.

Gerrit Parmele Judd came from the heart of New England. When he sailed from Boston in the fall of 1827 as a medical missionary to Hawaii, he was on the last leg of a westward migration which his ancestors had begun early in the seventeenth century from old England to North America. A seventh-generation American, descended from immigrants to New England before 1700 in all the branches of his family which can be traced,[1] he carried with him in undiluted form the accumulated Yankee experience of almost two hundred years in the New World. The same strong blend of conviction and piety which had nourished his forebears in Massachusetts, Connecticut, and western New York gave him spirit to face the challenge of still another frontier.

The founder of the family in North America was Thomas Judd of Langley in Essex. His name first appears in the records of Massachusetts in 1634, when he received a home lot in Cambridge. He later settled in Farmington, Connecticut, and served as a deacon of the church and as a representative in the Connecticut legislature. No known record gives the name of his first wife, cofounder of the American family which bears his name and mother of his nine children.[2]

By the time of the American Revolution, Thomas' descendants had firmly established themselves in the new continent and had participated fully in the colonial experiences which were shaping the new nation. They served as jurors, local officeholders, representatives in the Connecticut legislature, and as members of several Committees of Correspondence in the early stages of the rebellion. Two Judds graduated from Yale and became Congregational ministers. Members of the family fought in the colonial wars and in the Revolution.[3] They enjoyed varying fortunes. Thomas' grandson (also named Thomas, d. 1747) left an estate of £2279, then considered a substantial sum, but Elnathan (1724–1777), a grandson of the younger Thomas, was jailed for debt. At his death his insolvent estate was distributed among his creditors and his widow Meriam received only the personal household effects.[4] It is ironic that some fifty years later his grandson Gerrit argued hotly against abolishing imprisonment for debt.

Few Judd family papers have survived from this early period, so little is known of their personalities and private lives. But one receives throughout an unmistakable impression of their vigor, as year after year in an atmosphere of hard work, frugality, and prayer they won the battle for survival in the far-from-rich farm lands of colonial Connecticut. What sustained them was the stern and terrifying body of Calvinist doctrine, with its belief in the absolute sovereignty of God, the innate evil of mankind because of Adam's sin, and the utter helplessness of that part of the human race predestined by an inscrutable Deity to eternal damnation. They believed further that only a minority of the human race, the elect, through God's grace would find eternal bliss. Those men and women with a hope of salvation gladly endured all worldly trials and pains, for Jehovah, the Lord of Hosts, was fighting on their side. They felt both exultation and ecstasy, along with the need to lead moral lives in order to demonstrate their election. As they read or listened to the stirring words of the King James Version of the Bible they identified themselves with God's Chosen People, who had escaped from the oppression of Pharaoh to find in New England a new Promised Land. Such men and women were scarcely cosmopolitan. Their attitudes focused on the pietism of the seventeenth century rather than on the rationalism of the eighteenth. They felt more at home with the evangelism of John Bunyan than with the deism of Voltaire. But, by way of compensation, they developed a stoic toughness which in time of adversity carried them through trials which would have destroyed less determined people.

After the Revolution, land hunger seized New England. Veterans who had fought against Burgoyne told stories about fertile land in the still unsettled western part of New York. After Indian treaties opened the way for settlement, pioneers left the generally poor farm land of New England and poured by the hundreds through the Hudson and Mohawk valleys into the rich farm land of the new frontier. Their enthusiastic letters encouraged others to follow.[5]

4

Dr. Elnathan Judd, Gerrit's father, was among the men of Connecticut in the first wave of migration to the new West. In view of what is known of his early life, the fertile land on the frontier undoubtedly appeared more than usually attractive to him. Born on December 7, 1773, in the parish of Westbury (relocated in 1780 as part of Watertown), Connecticut, he was only three years old when his father, Elnathan the elder, died in January, 1777, and left the widow Meriam an insolvent estate and three minor children to support. Details of his childhood are lacking, but the probability is that he grew up in privation if not in actual poverty. At the age of 16, possibly earlier, Elnathan began to share the family's financial burden, and it is likely that he helped support not only his mother but also his sisters, two of whom never married.[6]

In 1795 Elnathan and his mother left Watertown, Connecticut, and undertook the 250-mile journey to Paris Hill, New York, about ten miles south of the present city of Utica.[7] Records of the Paris Congregational Church show that Meriam Judd was admitted as a member there on June 22, 1796, and Elnathan on July 10 of the same year.[8] At that time Rochester did not exist, Buffalo was not yet laid out, and Utica—called Old Fort Schuyler until 1798—contained less than 50 houses.[9]

Their journey to Paris Hill, in part through a countryside that was little more than wilderness, took several weeks. They moved slowly along roads obstructed by stumps and fallen trees, camping at nightfall in some clearing in the forest, on the alert for the bears, panthers, and wolves which roamed the area, as well as for Indians who were ordinarily peaceful but occasionally dangerous to encounter. Like most immigrants, they probably carried with them all their worldly possessions in a wagon, or, more likely, on a sleigh, since a journey by sleigh in winter or in early spring before the ground thawed presented fewer difficulties than forcing a wagon in later months along the deep-rutted, muddy roads. Other settlers, including the novelist James Fenimore Cooper, have left vivid accounts of the dangers and hardships that were commonplace on the New York frontier.[10]

Their destination, the village of Paris Hill, in the town (or township) of Paris, Oneida County, was first settled in 1789. The first church in the town, the Paris Religious Society (Congregational) in Paris Hill, was formed in 1791 with five members. It was this church that Meriam and Elnathan Judd joined five years after its foundation and seven years after the first settlement of Paris Hill. An indication of the small population then in the area is the fact that Elnathan was the fifty-eighth on the list of subscribers to the church.[11]

In 1797 Elnathan left Paris Hill and enrolled for one year in the academy conducted in connection with Williams College in Williamstown, Massachusetts, but he did not matriculate at the college.[12] How his mother managed without him for a year on a new frontier is not known. Probably she received help from her son-in-law, Joseph Cutler, who was in Paris Hill about that time, or from her eldest son, Richards Samuel Judd, who had settled in nearby Steuben. In any event, after a year Elnathan had to break off his formal schooling and return to Paris Hill because of her ill health.[13]

Thereafter, he studied evenings with his mother's help, and by day worked with his hands.[14] About this time he began to study medicine in the office of Dr. Seth Hastings of the neighboring village of Clinton—the usual means of acquiring a medical education in an era when few medical schools existed.[15] On April 13, 1802, he married Dr. Hastings' eldest daughter, Betsey, who was then 19 years old.

Elnathan settled down in the arduous role of a frontier physician, for a time as the partner of Dr. Caleb Sampson, who later sold out to him and moved to nearby New Hartford. He established himself in Dr. Sampson's house and "ride"—as a medical practice was then called—and in time became the leading physician of the district. His interest in medicine was genuine, and he brought to it the energy and high moral purpose of his pilgrim forebears. He was present as one of the twenty-nine charter members when, on July 1, 1806, the Oneida Medical Society was formed in Rome, New York. He took a lively interest in the new medical college in nearby Fairfield, from which his son Gerrit later graduated, and he served as trustee of that institution from 1824 to 1838.[16]

Elnathan emerges as a conscientious and rugged country doctor working under the enormous difficulties presented by the frontier, treating all manner of cases from tooth pulling to obstetrics;

6

traveling on horseback, on foot, or on snowshoes in winter, at all hours in all weather; operating without anesthetics and without the assistance of hospitals, nurses, and druggists, for the small fees in cash or farm produce—usually less than three dollars for delivering a baby—which frontier people could afford to pay.[17] His daughter's earliest recollection of his hard work was of being summoned to read to him from an old medical treatise as he lay exhausted on a wooden settee. Tall and slender, slightly stooping, with blue eyes and light hair, he was long remembered in Paris Hill for his affable personality and for his habit of covering his face with his hands and humming tunelessly for some minutes before prescribing for a difficult case. At the same time there ran through him a strain of Yankee individualism and primness. If he chanced to call on an untidy family, it is reported that invariably he refused to take off his hat or gloves until the room was neatened.[18]

Elnathan was far from wealthy, but he lived in comfort and respectability in a large white frame house facing the village green on the southern corner of the Sauquoit Road,[19] and he could afford to maintain a servant. Like many pioneer doctors of the day, he supplemented his income through farming, and here he worked as conscientiously as at his medical practice. At the first county fair held at Whitesboro on October 1, 1818, he won a set of spoons valued at $5.00 for the best half acre of potatoes.[20]

Like at least two of his forebears in the Judd line, Elnathan became a deacon of the church. To him, as to others in a bleak frontier environment, religion supplied both unshakable moral standards and inner satisfaction of a poetic intensity. He took his religion as seriously as did his seventeenth-century ancestors. Throughout his life it served him as a source of strength, but at one period it involved him in a dispute so bitter and prolonged that it undermined his position in the community and almost destroyed him. He faced the long crisis with stubborn courage, but the very firmness of mind with which he met the ordeal blinded him to all considerations of tactful compromise. In the end, he allowed the Calvinistic certainty of his convictions to lead him into a position from which no retreat was possible.

The dispute arose in part from petty jealousy and malice of the sort to be found in any community, and in part from the special

7

religious circumstances of the New York frontier. Here Presbyterians and Congregationalists, while generally agreeing in theology, disputed sharply over church administration, the former favoring centralized, and the latter favoring local, control of parish matters. At the same time, a new liberal Calvinism conflicted with the stern and dour faith of the immediate past. This new movement, called the New England Theology, had its roots in the pietism which had produced the Great Awakening of the 1730s, the Second Great Awakening of 1797, as well as the Wesleyan and Moravian movements. It stressed man's freedom of will to accept salvation instead of waiting helplessly for the predetermined grace of God. As such, it appealed to the individualism and self-reliance of frontier people, and it found expression in a number of wildly enthusiastic revivals. Ultimately this new Calvinism helped to generate that burst of energy which in the nineteenth century sent Protestant missionaries all over the world and which brought about a tremendous wave of social reform at home. But its immediate effect on the frontier was to add further turbulence to an already troubled situation.[21]

In Paris Hill, comparative harmony prevailed during the ministry of Eliphalet Steele, a Congregationalist of pronounced orthodoxy.[22] But after his death in 1817, controversy which had long smoldered burst into open, ugly flame. Hardly a meeting of the church committee passed without some accusation of indiscipline or heresy. Steele's successor, the Reverend John Waters, was a Presbyterian, and a year after his installation the church left the Oneida Association (Congregational) and joined the Presbytery. But in June, 1820, the parishioners, including Elnathan, decided to dismiss Waters.[23] The next incumbent was the Reverend William Raymond Weeks, a Presbyterian in active opposition to such evangelical revivalists as Charles Grandison Finney.[24] Weeks proved highly distasteful to Elnathan, who thoroughly approved of the "new measures" of the revivalists. Accordingly, on June 26, 1821, Elnathan and twenty others petitioned the Presbytery to be set off as a second Presbyterian church in Paris Hill, but the Presbytery refused to grant their request. A period of furious squabbling ensued, during which the Congregationalists in the church rejoined the Oneida Association, while Elnathan on June 18, 1822, was elected a deacon of the Presbyterian portion of the parish. A strange and possibly unique situation arose. Two separate churches worshiped under the same roof, served by the same minister as moderator, but receiving communion at opposite sides of the same table from deacons belonging to separate denominations. In 1823, at their own request, the two churches reunited under the care of the Presbytery, but two years later the church members repented of their decision and rejoined the Oneida Association.[25]

In the midst of this controversy, embroiled as it was with sectarian animosity, Elnathan faced charges of a scandalous nature. Gossip on the part of three women, one of them a former servant in his home, crystallized into a formal accusation on August 15, 1823, that he had made lascivious advances toward them. The purveyor of the charges, William Handy, Jr., was a Congregationalist and, as such, was opposed to Elnathan in the religious dispute. Although there is something incongruous in the spectacle of a deacon in his fiftieth year being accused of sexual misconduct, Elnathan insisted on an open hearing to put an end to the gossip. The church committee conducted a painfully detailed investigation, of which a verbatim record exists in manuscript. The committee exonerated Elnathan but resolved, "We do think facts proved which amount to imprudent and unguarded conduct; and that Brother Judd be, and is hereby admonished to be more on his guard in similar circumstances."

Apparently some of the committee voted for the resolution as a compromise measure to end the trouble without doing Elnathan serious harm. But the reprimand, mild as it was, threw Elnathan into a towering rage. A Calvinist to the core, imbued with rigid principles of absolute justice, he rejected any thought of compromise and demanded an unqualified vindication. He immediately appealed the committee's verdict to the Presbytery, which ruled on September 11 that the censure had been unjust. The Presbytery further ordered its ruling to be read from the pulpit at Paris Hill on the Sunday following and to be written into the church records. A later account, which may be exaggerated, states that Elnathan was present when his vindication was read, and never attended service there again. After protracted dissension, on July 3, 1824, Elnathan and Betsey joined the church at New Hartford, some ten miles away on the outskirts of Utica.[26]

The controversy did irreparable injury to his health as well as to his standing in the community. It certainly made an indelible impression on his serious-minded son Gerrit, then barely 21 years of age. It is perhaps more than a coincidence that Gerrit in his own fiftieth year and at the apex of his career faced a political crisis with the same brand of rigid and uncompromising determination, and that his refusal or inability to compromise brought about his downfall in almost the same way that it had ruined his father.

Ten years later Elnathan sold his house and practice at Paris Hill and moved to nearby Clinton, where he and Betsey were admitted to the Congregational church on September 6, 1835. Two years later, caught in a new westward fever, they moved to Troy, Michigan, a farming village nine miles east of Pontiac.[27] Here, on a relatively safe frontier, Elnathan lived out the remaining eight years of his life in moderate but hardly affluent circumstances.[28] His will, starting with the familiar phrase "In the name of God, Amen," signed in Paris on May 22, 1834, in his bold, oversize handwriting, was probated at Troy in the amount of $1,905.87—a fairly substantial estate for those days. It included bequests to the Oneida Institute, of which he was a founding trustee, and to the American Board of Commissioners for Foreign Missions.[29] His obituary stated, "Doct. Judd was for many years a professed disciple of Christ, and was distinguished for his active and fervent piety. He was a man of great energy, firmness, and decision of character."[30] Finney described him as "an earnest Christian man,"[31] a statement in agreement with the concluding words carved on his tombstone in the Union Cemetery at Troy: "He died as he had lived, Sept. 4, 1845, a Christian Father."[32]

Betsey Hastings Judd, Elnathan's wife and Gerrit's mother, was a descendant of Deacon Thomas Hastings, who emigrated from England to Watertown, Massachusetts, in 1634. Her father, Dr. Seth Hastings, a physician with rigid dignity and equally rigid religious principles, settled in Clinton, New York, in February, 1797. A stern and prominent figure in the new community, he took an active part in church affairs, and, like his pupil and son-in-law, Elnathan Judd, he became a charter member of the Oneida Medical Society.[33] Betsey was raised in the harsh Calvinism of old New England. A woman of fortitude and great personal charm, she gave unflagging support to her husband during their marriage of forty-three years. She bore her husband six children and outlived him by more than thirty years. In 1852, aged almost seventy, she had the hardihood to make the long voyage around Cape Horn to the Hawaiian Islands in order to join her son Gerrit, whom she also outlived.

She died on May 14, 1876, in her 94th year, and was buried in Nuuanu Cemetery in Honolulu, beside her son but more than four thousand miles from her husband's lonely grave in Michigan. Her tombstone bears singularly appropriate words from Ecclesiastes 1:4 and Job 5:26: "One generation passeth away, and another generation cometh: but the earth abideth for ever. Thou shalt come to thy grave in a full age, like as a shock of corn cometh in in his season."

Boyhood on the New York Frontier

Gerrit Parmele, the eldest child of Elnathan and Betsey Judd, was born at Paris Hill, New York, on April 23, 1803. His baptism on May 29 appears in the church records in the firm hand of Eliphalet Steele as "Garrit Parmale son of Do^t. Elnathan Judd and Beetsey his wife."[1] Steele's spelling tended to be somewhat erratic—in later entries Betsey's name is twice given as "Bettsey," then as "Elizabeth"—but during his youth Gerrit himself usually signed his first name as "Garrit," and it was undoubtedly so pronounced. Why he was named Gerrit is not known. His middle name, Parmele, was the maiden surname of his maternal grandmother.

At the time of Gerrit's birth, the high, rolling, wooded hills of Paris had been settled for only fourteen years, and the countryside still retained something of the raw appearance of a newly penetrated wilderness. The pattern of daily living remained much like that of pre-Revolutionary America in that the women still carded their own wool, spun thread, and wove on hand looms the cloth from which they fashioned clothes for their families. But in many ways the New York frontier, particularly in Oneida County, differed fundamentally from other outposts in America's thrust westward, for the great majority of the settlers there came from New England. Early emigrants to Oneida County included men with such typically Yankee names as Moses Foote, Elias Hopkins, Barnabas Pond, Seth Steel, and Asa Shepherd.[2] Many clergymen and teachers on this frontier were Yale graduates, such as Eliphalet Steele, minister of the Paris Hill Church; Noah Coe, minister of the New Hartford Church, 1814–1835; Dr. Asahel Strong Norton, minister of the Congregational church in Clinton, 1793–1833; John Niles and Robert Porter, principals of the Hamilton Oneida Academy in Clinton; and Dr. Azel Backus, first president of Hamilton College when it was chartered in 1812 as an outgrowth of the Academy.[3]

In less than a generation these enterprising and thrifty settlers managed to so transform the area that more than one observer commented favorably on the orderly appearance of the towns and villages, with their white clapboard houses, austere churches, and well-tended village greens. In Gerrit's childhood, Oneida County was a frontier as regards the energy and resourcefulness of its inhabitants, but it was at the same time a frontier tamed almost overnight into a western counterpart of New England.[4]

As a boy growing up in Paris Hill, Gerrit had ample opportunity to hunt in the neighboring woods, hard country much of it to traverse, for the hills in the area rise sharply and the ravines are both deep and narrow. He had opportunity, as well, to fish in the nearby streams, such as the clear broad creek that runs through the center of the Sauquoit Valley. It is certain that he helped with the household and farm chores, watering livestock, digging potatoes, and guiding a plow through the rich, hard topsoil of his father's fields. It is also certain that he felt, as all farm folk do, the slow tranquil rhythm of the seasons, as in solitude and with the silence broken only by the rustle of the wind and the chirruping of birds he had full time to ponder the mysteries of life and time and eternity. One may picture him as a husky, intent youngster in homespun clothes, stopping at the end of a furrow to wipe the sweat from his face and to glance briefly at the sky in the way farmers have of keeping an eye on the weather. At such moments he might well think deeply and slowly about religion, or what his father or mother had said about the faith, or the sermon of the Sunday before in the wooden church on the green.

Betsey Hastings Judd

In numerous talks with his parents and others he absorbed the Calvinist concept of an all-powerful God, along with the Protestant insistence on devotion to duty and the performance of good works. In childhood and early manhood he came to a full understanding of the religious controversies that convulsed the frontier, such as the continuing dispute between Congregationalists and Presbyterians on matters of church administration, and the theological differences between the strict predeterministic doctrines of the old-school Calvinists and the new free-will doctrines of the supporters of the New England Theology. Naturally enough, he and other members of the family became deeply involved, emotionally and intellectually, in the protracted battle which his father fought against various opponents in the parish. As time passed, by way of conscious or unconscious imitation, he patterned his own ideals of conduct on his father's rigid and strict moral standards.

On Sundays, scrubbed shiny and awed into decorum, he regularly attended church with his parents, probably both morning and afternoon. In the summertime, as he listened to the voice of Eliphalet Steele expounding the lesson from the pulpit, he might fidget in the warm, still air, and pray silently, as boys do, that the sermon would soon be over. In winter he felt discomfort of another sort, for all during his youth the church remained unheated, regardless of how high the snow lay banked outside, and it was not uncommon for snowdrifts to persist well into April. Then, with tingling fingers he could watch the breath of his neighbors, as Steele in the pulpit, wearing a cloak and woolen mittens, thundered out the word of Jehovah. Often, as he sat huddled in the narrow pew (one observer compared the pews to sheep pens), he would hardly be able to hear the sermon, since all around him, in a vain effort to keep warm, the congregation stamped their feet against the echoing wooden floor.[5]

Experiences of this sort, of course, he shared fully with his two younger sisters, Elisabeth Gertrude and Harriet Breck, and his two younger brothers, William Pitt and Henry Augustus. A third brother, baptized Henry Augustus Hastings, was born in 1805 but died in 1810 of scarlet fever.[6] No record remains of the family's grief on this occasion, and, indeed, little else is known about the family circle in these early years. One may assume that as time passed Gerrit became increasingly enmeshed in the bittersweet web of affection and heartbreak which characterizes any large family.

In 1830 Gerrit wrote an autobiographical statement which provides a brief outline of his education. "My honoured father and mother subjected me early to salutary discipline, watched with care my tender years, and spared no pains or expense consistent with their means in providing for my education. When about nine or ten years of age I was sent to Clinton to attend the grammar school where I remained, as near as I can recollect, about three years."[7] The words "salutary discipline" hint ominously at the severity of manners imbedded in the New England code. Children honored and feared their parents much as their parents honored and feared the God of John Calvin. They seldom spoke to adults unless spoken to, and replied with full deference and respect. They were industrious and tidy. If Elnathan refused to treat an untidy patient he certainly took steps to ban untidiness in his own home. Honesty, of course, was the best, indeed the only, policy, and humility stood high on the roster of the traditional virtues. At the other extreme lay the lures of Satan and the black sins of the liar, the sloth, and the sloven. Undoubtedly a full measure of corporal punishment helped Gerrit to distinguish clearly between virtue and vice.

The grammar school mentioned was the so-called Classical School in Clinton conducted in the years 1813–1815 by Comfort Williams and Moses Bristol, to fill the need created in the area when in 1812 the Hamilton Oneida Academy ceased operation as a grammar school and became Hamilton College.[8] Both Williams and Bristol were Yale graduates. Williams came from Wethersfield, Connecticut, but Bristol was born in Clinton, and after returning to Yale for a medical degree in 1816, practiced for a time with Gerrit's grandfather, Dr. Seth Hastings.[9] At the Clinton school Gerrit learned to write in a firm, neat hand, and he acquired a thorough grounding in English composition. His letters and state papers, which are both terse and clear, give ample evidence of sound academic discipline in his formative years.

Gerrit's autobiographical statement continues, "I then returned home and pursued classical studies under the tuition of Rev. Edwin W. Dwight (now of Richmond, Mass.)."[10] In Edwin Welles Dwight, Gerrit encountered an influence which may have helped change the entire course of his life. Dwight, a Yale graduate in the class of 1809, had studied theology under Dr. Lyman Beecher, one of the most influential preachers and theologians of the day, and had come to the New York frontier in 1816 for a year's home missionary service. In 1809, the year of his graduation from Yale, he had befriended Henry Obookiah, a native Hawaiian youth then in the United States, and in 1817–1818 he became Obookiah's tutor in the Foreign Mission School at Cornwall, Connecticut. When Obookiah died in 1818, Dwight published the youth's memoirs in the form of a biographical tract.[11] How far Dwight, a gentle, solemn man of deep religious faith, may have influenced Gerrit's later decision to go to Hawaii as a missionary does not appear, but it is suggestive to find an influence pointing in this direction when Gerrit was only thirteen years of age.

After Dwight left Paris Hill, Gerrit's memoir states, "In the year 1816 [?1817] I went to live with my uncle, Mr. Charles Hastings, of Utica. I remained with him six or eight months engaged in his bookstore."[12] In May, 1817, Charles Hastings, one of Betsey's younger brothers, a kindly and unassuming man of 24, opened with Andrew Merrell a bookstore and circulating library in Utica, located "At the Sign of the Bible" at 40 Genesee Street. Presumably Gerrit was sent in the capacity of clerk and errand boy to help launch the firm, which acted as agent for the Western Domestic Missionary Society and published a few books, such as *The Missionary Arithmetic*, a mathematics textbook utilizing as examples problems faced in a Christian mission, written by Elnathan Judd's bête noire, William Raymond Weeks, minister of the Paris Hill Church. This volume, it should be added, appeared in 1822, a year or so before Elnathan's long quarrel with its author. Charles Hastings apparently maintained close relations with the Judds. In 1834 he migrated westward to Troy, Michigan, and it was probably at his suggestion that Elnathan and Betsey joined him there three years later.[13] Gerrit's association with his Uncle Charles Hastings came at an extremely impressionable age. His stay in Utica undoubtedly sharpened his understanding of current religious questions, and it may well have awakened in him an interest in the foreign mission to which he was to devote so large a part of his life.

Gerrit's terse account hastens over the next seven years and leaves many pivotal questions unanswered.

Dr. Judd's birthplace, Paris Hill, New York

When I returned to Paris I assisted my father in the office, studied a little with a view to the profession of medicine. I attended a school taught in the place a part of the time. I spent some part of the time also in labouring with my brother and others on the farm. I afterwards engaged more directly in the studies of the profession my father had chosen for me. In the year 1820, when eighteen years of age, I went to attend medical lectures at Fairfield, in Herkimer County, which I continued to attend each term of four months in the year until the beginning of 1825 (at which time I graduated) spending the intervening time at home, partly at study and partly in practice and other employments. In the spring of 1825 I entered into a co-partnership with my father and commenced the practice of physic.[14]

The College of Physicians and Surgeons of the Western District of New York, more familiarly known as the Fairfield Medical College, was located about fifteen miles east of Utica, on the top of a huge hill with a spectacular view of the surrounding countryside. It received its charter from the state in 1812, and by 1840, when it finally closed its doors, it had a total of 609 graduates. In 1825, the year that Gerrit received his degree, it had 130 students. At that time there were only 14 other medical schools in the United States.[15]

As a center of medical education, Fairfield was in its day on a par with the older eastern schools and in some respects their superior. It attracted students not only from central and western New York but also from New Hampshire, New Jersey, and the District of Columbia. Beginning in the fall of 1825, the botanist Asa Gray of Sauquoit studied there, as did the Oregon pioneer Marcus Whitman, who entered in January, 1826. Another of its graduates was Dr. Seth Andrews, medical missionary to Hawaii in 1837. The college maintained a museum, anatomical theater, and dissecting room, but the real basis for its excellence lay in the caliber of its faculty. The most famous of Gerrit's teachers was Dr. Theodric Romeyn Beck, the foremost expert during his lifetime in the new field of medical jurisprudence.[16] Another of Gerrit's teachers was Dr. Joseph White of Cherry Valley, the college's second president (1817–1827) and lecturer on anatomy and surgery, said to have been the best surgeon in the state west of Albany.[17]

Classes at the college began in November, after the fall plowing, and lasted for three months; in 1822, the term was extended to sixteen weeks. Students paid $54 to attend the lectures. A dormitory room cost 30¢ a week or $4.50 for the entire session, with an additional charge of $1.25 for firewood. A student's total expenses per session came to about $100, which was at that time a large sum. But Elnathan undoubtedly felt that the money was well spent, for his son, as a graduate of a medical school like Fairfield, had received professional training far better than his own.

In addition to his work at Fairfield, Gerrit is said, on good authority, to have studied medicine for a semester in Auburn, New York, where in 1825 there was an unchartered but creditable medical school.[18] Aside from his formal schooling, of course, he profited greatly from the practical experience acquired in close professional association with his father.

While still a medical student, Gerrit joined in 1821 a local debating society composed of about thirty young men, who met once a week on Thursday evenings in Paris. The tone and purport of the organization appears in the preamble to its constitution: "We, the members of the Philosophronic Society, in order to improve ourselves in useful knowledge and good morals, and to form a more perfect union, harmony, and friendship, do ordain and establish this constitution."[19] Gerrit was a charter member, and from time to time served as censor, treasurer, and secretary. The Society's record book contains a number of entries in his hand. His signature, invariably as "Garrit," is at first quite plain, but toward the end is embellished with the bold strokes and flourishes characteristic of youth. He attended faithfully, and on at least two occasions the Society met at his house. At the meeting on March 21, 1821, he upheld the negative in the question "Ought imprisonment for debt to be abolished?" His side won on the merits of the question but lost on the merits of the discussion. On September 6, on the question "Are theatrical exhibitions on the whole injurious?" he again took the negative side. In this debate he won on the merits of the question, but the merits of the discussion were declared equal. He also participated in debates whether men with religious scruples should be exempted from military service, whether all people should be forced by law to attend church on Sunday, and whether all free citizens should become voters at the age of twenty-one. The Society was dissolved on October 25 by mutual agreement.

Four years later, on October 19, 1825, Gerrit and five other young men of Paris Hill formed "for the sake of improvement" a second debating club called the Ciceronian Society, which met Wednesday evenings to argue such questions as whether the hope of reward is a greater incentive to virtue than the fear of punishment, and, on November 16, 1826, whether slaves should be retained in bondage. On the latter question the negative won on the merits of both the question and discussion. Gerrit was not so active in this group as he had been in the earlier society. By this time he had finished his medical training, and other questions weighed upon his mind. On December 15, 1826, the Society resolved that G. P. Judd and several others be stricken from the roll and declamation list.

Such societies abounded on the frontier, along with moot courts and literary discussion groups. They appeared in hundreds of widely separated communities soon after the settlers had solved the basic problem of survival. It is apparent that they were social as well as intellectual gatherings, and that in general they served as a much-needed outlet for the active minds and emotions of a people in transit across the continent.[20]

On October 28, 1825, less than two weeks after the formation of the Ciceronian Society, Gerrit attended a gathering of the Republican young men of Paris Hill. At the meeting he was appointed to two committees, one to draft a resolution and the other to prepare an accompanying address in support of Governor De Witt Clinton, in particular to commend Clinton for the completion of the Erie Canal. The meeting further resolved that "Gerret P. Judd" and two others "be a committee of vigilance for the town of Paris."[21] It is a matter of record that in the election Clinton carried Paris by a two-to-one majority and was elected governor of New York.[22]

Gerrit at this stage in his life appears as an energetic and sober-minded young doctor, well trained in his profession according to the best standards of the day, capable of vast enthusiasms, and with a profound interest in the moral issues (along with the ways and means of reform) associated with the religion and politics of the time. In a way he seems to epitomize the character of the New York frontier, which, though disciplined in its morality, was, at the same time, restless, as if waiting tense as a coiled spring for the summons to a crusade. In Gerrit's case the summons was soon to come.

Appointment as Missionary Physician

Early in 1826 a religious revival swept through western New York. Its leader was Charles Grandison Finney, later president of Oberlin College, one of the most dynamic evangelists of his generation. Strikingly handsome, of athletic build, with intent eyes and a musical voice, he burned with the zeal of total conviction. Like other Protestant leaders of the day, he dreamed of evangelizing the whole world, and few could resist the fervor of his preaching. His opponents, notably Dr. Lyman Beecher of Boston, deplored his informal methods, which often verged upon the theatrical, but his tour of the New York frontier, known as the Western Revivals, achieved phenomenal success in the winning of souls. Whole towns made profession of faith. Casual travelers were converted and proceeded in an exalted state of mind on their various ways. A believer in the new Calvinism, Finney insisted on free will along with man's sacred duty to perform good works. Accordingly, over the years he helped to release a powerful humanitarian impulse. Hundreds of his converts devoted themselves to temperance, bible, and Sunday-school societies. Other reforms of the new Calvinism included campaigns to eliminate gambling and prostitution, better treatment of the blind and the insane, prison reform, foreign missions, and the explosive movement to abolish Negro slavery. In response to this humanitarian impulse, Protestant missionaries of the nineteenth century all over the globe emphasized secular labors in schools and hospitals far more than did the Catholics. At the time of the 1826 revivals, Finney was 34 years old and at the height of his powers. After preaching for some time at Rome, he proceeded on the first of February to Utica, where a revival had been in progress for about a month.[1]

Dr. Judd was among the throngs of men and women who came to Utica from the surrounding countryside to hear Finney preach. In his autobiographical statement, written four years later for the edification of his eldest son, he described in some detail his conversion by the great evangelist.

The spring of 1826 was a wonderful season in the county of Oneida. An extensive revival of religion prevailed in many of the villages, particularly Rome and Utica. My father and mother often visited these places to enjoy the Christian society and refreshing influences which they could there find congenial to their hearts. Their attention, their anxieties and their prayers were chiefly directed to their children who were all in an unconverted state. I believe they spent much time in agonizing prayer for their conversion. Business called me to Utica; my father urged me to stay a few days and attend the meetings and above all make the surrender of myself to God and the salvation of my soul, my first and most important business. When I arrived my friends made the same request and were so importunate that I could not deny them. I gave a half consent to stay and the carriage returned without me. I attended the religious meetings and in particular the preaching of the Rev. Chas. G. Finney, soon became anxious for the salvation of my soul, and by a blessing of God on the means of grace, I hope I was, about the 11th of April, brought to bow at the feet of sovereign mercy.[2]

An estimated five hundred people were converted at the Utica revivals, including the celebrated antislavery agitator Theodore Dwight Weld and Fanny Thomas of Clinton, who as Mrs. Gulick formed part of the missionary band which left for Hawaii in the following year.[3]

Other parts of Dr. Judd's autobiographical statement, as well as numerous passages in his diaries and correspondence, attest in lyrical language the intensity of his religious experience.

Oh my son! May you never dare to indulge the dangerous sentiment that you are too young to serve Christ—that you will indulge a little longer in sin and then seek religion. . . . It is often the case of those that resist the striving of the Holy Spirit that they are given up to hardness of heart and blindness of mind and left to follow their own choice and bring ruin on their own souls.[4]

His conversion at Utica was without question the turning point of his life. Everything which he thought or did thereafter derived from it. All other aspects of his career, including his medical and political labors, stand as secondary expressions of a fundamentally religious dedication. As he wrote in his memoir,

New views and motives of action now took possession of my heart; I felt in some small degree the value of a soul and the wants of a dying world; I desired to devote myself to the work of the Lord. I made this a subject of much meditation and without consulting any one read my bible and prayed and weighed the matter as well as I could for some months.[5]

On September 2, 1826, by profession of faith he joined the Presbyterian Church at New Hartford, to which his parents had transferred their membership after their difficulties with the church in Paris Hill.[6] The same month, so the memoir states, "I came to the determination to devote myself to the work of a missionary among the heathen."[7]

A family tradition traces his decision to a chaplain of a man-of-war, lately returned from the China seas, who spoke one Sunday in the Paris Hill Church of the pressing need for missionaries in the Pacific islands. The most concrete version of the tradition is in a poem, "Dr. Judd's Call," written many years later by his first cousin, Samuel George Arnold, who stated that he had the story from Dr. Judd's aged mother.[8] Arnold's account is unconfirmed and is improbable in detail, for Dr. Judd seldom attended the Paris Hill Church after his father's trouble there. But it is entirely possible that a chance encounter of this nature helped make up his mind.

On the other hand, the work of Christian missionaries at home and abroad received continuing publicity through a number of channels. During the previous fifty years, considerable information had been published on their activities in Africa, Arabia, Hawaii, India, and Persia.[9] As a boy of thirteen, Judd had become acquainted with Hawaii through his tutor, Edwin Welles Dwight, and slightly later he learned further about missions through his work on his uncle's newspaper, the *Western Recorder*, which in the mid-1820s printed numerous letters from missionaries. It is not at all extraordinary, therefore, that in the fervor of his religious conversion he turned to missionary service.

Accordingly, he addressed a carefully worded letter to the American Board of Commissioners for Foreign Missions in Boston, a nondenominational, but mainly Congregational and Presbyterian, organization with the stated purpose of "propagating the gospel in heathen lands." Founded in 1810 and chartered in 1812, the American Board had already sent missions to India (1813), the Cherokee Indians of Tennessee (1816), Hawaii (1820 and 1823), and Palestine (1821). In the next decade it was to extend its activities to China (1830) and Oregon (1835).[10] Its corresponding secretary was Jeremiah Evarts, a lawyer and philantropist of note,[11] and it was to him that Dr. Judd wrote from Paris Hill on September 6, 1826.

A young physician who has recently manifested a hope that he is "born of God" wishes to devote himself to the missionary cause. My object in thus addressing you is to inquire whether there is any want of a physician at any of the foreign missionary stations—what are the qualifications necessary in order to do good in that capacity—and what course he should pursue as the young man is ignorant of the things that are needful and does not choose to inquire of his friends and acquaintances at present. . . . Be so obliging as to write soon. . . . Pleas[e] direct your letter to Mr. E. Judson, Paris, Oneida Co., N.Y.[12]

Four months passed without a reply. In the interval Dr. Judd felt, as he later admitted, "much uneasiness." He finally asked the advice of Finney's disciple, the Reverend Daniel Nash, who was visiting the Judd family in Paris Hill. Dr. Judd also consulted his father and a few close friends, some of whom advised him to study for the ministry. The discussions proceeded in an atmosphere of soul-searching earnestness, undoubtedly accompanied by prayer.

Toward the end of the year he was making arrangements for President Henry Davis of Hamilton College to open a fresh negotiation with the American Board.[13]

At this stage in the proceedings he received from David Greene, Evarts' assistant, a belated reply dated January 9, 1827. Greene's letter pleaded press of business as an excuse for the delay, then proceeded to outline in frightening detail the qualifications which a missionary must possess.

He must be a decidedly and actively pious man; so much so as to secure the affections and the confidence of the religious community . . . with his whole heart be devoted to the work of spreading the gospel among the heathen, and willing to spend and be spent in making Christ known among them. He must be a man of energy . . . he must possess an amiable temper . . . he must be qualified to engage heartily and immediately in teaching and to be able soon to become a preacher of the gospel. . . .

Evarts added in a postscript the Board's wish that all missionary physicians should preach the gospel, and instructed "E. Judson" to show this letter, with its rigid standards of qualification, to all who should write testimonials on his behalf.[14]

During the next five weeks Dr. Judd busied himself in collecting eleven letters of recommendation for the Board.[15] Dr. Joseph White, president of Fairfield Medical College, stated that "Garrett" was industrious, competent, and of good moral character. Dr. Westel Willoughby, the College's vice president, wrote a formal note endorsing his professional qualifications. In a much warmer letter, Dr. L. H. Bishop characterized him as amiable and pious. Father Nash recommended him as "energetic, discreet, prompt, [and] very amiable." The Reverend Samuel C. Aikin of Utica's First Presbyterian Church, one of Finney's most active supporters, wrote in a similar vein. The Reverend Samuel Williams Brace, minister of the Second Presbyterian Church in Utica, added his signature to Aikin's letter.[16] Henry McNeill, postmaster in Paris Hill, spoke of him as affable and pious, and another neighbor, Abel Simmons, concurred in a short postscript. Thomas Hastings stated that his nephew "Garritt" was both amiable and enterprising. The Reverend John Waters, former minister of the Paris Hill Church, recommended him as coming from a respectable and pious family, and added, "I know nothing why he may not, in a short time, be qualified to preach the gospel."

These letters follow the usual pattern of formal testimonials, but the remaining three show evidence of mental reservation, possibly because of the high qualifications laid down by the Board, and they caused Dr. Judd much difficulty in obtaining the appointment which he was seeking. The Reverend Noah Coe of the New Hartford church, in a letter addressed to President Davis of Hamilton College and forwarded to the Board, emphasized the recent date of Dr. Judd's conversion, and predicted gloomily, "He can never hold a very distinguished rank among the missionaries. Still, I think that in some of the missionary stations he might be very useful."[17] Davis himself refused to give an unqualified recommendation because of the recentness of young Dr. Judd's conversion. It is likely that Davis relied heavily on Coe's prior opinion, and his notorious aversion to Finney's methods may have contributed to color his judgment. The final letter, which is no less than peevish in tone, came from Elnathan's adversary, the Reverend William Raymond Weeks of the Paris Hill Church. Weeks refused flatly to vouch for Dr. Judd's religious qualifications. "Though the young gentleman resides but a few doors from me, circumstances have been such that there has been very little intercourse between us, since the date of his hope, he having united himself to a church in another town, and not usually attending public worship with us." Weeks also stressed the recent date of Dr. Judd's conversion, and recommended that he study theology at Andover or elsewhere, so that the Board might have opportunity to observe him before reaching a decision. In addition to Weeks's known antipathy to the applicant's father, it may be pointed out that he also, like Dr. Davis, disapproved of Finney's revivalist techniques.

In spite of the discouraging tone of these three letters, Dr. Judd bundled them up with the other eight and forwarded them to Evarts, with a long covering letter of his own, dated February 15, 1827.[18] He began with an inspired account of his conversion and his decision to enter missionary work.

At the time when I hope through the mercy of God I found that joy and peace in believing which Jesus died to procure for sinful man there was an entire change in all my views and feeling. . . . Wealth, honors and worldly emolument had been presented before my imagination as a dazzling picture which I had pursued with all the eagerness of youth. But they vanished into insignificance before the objects which were then presented to my mind. My desire was to follow the path of Christ and his Apostles to live and die in the service of God. Nothing else seemed worthy the pursuit of an immortal soul. The immense value of the souls of my fellow beings who know not God was strongly impressed upon my mind and it became an important question with me what part I ought to act in the great work of evangelizing the world. The subject of a mission early presented itself to me in my closet. . . . I was of the opinion that as a missionary physician I might use my profession to as good advantage among the heathen as in our own land, and at the same time be able to do something more for the souls of those who perish for lack of knowledge.

He then explained the circumstances which led him to write his original letter under the pseudonym of "E. Judson." "As I am a son of Elnathan Judd [I] adopted the method I did, in order to obtain the information necessary to enable me to judge of my own qualifications before I informed any one of my determination. But God had otherwise ordered it."

After describing his talks with Father Nash and others, he stated frankly,

I have attempted to make you acquainted with me by procuring the accompanying letters from individuals of my acquaintance that you may be enabled to judge whether there is *any place* in the *whole missionary field* where I may soon [be] employed, or whether it is best for me to spend a season at study, or abandon altogether this object which lies so near my heart. It looks to me like a mountain which is difficult of removal, if I must lay aside my profession without a prospect of ever resuming it again and without funds endeavour to prepare for the ministry.

The thought of having to give up his medical career pained him. As a man of action, bred and raised on a restless frontier, he was torn between the otherworldly goals of religion and the Protestant ethic of hard work in a secular field. Further, Finney's preaching had stressed worldly activity as part of the good Christian life. Already Dr. Judd faced the basic conflict between religious salvation and the ethical pull toward practical good works which in later life impelled him to enter politics. But for the time being he was submissive and wrote, "I am willing to abide by the decision of the Prudential Committee as far as lies in my power whenever they are made acquainted with me and my desires."

With modesty becoming the occasion he then outlined his qualifications.

I would merely add that I have enjoyed the advantages of acquiring such an education as is necessary to make a good physician but have not improved them as I ought or as my friends may think I have done. Besides the common advantages of early education I have spent some time at a public academy where I studied as much Latin and Greek as was necessary to prepare me to enter upon the study of medicine to advantage, since which time I have attended to a few other studies not so directly connected with the profession but must confess myself to be wanting in those literary treasures which are to be obtained by a liberal education as well as that strength of mind which a regular course of mathematics is calculated to produce. I am of a good physical constitution, sanguine temperament, 24 years of age (next April), have labored some on a farm and am accustomed to fatigue. As for earthly goods— a full set of surgical instruments, part of an anatomical preparation, a few books, etc. will probably constitute the whole amount of what I shall possess when my affairs are arranged.

At the end of the letter he wrote:

I think I am willing to trust myself in the hands of God and go wherever His providence shall direct and with His assistance to undergo whatever may be His will. The great operations which are now in progress for the conversion of the world will go on whether I enter the field or not, but the command of God "Occupy till I come" will not allow me to rest in sloth while there remains so much land yet to be possessed. My prayer to Him is Lord what wilt Thou have me do. As far as I know my own heart I am willing to leave all those things which bind me to home and friends with ties almost as strong as life and spend and be spent in holding the light of the gospel of Jesus Christ before the feet of the benighted heathen who stumble over the dark mountains of death.

On March 2 the Reverend Rufus Anderson, another of Evarts' assistants and his successor as corresponding secretary of the American Board (1832–1866), acknowledged the application, and on May 14 Evarts reported the decision of the Board's Prudential (executive) Committee that Dr. Judd should take a thorough course in theology at Andover, beginning the next fall. Evarts added that the Committee wished to interview him in Boston.[19] Dr. Judd replied that he would come for an interview and that he was willing to take a theology course. [20] Evarts, apparently believing the matter settled, asked in his next letter if Dr. Judd knew of a pious, childless physician willing to go to Hawaii with the next missionary company, and inquired also if Dr. Judd's financial resources were sufficient to defray his expenses, estimated at $175 a year for room and board, at the Andover Seminary.[21]

In a letter misdated "June 31, 1827"—an indication of the agitated state of his mind—Dr. Judd notified Evarts of his intention to leave for Boston within the next three weeks. He explained at length his reluctance to ask his father for money. "My father is not a man of wealth. His former sources of gain are much diminished and now in the downhill of life [he] has a helpless family depending on him for support. Having designated me for his successor in business he has already expended much more for my education than he should have done in justice to the rest of the children." As for his own finances, he stated that he had no debts, that he owned a horse and a set of surgical instruments, and that he would sell the horse to pay the expenses of his trip to Boston. A few lines later he commented in a way which reveals the firmness of his resolution, "I have felt and do still feel that if God has called me into the missionary work He will provide for my wants." He closed with a promise to visit on his way to Boston a physician who might wish to join the missionary company.[22] The identity of this physician is nowhere revealed, and he may well have been as fictitious as "E. Judson."

Sometime in July Dr. Judd went to Boston and appeared before the Prudential Committee. Evidently he made a favorable impression, for Greene reported to Anderson on August 2, "Dr. Judd appears very well—very manageable and disposed to do what seems right. Things seem now as though he would go to the Islands next fall."[23] The very next day, so Dr. Judd stated in his autobiographical sketch, the Committee gave him the coveted appointment, which Evarts confirmed in a letter dated August 10: "You have been appointed to the responsible employment of physician to the Sandwich Island Mission, with the design of your ultimately preaching the Gospel to the heathen."[24]

Marriage and Farewell

Appointment as a missionary physician carried with it a vexing complication, for the American Board wisely insisted that none of the men sent to heathen lands should undertake their labors unmarried.[1] Dr. Judd faced, then, the double problem of speedily finding a wife who was willing to go with him on the mission to Hawaii and who could meet the strict moral and religious standards set by the Board. He found an extraordinarily felicitous solution to his problem in Laura Fish.

A descendant of John Fish, who by 1654 had settled in Stratford, Connecticut, Laura was born on April 2, 1804, in Plainfield Township, Otsego County, New York (just south of Paris Hill), the daughter of Elias Fish, a carpenter and sailor, and Sybil Williams Fish, who died when Laura was 23 months old.[2] The desolate story of her early years is best told in her own words, taken from the memoir which she wrote in the Judd family book:

My parents lived in Groton, Conn. . . . Somewhere near the year 1794–1800 they . . . moved to Plainfield, New York State, Otsego County, which was then considered *far west*. My father settled at the forks of Unadilla river at which place I was born. One month before the completion of my second year my mother died and I was left with six brothers to the charge of an only sister fifteen years older than myself. . . . Not many months after my mother's death my youngest brother, a seventh son, five years old, was choked to death with a bean which he was shelling by the side of my grandmother. . . . While my brothers and sisters were still weeping for their mother and this brother, my dear father received an injury in raising a bridge, which made him a cripple for the rest of his days and nearly cost him his life at the time. . . . When I entered my fourth year I was sent away from home to attend school. . . . I was an orphan; I felt it. My pillow was often wet with tears, and I think that turns of depression of spirit (which to this day come over me unbidden) had their foundation in those early trials of childhood.

A few months later she was seriously injured when a servant girl pushed her out of a hayloft. After her recovery her sister fetched her home.

I remained with her and at my grandfather Williams, till my sister was married to Mr. Benjamin Hubbel Tracy, and removed to Jefferson county. We resided in the village of Watertown till I was fourteen years of age. I attended the village school taught by Mr. Joel Everett. We removed to Sacket's Harbor in 1815, and I went thither also, for some time a member of his family as well as pupil. In the winter of 1819 my brother from Mexico, Oswego county, came to visit me, whom I had not seen since my infancy, and I went home with him and remained till the autumn of '23. . . . In Mexico, I first joined a Bible class, and taught in a Sabbath school. It was there also I first engaged in teaching a district school, and was subjected to the trying ordeal of "boarding 'round."[3]

Elsewhere she wrote,

I was but sixteen when I made my *debut* as school-teacher. I wonder if the little brown school-house still stands at the place where three ways meet?[4]

Fifty years later one of her pupils remembered her as "tall, commanding, slightly portly in figure, beautiful in feature, stately in carriage, engaging in manner. She was a queen fit to grace any court in christendom."[5] Another child, who first encountered her in 1855, left an equally vivid description. "Mrs. Judd was as stately as a queen. She wore her hair parted on the left side and her manner was attractive."[6] Her account continues,

In the winter of 1821, there was a revival in the congregation of the Rev. David R. Dixon, and many members of the Bible class were subjects of renewing grace, and I trust I was among that number. When I was just nineteen, I openly professed my faith in Christ by uniting with the Church in Mexico.[7]

In the winter of 1825–1826 she entered Miss N. Royce's Female Seminary in Clinton, New York. Here she encountered further privation.

I was poor—entirely dependent on my own exertions for support—not a friend to furnish me with a dollar; I was obliged to dress very plain and practise the most rigid economy in order to purchase books, pay my board, ½ tuition. My friends were kind, and waited till I raised money by teaching. I struggled hard—I suffered many mortifications—shed many tears, but my aim was high—I was as proud and independent as I was poor.

An unhappy love affair added to her distress.[8]

Under the circumstances it was natural for her to turn not only to her religion but to thoughts of missionary service. Her memoir states,

My interest in the cause of missions was first elicited in reading Mrs. Bingham's journal in the Missionary Herald, while spending a winter in Mr. Dixon's family. . . . I cherished an ardent desire to go in person to some part of the heathen world and carry the news of a Saviour's love.[9]

Family tradition has it that on the way back from his interview in Boston Dr. Judd made up his mind to ask Laura Fish, whom he scarcely knew, to marry him; that when he reached Paris Hill he commissioned "Hastings, his uncle," to do the actual proposing for him; and that at once she accepted.[10] Her own account of the courtship, recorded in the Judd family book apparently from her diary entries, gives tantalizingly few details:

Aug. 11, 1827. This evening I received an application to go to the Sandwich Islands as a missionary. . . . I will not decide for myself, but cast my burden on the Lord. May His unerring wisdom guide me.

Aug. 20. "The die is cast." I have in the strength of the Lord, consented Rebecca-like—"I WILL GO," yes, I will leave friends, native land, everything for Jesus.[11]

Four days later, Dr. Norton, pastor of the Congregational church in Clinton, wrote a certificate to the American Board that Miss Laura Fish was a member of his church in good standing.[12] On September 10 Greene acknowledged receipt of the certificate and informed Dr. Judd that she had been appointed to the Sandwich Island Mission.[13] Within a month after receiving his appointment, Dr. Judd had solved his twofold problem: he had located a bride, and the Board had approved his choice.

On September 19, the evening before his marriage, he wrote a hurried letter to Finney.

From New Lebanon I went to Boston, where after a stay of 2 weeks I received the appointment of missionary physician to the Sandwich Islands with the expectation of preaching the gospel eventually to the heathen, since which time I have been much occupied in visiting my friends and making my arrangements. . . . Miss Laura Fish is to be my companion—we are to be united tomorrow evening—and with pleasure do we take our lives in our hands and go out amongst the heathen. . . . We intend to leave Oneida County by the 15th of October—we wish very much to see you before we go—Shall we meet you and Mrs. F. in Utica at Synod? Friends all well—Do pray for us. O we need a great deal of faith and humility and every Christian grace. Laura sends her love to Mrs. F. She would write were it possible. Shall we hear from you soon?[14]

The marriage took place on September 20, with Dr. Norton performing the ceremony. Announcement of the wedding appeared in the *Western Recorder*, edited by Dr. Judd's uncle, Thomas Hastings.

On Thursday last, at an evening lecture in the village of Clinton, Gerrit P. Judd, M.D. of Paris, was married to Miss Laura Fish, of the Clinton Female Seminary. . . . Mr. and Mrs. Judd are to leave in a few days for Boston, where they expect to embark for the Sandwich Islands, about the first of November. . . . Mr. Judd goes out as physician to the missionaries at several stations, with the view of ultimately preaching the gospel.[15]

Unromantic as it may appear, their brief courtship was by no means unusual. All of the other medical missionaries to Hawaii, as well as a number of ministers in the various missionary companies, took brides less than five weeks before the date of sailing. Besides, short courtships were not uncommon at that time on the frontier.[16]

During the next three weeks the young couple visited their friends and made final arrangements. In a tense and tearful atmosphere they anticipated a journey which promised no earthly return. As day followed day, their emotions quickened with the agonizing thought that they might never again see their family and friends. Dr. Judd's letter to Finney, written on the night of October 4, gives unmistakable evidence of heartbreak and foreboding.

I received your message this day by Br. Kellogg. I have expected to see you and hear you preach at Utica before I leave and even now I do not altogether give it up. O Br. Finney I want to see you very much and so does Laura too. We have appointed the 15th inst. as a day on which our little missionary band will leave Utica on our way to Boston via New York. Should we not be able to see you before that time, I fear we shall never be able to do it, in this world. We regret exceedingly that our time is so much limited, as that we shall not be able to visit you at New Lebanon. I would travel 100 miles to behold your face if I had time, but as it is I must forego the pleasure unless you can meet us (in company with Mrs. F.) at Troy on the 16th. O do come to Troy and see us if you do not visit Utica. I write in the greatest haste imaginable and late at night but hope you will excuse. Mr. Finney you *must not omit to pray for us*. Farewell until we meet again.[17]

A week or so later his Uncle Seth Hastings gave him a religious book and in it wrote a long inscription containing the ominous sentence, "It is probable that we shall see each other no more in this world."[18]

Mrs. Judd carried with her a Book of Farewells, which her former pupils and friends, including Theodore Dwight Weld and Daniel Nash, inscribed with appropriate sentiments in prose and verse. In this book Dr. Judd's mother wrote,

My heart yearns over you with parental fondness. Shall I soon part with you and let you go to far distant Isles of the sea never to behold your face again? Yes, go and teach the poor benighted pagans the knowledge

Park Street Church today

of that Savior whom we hope we love and may long live in His vineyard and be the means of winning many souls to Jesus Christ.[19]

The day of their departure was one of anguish tempered with pious resolution. Elnathan's parting words to his son came from the heart of New England puritanism, "Never spend the hard-earned mite of the widow carelessly."[20]

Dr. Judd's memoir gives only the barest details, but it shows the deep emotion he felt.

This was a trying season to me but God gave me strength to endure it. I parted with my father and mother, all my brothers and sisters but one, who was absent, and all my relatives and friends in Oneida County, being commended in prayer by them to the care of the All-seeing God, and started for Boston on Monday [October 15]. We arrived in Boston on Saturday night.[21]

In Boston they stayed, so Dr. Judd stated, "in the pleasant and pious family of Mr. [Henry] Homes of Boudoin Place."[22] Here they met their associates in the Third Mission Company and a number of Bostonians prominent in church affairs, such as Dr. Lyman Beecher, at that time probably the most eminent preacher in New England, as well as Mr. and Mrs. John Tappan[23] and Theodore Dwight Weld—all later active in the antislavery movement. Their encounter with such people shows how closely related were the Board's missionary ventures to the main stream of humanitarian evangelism in the United States in the generation before the Civil War.

On Wednesday, October 31, they attended a public meeting at the Park Street church, where eight years before the first missionary company to Hawaii had worshiped.[24] The sailing was postponed from Thursday to Saturday, November 3. At 2 p.m. that afternoon they assembled at the wharf, where they heard a prayer by Beecher, so moving that almost everyone present wept. They left the wharf in small boats which took them half a mile out in the harbor to the *Parthian*, which was to be their home for the next five months.[25] They spent the remaining hours with their friends and well-wishers, as one witness later wrote, "in the crowded and lumbered cabin of the *Parthian* in the midst of confusion that denied the exercise of thought, with the deep waters of the Atlantic tossing under the

keel and signals of a long separation waving in the air."[26] The
Parthian weighed anchor at 3 P.M. The Reverend Charles Samuel
Stewart, a member of the Board's Second Company in Hawaii
1823–1825, along with Beecher, Evarts, Henry Hill (the Board's
treasurer), Weld, and several others stayed aboard for the first two
hours, and returned with the pilot boat. For Dr. Judd the time
passed quickly, since he was busy talking with Evarts and Hill
about the mission stores, which had been entrusted to his care.[27]
Once again it was a solemn leave-taking. As he wrote in his journal,
"Parted with these the last of my friends. Found it indeed a trying
season. It seemed truly as if all had been now given up, and as the
thought thrilled through my brain it left a pain at my heart which
I shall never forget."[28]

Mrs. Judd's feelings are vividly described in a letter to the
Finneys begun on October 30 and finished on the day of their
departure.[29] The letter is inscribed "Mr. Weld" on the cover, and
presumably she handed it to him before he left with the pilot.
The last lines are a highly appropriate quotation from Lord Byron.

Boston Oct. 30th 1827

Ever dear Mr. and Mrs. Finney,

Although my heavenly Father is sending me away from America without seeing your *dear* face again, still I must tell you, you hold a place
in my *warmest* affections and ever will. When I was in Troy I felt as if
I could not go without seeing you but it seemed duty, and I was obliged
to submit. I cannot say that I did, without murmuring however, for I
felt as if it was a gratification I *could not* be denied. I had the pleasure of
hearing from various sources, how the Lord is still prospering you in
your labors of love, how He is not only giving you stars to fill up your
crown, but how He is getting to Himself the glory in bowing and
breaking the stubborn hearts of His enemies. Dr. Beecher says, "he
would rather live in this day, than in the meridian splendour of the
Millenium." By the way, this same Dr. Beecher is a most wonderful
man. I wish you could have heard him lay down the law to sinners
yesterday. I tell the good folks of Boston how much he preaches like
the *madman* of Oneida County. I tell them perhaps they do not think it
a very great compliment, but they may be assured it is the best one I
could possibly pay him. If I am not mistaken the period is not far distant
when there will be a great and *tremendous* shaking in this eastern country.

39

Now a few words about my very important self and husband, and my words must indeed be few, for I expect Mr. Ibbetson every moment to accompany myself and the doctor to the ship. I am going to put my state room in order, as we sail day after tomorrow (God willing), and now, how do you think I feel? God has heard my prayer and granted me my desire in permitting me to go to [the] heathen. He has prospered me far beyond my most ardent wishes in every preparation, and what lack I yet? O I can tell you, there is great lack, a heart burning as it ought with love and anxiety for the souls of the heathen. I am ashamed of my *little feeling*, in such a glorious undertaking.

The natives that accompany us have arrived. They are very interesting. One of them I saw last evening at Mr. Evarts. He said on his way from Cornwall they stopped and had meetings. They made him preach. Mr. Evarts asked what he preached. He said, "O I tell them, 'Much to be done.'" We told [him] that was a very good text. They are all professedly pious, and we expect much from their influence. O you remember Fanny Thomas, now Mrs. Gulick, one of our happy number, she is well, we are very sociable when together. I shall leave you to guess the most common topic. She said to me last evening, "How is it that Boston people are sending *Finneyites* on missions? I should not suppose they would dare to."

Wed[nesday] morn[ing].

As I told you yesterday we went down to the ship. Everything is arranged for our convenience as much as it can be. Mr. and Mrs. Tappan of this city made a party last evening to which the missionaries and friends of missions were invited. We had prayers and at the close sung, "Blest be the tie that binds." It was an interesting season. Mrs. Hall from the Bombay mission attended.

I have many things to do today, as it is the last day I have to spend in my *dear native* land, it brings to mind the closing scene of life. It [is] a most solemn thought that this is the last day in which I shall ever exert a direct influence on Christian community and on the impenitent, but it is even so.

When I was in New York I saw Elisa Michell. She spoke of you with a great deal of affection, hopes to see you in that city.

One request and I have done. Will you always as long [as] we live pray for us, pray that we may be found faithful, that we may be very humble, that we may be the instruments of saving many heathen, that we may meet again where we shall ever hear the word.

Farewell. Pardon me, I have another request. May I not have the pleasure of a correspondence? I shall always feel a deep interest in your prosperity in all that concerns you. Dr. Judd and Mrs. Gulick send an affectionate remembrance and much love.

Ever yours affectionately
LAURA F. JUDD

I have just entered the room and read this letter given me by Laura. She has said all I think of just now. I will only add my request and expectation of a correspondence and our affectionate remembrance in your prayers so long as we shall live. Write this winter and direct to the care of Jeremiah Evarts, Cor. Sec., A.B.C.F.M., Boston. Good bye.

May the Lord sustain you under all your trials and missionary labours.

Affectionately yours
GERRIT P. JUDD

Nov. 1st. Dear brother Weld arrived yesterday, and leaves tomorrow, visits you at Stephentown. I can assure you my spirit goes with him.

I have just been out and met Mr. Frank. He gave me letters from you both. O how it makes my heart bound. I feel as if seeing you was almost the only *desired favor* the Lord has denied me, but it is undoubtedly for some wise purpose. God has always led me in a way I knew not, but it has always been with *great kindness*. I am anything but satisfied with what I have written. So many subjects rush into my mind at once, it is difficult to arrange them on paper, but br.Weld will tell you all. You ask us to write. O it will be the greatest pleasure [to] correspond with friends that are bound around my heart with so many tender cords of love and affection, but farewell, words are too poor and weak to tell you what I feel, pray for me, and my husband.

We shall meet in heaven I trust.

Ever yours
MRS. L. JUDD

This morning at nine the Parthian spread her light sails to the breeze, so "Farewell and if forever, still forever fare you well."

With much affection
L. F. JUDD

Nov. 3d, 1827

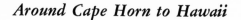

Around Cape Horn to Hawaii

The *Parthian*, which took the third missionary company from Boston around Cape Horn to Hawaii, was scarcely a commodious ship. Built in 1819, she was registered at 327 tons, 103 feet in length, 30 feet beam, and 19 feet draught.[1] This vessel carried the 20 members of the Third Company, a crew of 19, and two non-missionary passengers, Charles Taylor, on his way to assume command of a ship in the Pacific Northwest, and Josiah Thompson Marshall, the owner's son. The ship also carried 200 tons of freight and stores, including materials for two frame houses, a printing press, type, paper, and 40,000 tracts printed in the Hawaiian language.[2] Miss Maria Patton, one of the missionaries aboard, wrote dolefully that when she lay in her bunk her head was only one foot below the deck planking, so that her sleep was continually broken by the pounding of heavy feet. Both Dr. Judd and Mr. Stephen Shepard had to crawl several feet on their hands and knees to reach their berths.[3] Nevertheless, by contemporary standards the *Parthian* was, as Dr. Judd remarked, "a swift and good seaboat," and of a size then considered adequate.[4]

Almost immediately after sailing, the *Parthian* ran into heavy weather, which by Wednesday and Thursday (November 7 and 8) of the next week blew up into a gale. All the missionaries except Mrs. Theodosia Green became instantly and dreadfully seasick. On November 10 Dr. Judd wrote in his journal,

We continued sick about a week—had sleepless nights. During this time my mind was confused so that I do not now recollect much of what passed distinctly. . . . We were hardly able to stand even by holding on with both hands and every now and then we were called to belch up the contents of our stomachs without discrimination. O such a horrid appearance as we presented. It is enough to sicken me even now as I recollect the scene. We were crowded together (about 20 in all) in a small room say 10 feet either way—some 8 or 10 trunks, boxes and bags occupy the space intervening between our table and the inhabitants. The floor has not been visible since our embarkation owing to the super-abundance of grime and filth of every description. Such a horrid stream as issues from the cabin is quite enough to sicken anybody.[5]

Meanwhile, so one of the missionaries reported, a cat on board ship "mewed all night as if in the agony of death."[6]

Mrs. Judd was more fortunate than the others.

Monday morning [November 5] with great exertion I got on deck. Waves running mountains high. I had been seated but a few minutes when one broke over deck, and wet me completely. My mouth and eyes and ears filled with salt water. The effect was salutary. My sea sickness left me and returned not again.[7]

Further entries in her journal give a stirring account of the storm.

Thursday 8th. Yesterday about noon, the wind shifted. The sky darkened and there was every appearance of a tremendous gale. I was on deck. Capt. Blinn says, "Boys not a minute to lose." Things on deck were lashed with double caution, sails taken in or reefed closely. Orders were given and obeyed with the greatest alacrity, and many a fearful and anxious glance was cast to that part of the horizon where the storm was gathering. I remained on deck as long as my sensitive nerves could endure it. About 3 o'clock I went below and the hatchways were closed, the dead light put in, and the cabin converted into a perfect prison. . . . The timbers creaked and groaned like a human being in dying agonies. Three thunder showers followed each other in rapid succession, accompanied with lightning so vivid that the little which could enter my sky light (two inches bro[ad] and four long) almost blinded me. Once in a while between the gusts of wind I could distinguish the capt[ain]'s voice giving orders. About midnight the little green boat that we left the wharf in, was carried away and the railing on the side of the ship to which it was lashed with sixteen of our chairs in it; (leaving eight, for six families besides the young ladies and natives.) And it seemed as if the ship must rock to pieces. Never before did I feel so much the exceeding weakness and impotency of human will and human skill. . . .

Another morning dawned upon us on the waters (if not on the land) of the living. Towards noon the winds were entirely hushed, and this afternoon there is a great calm. Our language is, O give thanks unto the Lord for He is good, for His mercy endureth forever. Capt. Blinn (though an old and constant navigator) says he has not seen such a gale in ten years, and not one ship in fifty could have rode it. He had axes ready all night to cut away the masts if she capsized, so that she might possibly be righted again.

Gradually the missionary family recovered. By November 10 Dr. Judd felt well enough to begin his journal, but a second trial awaited them. As he reported to the American Board,

When I got able to go on deck, the captain told me that his orders from Mr. Marshall were to *supply the missionaries with wood and water only*— that he should accordingly serve out to us three quarts of water apiece daily and that it would be best for us to appoint a cook and steward from our company.[8]

Further details of their predicament appear in a joint letter written after the missionary company reached Honolulu.

In vain did Dr. Judd remonstrate—in vain did he inform him of our understanding of the agreement—in vain did he show him your letter of instructions; the capt[ain] was inflexible. . . . At length Dr. Judd succeeded in opening a box of crockery, and after much perplexity we managed to live independently of Capt. Blinn. Two of the ladies superintended during the week, in rotation. This with the assistance of one of the natives and their husbands, contrived to keep us from starvation. But you can easily conceive that this way of doing business was exceedingly incommodious. During a part of the time we had no more than 7 knives and forks, and at no time had every individual both a knife and fork.[9]

44

The American Board later stated that the owners of the *Parthian* had contracted to provide a steward and a cook to feed the missionaries. The Board exonerated the owners but flatly accused the captain, Richard D. Blinn, of having violated the agreement. Ironically, two copies of the contract were on board the *Parthian* during the entire voyage, one in Blinn's possession, which of course he did not reveal, and a second, which had been placed among other mission papers to be delivered to the Board's agent in Honolulu.[10]

The incident illustrates the latent animosity which existed between the seafaring and missionary groups. This animosity, of which the Third Company had a bitter foretaste, flared up again during the voyage, and in Hawaii reached the proportions of an open feud. But, for the time being, the missionaries adjusted to their discomfort. Mrs. Judd noted, "We possessed but little practical knowledge of the arts of the *cuisine* at first, but have sometimes astonished each other and ourselves at our success in producing palatable dishes, and most of all, light bread."[11]

Within a week or so after the storm abated, the voyage settled into the monotony of shipboard routine. Mrs. Judd commented on November 13, "All the members of the mission family better this morning. I succeeded in getting the ladies on deck. The voyage thus far has been uncommonly tedious."

On November 15 the *Parthian* encountered a mysterious ship. Mrs. Judd's account is graphic. "Capt[ain] fears it may be one of the *red* or *black flag* gentlemen. Accordingly all the fire arms put in order—says the ladies must put on hats and pea jackets, go on deck and the sight of so many persons would confound them." Piracy in these waters was at the time far from a chimera. In 1834 the novelist Richard Henry Dana had a terrifying encounter with a possible pirate in this vicinity.[12]

The next morning the mysterious vessel had vanished. The weather was sultry, and the sea was calm. Mrs. Judd wrote: "The *Parthian* glides along majestically through the deep never weary, never halting. Been sewing on deck, feel as quiet as on land, but that my ears are annoyed with oaths." On November 17 they evaded a waterspout. On December 6 it rained, and the company took full advantage of the opportunity to catch fresh water for cooking and washing. As Mrs. Judd stated, "We feel the value of water after being kept on allowance as we do at sea. We have three quarts apiece a day which is none too much for our cooking and drink in these warm latitudes."

On Christmas their minds turned naturally to thoughts of home.

The warmest Christmas I ever knew. The[r]mometer 84° in shade, sun vertical. Gentlemen stood in the shadow of their hats. We are but four or five hundred miles off the coast of S[outh] America, pass Rio Janeiro this evening. Crossed the tropic of capricorn five this afternoon, lost the trade wind. A Christmas dinner of stuffed boiled ham. It was very salt. Cannot help thinking of the friends and comforts of our native land, and hope our friends remember us.

For the next two weeks, as they approached and entered the roaring forties, they encountered a succession of storms known as pamperos, from heavy winds blowing off the heated plains (pampas) in the River Plate area, storms in which thunder and lightning alternated with periods of sunshine and hail.[13] The day after Christmas Mrs. Judd wrote,

I was making some salt risings for fresh bread (which we have occasionally) in a small jar, had it on the floor, with a pitcher of hot water and a keg of flour, which Mrs. Clark was holding for me. Suddenly the ship heaved, and away we went to the opposite side of the cabin. . . . At breakfast . . . I tried to help get away the dishes and tumbled about till nine o'clock, and then went to bed, which I have not yet been able to leave. Have had one of those very distressing turns I have been subject to. I thought of home, and the friends that used to take care of me, and I . . .

Here a page is missing from her journal, possibly because someone wished to suppress details of a heartbreaking episode. It is clear that she miscarried as a result of her fall.[14]

On January 7, 1828, she wrote cheerfully and in a way to indicate that she was recovering, "It is very grand to see the *Parthian* move along, as the white waves part, and comb up each side of her. Been mending clothes for my dear companion, an employment as delightful as new. I am more and more sensible every day of the blessing of an affectionate friend." On the 14th they passed the Falkland Islands. They saw whales, ice birds, Cape hens, and albatrosses, but did not see the land. On the 18th they sighted Cape St. John, on the eastern tip of Staten Island. Mrs. Judd wrote, "The rugged peaks of Staten Island appeared to the west of us. I have sat the live long forenoon feasting my eyes. It seems to give us all new life."

At this point they entered the most dangerous part of the voyage, the passage southward and westward around Cape Horn. Here they faced icebergs, snow, sleet, gales, prevailing head winds, and a strong current running against them from the southwest. The perils were not by sea alone, as one of the Hawaiians aboard the *Parthian* lugubriously reported, for in the valleys ashore were savages, reputed to be cannibals, who occasionally came out in canoes to attack passing ships.[15]

The temperature dropped from 72° on January 2 to 35° on January 11. On the 15th, in her unheated stateroom, Mrs. Judd wrote, "Am almost froze. Sat in my berth all day, and sewed while Dr. J. read to me. The sea is rough, and we are subject to sudden and violent commotions." On the 19th, the day after they sighted Staten Island, Dr. Judd noted, "Our situation is the same as it was yesterday. . . . We are almost becalmed. The current bears us out of our course." For the next nine days he wrote nothing in his Journal, but Mrs. Judd managed to make a few entries in hers:

Monday 21st. The current still drives us back. Meeting with the waves makes bad seas. Staten Island still visible at the north of us. . . . But we cast our burden on the Lord. He that led, guided and protected the wandering children of Israel through the wilderness will surely be our Guide and Protector.

Tuesday 22nd. The land still in sight. We have been driven back by the current all night. . . . Just after tea a squall struck us suddenly and unexpectedly. . . . I counted fifteen men on the main mast furling the sail. Waves rolled the highest I ever saw them. . . . In a short time, all was done that could be, the deck quiet, no one to be seen but the man at the helm, one mate and the capt[ain]. . . .

Wed[nesday] morn[ing]. The last night has been a sleepless one to most of us. The winds raged in all their fury. Capt[ain] up all night, said he feared the decks would be swept and the masts carried away in spite of him. Waves so high as to be seen above the foreyard, must have been 40 or 50 ft.

To make matters worse, the cask of drinking water opened on the 25th was unfit for consumption, even when served as tea.[16]

On January 28 Dr. Judd resumed his narrative.

It is nine days since I wrote in my journal. The only excuse I have for omitting it is that we have been doubling Cape Horn. To those who know what it is to double this Cape this is a sufficient excuse. As for those who do not I can only say I hope they never may except for the promotion of the cause of Christ.

Throughout, the reaction of the missionary family was of a religious nature in keeping with their calling. From the start of the voyage, just as soon as they had recovered from seasickness, they held regular services on Sundays as well as prayer meetings on Wednesdays and Saturdays. Mrs. Judd's journal contains a number of entries indicative of her faith. Dr. Judd's journal reveals a similar piety.

I feel it to be very important that a missionary have such a burning zeal for the cause as will enable him to endure the severest trials. . . . I am so wicked that it seems impossible that I can ever be of any use in the work of the Lord. . . . A few more fleeting years and our work will be finished, well or ill done. How insignificant it makes all our self denials when we look upward, when we *really think* of God and Eternity.

In passages such as these he shows a remarkable affinity to his ancestor, Thomas Judd, who had settled in puritan Massachusetts in 1634. Two hundred years later, as if they were of the same generation instead of six generations removed,[17] Dr. Judd invoked the Calvinism of his ancestor in all its militant fervor. "O my soul, trust thou in God. He is our refuge, a very present help in times of trouble. If God be for us who can be against us?"

By January 29 the greater part of the danger had passed. Cape Horn was safely behind them. Mrs. Judd commented happily,

I never saw so beautiful a prospect. The whole expanse of water visible is as smooth as glass, and if it does not reflect the trees, it does the clouds, the sun, the ship, and the large beautiful birds, that sail about continually. The colour of the clouds varies from the purest white to blue and red, all in curls, and with the most splendid embroidery. We are so far south and the days so long that the twilight meets the morning.

On February 5 the *Parthian* was heading north at eight knots in fair weather with the temperature at a comfortable 62°. Two days later the missionaries held a thanksgiving service in celebration of their safe passage around Cape Horn. On the 19th they encountered a waterspout. Dr. Judd wrote, "It approached the ship with such rapidity that the captain and other officers appeared to be much frightened. They loaded a cannon as quick as possible. They got ready and fired just in time to break it or without doubt it would have gone over or at least very near us. Had it passed over the ship the captain said we should have gone down in three minutes."

Two days later, on February 21, tension which had been building up for the sixteen weeks they had been at sea erupted into one of those ugly little episodes which mar any great enterprise. Taylor, one of the nonmissionary passengers, pointedly refused to speak to Mrs. Judd and returned to her unopened a note which she sent him requesting an explanation. This incident brought to a head the long-repressed animosity between the missionaries and the sailors. In a defiant mood Captain Blinn broke a well-established maritime custom by ordering several crew members to paint a longboat on the following Sunday. The missionaries, of course, were indignant at this violation of the Sabbath, and, as Dr. Judd stated in a letter to the American Board,

Mr. Green remonstrated with him, but with only partial success, for the work went on for a while, but finally they desisted. How much influence Mr. T[aylor] has over Capt. Blinn I cannot tell, but I think he has treated us very differently of late. Although they must know that Mr. and Mrs. Shepard, Mrs. Judd and myself hear their conversation in the after cabin, yet it has been of late not only shockingly profane but obscene beyond comparison.[18]

Shortly thereafter Blinn and his two associates hit upon a malicious device to taunt the missionaries, who made a habit of singing hymns on deck in the early evening hours. Dr. Judd noted with furious disapproval, "Capt. Blinn, Mr. Tailor and Marshall amused themselves in ridiculing us. They sing in the most vociferous tones the most profane, obscene and vulgar songs, one of their company lining for the rest as is our custom. We do not however appear to notice them."

Later Blinn, Taylor, and Marshall indulged in further malice by telling tall tales about the missionaries to John Coffin Jones, Jr., the American commercial agent in Honolulu. Jones reported, "This taking missionary freight at 18 dollars the ton must be unprofitable business. A more unwelcome cargo never was brought. . . . Their conduct on board the ship, I have understood was not the most proper. Capt. Blinn was apprehensive at one time that they would take the command of the ship from him, and got his arms in readiness to protect himself."[19]

Nevertheless, in spite of opposition from the maritime interest, the missionary movement gained strength. About the time of the boat-painting episode, four men sat down in Elnathan Judd's white frame house in Paris Hill to write short notes in a letter book destined for the Judds in Hawaii. Father Nash wrote cheerfully of the revivals in Hamilton and Madison counties; Charles Samuel Stewart, missionary to Hawaii in 1823–1825, who had bade them farewell when the *Parthian* left Boston, wrote a letter of reminiscence and encouragement; George B. Whiting told of his plans to go as a missionary to the Pacific Northwest; and Ashbell S. Wells stated his intention to undertake a domestic mission to Indiana.[20] Here in miniature is evidence of the mounting power of evangelism in the generation before the Civil War.

The last days of the voyage passed in heat and discomfort. On March 8 Dr. Judd noted, "Weather uncomfortably warm, awoke this morning with an inflammation of the eyes, the left eye very painful." As late as March 18 he commented that his eyes were so sore he could barely read. That day they ran into a gale, and Mrs. Judd became seasick. But both of them were up all of the night of March 20, ministering to Mrs. Green, who miscarried early on the morning of the 21st.[21] Mrs. Green was grateful for Dr. Judd's care. She wrote in her journal, "We have a kind, sympathetic and, I trust, skillful man for our physician, think he will be a devoted Christian and a useful man."[22]

On March 27 a crew member screamed "Land O!" from the masthead, but the announcement was premature. The next day, in a fever of anticipation, they saw a number of land birds, and on the morning of March 29 they caught their first glimpse of the Islands. Mrs. Judd wrote,

Among the passengers the excitement is intense and variously expressed; some rush below to their state-rooms to pour out their hearts in gratitude and thanksgiving, others fear to turn away lest the scene fade or prove a delusion, like our dreams of home land; some exhaust their vocabulary in exclamations of delight—others sit alone in tears and silence.[23]

At three o'clock on the afternoon of the next day, Sunday, March 30, 1828, after a voyage of 148 days and over 16,000 miles, the *Parthian* dropped anchor in Honolulu harbor.[24] In order not to break the Sabbath, the missionaries spent the night on board ship. Mrs. Judd wrote:

We passed a sleepless night; the vessel being at anchor we missed the accustomed rocking. At nine o'clock this morning we were handed over the ship's side (by our kind and unwearying friend Mr. S[ymmes], the mate), into the launch. . . . We were followed all the way from the landing by a crowd of natives, men, women and children, dressed and undressed. Many of them wore a sheet of native cloth, tied on one shoulder, not unlike the Roman toga; one had a shirt minus pantaloons, another had a pair of pantaloons minus a shirt; while a large number were destitute of either. One man looked very grand with an umbrella and shoes, the only foreign articles he could command. The women were clad in native costume, the *pau*, which consists of folds of native cloth about the hips, leaving the shoulders and waist quite exposed; a small number donned in addition a very feminine garment made of unbleached cotton, drawn close around the neck, which was quite becoming. Their hair was uncombed and their faces unwashed, but all of them were good natured. Our appearance furnished them much amusement; they laughed and jabbered, ran on in advance, and turned back to peer into our faces. I laughed and cried too, and hid my face for very shame.[25]

Surrounded by nudity, and embarrassed as only puritans can be embarrassed by a display of flesh, the Third Company proceeded to the mission house, some afoot, some in a one-horse wagon, and others in two carts drawn by natives, draft animals still being in short supply. On the way they visited briefly the pious and portly

Houses of the prime minister, Kalanimoku (from a drawing by A. Pellion)

Queen Regent, Kaahumanu, who went with them to the mission house.[26] Here they held religious services in an atmosphere of solemnity and pent-up emotions. With natives sitting on the floor and crowding around the door and windows, they sang the hymn beginning,

Kindred in Christ, for His dear sake,
A hearty welcome here receive;
May we together now partake
The joys which only He can give.

Mrs. Judd wrote, "Some of the company had sufficient self-control to join in the singing, but I was choking; I had made great efforts all the morning to be calm, and to control an overflowing heart, but when we knelt around that family altar, I could no longer subdue my feelings."[27]

After prayers they ate heartily and drank water brought from a mountain spring. Mrs. Judd wrote, "As we had not tasted fruit or vegetables for months, it was difficult to satisfy thoroughly *salted* appetites with fresh food." That evening she added, "Is it enchantment? Can it be a reality that I am on dear mother earth again? A clean, snug little chamber all to ourselves! I can go to the door, and by the light of the moon see the brown village and the distant, dark green hills and valleys. Strange sounds meet the ear. The ocean's roar is exchanged for the lowing of cattle on the neighboring plains; the braying of donkeys, and the bleating of goats, and even the barking of dogs are music to me."[28]

Hawaiian Islands in 1828

The newly arrived missionaries gazed in 1828 with curiosity and misgiving at the village of Honolulu, which sprawled untidily across the lowland plain between the harbor and the jagged mountains beyond. At that time, and for at least a generation to come, Honolulu looked parched and unattractive. In her memoirs Mrs. Judd mentioned "gray and red rocky hills, unrelieved by a single shade of green . . . not one white cottage, no church spire, not a garden nor a tree to be seen save the grove of cocoanuts."[1] Others shared her mood of disenchantment. Francis Warriner, a naval officer, complained, "Instead of the paradise which had been floating in my imagination, the island presented a barren and sunburnt appearance."[2] Sereno Bishop, a missionary descendant, described the Honolulu of his childhood with disdain. "This town was not then an attractive place. By May or June there was much heat and dust, and no verdure in sight. The small mission herd had thoroughly depastured the plain which extended unbroken by house or tree to Punahou, while brown Punchbowl with its dry slopes frowned darkly above. . . . Honolulu was a hard-looking old camp in those days. . . . Nothing could be less attractive than the general aspect of the town."[3]

Few observers neglected to describe Honolulu's native grass huts. To Mrs. Judd they resembled "straw bee hives," but Dr. Judd wrote dourly, "They look like pig styes rather than houses." Others compared them to wigwams or haystacks, oblong, rough-finished, and weather-beaten.[4] On close inspection, as Mrs. Judd later discovered when she made a "walk of usefulness" through the village, many of the huts turned out to be vermin-ridden and swarming with swine, ducks, and dogs as well as with human beings.[5] James Jackson Jarves, the journalist and art collector who came to Hawaii in 1837, wrote in his pseudo-autobiography, "Conceive a thousand or more thatched huts, looking like geometrical hay-stacks, most of them low and filthy in the extreme, scattered higgledy-piggledy over a plain, and along the banks of a scanty river, surrounded in general with dilapidated mud-walls, and inhabited by a mixed population of curs, pigs, Shanghae [sic] poultry, and unwashed natives."[6]

Barely fifty years before, in 1778, the exploring expedition of Captain James Cook of the British navy had chanced upon Hawaii. Although the Islands are larger in area than Connecticut and Rhode Island combined, they lie in isolation in the North Pacific, 2,000 miles from any major land body, and earlier voyages of exploration had missed them. At the time of Cook's voyage, the Islands supported a population of 300,000 natives in a state of relative ease and indolence, for Hawaii has fertile soil and a pleasant subtropical climate. Prevailing easterly trade winds counteract the heat of the sun, and the temperature usually hovers in the low seventies. In keeping with the mildness of the weather, the natives wore few clothes and subsisted for the most part in comfort on a simple diet of fish and taro, a starchy tuber which they pounded into a paste called *poi*. Like other Polynesians, they lacked metals, draft animals, writing, and the wheel. Upon occasion, cruelty and eroticism marred their social relationships, and despotic chiefs and a repressive tabu system brought a measure of misery into their lives, but on the whole it appears that they were not so barbarous as the New England missionaries alleged.[7]

In the decades after Cook's discovery, an increasing number of ships, especially those taking fur from the Northwest Coast to the Far East, stopped in Hawaiian ports for fresh water and provisions.

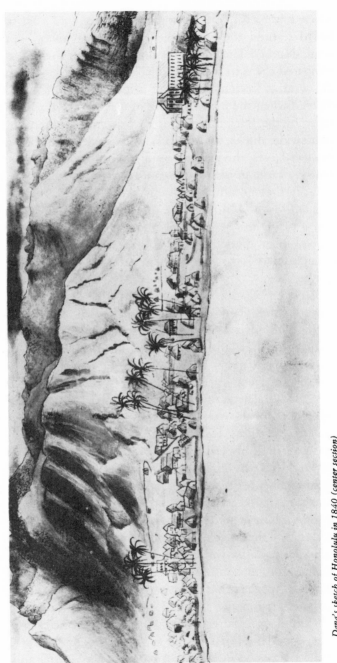

Dana's sketch of Honolulu in 1840 (center section)

At that time, European civilization, reinforced by the Industrial Revolution, was spreading all over the world. In Hawaii, as elsewhere, the motive forces at the start of the European imperialist movement tended to be economic rather than political. Only later did the flag follow trade. In particular, merchants from the United States and Europe sought native produce. Until the late 1820s traders dealt profitably in Hawaii's native sandalwood, for which there was a ready market in Canton. After 1820, when whalers began to operate in waters off Japan, a number of ports in Hawaii, especially Honolulu on Oahu and Lahaina on Maui, regularly serviced an expanding whaling fleet. In 1828, a typical year, 157 whalers, mainly American, touched Honolulu and Lahaina, and until the 1860s the recurrent visits of the whaling fleet in the fall and spring provided the Islands with their main source of revenue. As a natural consequence, the Islands soon acquired a foreign colony, mainly from the United States, Great Britain, and France. During the 1820s Hawaii had about fifty resident white traders; a hundred or more stranded sailors, an unruly and unreliable group; and at any time in the spring and fall no less than six hundred transient seafaring men who, as a contemporary saying went, hung their consciences on Cape Horn as they passed westward into the Pacific.[8]

The presence of mariners and traders created a number of problems which the natives were almost helpless to combat. Although in some respects the Hawaiians benefited from contact with Europeans and Americans in the premissionary period, it is plain that for such benefits they paid a prohibitive price, since the white man brought not only livestock, iron, and the wheel but also syphilis, smallpox, and rum. Under the impact of the white man's diseases, to which the natives had little resistance, the Hawaiian population fell from 300,000 in 1778 to about 85,000 in 1850.[9] For similar reasons many other primitive cultures, for example, those of Fiji and the New Hebrides, suffered comparable population decline.[10] Many of the surviving natives slipped into a dreamlike lethargy, compensated in part by alcoholism and sensuality, while the chiefs, infatuated by hitherto unknown luxuries such as silk, tobacco, and liquor, made scant progress in adapting themselves or their people to the Occidental civilization which Cook's voyage had thrust upon them. As Judge William Lee later commented, "Living without exertion, and contented with enough to eat and drink, they give themselves no care for the future, and mope away life, without spirit, ambition, or hope."[11] Overawed by the more powerful and better-educated traders and sailors, who came with iron, guns, and big ships, the Hawaiians, like other native groups throughout the world, suffered from a sense of inferiority which led them to feel contempt for their traditional primitive way of life. When they saw white men breaking the native tabus with impunity, they lost faith in their religion and in their institutions as a whole. In the language of the anthropologist, they felt social staleness and cultural fatigue.[12] In short, invaded by a more advanced civilization, the Hawaiian people almost lost their cultural identity and their will to live, and the traders, interested mainly in profit or vice, made little effort to check the progressive deterioration of the original inhabitants.

Jacques Arago, who visited the Islands in 1819, left a disheartening description of conditions at that time.

A miserable hut, built of straw, from twenty-five to thirty feet long, and from twelve to fifteen feet broad, the entrance to which is by a low and narrow door; some mats, on which several half-naked giants are reposing, and who bear the titles of ministers and generals; two chairs, on which are seated, on days of ceremony, a large, fat, dirty, heavy, proud man and a stout half-naked woman . . . such is the palace of the monarch of the Sandwich Islands; and such are the King and Queen of Owhyee, and such is their dignified court.[13]

Meanwhile, as a counterbalance to the sailors and traders, who roved the world mainly to exploit, there arose a kind of spiritual imperialism, the missionary movement. All over the globe, from Africa and Madagascar to Malaya and the Pacific isles, zealous and dedicated men and women undertook the gigantic task of evangelizing the world. The spirit of their enterprise is well expressed in the hymn written in 1832 by Dr. Judd's uncle, Thomas Hastings, "Hail to the brightness of Zion's glad morning," with its vision of Christian prayers arising from all lands and all the islands of the sea. The greater number of the Protestant missionaries came from Great Britain and the United States, supported by private funds, in contrast to the missionaries of the three previous centuries, such as those from Spain and Portugal, who enjoyed government support.[14] In 1820—the same year that whaling ships began to make regular, demoralizing visits to Hawaii—the first contingent of fourteen missionaries, sent out by the American Board, arrived in the brig *Thaddeus*, and in 1823 a second missionary company came as a welcome and much-needed reinforcement. Their goal, in harmony with the new liberal Calvinism preached by such men as Finney, was to bring not only Protestant Christianity but also social reform of an Occidental variety to primitive peoples throughout the world. As stated in the instructions of the American Board's Prudential Committee to the first company,

Your views are not to be limited to a low or a narrow scale; but you are to open your hearts wide, and set your mark high. You are to aim at nothing short of covering those islands with fruitful fields and pleasant dwellings, and schools and churches; of raising up the whole people to an elevated state of Christian civilization; of bringing, or preparing the means of bringing, thousands and millions of the present and succeeding generations to the mansions of eternal blessedness.[15]

The American missionaries, convinced that theirs was the only true religion, quite naturally regarded the Hawaiians as heathen wallowing in unspeakable depravity. Hiram Bingham of the First Company, who became the unofficial leader and spokesman of the mission, commented on the "destitution, degradation, and barbarism, among the almost naked savages."[16] The Reverend Charles Stewart of the Second Company spoke in disgust of "the dreadful abominations daily taking place around us, drunkenness and adultery, gambling and theft, deceit, treachery, and death."[17] James Jackson Jarves characterized the situation as an "extraordinary intermixture of civilization and barbarism. . . . Within sound of one of Watts' hymns, as sung by a native choir, the curious visitor would be cautiously conducted into the premises of a high chief, who was surreptitiously indulging himself in witnessing wanton dances by young, half-clad maidens, followed by scenes not to be described."[18] Others, including Chester S. Lyman and Mrs. Oliver Emerson, have left appalling yet credible accounts of drunkenness, incest, sodomy, and prostitution.[19] Parents in the mission, fearing contamination, as a rule forbade their children to learn the native language.[20] Henry A. Wise reported that native living conditions in Honolulu were "in all save absolute want or destitution, far below in the moral scale, the worst hovels of iniquity in the great cities of the Old World."[21]

In particular, the missionaries were appalled at the seminudity of the native population. All shared the revulsion expressed by Mrs. Judd on her first day ashore. In 1840 Joseph G. Clark stated, "The males are clad, some of them in trowsers and hat, and no shirt or shoes; others with shirts and minus the trowsers; and one I saw with hat and shoes, without either shirt or pants."[22] Sereno Bishop has recorded a family anecdote that one day before his birth in 1828 a group of Hawaiian women led by a royal dame entered his mother's sitting room stark naked after a sea bath. They carried their clothes with them and chatted unconcernedly as they proceeded to dress.[23] With unconcealed irritation Mrs. Jarves spoke of Honolulu in 1839 as "a most disagreeable, filthy place, where you are subjected to sights, which would make any city lady blush fifty times a day."[24]

For a number of reasons the missionaries made fast progress toward the realization of their objective. In Hawaii, as elsewhere in the world, the disintegration of the primitive culture because of the impact of Occidental civilization weakened the native resistance to Christianity. The missionaries shared the power, and therefore the prestige, of the commercial imperialists, so that the natives viewed the power of the Christian God with particular awe.[25] The abandonment of ancient practices, such as the abolition of the tabu system in 1819, left a vacuum in Hawaiian culture which the introduction of Christianity helped to fill. In this light, the institution of the New England Sabbath, proclaimed as law in December, 1823, and docilely observed throughout the kingdom, took root largely because the natives regarded it as a new form of tabu. Further, the dedication of the missionaries themselves lent an atmosphere of good faith to the entire undertaking. The presence of women in the missionary companies helped convince the native chiefs that the evangelists came with amiable intentions, in contrast to the baser motives which generally prevailed in the commercial community. The skill of the mission women in needlework, as well as the skill of the mission physicians—Thomas Holman in the First Company and Abraham Blatchely in the Second—served further to placate chiefs and people alike. As a matter of practical necessity, the missionaries first concentrated their attention on the chiefs, without whose help the mission had little chance of success. Once having converted the chiefs, the mission used the authority of the native government to enforce at least the outward forms of Christianity among the people at large. The conversion of the matriarch Kaahumanu, regent from 1823 to her death in 1832, contributed vastly to the Christianizing process. By 1825 the missionaries were in a position to dictate public policy in the Islands.[26]

The successful efforts of the missionaries to initiate a regime of religious and social reform infuriated the trading and seafaring population. The missionaries made strenuous efforts to suppress gambling, prostitution, and the sale of firearms and liquor to the natives. Also, they tried to protect the natives from economic exploitation by the commercial interests. In Hawaii as elsewhere in the Pacific, in Africa, and indeed wherever in the world the two groups met, there arose a furious antagonism between the missionaries on the one hand and the sailors and traders on the other. The hostility from the crew which the Judds and others in the Third Company encountered on the *Parthian* was part of a world-wide pattern at this time.[27] Richard Charlton, the British consul in Honolulu, agitated tirelessly against the mission.[28] John Coffin Jones, Jr., the American commercial agent, attacked the evangelists with venom.

Trade never will again flourish at these Islands until these missionaries from the Andover mill are recalled. They are continually telling the King and Chiefs that the white people traders are cheating and imposing on them, consequently have depreciated the value of most articles. I believe it is a fact generally acknowledged by all here, that the natives are fifty per cent worse in every vice since the missionaries began their hypocritical labour here; these blood suckers of the community had much better be in their native country gaining their living by the sweat of their brow, than living like lords in this luxurious land, distracting the minds of these children of Nature with the idea that they are to be eternally damned unless they think and act as they do: and that Providence would put a whip in every honest hand to lash such rascals naked through the world.[29]

Such antagonism easily flared into physical violence. In 1825 the crew of a British warship mobbed the house of the Reverend William Richards at Lahaina. In 1826 the crew of the U.S.S. *Dolphin*, enraged at a missionary-inspired decree prohibiting native women from boarding ships in the harbor, stormed the house of Governor Kalanimoku (Billy Pitt), and threatened the life of Hiram Bingham. That same year the antimissionary party petitioned the chiefs to expel Bingham from the Islands, and at Lahaina Richards' house suffered a second attack by an angry mob. In 1827 the crew of the *John Palmer* opened fire with cannon on the Lahaina mission house.[30]

Understandably the missionaries resented the opposition of the trading group. As Dr. Judd wrote to the American Board in 1831,

National affairs appear now to be in a very prosperous state as it respects the native population. Good order, peace, and faithful obedience to the laws are observed. But the foreigners cause the chiefs no little trouble by withstanding and throwing obstacles in the way of the execution of the laws among them. Some individuals have added personal insult and threats to their opposition.[31]

Hawaii in 1828 presented the spectacle of a semicivilized outpost where the forces of puritan morality, already entrenched and well on their way to dominance, did daily battle in an atmosphere of resentment and turbulence not only with native lethargy but also with the often vicious impulses of the commercial community. The natives, fast declining in population, stood by in a condition of shock as their culture disintegrated, and watched like shadow-people the furious rivalry of the invading whites. American, British, and French traders competed hotly with one another. The American missionaries, representing the Protestant interest, stood firm against the missionaries of Catholic France. Upon occasion, warships from rival nations came to Hawaii, as they went to Tahiti and the Tonga Islands,[32] to protect the real or fancied interests of citizens in both the missionary and commercial groups. In short, when the *Parthian* reached Honolulu, her missionary passengers faced the challenge of a raw, semitropical frontier. Small wonder that they felt misgiving as well as curiosity as they gazed at the land which was to be their new home and their life work.

While the newcomers rejoiced in their release from almost five months at sea, their hosts in the mission house felt equally profound emotion of a different kind. Bingham wrote simply, "Their arrival was opportune."[33] The implications of his remark are clear, for of the twenty-eight members of the first two companies of 1820 and 1823 only sixteen (nine men and seven women) still remained to convert the heathen and to combat the demoralizing tendencies of the commercial colony. In particular, ever since the departure of Dr. Blatchely on November 6, 1826,[34] the Islands, with a population of almost 125,000, entirely lacked a resident physician. As a portent of future demands to be made on his services, Dr. Judd prescribed for several cases of sickness among the natives within hours of his arrival on shore. On April 2, their third day ashore and, incidentally, Mrs. Judd's twenty-fourth birthday, she noted with gratification the welcome which the natives extended to her husband. "They all express themselves delighted in having a physician among them, and one man said, on being introduced to Dr. Judd, 'We are healed.' "[35]

A welcome of this nature had both sincerity and charm, but uppermost in the minds of the newcomers and veterans alike on the mission staff was the staggering challenge of their surroundings along with the high moral purpose of their calling. " 'Here we are to live and labor,' " Mrs. Judd wrote, echoing the original instructions of the American Board, " 'until the land is filled with churches, school-houses, fruitful fields and pleasant dwellings.' When will it be?"[36]

Life in the Mission, I

The Judds soon found that their chosen field of labor carried with it a full measure of privation. In August, 1828, Mrs. Judd wrote.

Housekeeping at last in two little rooms and a chamber, under the same roof with the Binghams! The clapboards are bare and admit quantities of dust which the trade-winds bring in such fearful clouds as to suggest the fate of Pompeii. . . . We have had a very hot summer, no rain, the earth parched, and clouds of dust blowing day after day. I have emptied quarts of it from my bed cover at night, and it pours in so thickly that in a few minutes it is impossible to distinguish the color of the different articles of furniture.

Our yearly supply of sugar, flour, and other stores, sent from Boston in a whale-ship, was carried by mistake to the Japan whaling grounds, consequently we have been on short allowance. The drought almost produced a famine in the vegetable kingdom. Our good queen-mother [Kaahumanu] has been often absent, and we have missed her presents of kalo [taro], fish, and other good things. The poor cattle have almost starved, and of course our supply of milk has failed.[1]

Others in the mission encountered similar discomfort. Sereno

Bishop and Oliver Emerson, missionary sons, have left accounts of the condition of the flour when it finally reached Honolulu after its voyage around the Horn. Soaked with sea water and encrusted with a moldy cake, its interior filled with large white worms, the flour barrels often had to be cut in half with a saw. In the Dwight Baldwin and Titus Coan households the flour was so hard that it had to be chipped off with a chisel or an axe.[2]

Mrs. Judd wore secondhand dresses sent to her from the United States as acts of charity. Stephen Reynolds, a member of the commercial colony who was particularly outspoken in his dislike of the mission, reported spitefully in May, 1828, that some of the native women were better dressed than the women of the newly arrived Third Company.[3]

The financial resources of the mission were meager and administered in the common-stock system, whereby each member drew supplies as needed from the Board's agent, Levi Chamberlain. All presents and earnings became the common property of the group.[4] Until he left the mission in 1842, Dr. Judd retained no fees for his medical services. At that time—with a wife and six children to support and with many demands made on him for food and lodging by travelers and by his colleagues as they visited Honolulu—his salary amounted to only $760 a year.[5]

An ordeal confronted the missionaries when they went from one island to another. The voyages from outlying islands for the annual convention in Honolulu in the spring presented terrors equal to those on the passage around Cape Horn. Mrs. Judd wrote, "They are made in a little schooner, stowed to its utmost capacity with men, women, and children, lumber, poi, poultry, horses, horned cattle, pet pigs and dogs, and all manner of creeping things. . . . The native navigators often go to sleep even at the helm, though the trade-wind may blow a gale. . . . If I had ever dreamed of 'yachting by moonlight among the Isles of the Pacific,' one trip has dispelled the illusion forever." On another occasion she spoke of "the comfortless days and nights in these little floating prisons."[6] Bates characterized interisland travel as repulsive, and wrote a description of natives alternately eating and vomiting poi while pigs and passengers alike wallowed in the mire. Titus Coan reported that women often became so weak from suffering that they had to be carried ashore.[7]

On a Monday in 1830 Dr. Judd, along with his wife, infant son, and about thirty other passengers, left Honolulu for Lahaina, Maui, in the *Missionary Packet*, a small coasting vessel. Although the distance between the two ports is just over a hundred miles, the trip took four days. Caught in a storm off the north coast of Molokai, Dr. Judd and his family landed Tuesday night on the Kalaupapa Peninsula, crossed the island to Kamalo on the south coast, and re-embarked there on Friday morning, only to become becalmed in the Lahaina Channel. They did not reach their destination until late that afternoon.[8] On another occasion they spent ten days at sea on the whaleship *Superior* en route from Honolulu to Kaawaloa on the island of Hawaii. They took three whales on the way, suffered from seasickness, and almost met their death in a storm.[9]

On land they had reason to complain of mosquitoes, recently introduced to the Islands from the water cask of a merchantman. From Waialua, on the windward side of Oahu, while visiting the Emersons in 1834, Dr. Judd wrote to Chamberlain, the Board's agent, "But O the mosquitoes! Do buy all the mosquitoe curtains necessary for the use of all who are bitten. Ewa, Waialua, Honolulu, and Lahaina have all complained generously of them lately." But the netting was not provided. Three years later, in the same place, his children, Gerrit, Jr., and Elizabeth, found sleep impossible, despite two native women who waved branches of ti leaves over their faces the whole night through. "The next day," so Elizabeth recalled, "mother made nets of ordinary calico, and, as we nearly smothered, all the windows and doors were left open. Toward morning, a pig came in grunting, and we climbed into mother's bed in great fright."[10]

Violence lent a further note of harshness to their lives. In 1830 Dr. Judd wrote, "A bear brought from the North West Coast, has been set up for a mark to shoot at near our house today. Thousands of natives and most of the foreigners have passed the door going to the cruel sport."[11] Two weeks later Mrs. Judd reported the death of a drunken sailor from a blow on the head received in "the house of strange women."[12] In the spring of 1831, three men robbed a store of over $1,000. One of them, a white man named Mackey, was sentenced to be flogged through the village at the cart's tail. He received 100 lashes, as Dr. Judd reported, "applied with no sparing hand. His back was cut and mangled dreadfully with the cat. He however lived it through."[13] On October 20, 1840, the authorities hanged from the wall of the old fort in Honolulu a chief and a native found guilty of murder. A crowd of about 12,000 natives, shouting and weeping, witnessed the execution.[14]

Isolated in such surroundings, at times without news of their families in the United States for a year or more, the missionaries frequently felt pangs of homesickness. Early in 1831 Dr. Judd noted in a journal letter to his parents that he had received no mail from them in over a year. From Kauai in 1832 he exclaimed to Levi Chamberlain, "My cry to you is send the news. O how I long to hear from America."[15]

To the task which lay before him Dr. Judd brought the same faith which had sustained him in the voyage from Boston. On his arrival in Honolulu he wrote in his journal, "O my God support me under this weight of feelings which rushes upon me, prepare me to hear whatever else there is to be told with undaunted fortitude resting on Thee." In Hawaii his faith remained firm and his hopes continued high. To the American Board he wrote cheerfully in October, 1828, "Although I am not unconscious of the difficulties and trials of my situation yet I think it is on the whole pleasant and desirable."[16]

The same optimism appears in a letter which he wrote two months later to Finney.

Since we landed on these shores we have been happy—we have our work—though have much unfaithfulness to lament. I think a life spent among the Heathen if spent in doing good is all *we* ought to ask. As for inheritance Christ shall be sufficient. We suffer for none of the comforts of life. Laura minds the affairs of the house and labours like a missionary among the native women. My hands are full of my professional business, etc., yet contrive to spend a good portion of every week in attending to the study of the language and other studies preparatory to engaging more *actively* into missionary work. In these employments time passes swiftly by us, 14 months have glided imperceptibly away, and thus no doubt will life if it is the will of God. . . . The natives are our best friends. If they do not favour our plans, they are unwilling to oppose us from selfish motives. The cause of religion is gaining ground among them though the novelty of the thing is partly worn away. . . . The candle of the Lord is shining about this mission. In the midst of opposition the cause triumphs.[17]

One sentence in this letter requires special comment. When he mentioned "other studies preparatory to engaging more *actively* into missionary work," it is clear that he still contemplated becoming a minister. Without ordination, he was only an assistant on the mission staff and not a missionary proper.[18] Precedent existed for ordaining assistants in the field. In the years 1825–1826 James Ely, Joseph Goodrich, and Samuel Whitney were ordained in Hawaii. Two other physicians later sent out by the American Board, Dwight Baldwin and Thomas Lafon, were also preachers.[19] In view of these circumstances, and especially in view of his religious convictions, Dr. Judd's wish to be ordained is understandable.

At least his colleagues so considered it. The general letter of the mission of June, 1828, mentioned "a vote of the mission . . . that Dr. Judd, agreeably to the design expressed in his appointment, be allowed such facilities, as to time and the means of instruction, as will enable him to prosecute the study of theology, with a view to his preaching the Gospel." The mission report of the following year stated, "Dr. J. has been desirous to direct his attention to the study of theology, and no pains have been taken to seek or solicit business in the medical line."[20]

With Bingham and Emerson he labored to train native choirs, but they met with only limited success. Sereno Bishop recalled a church service in Honolulu during his youth: "Well in front was quite a company of singers, led by Dr. and Mrs. Judd, among whom were several large and fleshy women. I remember thinking that their voices were inharmonious."[21] Nevertheless, Dr. Judd's interest in music remained unabated. In 1832 he wrote to his uncle, Thomas Hastings the hymn writer, to ask for a copy of his *Juvenile Psalmody* for possible translation into Hawaiian. Two years later Asa Thurston asked his help in making a report on music. "I write to you on this subject because of your known skill in the art of music, and also because you have had the principal labor in teaching it at your island." Thurston's report contains the enigmatic statement, "In 1832 a Gamut was printed and a few rules: and eight tunes were engraved by Dr. Judd." Nothing more is known about the gamut and tunes, but in later years Dr. Judd retained his musical aptitude. During his diplomatic journey of 1850, he played briefly on a piano in the East India Company's museum in London.[22]

Upon occasion he preached to the native population. He wrote in his journal in January, 1831, "Rode to Waititi [*sic*] to day and held meeting. The school house proving too small the congregation assembled in the open air under a clump of trees close to the shore. There might have been 6 or 8 hundred who collected around me and gave good attention to my remarks from Luke 10:27 on the duty of love to God. In the afternoon the duty of love to our neighbor was concisely treated." In May of the same year he wrote, "I attended and directed the attention of the people to the solemn and important fact that 'the wages of sin is death: but the gift of God is eternal life through Jesus Christ our Lord.' " He preached on a number of other occasions in the years 1830–1833.[23]

Thoughts of religion remained uppermost in his mind. The Reverend Sheldon Dibble's preaching in June, 1831, reminded him of his friend Aikin in Utica, and when he heard Tinker preach the next Sunday he wrote, "I was forcibly reminded of Mr. Finney and the revival scenes of 1826." A few months later he wrote fervently in his journal, "Awake O Zion, put on strength. Let a cry be heard throughout her border and let all the chosen of the Lord come forth to the battle, for the time is at hand."[24]

Others on the mission staff shared his enthusiasm. In the summer of 1829 the natives built a new thatched church in Honolulu capable of holding three to four thousand persons. It had a mahogany pulpit and a glazed window draped with crimson damask, and represented a vast improvement over the older building, the walls of which had been eaten away by hungry goats and cattle. At its dedication in November, 1829, Mrs. Judd reported, "Kaahumanu made a very interesting address to the people, and, to the surprise of all present, the king followed with a speech and a prayer. He not only dedicated the house to the worship of the only living and true God, but solemnly, then and there, consecrated his kingdom to the Lord Jesus Christ."[25] In an atmosphere of jubilance on November 14 the members of the mission wrote a joint letter to Captain Finch of the U.S.S. *Vincennes* expressing satisfaction at the improvement which they saw all around them.[26]

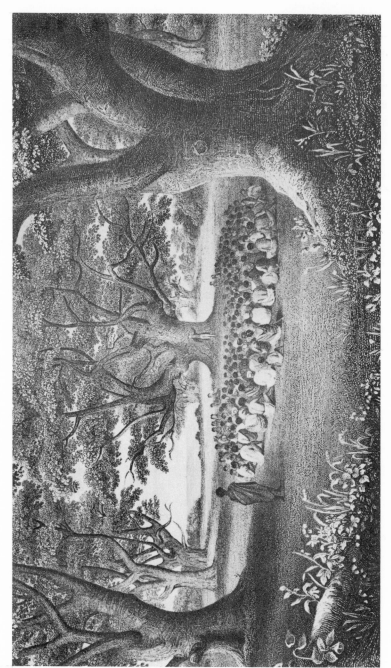

Missionary preaching to Hawaiians in a kukui grove (from a drawing by A. T. Agate)

In 1831 the mission had further cause to rejoice, for that year the native government banished a group of French Catholic priests who had come to the Islands four years before. The banishment was inspired by the Protestant missionaries, who formally approved the expulsion of their rivals and used their influence with the chiefs to keep the banishment in effect. In December, 1839, Dr. Judd wrote to Chamberlain, "If the *Europa* goes before I return—which is quite probable—I will thank you to do what I think would be my duty to do were I there, viz., to request Mr. Ladd to arrange his meeting with Capt. Shaw so that no priests or propagators of the Romish religion be brought here on her return. A hint will be sufficient no doubt."[27] Two years earlier he had written to Finney, "The Jesuits who were expelled from the islands very lately returned and are now here. Come and help confound them and pull these foreign residents out of the fire."[28] But a number of missionaries, including Bingham and Dr. Judd, remonstrated when the government embarked on a persecution of native Catholics. The expulsion and persecution of the Catholics later caused serious political repercussions with the French government, and in 1839, in part because of missionary pressure, the Hawaiian authorities put an end to the persecution. The leaning of the Calvinist missionaries toward religious toleration showed itself also in the warm reception which they gave in 1835–1836 to the Quaker preacher, Daniel Wheeler. On one occasion Dr. Judd acted as interpreter for Wheeler, who preached to a native congregation of 2,500.[29] In welcoming a Quaker and in urging toleration of Catholics, the missionaries of the 1830s differed from their seventeenth-century ancestors, who had persecuted both denominations.

The early optimism of the mission, however well founded it had appeared to be in fact, soon faded as the Islands entered a period of moral decline. The missionaries had underestimated the difficulty of converting pagans to Calvinist Christianity, and their reports home of late 1832 and 1833 reflect discouragement. In October, 1832, Dr. Judd wrote to Hunnewell that he could see no improvement in the conduct and attitude of the natives. Two years later, on a tour of Oahu, he reported that the natives were indifferent to religion. For several months they did little more than play with marbles, newly introduced to the Islands, and a similar childlike lapse occurred with kites.[30]

Nowhere was the moral lapse more apparent than in the household of the king. After the death of the pious regent Kaahumanu on June 5, 1832, so Mrs. Judd reported,

The young king (Kamehameha III) threw off the restraint of his elders, and abandoned himself to intemperance and debauchery. . . . Vile heathen songs, games, and shameless dances, which had gone out of use, were revived. Rum and wretchedness became rampant; and the quiet of our lovely dells and valleys was disturbed with bacchanalian shouts and the wild orgies of drunken revelry.

The mission deplored the king's conduct and prayed for him, but his debauch continued undiminished for almost two years.[31]

The king's behavior distressed his pious half-sister Kinau, successor to Kaahumanu as *kuhina-nui* or premier. Kinau had long been on intimate terms with the missionaries, and as a token of friendship the Judds had named their eldest daughter after her. At one period Kinau thought of resigning her office. In despair she called on the Judds. "We assured her," Mrs. Judd wrote, "that she was called to her present position and dignity by Divine Providence, and that she must nerve herself to fulfill her high destiny. We knelt around the family altar, and asked for her strength, and wisdom, and patience, and for light on her darkened pathway." In a letter written many years later Dr. Judd reported, "Our arguments convinced her. By our advice she presented herself before the king and claimed her rights, which were acknowledged, and she was in due time proclaimed as kuhina."[32]

By 1835 the missionaries regained their pre-eminent position in the government. The British Consul observed that the king "trusts Kinau his half sister with the reins, she is entirely governed by the American Missionaries who through her govern the Islands with unlimited sway." Two years later the missionaries reaped a full harvest from their persistence, for in the Great Revival of 1837–1840 nearly 20,000 natives joined the church.[33]

Throughout the troubled thirties the Judds savored not only the alternate discouragement and elation of their co-workers in the mission but also the challenge of raising a family in a crude frontier environment. Their eldest son, Gerrit Parmele, Jr., was born in circumstances which Dr. Judd noted briefly in a letter to the American Board. "On the morning of March 7th [1829] Mrs. Bingham was, after only two hours' illness, delivered of a daughter. In the evening Mrs. Judd, who had attended on Mrs. B. during the day, began to make similar complaints, and by eleven o'clock became the joyful mother of a son. The united weight of both children was 21 lbs. 12 oz. Mrs. B.'s little one weighed 10 lbs. 10 oz."[34] On July 5, 1831, their eldest daughter, named Elizabeth Kinau in honor of their royal native friend, was born. The child's weight, so Dr. Judd recorded, was ten and three-quarters pounds.[35] A second daughter, Helen Seymour, was born on August 27, 1833. Two years later, on September 8, 1835, Mrs. Judd gave birth to twins, a boy and a girl, whom they named Charles Hastings and Laura Fish. By way of understatement Dr. Judd wrote to the Reverend David Greene, "If you wish to know what Mrs. Judd is doing she is nursing twins six weeks old and taking care of three older children."[36] The three older children, it may be noted, were aged six, four, and two. There were four more children still to come.

In the spring of 1835 they left the mission house, which they had shared with the Binghams since their arrival, and moved across the street to the cottage formerly occupied by Stephen Shepard, the mission printer.[37] Here in true Yankee style they set about improving the appearance of their new home. Two years later Mrs. Amos Starr Cooke remarked, "Dr. Judd has a beautiful garden, many pretty flowers, some of the most beautiful little trees with elegant blossoms." For all this he gave credit to his wife.[38]

Their lives were rich in personal satisfaction if not in material wealth. In a journal intended as a letter to Dr. Judd's parents in Paris Hill, Mrs. Judd wrote, "I think few men are as happy as Gerrit. He loves his wife a great deal more than she deserves to be loved and he thinks no children are like his own; has a heart to enjoy with gratitude whatever comforts God in His kind providence sends him; has a remarkable flow of spirits; is habitually cheerful, enjoys the confidence of his brethren, has favor with the heathen, and is willing to spend and be spent in doing them good and what more can you desire for your son?"[39]

Life in the Mission, II

In keeping with the nineteenth-century Protestant emphasis on good works and social reform, the American missionaries in Hawaii, like the British in the South Pacific, sought to bring to the heathen not only the word of God but also the benefits of Western civilization.[1] As John Thomas Gulick expressed it, in a statement which both Finney and Dr. Judd would have approved, "The mission of our parents was the training of the people of this island kingdom not only how to prepare for the other world, but how to achieve this great end while improving their condition in this world."[2] It was precisely because of this dual purpose, to serve both God and man, that Dr. Judd was reluctant to give up his medical career. Everywhere, Protestant missionaries stressed education and social betterment, and tried to train the natives in the New England virtues of industry and temperance. Protestant missionaries in both Africa and Hawaii believed laziness to be a cardinal sin and hard work to be a prime Christian virtue. Artemas Bishop of the Hawaiian mission remarked ingenuously, "An idle, improvident Christian is a contradiction in terms."[3] So strong was their faith in the secular aspect of Calvinist Christianity that the American Board warned them that teaching the natives to be literate and industrious would avail little unless such virtues went hand in hand with knowledge of the gospel.[4]

Soon after their arrival the missionaries began an extensive educational program, because New Englanders admire learning and for the practical reason that the *palapala*, or the written word, proved a potent way to win souls. In 1831 there were about eleven hundred schools in Hawaii with more than fifty thousand adult pupils, or about two-fifths of the native population. That same year a native high school, later a seminary, was founded at Lahainaluna, Maui, on a plan later adopted by Hampton Institute in Virginia.[5]

By the summer of 1830 both Dr. and Mrs. Judd found themselves occupied in teaching arithmetic, reading, and writing to upwards of 100 natives, many of whom later became teachers themselves, for it was obvious that the only sound solution to Hawaii's educational problem was to train teachers from the native population. In 1831 Dr. Judd inspected thirty-two native schools at Waikiki, and three years later Emerson persuaded him to lend a hand with the native school at Waialua.[6] Mrs. Judd managed to teach geography, the Scriptures, and arithmetic to native shipmasters and schoolteachers. How many times, as she taught the gentle, laughter-loving natives that crowded around her, did she remember her days as a schoolmistress in western New York, "where three ways meet"? Her teaching continued despite the demands of her household, but Dr. Judd found that the pressure of his medical and other duties left him little time for schoolroom labors. Still, in 1835, he taught arithmetic, reading, writing, and "the art of making pens and ink of native materials" to forty teachers and sixty young boys.[7]

From the first, the mission faced an almost complete lack of educational facilities. The first school for native children met in 1832 in an unfurnished building with adobe bricks as seats. Mrs. Judd was proud of this improvisation. "One step in the ladder of progress was gained," she wrote cheerfully. But this school soon met with disaster, as Dr. Judd reported to the American Board.

The fine, large school house built at our station was blown down last fall, and all the benches, doors, etc., were crushed in the ruins. It was a miserable house, notwithstanding all the praises bestowed on it. . . . It was altogether too large—120 ft. long, of too temporary a structure, badly lighted, having no glass windows, the seats and desks of the rudest kind imaginable, the former being made of mud bricks piled up in rows, and the latter of boards nailed to legs driven into the ground.[8]

Nevertheless, the work of educating the natives continued, and two years later Dr. Judd was able to report the construction of a new school with better seats and desks. The building had mud walls plastered with clay, and a thatched roof, but at the time of writing it still lacked a wooden floor. In rude buildings such as this, missionary and native teachers ultimately made the Hawaiians one of the most literate peoples in the world.[9]

In 1839, after discussion with Governor Kekuanaoa and others, Dr. Judd became a trustee of a newly established school for the young chiefs. The Chiefs' Children's School, or Royal School as it was sometimes called, operated under the direction of Mr. and Mrs. Amos Starr Cooke, A year after its establishment Mr. Cooke reported, "Dr. Judd has also lent his constant and efficient influence to the school, and owing to his long and intimate acquaintance with the chiefs, he has been exceedingly serviceable." For a time the Judds sent their own children to this school, but the chance appointment of a brutal schoolmaster, whom Dr. Judd recruited on a trip to Maui in 1843, led to Mrs. Judd's tearful decision to remove them.[10]

Naturally, the missionaries felt concern for the education of their numerous children. In the early days of the mission it had been customary to send them to the United States, but this arrangement told heavily in heartbreak for parents and children alike. Mrs. Judd wrote,

I shall never forget some of those heart-rending parting scenes. Little children, aged only six or seven years, were torn away from their parents, and sent the long voyage around Cape Horn, to seek homes among strangers. . . . On one occasion I accompanied some friends to a ship just starting for America. As the vessel moved from the wharf, there was one affectionate little girl, not more than seven years old, standing on the deck and looking at her father on the shore, the distance between them widening every moment. She stretched out her little arms toward him and shrieked with all her strength, "Oh, father, dear father, do take me back!"[11]

As early as 1836, a group including Dr. Judd, Bingham, and Chamberlain chose a site for a mission school at Punahou, at the entrance to Manoa Valley on land given to Bingham by Governor Boki, and the next year a committee, on which Dr. Judd served, informed the American Board that a school there would meet a definite need. But the matter slumbered until 1840, when the general meeting of the mission appointed Dr. Judd chairman of a committee to take definite action. Accordingly, he wrote to the American Board asking for support and especially for a teacher to supervise the school, now designed not only for mission children but also for children of "pious foreign residents who may be expected to settle permanently in the country." In 1841 the Reverend Daniel Dole, newly arrived in the Islands, became principal, and the construction of Punahou School began, with Dr. Judd in charge of putting up the first buildings of adobe on coral foundations, on the land which Bingham had turned over to the mission.[12]

Dr. Judd's diary indicates the extent of his labors. "June 30th, 1841. Engaged to take laying foundation and cellar at Punahou. Sent stone and rafters. Bargained for cellar. . . . Ordered out all Punahou and Makiki to work. . . . July 12, plough and scrape. . . . 17, plough and scrape till 4 P.M. 19, Punahou all day on cellar. 23, at Punahou. Making dobies." From time to time he wrote short notes to Chamberlain, the Board's business agent, for supplies such as dobie boxes and rope. In March, 1842, just before Punahou opened its doors, he donated $50 to the school, almost a month's salary.[13]

While Punahou was being built, Dr. Judd had charge of an even grander construction project, Kawaiahao Church, for many years Honolulu's largest building, with a capacity of more than two thousand people, and still in daily use. With funds provided by the Hawaiian government in 1837 he supervised the laying of its 14,000 coral blocks, cut by natives from the reefs, and tradition has it that when the walls were finished he climbed up and paced off the perimeter before the roofing began. In his diary he noted,

July 8, 1840, I started for Waialua to hire 100,000 shingles made. 9th. In the mountains all day. Horse proved weak and lame. Arrived home at 4 o'clock A.M. July 16, went to Waipo to look for timber to make shingles. August 29. Made patterns for stones for pillars today. June 12,

Kinau returning from church accompanied by her maids of honor (from a drawing by J. Masselot)

1841. Timber for meeting house being brought. July 10. Drew plan of roof for native church. August 5, went to Waialua. During my stay made a model of a roof for the meeting house. August 27. Wrote contract for roof of church. October 29th. In raising a frame the beam broke and all came down with a crash. November 6. . . . Six pairs of rafters up. Worked hard all the week. 11th. Raised last rafters. Three times three cheers.

On April 19, 1842, he wrote to the American Board, "Our house is nearly ready for use, though 3 or 4 thousand might be very properly expended on it yet." The old meetinghouse, so he noted in his diary, was used for the last time on July 10, and the new church was dedicated eleven days later.[14]

Man of action that he unquestionably was, Dr. Judd took satisfaction from this and other buildings erected under his direction. In company with his Yankee colleagues, he enjoyed hard work. When, about the year 1839, in appreciation of his medical services he received from the king 22 acres of waste land at Pawaa on the Waikiki plain—land which was sandy and swampy, with no taro on it and only a few cocoanut trees—he fenced, drained, and plowed it himself, and planted grass to convert it to pasture.[15] How many times, as he slogged behind the plow through the hot, sandy furrows, did he think, with nostalgia and perhaps a pang of regret, of the rich acres which he had plowed as a boy in faraway Paris Hill? On this the record is silent. But here, as elsewhere, he exemplified the puritan virtue of industry, which the mission was trying with scant success to bring to the indolent native population.

Dr. Judd and others in the mission worked with equal fervor in the temperance movement, not only to curb the orgies of sailors but also to protect the natives, who, in Hawaii as in the entire Pacific, proved unusually susceptible to alcohol. Reliable witnesses, including Herman Melville and Robert Louis Stevenson, have left appalling accounts of drunkenness leading to hot-blooded debauchery even on the public streets.[16] The Hawaiian king himself was sometimes drunk for days and weeks or even longer periods. What good purpose did it serve, the missionaries asked, to teach letters and habits of industry to a people that frequently lapsed into helpless intoxication?

Consequently, the members of the mission practiced strict tee-totalism. As Dr. Judd reported to Finney, "They are temperate in all things. Only a minority use tea and coffee. Spirits and tobacco excluded, and wine except as a prescribed medicine." In 1831 the Judds took into their home an alcoholic from the foreign population, only to discover several months later that their efforts to reform him had failed. Dr. Judd reported sternly, "Today I saw him drunk. He has returned to his wallowing in the mire." But in April of the same year there was cause for rejoicing in the mission-inspired decision of Governor Kuakini to suppress the grogshops and gambling houses on Oahu, however much the foreign colony might grumble and make threats.[17] Despite complaints, such as General Miller's, that the mission reform program was "despotic and vexatious," and despite evasion of the liquor regulations— some grogshops sold coffee and gave away rum—Dr. Judd found reason to state in 1832 that "intemperance has received a check which it will not soon get over."[18] Early in 1834, at Kinau's request, he made a temperance tour of Oahu to address native crowds on the evils of drink. Many years later he recalled, "All the distilleries (which were nothing more than an iron pot and a gun barrel, or other tube) were overthrown and destroyed."[19]

As time passed the temperance movement made progress, co-incident with the rise of prohibition sentiment in the United States, and on April 26, 1842, the king and a number of chiefs took the total-abstinence pledge. Mrs. Judd wrote exultantly,

Temperance laws are now triumphant, and the nation is a temperance nation, from the king on the throne down to the little children. All are collected into a "cold-water army." We have had a grand festival. *Fourteen hundred* children marched in procession with music and banners, dined together, made speeches, and hurrahed in the most approved style. One needs to have lived among such a people, when there was no restraint upon the natural love for stimulants, and to have been a spectator of the excesses when a whole village was drunk. What pencil can portray the loathsome picture? The king adheres to his pledge nobly, and appears to be fully aware that his temporal salvation depends upon it. We indulge in renewed hope that his soul will be saved.[20]

When, in 1843, the missionaries gave a formal dinner to the king and diplomatic corps, they pointedly omitted to serve liquor. This omission worked a hardship on Admiral Richard Thomas of the British navy, who stayed gamely at the banquet table for three hours, but excused himself when the cloth was removed for tea and coffee on the pretext that it was time for his evening walk.

Two years later the king gave a birthday feast with two hundred guests, once again without wine or spirits. The independence celebration of 1847 followed the same "strict temperance principles," and at this feast, so his daughter recalled, Dr. Judd took firm measures to enforce them. When two Englishmen present became somewhat boisterous from the effects of a bottle of Scotch, Dr. Judd reportedly took the bottle away from them and smashed it on a stone, exclaiming, "Cursed stuff! it will be the ruin of Hawaii."[21] Such conduct, of course, hardly endeared him to the more broad-minded elements in the foreign population.

Dr. Judd took temperance as seriously as his religion, and it may be said that the temperance movement, as it embodied the puritan virtue of self-discipline, became part of his religion. He wrote in 1844,

The cause of Temperance remains unshaken among the natives. . . . Among foreigners it has opened a character never before known. . . . The existing regulations tend to confine the use of the poison to the narrowest possible limits, which I trust will become still narrower when the influences now at work have their full effect upon the population.[22]

In July, 1845, he was elected president of the Hawaiian Total Abstinence Union, which later became the Oahu Temperance Society. His strict teetotalism became proverbial. Steen Bille of the Danish ship *Galathea*, who attended a teetotal party at the Judds' in October, 1846, reported that Queen Kalama in a superb gesture of disdain spat out a mouthful of tea onto the hall floor "with an explosion as were it the spouting of a large fish." Later in the month Bille entertained the king and chiefs on board the *Galathea* with wine as well as lemonade and chocolate. "I was pleased to see," he wrote, "that several of the good people had a very good taste of the champagne whenever Mr. Judd turned his back."[23] Six years later the officers of the Swedish frigate *Eugenie* found themselves in a similar situation when the royal party came aboard, but this time, so Lt. C. Skogman reported, Dr. Judd kept a closer watch. "A couple of us sought to prevail upon Governor Kekuanaoa to take a glass of champagne with us, but he indicated only the water carafe although we thought his eyes meanwhile were looking in another direction; rather perfectly seen, too, were Dr. Judd's sharp and lively eyes fixed upon him through his eyeglasses from the other side of the cabin."[24]

Such anecdotes naturally multiplied. It was even said that on one occasion he helped with his own hands to unload at the wharf a barrel of smuggled brandy in the belief that it was a barrel of beef.[25] His teetotalism even after he entered politics lent itself to gossip and ridicule. It was to cause both him and the Hawaiian government much trouble in years to come.

Dr. Judd's support of the mission program extended beyond temperance agitation, building, and teaching to a number of lesser yet time-consuming tasks. From 1832 to 1842 he was a member of the mission printing committee, and in 1834 he sent to the American Board a long list of the needs of the printing department. In 1831 he undertook to bind two thousand copies of a mission tract. In June of that year the mission instructed him to prepare a set of maps.[26] Apparently he found little time for this new assignment, for in December, 1832, Mrs. Judd complained that she still had to draw the maps which she used in the classroom.[27] But by the end of the next year he had received from the American Board stereotype map plates, "exactly what was needed," and he reported besides that a surveyor in the employ of the mission was making a series of maps of the Islands. In 1834 he drew diagrams for Lorrin Andrews' Hawaiian geometry book, the *Ana Keonua*, published at Lahainaluna.[28] In 1838–1839 he edited *Ke Kumu Hawaii* ("The Hawaiian Teacher"), the mission's periodical in the native language.[29]

Characteristically, he took a prominent part in the Sandwich Island Institute, founded in 1837 for the intellectual and moral improvement of its members and particularly to gather scientific information about Polynesia. He delivered to this group three medical lectures, one of which was published in the Institute's journal, the *Hawaiian Spectator*, the first quarterly review published in the Pacific.[30] By the end of 1839 the Institute suspended its meetings, and the *Hawaiian Spectator* ceased publication, but, short-lived as it was, the Institute serves as a splendid example of the transference of New England folkways to the Pacific frontier. In purpose and composition it closely resembled the debating societies which Dr. Judd had joined as a young man in Paris Hill.

Contemporary observers noticed with approval and astonishment that the mission, along with some Americans in the trading community, had brought a thoroughly Yankee way of life to the Islands. After taking tea with the Binghams in 1832, Francis Warriner wrote, "The party was so much like one in America, that had I been placed there by accident, or could I have forgotten the circumstances of my visit, I should have fancied myself in New England." In 1840 Lt. Charles Wilkes of the United States exploring expedition described Coan's home at Hilo as "an old-fashioned, prim, red Yankee house, with white sills and casements, and double rows of small windows." A generation later Charles Nordhoff saw even more evidence of New England civilization in the Islands.

The white frame houses with green blinds, the picket-fences whitewashed until they shine, the stone walls, the small barns, the scanty pastures, the little white frame churches scattered about, the narrow "front yards," the frequent school-houses, usually with but little shade: all are New England, genuine and unadulterated; and you have only to eliminate the palms, the bananas, and other tropical vegetation, to have before you a fine bit of Vermont or the stonier parts of Massachusetts.[31]

In effect, the transit westward of New England civilization was accomplishing much the same result in Hawaii as on the New York frontier. Insofar as possible the missionaries followed literally the precept of the American Board to cover the Islands with churches, schools, and fruitful fields.

As he participated earnestly in the secular labors of the mission, Dr. Judd had his part in bringing Yankee civilization to Hawaii. How his work was regarded appears in a letter which he received in 1835 from Hiram Bingham, the mission's *de facto* leader. "I look upon you as a *tried* friend; *tried* by the occasions you have for *hoomanawanui* [patience] and *tried* in the sense of having been proved to be faithful and trustworthy in the estimation of your Brother, H. Bingham."[32] From Bingham, a tough-minded puritan of the seventeenth-century variety, this was high praise.

Medical Practice

Despite his many general assignments, Dr. Judd's main task in the mission was medical. For a few years he continued his theological studies, and for a time he thought seriously of preaching the gospel. But in 1832 a mission committee decided that physicians need not seek ordination.[1] Dr. Judd welcomed this decision, for it left him free to concentrate on his profession and, in accordance with Calvinist precepts, to please God by doing good works in the world. As he told the American Board, "About a year since, I came to the same conclusion although expecting to receive a license in the course of a year. . . . That I should have a pastoral charge seemed incompatible with the most important duties of a physician, particularly in regard to visiting distant stations."[2] Henceforth medicine came first.

Until the arrival in June, 1831, of Dr. Dwight Baldwin, who was sent to Waimea on Hawaii, Dr. Judd was the only physician in the mission. Dr. Thomas Charles Byde Rooke, who came to Honolulu about 1830, and Dr. Alonzo Chapin, who was attached to the mission 1832–1835, gave him some assistance, but for the most part he had to rely on the help of his nonmedical colleagues and the co-operation of surgeons from passing ships. In 1835 he noted "the perplexing situation I feel myself in reference to two calls now made on my services, in anticipation not five days apart—at the two extremes of the Sandwich Islands—Hilo and Kauai, which by the bye is no uncommon predicament for me to be in." After Dr. Chapin left late in 1835, and until the arrival of Dr. Seth Andrews and Dr. Thomas Lafon two years later, he resorted to desperate improvisation and wrote repeatedly to Boston asking for help.[3]

He soon learned from personal experience the effect of a tropical disorder. In May, 1829, he wrote to Evarts,

I was attacked with a bilious remitting fever. I never knew before what it was to languish with severe illness. A part of the time I was slightly deranged, but did not lose confidence in my own capacity to prescribe for myself, and took some medicines which were improper. . . . I was so much debilitated that I did not go out until the expiration of four weeks from the first attack.

But when he was barely well enough to walk he had to look after Mr. and Mrs. Shepard, both of whom fell ill. About the same time William Richards had a month's bout with rheumatism, Mrs. Green caught a fever, her infant died, and Mrs. Chamberlain had a long convalescence from childbirth. To make matters worse, word came from the island of Hawaii that Mrs. Samuel Ruggles had had a stillborn child, that Mr. Ruggles was failing, and that their daughter Huldah had suffered six attacks of fever. From Lahaina on Maui he heard that Mr. Andrews was ill, and from Kauai came a plea from the Gulicks to visit their sick child. With perfect truth he could assert, "To me it has been a season of great care and anxiety." In July, 1831, he fell sick again and was confined to the house for a month.[4]

His primary concern was the health of his associates in the mission, many of whom were overworked and despondent. His practice varied from obstetrics to vaccinating the teachers in the Royal School, and from advising Ruggles about his diet to treating Mrs. Cooke, who had poured tincture of castor instead of eyewash into her eye. In describing a typical situation he stated, "I attended Mrs. Parker at Kaneohe four days since. They were alone and their little son being sick, I had all the honorable offices of physician, midwife, nurse, kitchen, and house maid, to perform. Mr. P. was hardly able to leave his sick child a moment of the time. They have a daughter."[5]

He traveled continually from island to island, usually in native craft. His work took him to Maui and Hawaii, and upon occasion to Kauai.[6] In 1829, in an effort to rehabilitate its failing brethren, the mission sent him to the island of Hawaii to establish a rest haven there. The site ultimately chosen was at Waimea, some two thousand feet above sea level on the plateau facing snow-capped Mauna Kea, where the cool air offered welcome contrast to the sultry lowlands in which most of the missionaries labored. Along with his wife and infant son he reached the island of Hawaii on November 26, and, with the exception of a brief trip back to Oahu in January, 1830, he stayed at Waimea until July 13, his time occupied not only with building the health station but also with establishing a church and a school for native teachers. His report to the American Board struck a cautious note. "Whether the station at Waimea will prove all that has been hoped in restoring the feeble health of missionaries is yet to be determined. . . . In a climate like this we cannot expect that any means will invariably succeed."[7]

From the beginning his practice extended beyond the mission to Hawaii's foreign population. As he stated in 1839, "Owing to want of physicians in the village or to some other cause I have had an unusual number of calls from foreigners, many of whom are enemies of the mission—some persons of bad character—and all fully aware that my services are gratuitous."[8] From time to time he wrote up cases in his journal, to be sent to his father. Early in 1831 he wrote, "Was called in consultation yesterday in the case of a foreigner who has a fracture of the tibia supposed to be comminuted. It appeared to me to be a simple fracture and the bones have never been in apposition. The poor fellow has lain 68 days and will I fear be a cripple for life." On April 16 of the same year he accompanied Dr. Rooke on board a ship in the harbor to do what he could for three sailors who had fallen from the rigging.

We found one lying just where he fell—his thigh fractured, the bone driven through the flesh, his chin injured and several of his teeth knocked out, another with a fracture of the ribs, and the third much bruised but no bones broken. We dressed them as well as we could and brought one of them on shore. Today [April 17] I have visited him again. He is lying in a grogshop (apparently *without liquors*) well attended—is somewhat deranged and in a very critical state.[9]

A month later he noted, "My professional business has been very pressing for some weeks past. I frequently make from 20 to 40 prescriptions a day. The man who was mentioned 17th April is in a very low state. We took from his thigh a piece of bone the other day two inches long and something more than half the bulk of the middle of the femur, discharge profuse—hectic."[10] Whether the sailor survived is not stated.

The medical needs of the native population posed a more pressing problem, for the Hawaiians were not only susceptible to the white man's diseases but ignorant of even the simplest rules of hygiene. It was not uncommon for missionaries to encounter native infants, unwashed since birth and covered with sores, being fed sugar-cane juice, taro, and even fish and poi. Naturally many perished. Further, during epidemics of measles, whooping cough, and smallpox, the stricken natives rushed by the hundreds into the sea or exposed themselves to a high wind to cool their fever. The majority, of course, soon died.[11] As Dr. Judd wrote, "The state of the natives too cries loudly for help. They are fast decreasing in numbers. Go where we may we find the poor improvident creatures left to suffer on a sick and perhaps a dying bed. The native doctors are a miserable set of quacks who often shorten the lives of their patients by their remedies."[12]

He spent many hours in the dispensary in the cellar of his house, tending the natives who flocked to him for treatment. His daughter recalled, "Our yard was generally full from daylight to dark, of Hawaiians waiting to see him." Levi Chamberlain's daughter, who lived across the street, remembered as a child peeking into the doctor's cellar, where she saw "crowds of half-clad, barbarous native patients," some being bled.[13]

On a number of occasions he performed surgical operations on natives, who bore the dreadful ordeals without anesthesia. In 1830 Chamberlain noted in his journal, "The Doctor performed an operation of amputation on a native in the neighborhood this morning.

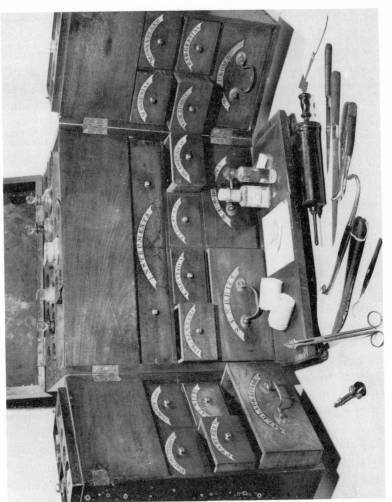

Dr. Judd's medicine chest

It was taking off the arm just above the wrist-joint in consequence of a disease in the hand which had so affected the bones that a cure had become hopeless. He was assisted by Dr. Rooke. Mr. Clark, Gulick and myself were present."[14]

In his own journal the same year Dr. Judd described a similar case.

Yesterday a native came to me with two silver dollars in his hand, begging I would cut off his hand which has been diseased 5 years and become entirely useless. The disease appeared to be a malignant kind of ulcer which had affected the wrist, destroyed the thumb and nearly the fore finger and was spreading fast. I amputated it to day, at 10 A.M. assisted by Mr. Richards and Green and Capt. Morgan. Two other captains were present beside a number of the chiefs. There was a great crowd of common people about the yard. The operation was performed in the usual manner, and made a good stump. The house being very hot it bled this afternoon. I changed the dressings and placed him in a cooler situation. No hemorrhage since.

That the operation succeeded appears in a note which he added five weeks later, "The stump healed, quite well." The latter patient, and possibly the former also, may have been afflicted with leprosy.[15]

In 1832 he attended the Queen Regent Kaahumanu, who died on June 5 in her retreat in Manoa Valley. Dr. Chapin assisted him in her illness and commented, "Dr. Judd attends her, as he does also most of the chiefs and their families."[16]

Nine years later he performed a major operation on Kapiolani— the chiefess of Alfred Tennyson's poem "Kapiolani"—who, in 1824 had broken a sacred tabu and in defiance of the goddess Pele had descended into the volcano at Kilauea. Her bold act persuaded thousands to embrace the Christian faith. In the spring of 1841 she came to Dr. Judd to be operated on for cancer of the breast. The operation took place on March 23 at noon, without anesthetics. It demanded courage at least equal to that which she had shown in the volcano. As Dr. Judd's daughter stated, "The brave Chiefess walked calmly about while the bandages and instruments were prepared, and then, after a short prayer, submitted herself to the knife for half an hour, bearing the terrible pain with remarkable fortitude, uttering neither cries nor groans."[17] Dr. Judd removed her entire right breast and described the operation as "severe." The sequel is best given in his own words.

Dr. Wood, of Honolulu, and Dr. Fox of the U.S. Ship Vincennes, who were present, united with me in the opinion that the disease was removed and we might expect a perfect recovery. The wound healed kindly, and at the end of a fortnight was nearly closed. . . . About six weeks after the operation, deeming my attendance no longer necessary, I gave her permission to visit Maui as soon as she could procure a passage. In preparation for leaving she took a long walk in the heat of the day, which brought on a pain in her side. The next day, April 29, she visited each of the missionaries at their houses, including those from other islands. Erysipelas now made its appearance, which after two or three days affected the brain by *metastasis* and she sunk away into palsy and death.[18]

Whenever possible, Dr. Judd used natives as medical assistants. In May, 1828, John E. Phelps, who had sailed with the Third Company on the *Parthian*, was assigned to him as a student and assistant. Somewhat later he obtained the services of another native, Hoohano, whom he described as "a valuable assistant both in the preparation of medicines and in prescribing for office patients." But Hoohano died in June, 1840, and another assistant, Kalili, quit because he was unwilling to work without wages.[19]

Consistently, he did what he could to educate the native healers. As he reasoned, "It has been an object with me not to oppose the practice of the native physicians in mass, but to endeavor by the best means in my power to correct and modify their practice. . . . It is out of the question for us to think of putting down the native practice unless we will attend all the sick ourselves." Similarly he tried to persuade the natives that certain rituals of the Catholic priests in Hawaii had a spiritual rather then a medical purpose, for some natives identified the Catholic use of holy water with the ancient Hawaiian custom of sacred sprinkling to purify contaminated persons.[20]

As a practical measure, he devoted much energy to the medical education of his colleagues, especially those in outlying districts, so that they might be able to give rudimentary medical treatment to one another and to the natives in their congregations. In 1834, after a survey, he wrote the American Board requesting that medical books be sent to the mission stations. He argued persuasively, "Every station must be supplied with medicines for the use of both missionaries and people and the need of books is obvious in order to guide those who administer them." For the immediate use of missionaries and natives alike, he prepared a handwritten treatment book in the Hawaiian language. His colleagues had reason to be grateful for his help. Repeatedly they were called upon to treat sick natives in their districts. In time of epidemic they even turned their sermons into medical lectures.[21]

In response to mission orders of 1835, Dr. Judd prepared for the students of the Lahainaluna Seminary a 60-page textbook on anatomy, written in Hawaiian. His *Anatomia* was published by the mission press early in 1838 in an edition of 500 copies. In it he contributed almost all the anatomical words in the Hawaiian language.[22] The work contains 58 superb copperplate engravings, all copies by native students at Lahainaluna from illustrations in Jerome V. C. Smith's *Class Book of Anatomy, designed for Schools* (1834). The engravings are all the more remarkable in that the artists were untrained natives working with crude tools on odd pieces of copper acquired from passing ships.[23]

From time to time he lectured on medical topics to the Sandwich Island Institute. After a discourse on the Hawaiian climate in December, 1837, he gave a talk on electricity on June 18, 1838, and, as the affair was reported, "the lecturer kindly offered to *shock* any of his audience," probably with the same "electrical cylinder machine" which Sereno Bishop remembered as a child. On November 2, 1838, he discussed the bones of the skull, and, as his talk was reported, "wrapped solemn facts in a sweet coating of dry humor." About the same time, the mission invited him to give annual medical lectures at the Lahainaluna Seminary, but this project never materialized.[24]

Throughout, he showed himself to be a conscientious pioneer physician coping with much the same problems that his father faced on the New York and Michigan frontiers. Like his father, he worked to the limit of his knowledge and strength. Both traveled under primitive conditions, performed surgery without anesthetics, and received payment for their services in kind. Kauka (Doctor) Judd, as he was known to the natives, received only one dollar in

ANATOMIA.

HE PALAPALA IA E HOIKE AI

I KE ANO

O KO KE KANAKA KINO.

———————

Ua kakauia ma ka olelo Hawaii, i mea e ao ai na haumana o ke Kula
Nui, ma Lahainaluna.

———————

OAHU:
MEA PAIPALAPALA A NA MISIONARI.
———
1838.

Title page from "Anatomia"

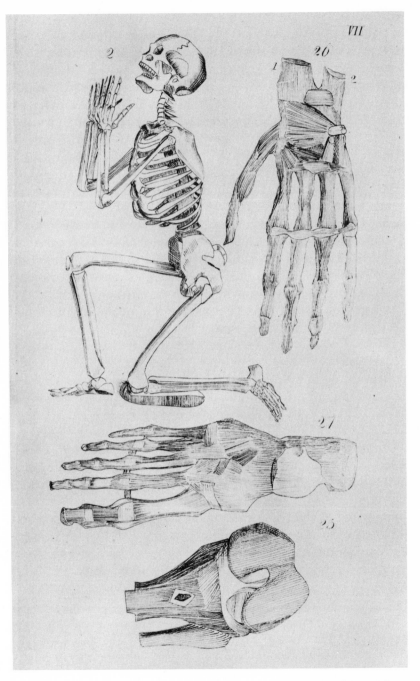

Engravings from "Anatomia"

cash fees in 1834–1835, but his patients gave him a vest, a pump, beef and mutton valued at $15, a lamp, gingham, sugar, figs, and three pairs of children's shoes. His daughter recalls that the natives often brought a *hookupu* (contribution) of food, varying from a live pig that got loose in the living room to a bowl of eggs, a scarce commodity, which the twins, Charles and Laura, broke over one another's heads while Mrs. Judd was dreaming of long-untasted custards and cake.[25] But at any event, all the fees, either in cash or in kind, belonged to the mission and were deducted from his share of the common stock. Usually he received no fees at all.

Mrs. Judd had reason to complain of this situation. "My husband's practice in the foreign community," she wrote, "increases every day, and if our rules allowed him to receive pay for it, a day's earnings would support his family a week. It does not seem right to draw our support from the treasury of the A.B.C.F.M., when ample opportunity is afforded to take care of ourselves without abridging our usefulness to the nation or mission."[26] Under the circumstances, it was hard to reconcile the mission's communal practices with her ingrained Yankee ideals of industry and thrift.

Dr. Judd made an effort to keep abreast of new developments in medical science. He read the *Boston Medical and Surgical Journal* as it appeared;[27] Smith's *Anatomy*, which he used as the basis of his own anatomical book, was not published until 1834, six years after his arrival in Honolulu. But with cruel irony his medical knowledge failed him when most he needed it.

On the afternoon of November 10, 1839, his first-born child, Gerrit Jr., then in his eleventh year, had an attack of appendicitis. Dr. Judd diagnosed the case as "inflammation of the bowels," and, in accordance with prevailing medical usage, treated him with cupping and leeches. This therapy only increased the child's pain. About 11 o'clock on the evening of November 13, Gerrit Jr. died of what is now known to have been a ruptured appendix with generalized peritonitis. Some years later Mrs. Judd wrote,

He was beautiful in form and feature, and lovely in disposition—manly beyond his years—and gave promise of uncommon worth—but the Master called him, and we resigned what was so precious to us, without one murmuring thought or word. . . . He died perfectly tranquil, took leave of us all, as though going on a journey, taking each by the hand, saying, "good-bye, dear father and mother: I shall meet you in heaven. Good-bye dear sisters and brothers, prepare to meet me in heaven."

He was buried on November 15 in Kawaiahao Cemetery. Bingham preached at the funeral. Dr. Judd's medical student, Hoohano, wrote a long and affecting poem about his death.[28]

Almost immediately death struck again. The day after little Gerrit's funeral, Midshipman Robert S. Morris of the U.S.S. *John Adams*, who had lived as a patient in the Judd household for over a month, died of consumption. As Mrs. Judd wrote, "He was fully aware of his condition, and earnest in his preparation for death. Gerrit spent hours each day in reading to him, and they formed a warm friendship for each other. We used to pray with him daily; and little thought the Lord was preparing us in attendance on this young stranger to perform the same tender office for our own dear boy." He was buried on the 17th beside Gerrit Jr.'s freshly closed grave in Kawaiahao Cemetery.[29]

But even in the midst of grief new medical duties pressed upon Dr. Judd. Right after his son's death he was called to Wailuku on Maui, where the native students in the female seminary were suffering from malnutrition. Accompanied by his wife and five surviving children, he spent several weeks on Maui, where he recommended better food and more outdoor exercise for the languishing scholars. By May of the year following, he could report that their health was much improved.[30] He had barely finished his report when a new medical burden was placed upon him. Early in June he took into his home four shipwrecked Japanese sailors who were suffering from the aftereffects of exposure.[31]

Many times his work as a physician drove him to heartbreak and exhaustion. But equal sorrows, and even greater challenges, soon confronted him in an entirely different field.

Adviser to the Chiefs

From the beginning the missionaries recognized the practical necessity of learning the native language, for obviously it was more effective to preach the gospel in Hawaiian than in an idiom foreign to the heathen population. Accordingly, they standardized the alphabet and soon used Hawaiian exclusively in the native schools. By 1839, through a co-operative effort in which Dr. Judd participated, they had finished their translation of the Bible into the native tongue.[1] Naturally enough, their proficiency in the language endeared them to the chiefs. It contributed immeasurably to the mission's success in Christianizing the nation, and did much to bring the native government under mission domination.

Before the *Parthian* left Boston, Elisha Loomis, who had just returned from the Islands, gave to the Third Company a Hawaiian vocabulary. Along with their colleagues, the Judds studied the language conscientiously on board ship. Five weeks before they landed, Dr. Judd wrote in his journal, "I have after seven days of severe labour finished copying a vocabulary of the Hawaiian language. I have bound it in a little volume containing 128 pages. I am now about to learn what of it I can before I arrive. Laura joins me in it or rather precedes me for she can speak many more words than I can." The day after their arrival, when they took their first walk among the natives, Mrs. Judd noted with satisfaction. "We could converse with them a little which pleased them much."[2] Ultimately, both she and Dr. Judd became fluent in the native tongue.[3] In the 1830s, using the language of the people, he was able to teach in the native schools and to preach in the native churches. His textbook on anatomy, published in Hawaiian in 1838, gives formal testimony to his linguistic skill.

On numerous occasions he acted as interpreter for visiting clergymen and officials. He interpreted for Francis Warriner of the U.S. frigate *Potomac* in 1832, when Warriner addressed a native Sunday school. Four years later he interpreted for the Quaker Daniel Wheeler, who preached to a native congregation of twenty-five hundred.[4]

As time passed he became intimately associated with the native chiefs, not only as their interpreter but as their physician, too. Soon enough, and almost inevitably, he became their adviser. In his wife's words:

As Dr. Judd was not a clergyman, and had been the medical attendant and personal friend of the royal family, it was natural that they should often apply to him. He taught clerks to keep, in the native language, records of all important business, and to preserve all receipts on payment of debts, in order to prevent being compelled to pay them twice, which had not unfrequently happened.

By 1839 he could report significantly to the mission, "Some time has been occupied during the year as interpreter and translator for the government, an employment of much importance."[5]

Along with others in the mission, he became increasingly involved in the politics and diplomacy of the Hawaiian nation. Gradually also he developed a feeling of patriotic attachment to the Hawaiian government, as appears in a sentence which he wrote to Levi Chamberlain in the summer of 1837. "Let us hope still for this feeble and struggling nation, and pray for them and their enemies."[6]

The extent of his involvement in native politics appears further from his correspondence over the British brig *Clementine*, which

97

had brought two Catholic priests to Honolulu in April, 1837. When the Hawaiian authorities tried to deport the priests on this ship, the owner complained to the British consul, Richard Charlton, who demanded damages from the Hawaiian government. The affair precipitated a bitter paper war.[7] Dr. Judd wrote to Chamberlain from Waialua on July 11, "Probably the complaint against Charlton should be presented and the papers looked up. If there is no copy of the English of that in the hands of the chiefs, I believe I have one among my papers at Honolulu. Do give Br. Brinsmade a jog and use every effort to keep him awake *now*. He and those with him can and ought to do much." He added characteristically, "and do you, my well tried brother, remember to *work* as well as pray."[8]

Further particulars of his activity appear in Lorrin Andrews' journal.

In the evening [October 9, 1837] I went with Dr. Judd to the chiefs. Dr. J. carried some papers relative to the affair of the *Clementine*—had also some conversation respecting the Jesuits. . . . At ten o'clock [October 11] I returned to the mission house. In half an hour I was sent for with Dr. Judd who went with me. We found the chiefs wanted assistance in preparing the document to be sent, that is, the accusations against Mr. Charlton. . . . I spent the evening [October 12] with Dr. Judd in conversation and instructing the king and chiefs relative to their future proceedings. In the mean time the documents relative to the history of the Jesuits and the *Clementine* were written and were put in a course of translation. . . . Mr. Bingham and Mr. Bishop were engaged in the translation, and Dr. Judd compared and put the documents together.[9]

Two years later he figured in another political crisis, when Captain Laplace of the French frigate *L'Art'mise* presented an ultimatum to the native government, demanding equal rights for Catholics and exacting $20,000 as security that their rights would be respected. Under threat of war the chiefs yielded to the French demands. Dr. Judd was at the time touring the windward side of Oahu with Mr. and Mrs. Jarves. A messenger summoned him to Honolulu. Shortly after his arrival, he forwarded to the American Board an important communication on the subject from the Hawaiian chiefs.[10]

James Jackson Jarves, the journalist and art collector, who was at the time living with the Judds, has left a striking character sketch which can only refer to Dr. Judd. In it Jarves gave due weight to his activities as governmental adviser.

I have seen the same individual perform skilful surgical operations, practice medicine extensively, plough, and direct natives in the culture of their farms, build the stone walls, and raise the massive roof of a church, a tinker and carpenter at home, a music-teacher, and a school-master, an interpreter for government, a translator for foreigners in drawing up deeds, in fact, an adept in every good and useful work, whether medical or manual. Beloved by all classes, he is constantly laboring for all. With all this multifarious labor, he, with his spouse, a lady well worthy of such a husband, finds time to educate six children; and a better regulated and more happy family, I have never seen.[11]

It is fully apparent that Dr. Judd, like many other leaders of his generation in the United States,[12] displayed throughout his life a phenomenal virtuosity, as with energy and good will he undertook a wide variety of challenging tasks.

In the winter of 1840–1841 he took on still another assignment, which nearly cost him his life, and in its unpleasant aftermath had much to do with shaping the course of his future career. For three months he accompanied as overseer and interpreter the United States exploring expedition under the command of Lt. Charles Wilkes, a great-nephew of the English politician. Wilkes's expedition surveyed in the years 1838–1842 the Pacific Northwest, 280 Pacific islands, and large stretches of the antarctic, including that part which still bears his name.[13] He reached Honolulu in 1840.

The year previous, at the request of Lt. A. K. Long of the U.S.S. *Relief*, Dr. Judd had sent a circular letter to his colleagues requesting detailed data on such subjects as soil, climate, schools, churches, and population.[14] At Wilkes's invitation and with the concurrence of his brethren in the mission, Dr. Judd left Honolulu for the island of Hawaii on December 3, 1840, as "physician, interpreter, adviser, and manager of the natives." The expedition, including six hundred Hawaiians, spent several weeks near the summit of Mauna Loa, almost fourteen thousand feet above sea level. On January 16, 1841, Dr. Judd descended into the crater of Kilauea, the world's largest active volcano, in order to gather specimens of gas and lava.[15] Here he almost lost his life.

He wrote in his annual report to the American Board,

While at the Volcano of Kilauea I narrowly escaped a horrible death through the merciful interposition of Providence. Let down by the hands of a native, I had descended 6 or 8 feet of the brim of a cooled caldron 28 feet deep and 200 wide, and crept along under a ledge where I was crouched down on my feet collecting *Pele's hair*, when the falling of a few stones warned me that an eruption was about to take place, and the next instant the bottom opened 50 feet from me like an immense bubble 8 or 10 feet in diameter and with a tremendous noise projected a column of lava to a height far above the bank or margin of the caldron. The color of this jet was of the most perfect crimson and the heat and glare too great for the eye to look on. I raised myself to an erect posture, turned my face to the wall with my hands upon a projecting ledge above me, which I found it impossible to mount without assistance, nor could I resume my former position and retrace the way I came on account of the intense heat.

There I stood perfectly helpless. God heard my prayer. When I had given up all and resigned myself into His hand, Kalama appeared on the bank, put out his hands, seized one of mine, which enabled me by an extraordinary effort to throw myself out.

It seems that at the moment of the eruption the whole of the five natives who were with me ran off, but Kalama, more bold than the rest, bethought himself of me and turned back only just in season for my rescue, for just as he approached the brink the accumulated flood, having filled the inequalities of the bottom, flowed directly under my feet. As I went over the ledge I felt that I was burnt, although as it proved but slightly on each elbow and one wrist. Kalama's face and ear were blistered by the heat radiated from below.[16]

Elsewhere he added,

We both ran a short distance till we thought we were safe. On looking back I saw that the column of lava was much lower, and that I had left my memorandum book on the bank. With caution I approached and finding the crater nearly full to the ledge on which I had been standing, the wind in my favor and the lava about to flow over the lower edge of the crater, I called to the natives to bring the frying-pan which I lashed to a long pole. By this time the stream of liquid livid lava, fully 40 feet wide, was passing by me and I thrust out the pan midway of the stream which rolled into it filling it full. The first time the cake was spoiled by the grease of the pan flying out. The next trial was successful, and the

101

fine black and shining cake of lava was preserved and carried away to grace the cabinet of curiosities at Washington.[17]

When he reached the tents he found that his burns were severe. His wrists, which were inflamed with sores the size of a silver dollar, gave him much pain, and for a time he was stricken with a fever. As for the heroic Kalama, Wilkes reported that his "whole face was one blister, particularly that side which had been most exposed to the fire."[18]

Wilkes and Dr. Judd developed admiration and respect for one another. When Dr. Judd's fourth son was born on April 20, 1841, he was named Allan Wilkes in honor of the naval commander. For his part, Wilkes insisted on giving Dr. Judd more than $700 in recognition of his hospitality and services.[19]

Dr. Judd's work in the exploring expedition, and particularly his acceptance of money from Wilkes, caused jealousy and resentment among his colleagues in the mission. Armstrong, for example, commented acidly, "Dr. Judd is living—at least to the Squadron if he is dead to every thing else."[20] In May, 1841, he received formal word from Levi Chamberlain that in accepting money from Wilkes he had broken one of the mission's regulations. Chamberlain insisted on laying the matter before the mission at the forthcoming annual meeting.[21]

The issue involved was a delicate one, and it caused much wrangling before it was settled. Dr. Judd's reply to Chamberlain revealed indignation and bruised feelings. "It is not so pleasant after walking 13 years hand in hand with my brethren to have the suspicion thrown out that I have so far turned aside from them as to need such decided measures as have been proposed." In his annual report to the American Board he argued that he was entitled to keep the money. "I went on this expedition in no other capacity than as companion of Capt. Wilkes and aid and director of the natives, having no other expectation of reward than a consciousness of doing good and serving our common cause. . . . I received a valuable present from Capt. Wilkes, under the positive restriction that it should be entirely at my disposal and not a donation to the Board." He later explained that the gift was intended to benefit his children.[22]

After protracted discussion the matter was referred to Boston. The American Board suggested as a compromise that part of the money represented pay from Wilkes for services rendered. This sum, according to the regulations, should be turned over to the mission. The balance, regarded as Wilkes's donation, he might keep. Dr. Judd accepted the Board's ruling and offered to give up the entire amount. As he stated, "I believe that those brethren best acquainted with me will allow, that I have not unduly sought my own. In my pecuniary transactions I have endeavored to maintain strict integrity. . . . If the brethren think I took too low a standard in adjusting the ordinary pay I do not feel strenuous upon the point. I would sooner relinquish a larger or the whole amount, than be branded with avarice or dishonesty." Satisfied with his submission, the brethren ruled on May 27, 1843, that he might keep the money.[23]

Amicable as it was, the settlement came at a peculiar time. Dr. Judd had already left the mission. At the very moment that the brethren ruled in his favor he had become a central figure in a crisis of far-reaching political consequence to the Hawaiian nation.

11

Translator and Recorder

In the 1840s Hawaii throbbed with conflict as the expansion of
Europe and America sent dynamic social forces into the Pacific.
The Islands acted as a funnel through which these forces entered
Oceania and as a warm frontier in which they did daily battle. The
shipping interest, especially the whalers, made Honolulu a regular
port of call. Business firms of several nations took root and flour-
ished. At the same time, the powerful American mission set its
high-flung aims of puritan godliness against the baser goals of the
commercial population. The two groups quarreled furiously. Meanwhile, representatives of various nationalities referred a number of
disputes to their home governments. All too often the reply came
in the form of a ship of war. Consequently, many Island residents,
knowing that the native administration was incompetent, feared
that at any time Hawaii might be seized outright by a major power
such as England or France.

In this troubled situation the missionaries played a vital part.
They did what they could to Christianize the Islands, and as
followers of liberal Calvinism they stressed social reform in such
fields as education and public health. They were in close association

with the wavering chiefs; it was a small and almost unavoidable step to take control of the kingdom's political arrangements. During the 1830s they operated as the power behind the throne, but their involvement, or, as their opponents termed it, their meddling, in politics, led them into an impossible position. By advising, they assumed indirect responsibility for the unstable Hawaiian government, yet the instructions of the American Board stated clearly, "You are to abstain from all interference with the local and political interests of the people. The kingdom of Christ is not of this world, and it especially behooves a missionary to stand aloof from the private and transient interests of chiefs and rulers." In recognition of the issues involved, the Reverend William Richards left the mission in 1838 to serve the government in an advisory capacity as chaplain, teacher, and translator to the king.[1] Richards' action prepared the way directly for Dr. Judd's political career.

Under mission tutelage the nation made much progress. By 1840 the government had adopted a code of laws and a liberal constitution with a representative assembly. Dr. Judd advised Richards about some of the earlier legal arrangements. Richards also turned his attention to economics and diplomacy. There evolved a naive scheme whereby all unoccupied lands in the Islands were secretly leased in 1841 to Ladd & Co., an American firm sympathetic to the mission. The scheme had two objectives: to attract colonists of good moral character and to discourage imperialist designs of European powers by disposing of the vacant lands. In the winter of 1841–1842 Peter Brinsmade, one of the partners of Ladd & Co., left Hawaii to promote the scheme and to seek diplomatic recognition of the Kingdom's independence in Britain, France, and the United States.[2]

The Ladd & Co. enterprise reveals both the good will and inexperience of its sponsors, for it was not based on sound knowledge of land speculative practices. It was also vulnerable, as Dr. Judd later decided, because little worth-while land was unoccupied and because colonization by whites might submerge the natives as completely as an imperialist seizure.[3] The missionaries, it is apparent, faced the difficult Hawaiian situation with few qualifications beyond courage and devotion to duty. Their puritan code of ethics was unsuited to Hawaii's climate and native culture, and their political thinking tended to be theocratic. Almost without exception they lacked experience in politics and finance. The Hawaiian government, while it could not have survived without their help, needed also worldly advice.[4]

Such advice came opportunely when in February, 1842, Sir George Simpson, governor in North America of the Hudson's Bay Co., arrived in Honolulu from California. The Company had had an agency in Honolulu since 1834, and its employees there tended to be pro-American. Despite efforts on the part of the British consul, Richard Charlton, to poison his mind, Simpson took a sympathetic interest in the mission, and especially in its attempts to bolster the weak native government. He discussed native problems with Kekuanaoa, the governor of Oahu, and with Dr. Judd. On March 20 he made a trip to Lahaina on Maui to see Richards and the king. A letter from Dr. Judd put him, as he stated, "on a confidential footing," and a number of conferences followed.[5]

Simpson recommended that the government send Richards abroad to negotiate treaties with Britain, France, and the United States, to guarantee Hawaii's independence, and he agreed to act with Richards as a diplomatic representative of the Hawaiian king. He felt that such formal proceedings would be more effective than the informal mission of Ladd & Co.[6]

At the same time, Simpson advised the creation of the office of recorder, translator, and interpreter to the Hawaiian government. It is virtually certain that he also recommended Dr. Judd, of whom he had a high opinion, for this new post.[7] Simpson left for England by way of Alaska on March 24. He planned to be in London by November to help Richards in the treaty negotiations.[8]

Shortly thereafter the king invited Dr. Judd to take Richards' place in the government. At that time Dr. Judd faced the first major crisis of his life after his conversion. He knew that if he accepted the king's offer he would have to leave the mission to which he had dedicated his life. On the other hand, from Finney and other advocates of the new Calvinism he had learned that good works were a part of the duty of a Christian. Richards had already set an example by leaving the mission to serve the new nation. In the past, Dr. Judd had faced a similar dilemma when he decided to continue with his medical career instead of preaching the gospel.

With complete consistency he now decided that, although he lacked political experience, it was his Christian duty to enter the government, since secular service of any kind was, so he believed, pleasing to God. Nonetheless, the decision caused him untold anxiety. As he later told the mission brethren, "I did not break my connexion with you without greater mental conflict and sacrifice of feeling than is known to you."[9]

Just before leaving for Lahaina on April 19, Dr. Judd wrote to the American Board requesting a temporary discharge from the mission. At the same time, he stated that he would seek the approval of his brethren before accepting the government post. He reached Lahaina on April 22, where he attended the legislature and conferred with Dwight Baldwin, who advised him to take office in the government without resigning from the mission. On the other hand, Richards advised him to leave the mission and to take office without consulting the brethren, so that the mission could not be held responsible for his political acts. Dr. Judd took Richards' advice, but instead of accepting Richards' old post, which was mainly advisory, he urged the formation of a national treasury board.[10]

To this proposal the king and chiefs agreed, and on May 10 the board was created by legislative action. On the same day, the king and premier appointed to the board Dr. Judd and two chiefs, Timothy Haalilio and John Ii. Two days later, another law created the office of government interpreter and recorder, and on May 15 the king and premier appointed Dr. Judd to this office in addition to his duties on the treasury board. His letter of appointment set his salary at $760 a year. The figure was of his own choosing. As he stated, "I receive the same amount from the Government as I was allowed by the mission, and am exposed to extra expenses, but did not like to ask more lest the enemy should say with a semblance of truth, as they have said falsely, 'You have left the service of your God for filthy lucre.' "[11]

He soon realized that his previous request for a temporary leave of absence from the mission would not suffice, and on June 11 he asked the American Board for an honorable discharge. On July 18, the day that Richards and Haalilio left on their diplomatic journey, he received a new responsibility from the king and premier. "We hereby appoint you to be our officer, whose duty it is to collect certain information and report to William Richards and Sir George Simpson, who are to act according to your words."[12] His various duties, broadly and loosely stated as they were, conferred power little short of dictatorship.

As was only to be expected, Dr. Judd prepared an elaborate justification for leaving the mission. His defense became particularly labored when he discovered that neither the brethren nor the American Board approved his entrance into public life. He wrote,

It is a fact well known to me that since I came to the Islands the government have depended on individuals of the mission for advice on all important measures and for aid in carrying them into execution. I will not go into details in illustration of this, but will state that for the last three or four years, an increased share of this labor has fallen upon me, and I have done it with the approbation of my brethren, using great caution, however, lest I should appear to the world too conspicuous an actor. This I was the better able to do by reason of my being a medical man, often called about the persons of the chiefs. . . . The services which I have been called to render in this way have at length become so numerous and burdensome, and at the same time so threatening to my reputation as a missionary, *who professes not to direct the counsels of the nation*, that I had determined that I must at any rate decline the service altogether, or leave the mission. My own feelings are in favor of the former course; I greatly prefer my own profession, and to maintain my connection with the Board, but there is no one here who could be found to do what the exigencies of the government require. . . . The motives which induced me to take this step, were a desire to be more useful to the nation for whose welfare I had left my native land, the fact of Mr. Richards being about to visit Europe, the absolute necessity that some one should aid the king and chiefs in conducting their affairs, and the impossibility of their procuring any other secular man with a knowledge of the native language to aid them.[13]

All the enthusiasm which had led him to join the mission in the first place still flowed with undiminished vigor in a secular or nationalistic channel. As he admitted to Sir George Simpson in 1844, "It is impossible for me to express to you the deep anxiety I feel for the young government of these Islands. I have unawares been drawn into the deepest assimilation of all my interests with theirs, and am ready to sacrifice every thing for the welfare of the nation."[14]

The king and chiefs were delighted with his appointment. In the past, when he had been a mainstay of the government in fact if not in title, they had come to trust him completely. In succeeding years their faith in him increased. Throughout the eleven and a half years that he held office, Dr. Judd owed his power mainly to the forcefulness of his own personality and the trust of the king and chiefs. No other white man in the government could rival him in their affection.

Although the native rulers welcomed him warmly, many foreign residents greeted his appointment with hostility, for the commercial colony feared that through him the mission would dominate the nation. Alexander Simpson, a cousin of Sir George Simpson and a partisan of Charlton, the British consul, attacked him as "narrow and illiberal" and insisted that he "rode rough-shod over residents, chiefs, and people." Simpson wrote further, "Thus did individuals, who came out for the avowed purpose of teaching the religion of the meek and lowly Jesus, use the influence which they had acquired for the furtherance of their own ambitious purposes." Stephen Reynolds, an American merchant, referred to him as "King Judd" and added that he "rides us down to the dust. We have no mercy to expect from him. The king is nothing—nobody. Judd orders him as you would a boy."[15] The chorus of opposition, which began as soon as he entered the government, became even more vociferous as the years passed. It reached a climax in Herman Melville's characterization of him as "a sanctimonious apothecary-adventurer."[16]

The brethren in the mission also objected to his appointment. To preserve appearances they thanked him formally for his past services and accepted his offer to continue as mission physician. In return, as he had requested, they allowed him to occupy his house, which was, of course, mission property, and to use the mission herd.[17] But under the surface a bitter current of resentment welled. Some feared that they would lose his services as physician. Armstrong told the American Board in September that he was too busy with politics to tend the mission's medical needs—a charge which Dr. Judd flatly denied.[18] Others objected to the haste and apparent secrecy of his appointment. Lowell Smith complained that he had consulted none of the brethren—he had in fact consulted

Baldwin—and Dr. Judd himself admitted that he was "out of order" on this score.[19] Armstrong believed that the mission would have approved his departure had he laid the question before them "in a proper manner" at the general meeting, and Chamberlain, although generally sympathetic to his appointment, pointed out that it might be construed as a missionary plot to take control of the Hawaiian Kingdom.[20]

The American Board shared Chamberlain's apprehension. The Prudential Committee reproved Dr. Judd for accepting the appointment and invited him to return to the mission, on the ground that it would injure the entire evangelical movement, which was worldwide in extent, if the public learned that missionaries were leaving their spiritual labors to take part in local politics. The case of Richards, it was argued weakly, should not be regarded as a precedent. The Committee also objected that his entrance into politics might encourage Catholic missionaries to do likewise, and that it might displease certain foreign governments.[21]

After reviewing the Board's reasons, Dr. Judd replied stubbornly, in a statement which reflects Finney's emphasis on good works, "They are correct and ought to be maintained by the Board, but I have believed it to be my duty to take steps contrary to them both for the safety of the mission and for the good of the nation. . . . My prayer is that I may be useful, and in that way best adapted to glorify God."[22] He had searched his conscience and made up his mind. No amount of persuasion could move him.

At the same time, the brethren opposed his return on the ground that if he rejoined them in the spring of 1843 the mission might be held responsible for his political acts in the interval since he had taken office. It was argued also that if he were forced out of office a new administration might retaliate against the mission. The dispute over his gift from Wilkes was still unsettled, and the element of pique was not absent from the deliberations. Lowell Smith in particular attacked him and ended by calling him "King Judd." In view of the circumstances, the American Board reconsidered the case, and in November, 1843, accepted his resignation.[23]

Dr. Judd's uncertain status while his resignation was still pending aggravated the difficulties which he faced in the government. By the end of 1842 he had encountered, as a sort of bitter preview, almost all the problems that harassed him during his long tenure of office: the personal conduct of the native rulers, many of whom were addicted to drink; threats of imperialist seizure; dissension with the foreign colony and its diplomatic representatives; and the morass of native finance, including a soaring national debt.

From the beginning he kept close check on the behavior of the king and chiefs. On April 26, 1842, four days after Dr. Judd landed at Lahaina and just before he took office, Kamehameha III and thirteen chiefs signed a temperance pledge. In view of Dr. Judd's uncompromising teetotalism the event cannot be a coincidence. Almost certainly he made the pledge a condition of his assuming office. Similarly, he later bought the king a billiard table for the palace, as Mrs. Judd commented, "so he need not be tempted to seek amusement beyond his own premises." She added characteristically, "We are ready to contrive anything that is innocent to withdraw him from low associates."[24]

Soon after the departure of Richards and Haalilio, Dr. Judd faced another vexing problem, one which he had recognized as early as 1831, when he wrote, "It appears to us that unless some counter influence is exerted the country will soon come under the influence of a foreign power." Early in August, 1842, came frightening news that France had seized the Marquesas Islands, and on August 24 a French man-of-war, commanded by Captain S. Mallet, entered Honolulu harbor. Mallet accused the Hawaiian government of breaking the Laplace treaty of 1839, and made a number of unreasonable demands, one of which would have given Catholic priests in the Islands the right to appoint certain officials of the Hawaiian government. Dr. Judd and others believed that the French intended to seize the Islands. It was the first diplomatic crisis which he faced in full command of the Kingdom, and as he later stated, "No one can tell how much I suffered of anxiety and mental labor on this occasion." He wrote the king's reply to Mallet, which stated that the government would observe the Laplace treaty and that negotiations for a new treaty were already under way. Apparently satisfied, Mallet left in September, and the crisis passed.[25]

A second crisis followed on the heels of the first. Richard Charlton, the British consul, left Honolulu on September 27 for London, where he hoped to thwart the treaty negotiations of Richards and

Haalilio. The day before he left he notified the Hawaiian government that he had appointed Alexander Simpson acting consul in his absence. Simpson was notoriously hostile to the government. He had quarreled publicly with Dr. Judd, and on one occasion he had challenged Dr. Judd to a duel.[26] Consequently, although declining the challenge, Dr. Judd retaliated by advising the chiefs not to recognize Simpson's appointment. In October the two men had a further dispute over whether Simpson had returned an official letter unopened or with the seal broken. Shortly thereafter, when a Hawaiian court attached Charlton's property in the course of a lawsuit, Simpson wrote an angry letter through British diplomatic channels asking for a naval expedition to protect the rights of British nationals in the Islands.[27] As events were to prove, this letter precipitated a crisis in which the Hawaiian government almost lost its independence. Dr. Judd's quarrel with Simpson had a tremendous aftermath, but it was only one of a series of quarrels in his stormy political career.

The confused state of native finances created equally disturbing problems. Up to the time that Dr. Judd took office, as he later stated, "the government kept no accounts, debts were often contracted by irresponsible persons without any provision for their payment, and in many cases where payments had been made, no sufficient vouchers or proof could be found. There was very little government property, and neither a public chest or a dollar on hand."[28] Public credit, he added, was "at a low ebb." The exact amount of the public debt was unknown. Later determinations placed it at about $60,000.[29]

Dr. Judd set out conscientiously to put the government finances in order. The very day that he entered office he established a set of books.[30] Within a week, regular authorizations for payment began to issue from the treasury.[31] Before the end of May the government imposed a three per cent duty on imports of goods and exports of money. About the same time, he set up an office in Honolulu to transact the government's financial business, and he began to train native clerks in bookkeeping. For a time he tried vainly to get a white man as a clerk, but by November he had hired Joseph Slater, a tailor, to record the minutes of the treasury board.[32] Meanwhile, to tide over the emergency, he obtained a credit of £10,000 from the Hudson's Bay Company, and he authorized Richards to negotiate a foreign loan.[33]

Dr. Judd threw himself into his political labors with the same energy and high moral purpose which had characterized his work in the mission. Even Alexander Simpson, one of his most severe critics, admitted, "Judd's motives are not mercenary." He pursued his task wholeheartedly. In dealing with a white man accused of selling liquor without a license he revealed, so Stephen Reynolds reported, "a great deal of anger. I never saw a man show more temper than Judd did."[34]

The immediate results were gratifying. By the end of the year the government had a regular system of accounts and a regular revenue from taxes. Public credit had been restored, and the national debt reduced by well over $20,000.[35] Frugality of the New England variety, along with Yankee orderliness and horror of debt, had gone a long way toward putting the native government on a sound financial foundation. Even before the year ended, Dr. Judd could write to Richards, "King and chiefs remain *ma ka pono* [righteous]. Taxes coming in. Peace and good order prevailing."[36]

In view of such progress in Hawaii's domestic situation, Dr. Judd had reason to feel hopeful for the future. He did not know that already forces outside the Islands were poised to strike a devastating blow.

The Paulet Episode

On February 10, 1843, the British frigate *Carysfort* anchored off Honolulu. In command was Captain Lord George Paulet, a handsome and capable officer. Then in his fortieth year, he was midway in a distinguished career which brought him eventual promotion to admiral. His presence in Hawaii resulted from the complaints of Alexander Simpson and Charlton, which had come to the attention of Rear Admiral Richard Thomas, commander of the British squadron in the Pacific. His mission was to protect British interests in the Islands, and, in particular, to restore Charlton's property, which a Hawaiian court had seized.[1]

When he reached the Islands, Paulet was unaware that the British Foreign Office had recently instructed the Admiralty to respect the political independence, laws, and customs of native governments in the Pacific. Britain had not yet become a consistently imperialistic power. At this time British opinion was generally indifferent to or opposed to colonization overseas, and such expansion as there was took place haphazardly. Nonetheless, from time to time the British seized territory, such as New Zealand, to prevent it from falling into French hands, just as the French took New Caledonia to keep it away from the British.² The situation was, to say the least, uncertain. Paulet's presence in the Islands immediately created an atmosphere of crisis and foreboding.

Right after the *Carysfort* anchored, Simpson went on board to give Paulet his version of the troubled Hawaiian situation. He urged Paulet not to exchange the traditional courtesies until the government recognized his appointment as acting British consul. Paulet agreed. Consequently, when Dr. Judd came on board, Paulet refused to receive him officially. Instead he wrote to Governor Kekuanaoa demanding an interview with the king.³

Kekuanaoa replied that he would send for the king, who was on Maui. Meanwhile the U.S.S. *Boston*, a sloop of war, arrived from Tahiti and added to the excitement. When Kamehameha III reached Honolulu on the 16th, Paulet again wrote asking for a private interview the next day. The king and premier replied on the 17th, in a letter which Dr. Judd both advised and translated, that the government refused. "In case you have business of a private nature, we will appoint Dr. Judd, our confidential agent to confer with you, who being a person of integrity and fidelity to our government, and perfectly acquainted with all our affairs, will receive your communications."

Paulet's response was firm and uncompromising. "I shall hold no communication whatever with Dr. G. P. Judd, who, it has been satisfactorily proved to me, has been the prime mover in the unlawful proceedings of your government against British subjects." Alexander Simpson, it is clear, had done his work well, for Paulet continued with a series of demands: restoration of Charlton's property, recognition of Simpson as acting British consul, and a general settlement of British grievances. Paulet added that he would attack if these demands were not complied with by 4 P.M. the next day.

"Many persons of good judgment," so Dr. Judd stated, "advised the king to let them fire, but the usual pacific course prevailed. The English families went on board a brig, in the outer harbor, and the Americans were ready to go to the *Boston*. As for myself I knew very well that the *Carysfort* would not wish to fire, but I believed their object was to get possession. I therefore joined with those who advised a compliance with the demands under protest."⁴

115

Accordingly, the king and premier on the 18th addressed a letter to Paulet offering submission under protest and adding that commissioners of the Hawaiian government were already in England to make a general settlement of the diplomatic difficulties.

A statement of this nature, which had proved successful with the French Captain Mallet in the September previous, now failed to achieve its desired object, for Paulet, prompted by Simpson, followed his ultimatum with further demands: that certain court decisions be reversed (a proceeding clearly illegal under existing law) and that the Hawaiian government pay indemnities amounting to more than $100,000.

Between February 20 and 23 the king and Dr. Judd had daily conversations with Paulet and Simpson. After the interview of the 23rd, so Dr. Judd reported,

. . . the king declared himself a dead man, and expressed his conviction that his ruin was determined. All the claims he considered unjust, but was willing the cases should be heard, before a proper tribunal, but that was denied him. The object was to rob him of his money, and destroy his laws. Money he had not and could not raise it. He could not overturn the decisions of the courts, without destroying the credit of the government, and exposing it to attack on all sides. He would sooner give up all. "Let them take the Islands." He spent a sleepless night.[5]

On the evening of February 23 Dr. Judd met with Captain Long of the U.S.S. *Boston*, Jules Dudoit, the French consul, and William Hooper, the American consul, to discuss placing the Islands under the temporary protection of France or France and the United States jointly. Documents were prepared for the king's signature, but the next morning the king refused to accept either proposal.

Dr Judd then advised a provisional cession of the Islands to Great Britain. The king and chiefs agreed on the grounds that "Charlton and Simpson are their enemies, but they consider England their friend."[6] After Paulet and Simpson assented to the proposal, Dr. Judd drafted the cession terms.

Early on the 25th the king sent for Dr. Judd and once again asked his advice about ceding the Islands to France and the United States. Dr. Judd advised against such a course and offered to resign, but the king refused to accept his resignation. Upon reflection the king decided, so Dr. Judd reported, "to throw himself into the arms of England, trusting in the justice of his cause, and hoping still for independence."

In an atmosphere of tearful solemnity, the king and chiefs then read the deed of cession. Dr. Judd wrote,

Sorrow and distress marked every countenance. Went to prayer. During prayer, sighs suppressed were often heard. After prayer, not an individual left his knees for a full minute, and I then saw that tears had come to their relief. They sat in silence. The king seized a pen and signed the deed of cession. "Let it go," said he. "If I get help I get it, if not let it go. I can do no more." The premier then added her signature.[7]

At 3 p.m. that afternoon, so Mrs. Judd wrote,

The Hawaiian flag we loved so well, was lowered in the fort, and an English one run up in its place and saluted by the batteries of the fort and the guns of the *Carysfort*. English soldiers marched into the fort and the band played "God save the Queen," and "Isle of Beauty, fare thee well." The latter was played by the request of some lady friends of Lord George, and regarded by us as a refined cruelty, which could only emanate from a woman. . . . After the cession my husband came home and threw himself down, utterly exhausted in body and mind, after the sleepless week of fasting and torture. I sat by him two hours, ransacking heart and brain for arguments of consolation.[8]

In the eyes of many missionaries and American residents Paulet became "a hot-headed young nobleman" duped by Alexander Simpson, whom Mrs. Judd described as "the surly mastiff." William Paty, a patriotic supporter of the Hawaiian government, wrote indignantly, "Cession forsooth! Why don't they call it by its right name, robbery?" In later months the press in the United States raised a similarly furious howl of denunciation.[9] But Paulet and his associates had another view of the matter. They spoke openly of rumors that France was preparing to seize the Islands, as she had just seized the Marquesas and Tahiti, and they defended the cession as a shrewd maneuver to forestall French aggression.[10] Some members of the mission, such as Armstrong and Chamberlain, accepted Paulet's explanation at its face value, and added that if the Islands could not remain independent it were far better to be ruled by Protestant England than by Catholic France.[11] On the other hand, most Americans, including the Judds, distrusted Paulet's motives and regarded the French threat as a pretext rather than a valid reason.

The provisional British government was to operate through a commission consisting of Paulet, Lt. John James Bartholomew Frere of the *Carysfort*, Duncan Forbes Mackay, who resigned on March 4, and either the Hawaiian king or his deputy. As was only to be expected, the king asked Dr. Judd to serve as deputy, but at first Dr. Judd refused. He knew at that time that the American Board wished him to rejoin the mission, and, as he wrote to Rufus Anderson, "it was a season of horrible mental conflict. . . . O my dear sir, you cannot know how much this vexatious business has cost me. My health, my eyesight, my reputation, my family, my hope of a future support—all injured."[12] On February 27 he told the king that he would not consider the appointment unless Paulet declared in writing that it was acceptable, but when Paulet and the other commissioners gave their approval he still declined the office. The king then suggested William Paty, whom Paulet rejected. Finally and reluctantly Dr. Judd agreed to serve.[13] Paulet's approval of his appointment appears strange, but Paulet undoubtedly realized that without Dr. Judd, or someone else equally well acquainted with Hawaiian politics and the Hawaiian language, the newly established commission could not function at all.

Once again a storm of adverse criticism arose to torment him. As Armstrong noted sympathetically, "In the recent transactions the Dr. has been a severe sufferer; the English party charged him with the blame of all their grievances; and now that the government has gone into the hands of the English, he is blamed by the Americans. Poor man! It has well nigh crushed him."[14]

Meanwhile, since the cession was provisional, both Paulet and the king prepared appeals to the British government. It was decided that Simpson should go to London, the first part of the journey to be undertaken on the native schooner *Hooikaika*, which the commission had seized and renamed *Albert*. At the same time, Paulet tried to prevent the Hawaiian authorities from presenting their case by closing the normal channels of overseas communication. Dr. Judd and the chiefs realized the imperative necessity for countering Simpson's representations, which were certain to be highly colored. The chiefs authorized Dr. Judd to select an envoy who would present the Hawaiian side of the dispute not only in London but in Washington as well.

Dr. Judd chose James Fowle Baldwin Marshall, an American merchant only 24 years of age. At a ball on board the U.S.S. *Boston,* at which the English officers were not present, young Marshall was asked into the cabin, where he found Dr. Judd with Captain Long and several others. Marshall heard the proposal and accepted without hesitation.[15]

Dr. Judd took extraordinary and dramatic precautions to keep the plan secret. He drew up Marshall's credentials and accompanying papers, including letters to President John Tyler, Queen Victoria, and King Louis Philippe of France, at night in the old royal tomb, a small coral structure on the palace grounds. The tomb, which was only a block or so from his house, offered an excellent place of concealment, for it had no windows, and its door facing King Street was solid, so that a light burning inside was invisible to passers-by.[16] For a desk he used the coffin of his old friend, the Queen Regent Kaahumanu. A confidential clerk assisted, but as an extra precaution the name of the envoy was left blank. The wording of the credentials was taken from those of John Adams, the first minister of the United States to England.

By night a canoe summoned the king from the island of Maui, where he had gone after the cession. The king and suite came at once to Waikiki, and at a council by night gave final approval. Dr. Judd delivered the signed papers to Marshall, who sailed on the afternoon of March 11, ostensibly as the agent of Ladd & Co., on board the *Albert,* the same ship which was carrying Alexander Simpson on his way to London. Some American residents knew about Marshall's mission, but Paulet and Simpson remained in ignorance of his status as an accredited diplomatic agent of the Hawaiian government.

Two days later Dr. Judd sent to Richards a full account of Marshall's mission by way of the U.S.S. *Boston,* and, about the same time, the Honolulu office of the Hudson's Bay Company forwarded to London a letter which sharply criticized the conduct of Paulet and Simpson.[17] Through channels such as these, and in spite of Paulet's efforts at censorship, voices sympathetic to the Hawaiian government managed to make themselves heard.

119

On March 16, while the political crisis simmered, Dr. Judd assisted at the birth of his eighth child, Sybil Augusta, the only one of his children born under the British flag.

On April 4 he left Honolulu to attend the annual meeting of the Hawaiian legislature at Lahaina on Maui. In the House of Nobles, which remained in session until the 28th of the month, he took a prominent part. Although Melville ridiculed his efforts, there is something touching about the extant record of the legislative proceedings, especially the entry for the day of adjournment, when the clerk wrote, "G. P. Judd then spoke about being in touch with God's laws, and also of his regrets that the country had been taken by Great Britain."[18] Little imagination is required to picture him, broad-shouldered, heavy-set, and dressed in a plain black suit, the only white man in the assemblage of brown-skinned chiefs, soberly and earnestly exhorting them in their own language to trust God in their time of trial and need.

In the new appropriation bill, which generally raised salaries, his annual stipend was increased to $1,500. But the chiefs wished to provide for him in case, as seemed likely, the British should take permanent control of the Islands and dismiss him from office.

The chiefess Kekauluohi (or Auhea), who was premier of the Kingdom from 1839 to her death in 1845, offered him as a gift the whole of Manoa Valley.[19] This valley, which faces Honolulu's celebrated Waikiki Beach, was at the time a fertile and verdant place, productive of sugar cane, taro, potatoes, grass, and shrubs, in contrast to the dusty and barren plains nearby. Dr. Judd knew the valley well. As early as 1832 he had had a small rustic retreat there.[20] But he refused the magnificent gift.

Instead, on April 15 the king and premier agreed to assign to him for 33 years rents in the amount of $1,500 per annum from two wharf lots in Honolulu, which the government had leased to Ladd & Company. Dr. Judd later commuted the rents for an annuity of $1,000 to run until 1876.[21]

When he returned to Honolulu on May 4, he found that in his absence the two remaining members of the British commission, Paulet and Frere (Mackay having resigned), had violated the terms of the cession as stated in Paulet's proclamation. They had modified the Kingdom's fiscal and judicial systems, and in an action to which Dr. Judd and the missionaries strenuously objected, they had relaxed the laws against fornication to the point that flagrant immorality resulted. Dr. Judd protested with vigor, but Paulet and Frere refused to rescind their acts. On May 8 a furious scene ensued, in which Paulet, with "many overbearing and insulting expressions," declared that Dr. Judd would no longer rule the Islands. On May 10 Dr. Judd wrote a formal protest, with especial emphasis on the fornication law, and on the 11th he resigned as king's deputy on the commission.[22]

At the same time, he had strained relations with the mission. The question of his gift from Wilkes was in the final stage of settlement—it was settled on May 27—and the brethren, fearful of becoming involved in a political fracas, refused flatly to print his protest on the mission press.[23]

By resigning, Dr. Judd placed Paulet in an extremely awkward position, for unless there were a deputy of the king to share responsibility for the commission's acts, the British government might be held responsible for any damages resulting from Paulet's rule. Paulet, it is clear, understood the danger involved, for he lost little time in asking the king to appoint another deputy. Dr. Judd kept the king, who had remained on Maui, fully informed of the changing situation by means of a series of letters which were read and then burned.[24] It is possible, therefore, that he actually drafted the firm refusal which the king made to Paulet's request. "In case you will consent to restore the laws which you have set aside and firmly maintain the words of the treaty, then Dr. Judd can take his place with you again, but otherwise, I am sure I shall neither transact business with you or appoint another deputy." Paulet replied indignantly that nothing would induce him to accept Dr. Judd "or any person possessing similar sentiments" as a member of the commission, and on May 29 he left for Maui to confer with the king. But his efforts at persuasion failed. Although he suggested as candidates a number of prominent chiefs, the king refused stubbornly to appoint a new deputy.[25]

When Paulet returned he handed Dr. Judd a sealed order from the king not to pay out any public money for the native troops which the commission had enlisted. Dr. Judd, while he had resigned from the commission, still remained an officer of the Hawaiian

Assembly of Hawaiian chiefs in conference, 1837 (from a drawing by J. Masselot)

treasury, and without delay he communicated the king's order to the commissioners. At once Paulet returned to Maui, but the king would only direct Dr. Judd (probably at the latter's prompting) to pay the money under protest and take a receipt. When on June 20 Dr. Judd so informed the commission, he was told to obey the commission's orders or lose his post in the Hawaiian government. The occasion did not lack drama. As he noted in a memorandum, "This order brought by Lt. Frere in person in full uniform and with his side arms. I complied and paid the money. Have since learned that it is the intention to turn me out and take possession of the treasury. *Carysfort* left the same evening."[26] Four days later the king issued a formal statement disclaiming responsibility for the acts of the commission.

At this point, when the commission had almost no prestige and only the limited authority which it could command by military force, Dr. Judd resolved upon a bold and defiant course of action. As he later wrote, "I took away all the records and papers of the government to the royal cemetery where at night and alone I was obliged to do my business. The commission was by this means thwarted and in fact broken up."[27]

Although by night he labored in the royal tomb, he spent some time by day in the treasury office in order to preserve appearances, as official letters attest. Few further details are available, but it is certain that he was fully aware of the danger to which he had exposed himself. A short note written to Levi Chamberlain on July 3 shows precisely his state of mind. "If possible do come over to my house a few minutes before 9 o'clock. If you find the English officers here it will be too late and you will have to return."[28]

On July 26 tension in Honolulu rose to new heights with the arrival from Valparaiso of Paulet's superior, Rear Admiral Richard Thomas, commander of the British Pacific squadron. "What was his errand?" asked Mrs. Judd. "Had he brought relief, or had he come to declare our bondage perpetual? We held our very breath to await the answer."[29]

It soon became apparent that Thomas intended to dissolve the provisional government and restore the kingdom to independence. He held long conferences with the king and Dr. Judd on the 27th and 28th, at which articles were drawn up guaranteeing the rights of British subjects in the Islands. Dr. Judd objected to some of the terms. Thomas yielded on a few points, but insisted on the major part of the articles, and, although not fully satisfied, Dr. Judd advised the king to sign.[30]

The actual restoration of the kingdom's independence took place on the morning of July 31 in an atmosphere of hysterical celebration. Dr. Judd wrote to Richards, " 'Tis done! The swoon is passed away! The Hawaiian flag is restored and people once more enjoy their freedom under the mild dominion of Kamehameha III. . . . Never did Honolulu witness such a glorious day and such rejoicings. The residents seemed almost frantic."[31]

Mrs. Judd's account states vividly,

Marines from the *Dublin, Carysfort,* and other English ships, under their respective officers, were ordered to be on the parade ground on the plain, in full uniform, at eight o'clock A.M., under Lieutenant Frere. A pavilion was erected for the ladies. Foreign residents of all classes, missionaries, and thousands of natives assembled at an early hour. Admiral Thomas preceded the king in the carriage of the latter. When the king, on horseback, arrived upon the ground, the admiral gave him a salute of twenty-one guns from the field artillery of the squadron. Lord George was not present.

At a signal given, the English flag-officer advanced toward the king, surrounded by his guards, bowed his colors most gracefully, while the splendid Hawaiian standard was unfurled, and, as the breeze caught its ample folds, displaying the dove and olive branch in the center, the guns from the *Carysfort* fired first, then the *Dublin,* and the other English ships, followed by two American ships-of-war. Each poured forth a salute of twenty-one guns, which was responded to by the fort and battery of old Punch Bowl. The roar and reverberations were loud and long, and one would think the royal slumberers in the adjacent tomb might be startled in their long sleep. As the cannons ceased, thousands of human voices mingled in one patriotic cheer. Men and boys, black, white, and red, shouted themselves hoarse, as the king returned from the plain. The king and chiefs proceeded to the stone church [Kawaiahao], where, in the midst of the great congregation, they gave thanks to their God for deliverance from a foreign yoke.[32]

At the thanksgiving service Dr. Judd read the admiral's communication restoring the kingdom's independence. The king made a moving speech, in which he is reported to have used the words, *Ua mau ke ea o ka 'aina i ka pono*, the life of the land is preserved by righteousness—words which have become the official motto of Hawaii.[33] In further commemoration, the site of the restoration ceremony is still called Thomas Square.

After the restoration Dr. Judd collapsed from the strain which he had undergone,[34] but in time he had reason for more rejoicing. The diplomatic mission of Richards and Haalilio, as he was soon to learn, resulted in a joint declaration by England and France, signed November 28, 1843, which recognized the independence of the Hawaiian Kingdom. While the United States did not sign the declaration, President Tyler in a previous message to Congress had already recognized Hawaii as an independent state and had in effect extended the Monroe Doctrine into the mid-Pacific.[35]

During the entire crisis, Dr. Judd managed to discredit Paulet and to maintain order in Hawaii's internal affairs. At the same time he took steps to get a satisfactory settlement with the British authorities in London. Despite prevailing British policy, it is likely that Admiral Thomas would not have restored the kingdom's independence if he had found Hawaii's internal affairs in disorder. Had Dr. Judd not been a skilled administrator it is possible that Hawaii would still be under the British flag.

Minister of Foreign Affairs

Recognition of Hawaii's independence had the welcome effect of clearing for the time being the troubled political atmosphere. It provided a temporary breathing spell and gave reason for cautious hope. As Dr. Judd stated in a letter to the American Board in October, 1843, "I'm plodding on in my new and strange course much better than I feared I would. Our troubles are not yet over with, either with England or France, but I think the day is dawning, and trust my watch will be soon over. Astonishing changes seem to be at hand in these Islands—for good no doubt in the end."[1]

Nevertheless, as he well knew, he faced a new and vexing series of administrative problems, as increasingly the need arose to strengthen the political institutions of the infant nation. A system of government, as well as a policy, had to be created so that the little Kingdom could assume the responsibilities of its still uncertain sovereign status.

A typical emergency presented itself with the arrival on October 16 of George Brown, the newly appointed United States commissioner. When Brown asked with whom he should transact official business and the king referred him to Dr. Judd, Brown objected that Dr. Judd lacked the proper formal authority. In consequence, Dr. Judd was appointed secretary of state for foreign affairs, his commission being signed at Lahaina on November 2. He accepted the new post with misgiving. As he wrote to Richards, "I was greatly perplexed on this subject, and accepted the office under great doubt as to the expediency of it. The Admiral [Thomas], however, approves, and thus far all seems favorable." In a later letter he added characteristically, "I, of course, take the bull by the horns. I don't like the situation." The appointment pleased Brown, who described him as "gentlemanly and mild in his deportment but firm in his actions." Brown continued enthusiastically, "The choice of the king could have fallen upon no better man."[2] At a later date, both Thomas and Brown expressed less flattering sentiments.

Dr. Judd's basic policy derived from a realistic appraisal of the Hawaiian situation. He knew that neither chiefs nor people were competent to assume full control of the government, either in its internal affairs or in its relations with the more advanced Western powers. He faced, in fact, a problem still familiar to colonial administrators, and his proposed solution was both enlightened and benevolent. He had no wish to subject the Islands to permanent white domination of an imperialist order. (He particularly deplored the brutal displacement of red Indians by the American frontiersmen.) He hoped instead that in time the Hawaiians through education and practical experience would learn to govern themselves. For the time being, therefore, he proposed to employ a few white men of good character in key government offices. These men, he assumed, should govern openly, for he disliked the old system, which had obtained in the 1830s, of having white foreigners secretly direct the government behind the scenes. The king readily agreed to having, as he put it, "ministers of the white skin." With grave simplicity he explained to his subjects, "They know more than we, and I have chosen them for the sake of knowledge."[3]

Dr. Judd felt especially the need for legal assistance. In 1842 Sir George Simpson had advised the government to hire a lawyer, and Dr. Judd had written repeatedly to Richards to recruit one in the United States or in England. It was singularly opportune, therefore, that John Ricord reached Honolulu on February 27, 1844, on the barque *Columbia*.[4]

Ricord, then 32 years of age, was a tall, handsome Yankee of Huguenot extraction, who had studied law in western New York. After being called to the bar in Buffalo, he had lived in Louisiana, Texas, Arizona, Florida, and Oregon. When, after three years, he left Hawaii, he visited Tahiti, Siam, Liberia in Africa, and Paris, where he died in 1861. This headstrong and restless global adventurer carried with him to Honolulu a letter of introduction from the Oregon pioneer, Marcus Whitman. Although ill at the time, Dr. Judd sent for Ricord and on his own responsibility, hired him immediately, not only because the government urgently needed a lawyer but also because he feared that Ricord's services might be used against the government in a number of pending lawsuits. Although Commissioner Brown and some of the chiefs remonstrated, Dr. Judd had his way, and Ricord received official appointment as attorney general on March 9.[5]

Ricord threw himself into his new duties and performed valuable service in reorganizing the Kingdom's legal structure. Mrs. Judd was especially pleased with his appointment. "I feel," she wrote, "as if a kind Providence had sent him just now to save my husband's life, for I am quite sure he can not sustain such a load of toil and responsibility much longer without assistance."[6]

In legal matters, in which he had no technical competence, Dr. Judd relied implicitly, perhaps too much so, on Ricord's judgment. Ricord's influence over him became a matter of acrimonious comment on the part of a number of disaffected persons. Commissioner Brown, on the brink of a furious quarrel with the government, wrote, "At present, the king is completely under the guidance of Judd, and Judd completely under the thumb of Ricord. Everybody is disgusted. . . . Dr. Judd is not a bad man, far from it. I believe he has the interests of this people much at his heart, but he has little experience and Ricord who is a designing if not unprincipled man has got him entirely under his control." Stephen Reynolds commented in much the same vein. From California, John Coffin Jones, Jr., reported acidly, "Leidesdorff says it is a perfect hell there, Judd and Reord [sic] in supreme command ruling with despotic sway."[7]

Shortly before Ricord's arrival, there came to the Islands another man destined to have an even more dramatic role in the Kingdom's political life, Robert Crichton Wyllie, who richly deserves a full-scale biography. A native of Scotland and educated as a physician, he had lived some years in Spanish America, where he accumulated a fortune. In the company of General William Miller, the new British consul, Wyllie came to Honolulu from Mexico with the intention of continuing home to the British Isles by way of China. Instead he remained in Hawaii for 21 years, until his death in 1865.[8]

Impulsive and puckish, given to intrigue, and on occasion ridiculously long-winded, Wyllie nonetheless was a man of substantial abilities and unshakable integrity. A worldly bachelor with the sensibility of an artist, "the Laird of Rosebank," as he sometimes called himself, was in many ways the direct antithesis of Dr. Judd. Ultimately the two men came into savage conflict.

Between July, 1844, and March, 1845, Wyllie served as British proconsul while General Miller was absent in Tahiti. Miller was not entirely satisfied with his conduct of the office. When Dr. Judd suggested that the Hawaiian government might avail itself of Wyllie's services and asked for a recommendation, Miller replied curtly that Dr. Judd knew Wyllie well enough to decide for himself.[9] In spite of Miller's negative attitude, Dr. Judd invited Wyllie to join the government, and Wyllie accepted.

About this time, Ricord, Wyllie, and Charles Gordon Hopkins, an English law student who later held high political office in the kingdom, all lived as boarders in Dr. Judd's home. The situation is ironic. Within the next few years Dr. Judd became estranged from each of the three, as he did from James Jackson Jarves, who had returned to the Islands to resume editorship of the government newspaper, the *Polynesian*. But, for the time being, all was amiable. Dr. Judd was making steady progress in recruiting white officials into the government service. By September, 1844, officials of foreign birth numbered fourteen; in 1851 they numbered forty-eight.[10]

Recruitment of white officials, although of critical importance, formed only part of Dr. Judd's larger objective, as he later stated it, "to unite the foreign with the native element as subjects and as officers of government." On March 9, 1844, when Ricord received his commission as attorney general, both he and Dr. Judd renounced their United States citizenship and swore allegiance to the Kingdom of Hawaii. Dr. Judd was the first to take the oath.[11]

A new nation was quickening into life, along with the perfervid nationalist loyalty so characteristic of Western civilization in the mid-nineteenth century. In a frenzy of patriotism Dr. Judd rhapsodized, "Although born in the United States I am not an American, having not only renounced all allegiance to the United States, by a solemn oath, but having cultivated in my own heart a sentiment of attachment to Hawaiian interests, stronger than my attachment to life itself."[12]

As a further means of strengthening the Kingdom, he wrote an official letter to the American Board requesting that the American missionaries in the Islands become naturalized Hawaiian subjects. At first the Board took a neutral position, and made no objection if the missionaries themselves wished to change their citizenship, but a year or so later Rufus Anderson advised against it. In the Islands the brethren objected heatedly to the proposal. As Levi Chamberlain stated, "The missionaries desire to keep aloof from the excitements of other foreigners, and they wish to be regarded by the nation as friends without the necessity of the oath of allegiance."[13]

The Reverend Artemas Bishop went further. When Dr. Judd told him that government aid to the mission would be given only if missionaries became Hawaiian citizens, he replied with a stinging letter of reproach.

Give me leave to say to you that the garrulity of your last came very near betraying you into egotism. . . . You speak of "advancing the course of the Hawaiians." This is all very well, but it does not go far enough for a Christian and a quondam missiona[ry]. The cause of Christ with us should stand first and foremo[st]. You in your exalted station (if to be a Hawaiian Sec[retary] of State may [be] called such?) must not, in all your intercourse and collisions with the world, forget the object for which you renounced country and Christian society some 17 years ago. Keep humble, Brother Judd, cultivate a spirit of prayer and meekness, and be diffident of self-esteem, and I will not doubt of your eminent usefulness in the midst of the temptations which surround you.

But ultimately Dr. Judd had his way. In the end a large proportion of the American missionaries, including Bishop, took the naturalization oath.[14]

Dr. Judd's policy met equal resistance in the commercial colony. At his insistence, the government passed laws that no alien could acquire fee-simple land. Since the land laws provided a strong incentive for foreigners to become Hawaiian citizens, Dr. Judd hoped that many would take the step and in so doing provide additional support to the government. As Mrs. Judd explained,

The principal disputes and difficulties in which the nation had been involved for years have arisen from the complaints of foreigners holding lands and real estate in the Islands (some of them married to native wives), and yet claiming the protection and interference of their home government, exercised here through its representative. Now it was thought that if fealty to the rightful sovereignty of the realm was required, in order to hold landed property, it would be necessary to bring all disputes arising therefrom before the Hawaiian courts, to be settled by the only legitimate authorities.[15]

But, as it happened, Dr. Judd was over-optimistic in his expectations, for many foreign residents refused to take the oath. James Marshall, who returned to Honolulu early in 1844, made a typical objection. "The present advisers or *rulers* of the king seem bent on breaking down all opposition, and are vexing and if possible driving off all foreigners who refuse to take the oath of allegiance. Mr. Richards at heart disapproves of such harsh measures, but he does not feel strong enough openly to confront such determined men as Judd and Ricord." Nonetheless, by 1848, five hundred white aliens had become naturalized Hawaiian citizens.[16]

Consistently, Dr. Judd tried to build up the dignity of the government. He made heroic efforts to keep the king from liquor. Regularly on Sundays, he and Mrs. Judd went with the king and queen to church, where they sat together in the royal pew near a window curtained in orange and crimson satin. The new palace, completed in 1845, had a spacious reception room with handsome carpets, green Venetian blinds, and furnishings appropriate to royal pomp.[17]

Dr. Judd wished especially to have a code of etiquette in the court comparable to that in vogue in European capitals. Accordingly, an order in council of June 20, 1844, established formal rules as prescribed at the Congress of Vienna in 1815. One regulation stated that a diplomatic agent must apply for an audience in writing twenty-four hours in advance and must appear wearing full diplomatic costume. At one such audience, the king wore the Windsor uniform, which Hawaiian sovereigns had adopted at the request of George IV of England.[18] At another, Dr. Judd "was dressed in a blue coat with large gilt insignia buttons and gilt crowns on each shoulder, with white pants and vest and a heavy gold watch chain." Lt. Wise of the United States navy, on being presented at court in 1848, described Dr. Judd as "not an ill-looking nobleman—in full court costume, and a field-marshal's chapeau tucked under his arm." Wise added maliciously, "The king, premier [John Young], and Judd had broad red ribbons thrown baldric fashion over breast and shoulders, of such extreme breadth as to give the idea of the wearers having burst their jugular arteries."[19]

Critics of the government, of course, dismissed such pomp as ridiculous.[20] But an American, who happened to be present when the king opened the legislature in the Kawaiahao Church in 1845, wrote a glowing account of the proceedings.

The king was dressed in a costly and splendid uniform. He came attended by the queen, his cabinet, and military escort. As he entered the building, the new royal standard, containing the national coat of arms, designed at the herald's office in London, wholly from national emblems, was hoisted for the first time. The brass band, all native musicians, struck up the national anthem; guns from the fort thundered forth twenty-one times. The whole company arose, and the king walked with much dignity to his throne. A prayer was offered by Rev. Mr. Richards, chaplain of the court, after which, at the command of the king, all seated themselves. The king then covered his head with his chapeau in a graceful manner and read his speech. . . . I must confess that gratifying reflections filled my mind upon viewing the well-ordered and appropriate ceremonies of the day. . . . Still more gratifying is the reflection that this order has been brought out of disorder and savage barbarism in the short space of twenty years by my countrymen.[21]

In the midst of governmental reorganization and with the dispute over naturalization reaching its climax, Dr. Judd faced several thorny problems arising as an aftermath of Richards' diplomatic mission to England. The general settlement included a treaty which the new British consul, William Miller, brought with him to Honolulu early in 1844. Dr. Judd objected to three of the articles in the treaty: the second, which might restrict the king's power to grant preference to his own subjects; the third, which might require a white jury trial for British subjects accused of a misdemeanor; and the sixth, which permitted the import of liquor at a duty of only five per cent. Since Miller had no power to alter the treaty, Dr. Judd advised the king to ratify it as it stood, and it was signed at Lahaina on February 12. But five days later Dr. Judd wrote to Lord Aberdeen in London requesting that the treaty be modified.[22]

Miller also brought with him the British government's decision on Richard Charlton's land claim, a vexatious matter which did not reach its final settlement until three years later. The claim covered a valuable piece of property in Honolulu, which Charlton asserted he had received on a 299-year lease in 1826 from the Hawaiian chief Kalanimoku, familiarly known as Billy Pitt. Although Richards had argued correctly that Kalanimoku did not have legal authority to make the grant, Lord Aberdeen had ruled in Charlton's favor—provided that the deed, then in Honolulu, could be certified. Richards had accepted the ruling on behalf of the Hawaiian Government. Consul Miller believed that the deed was entirely in order, and he took the straightforward view that just as soon as it was certified Charlton should have his land. Dr. Judd, on the other hand, believed that the lease was a forgery and that Kalanimoku, premier but not regent in 1826, lacked authority to have made the grant in the first place. On Ricord's advice he insisted on submitting the whole question to arbitration and sent to Miller a long series of letters filled with legalistic jargon which Ricord supplied. Had he confined himself to proving the lease a forgery, instead of arguing also against Kalanimoku's right to grant it, he probably would have made a stronger case. From Miller's viewpoint the correspondence was "irrelevant" and filled with "special pleading," and he was not long in deciding that the Hawaiian government was guilty of bad faith. After protracted bickering, Miller received fresh instructions from his government, and in August, 1845, he presented an unequivocal demand, which amounted to an ultimatum, to give Charlton the land. The Hawaiian government yielded. A review of the case, which lasted until 1847, did not alter the final result.[23]

The correspondence in the case, which exceeds seven hundred

Kamehameha III

printed pages, reveals how completely Dr. Judd had transferred the religious values of the mission to politics. A typical letter, which he wrote to Miller in April, 1844, when the dispute was in an early stage, overflows with moral fervor. He wrote,

this government being weak as to physical force, neither boasting of armies nor naval appliances with which to compel its behests right or wrong, must rely upon the judgment and reason of mankind, and upon the ethical and virtuous sense of public opinion. . . . And this government, intending as other nations have, to make public its diplomatic correspondence . . . is desirous to present a clean and virtuous sheet in her history.

To the American Board he wrote of his determination "to concentrate a moral power adequate to maintain that high attribute called sovereignty, in the estimation of the world."[24]

In such an exalted state of mind he overworked himself to the point of collapse. As he wrote to Richards,

The transactions of government are becoming daily more complicated and intricate. Those affecting foreigners are quite sufficient to engage the undivided attention of one man, and those affecting the interior administration of the kingdom another; yet much of both devolve upon me, and thus I am overborne with mental and physical labor and anxiety.[25]

He suffered from giddy spells and ringing in the ears. For well over a year his eyes had been failing. Early in 1845 his left eye became completely blind from a cataract, and he could scarcely see to read or write with the other. Facing total blindness he contemplated retiring from public life. "I only wait," he wrote in January, 1845, "to find a man on whose fidelity and skill his Majesty can rely, to tender my resignation."[26]

Richards returned from Europe on March 23, bearing the sad news of Haalilio's death at sea on the long voyage homeward. Three days later Dr. Judd resigned as foreign secretary, and on his recommendation Wyllie received the office. But instead of retiring he remained as head of the cabinet, and on March 28 he assumed the newly created office of minister of the interior.[27]

Minister of the Interior

Coincident with Dr. Judd's appointment as minister of the interior, further political difficulties arose, in large measure precipitated by George Brown, the American commissioner. Brown had objected heatedly in the fall of 1844, when the government refused to let him name the jurors in the trial of John Wiley, an American accused of rape. Because of Brown's intemperate language the king wrote to the president of the United States on September 20 asking for his recall. At this time, Brown's complaints focused mainly on Dr. Judd, who had assisted Ricord and Governor Kekuanaoa in the judicial proceedings.[1]

A second dispute occurred early in 1845, when Brown appeared as counsel for James Gray, an American who sued the government to recover a fine for drunkenness, on the grounds that he had been denied a jury trial. As before, Dr. Judd, Ricord, and Kekuanaoa presided. The trial, which was held on February 28 and March 3, degenerated into a verbal brawl, with Brown and Dr. Judd shouting at one another, while Ricord, who alone might have kept order, remained helpless to control the situation. As was to be expected, Gray and Brown lost the case.[2]

On the afternoon that the trial ended, Brown attended a picnic at Waikiki at which a large number of American residents were present, and made a fiery speech to the effect that he would uphold the dignity of the United States.[3] Exactly a week later Brown saw the king and brought charges against Dr. Judd accusing him of misconduct in office.

Brown based his case on conversations which Dr. Judd had had with two American merchants, Charles Brewer and James Marshall, late in December, 1844. Both men, it appears, had reason for dissatisfaction, Brewer because of the government's conduct in a lawsuit and Marshall (so Jarves reported) because of Dr. Judd's settlement of his expenses on his diplomatic mission to Europe in 1843. In consequence, Brewer and Co. had withdrawn its advertising from the government newspaper, the *Polynesian*. With characteristic directness, Dr. Judd warned Brewer and Marshall not to persist in their opposition. "I have begged them," he reported "not to go to war with us. . . . If they withdraw from our press we will withdraw from them. If they oppose us we must oppose them." In Brown's eyes, Dr. Judd's warnings became "improper threats against American merchants."[4]

Tempers flared high. In an official despatch Brown complained of Dr. Judd's "imbecility." In another he wrote, "No dependence can be placed on anything while Messrs. Judd and Ricord still hold office."[5] Brewer called Dr. Judd "a damned rascal," and in an indignant letter he stated, "This government . . . have become arrogant and oppressive in the extreme towards all foreigners, and should they not be checked soon, it will be intolerable to reside here. . . . Dr. Judd is extremely unpopular with the residents in general, and all the missionaries. The latter very severely and openly condemn his official deeds. Government affairs never were in more confusion."[6]

The king and chiefs took a lighter view of the situation and laughed at the charges. As a measure of his contempt, the king appointed Ricord along with two of Dr. Judd's loyal supporters among the chiefs, John Ii and John Young, as an investigating committee. The impeachment proceedings, which lasted from the 14th to the 26th of March, consisted mainly of testimonials on Dr. Judd's character given by his well-wishers, such as Jarves and

William Paty of the government service; George Traill Allan and George Pelly of the Hudson's Bay Co.; and Levi Chamberlain, Edwin O. Hall, and Samuel N. Castle of the American mission. The testimony at times reads as if Brown and not Dr. Judd were on trial, and the verdict of the commissioners was to dismiss the charges as "frivolous."[7] Fully vindicated in the eyes of his government, Dr. Judd resigned as minister of foreign affairs in order to assume the new post of minister of the interior.

In spite of his defeat, Brown continued his tirades, and on July 29 the king gave orders that henceforth the government would receive no further official communications from him. Brown remained in the Islands for more than a year in a sort of diplomatic limbo. He finally left Honolulu on August 5, 1846, on the ill-fated brig *Wm. Neilson*, which disappeared at sea with all hands.

During and shortly after his impeachment, Dr. Judd faced formidable opposition from David Malo, a prominent native leader, who wished to dismiss all naturalized foreigners from the government. The movement took the form of petitions, one of which from Wailuku on Maui had 2,181 signatures.[8] As a means of combatting the opposition, the king and John Young made a number of speeches on Maui in the summer of 1845. In a typical speech, which Dr. Judd may have written and which he certainly inspired, John Young argued,

Formerly, when important business was done, Dr. Judd would be present, but must keep silent, or be sent away. When Kamehameha III put on him his own garments, then he was heard. He took the oath of allegiance, and stood in the gap to save us. This year you have petitioned against him—you and the people of Lahaina. Did you ever hear of a people destroyed by allegiance? America was overrun, as you have been told, and the red-skins were destroyed. But the white men owed them no allegiance. Do you think that I or Paki can do the work of a white minister? No. The young chiefs will, we hope, be qualified, but now we must have these white men.

Gradually the opposition subsided, but while it lasted it caused the government no little anxiety. Some years later, Dr. Judd expressed the belief that had he resigned in March, 1845, instead of taking office anew as minister of the interior, the rest of the cabinet (that is, Richards, Ricord, Wyllie, and John Young) could not have held together for more than three months.[9]

Fresh difficulties arose from the tangled affairs of the American firm of Ladd & Co., which since 1841 had held a lease from the Hawaiian government to all undeveloped lands in the kingdom.[10] Peter Brinsmade, who had left the Islands to promote the company abroad, having failed to find investors in Britain, France, and the United States, turned his attention to Belgium. In May, 1843, in Brussels he signed the so-called Belgian contract, whereby Ladd & Co. transferred its property and rights to the Belgian Company of Colonization. According to the contract, Ladd & Co. would receive a cash payment from a Belgian subsidiary company which would exploit the Hawaiian holdings. Richards and Haalilio signed on behalf of Kamehameha III, but the subsidiary company was never formed, and Brinsmade finally left Belgium in 1845 without the financial support which the contract had promised.

Meanwhile, in Hawaii, Ladd & Co. fell upon evil days, particularly with respect to its sugar plantation at Koloa on Kauai. On November 1, 1844, the company closed its doors, carrying on its books a large unpaid debt to the Hawaiian government.

Dr. Judd disliked the entire Ladd & Co. operation, including the Belgian contract, which he later called "humbug," mainly because it granted to aliens the right to hold land in fee simple. Wishing to preserve the Islands for the benefit of the Hawaiian natives, he set himself wholeheartedly against any such scheme of mass colonization. Moreover, the failure of Ladd & Co. had deprived him of much needed personal income from the company's lease of the wharf lots in Honolulu which had been assigned to him in 1843.[11]

When Richards returned in the spring of 1845 with the disheartening news of Brinsmade's failure, Dr. Judd and Ricord set about to recover through legal process the Ladd & Co. properties. In May Dr. Judd employed a Belgian lawyer, J. B. de Fiennes, to report on Ladd & Co.'s plantation holdings, and the liquidation proceeded with dispatch.[12]

In March, 1846, Brinsmade returned to the Islands. Soon thereafter Ladd & Co., with the support of Commissioner Brown and his successor, Anthony Ten Eyck, brought suit for $378,000 against the Hawaiian government for breach of contract. While Richards, who had been a party to the contracts of 1841 and 1843, wished to make a settlement, Dr. Judd and Ricord were determined to stand their ground. The proceedings in arbitration dragged on for about a year and evoked rabid hostility on the part of the American residents. Dr. Judd, as minister of the interior, had a large share of the responsibility for presenting the government's case. Ultimately, in 1847, Ladd & Co. withdrew from the arbitration, and the Hawaiian government won the suit by default.

The aftermath only added to the already existing political tensions. "There was a great deal said by both parties," wrote Mrs. Judd, "and time enough consumed to have made a little fortune, but breath, time, and money were expended to little purpose, except to widen the breach. The arbitration produced no beneficial results, and ended in the entire alienation of old and long-cherished friendships." To justify its conduct the Hawaiian government published a large volume containing a fully documented account of the dispute.[13]

Quite aside from major cases, such as the Ladd & Co. arbitration, Dr. Judd found himself overwhelmed with routine responsibilities. He made a regular practice of acting with Ricord and Governor Kekuanaoa as a judge, in surroundings which added little to the dignity of the legal proceedings. "The court," as Judge Lee later recalled, "met in an old grass house, floored with mats, without benches, seats or comforts of any kind, with one corner partitioned off with calico, for judge's office, clerk's office, police court, and jury room." On one occasion the privy council appointed Dr. Judd sole judge in a land dispute.[14]

As minister of the interior he had charge of government buildings, including prisons. He supervised the cutting of stone and the construction of the new customs house. He was responsible for the government vessels and cattle. He formed the soldiers into watches to guard the king's person. He hired laborers to work on the Lahainaluna ditch.[15] Early in 1844 he communicated to the United States commissioner the permission of the Hawaiian government to build a naval base at Honolulu. In the spring of 1845 he coped with runaway sailors, unlicensed retailers, transit dues on cargo, and a proposal to form a fire department. Four years later he arranged for the purchase of cast-iron pipes for Honolulu's water supply.

The extent of his miscellaneous labors cannot be determined, since it was the custom of Governor Kekuanaoa to supplement written instructions for a specific task by verbal orders that the work parties should follow Dr. Judd's directions.[16]

Early in 1845 he supervised construction of a road through Nuuanu Valley. A part of this road was a horse trail down the *pali*, a steep and forbidding cliff 1,186 feet high, which leads to the Koolau district on the windward side of Oahu. On the evening of June 27, the king, John Young, and Dr. Judd officially opened the trail by riding down it on horseback. The king, who led the way, is said to have been the first person to ride a horse down the narrow and dangerous path. Sixteen years later, on September 9, 1861, after the roadway had been widened considerably, Dr. Judd and the Reverend Eli Corwin of Honolulu's Fort Street Church drove down it in a one-horse express wagon—an unprecedented feat.[17]

Dr. Judd's interest in road building led to the passage of a resolution by the privy council on May 23, 1849, directing him to make a road on the island of Hawaii "between Kailua, the seat of the local government, and Hilo, the principal port." He chose a direct route across the high plateau between Mauna Kea and Mauna Loa. The road was under construction for several years, but ultimately the government gave up the project, as part of the route lay in the path of recurrent lava flows. It is still known as the "Judd road."[18]

Dr. Judd shared with the American mission a desire to encourage agriculture in the Islands. As early as 1834 he was exploring the possibility of raising cotton, and in 1840, while still in the mission, he acted as Governor Kekuanaoa's agent in a sugar plantation near Honolulu. In his first report as minister of the interior, delivered to the Hawaiian legislature on May 21, 1845, he presented a summary of Hawaii's agricultural potential, with special reference to sugar, coffee, flax, sheep and cattle.[19]

In the same report he made a suggestion, which had far-reaching consequences, that "commissioners be appointed to inquire into and determine the validity of all titles to lands and houses." He proposed besides a review of the entire system of land tenure. In accordance with his recommendations, legislation was enacted toward the end of the year to establish a Board of Commissioners to Quiet Land Titles, familiarly known as the Land Commission. This board, which first met on February 11, 1846, consisted of Richards and Ricord plus three Hawaiians, John Ii, Z. Kaauwai, and James Young Kanehoa. It remained in existence (with personnel changes) until 1855, reviewed 13,514 claims, and made 9,337 awards.

From its inception the Land Commission faced an overwhelmingly difficult problem. As Dr. Judd later stated,

It had been employed a year or two upon claims of foreigners principally, but no claims of natives could be decided until the breaking up of the old feudal system which allowed to the king, chiefs and people an interest in the soil, the tenure of each subject to the will of his superior. The king and chiefs labored in vain for two years to make some division among themselves which would enable each to own some land independently. It could not be done. There was no one but myself had the knowledge, and I may say the resolution, to act efficiently. I therefore volunteered my services to the king, and on condition of his appointing as my fellow-laborers those whom I named, pledged myself to make the division.

The privy council accordingly resolved on December 18, 1847, to appoint a special committee consisting of Dr. Judd and three Hawaiians, Kekuanaoa, Piikoi, and James Young, to undertake the *Mahele*, or division of lands. The committee began operations three days later. Between January 27 and March 7, 1848—a total of only 41 days—it made 245 awards, duly recorded in the Mahele Book.

The committee's work, often referred to as the *Great Mahele*, brought order and equity to Hawaii's troubled land situation. Some years later Dr. Judd commented to Wyllie, "You know that the work was *done*, and how thoroughly; but you can never know what obstacles had to be encountered; whose feelings were hurt; whose rights, in his or her estimation, were disregarded; but I have the satisfaction of knowing that, on the whole, the division was fair, and a great blessing to the Hawaiian nation."[20]

The awards in the *Mahele*, along with the awards made by the Land Commission, form the basis for all existing land titles in the Hawaiian Islands. A further and equally significant result of the commission's work appears in its final report. "But perhaps the greatest benefit that has resulted from the labors of the commission . . . is the securing to the common people their *kuleanas* [properties] in fee simple; thus raising them at once from a condition little better than that of serfs or mere tenants at will of the *konohikis* [landlords], to the position of absolute owners of the soil."[21]

Consistently and with Yankee thrift, Dr. Judd devoted much attention to problems of government finance. His first report as minister of the interior contained recommendations for new taxes, and in June, 1845, at his suggestion the government raised the rate of its import duties from three to five per cent. He later stated that he had devised all but one of the taxes which the government levied during his tenure of public office and for six years thereafter.[22] His first report also recommended the issuance of a copper cent, which the legislature approved in the year following. By 1847, $1,000 worth of the new coins were in circulation.[23]

His control of government finances led to the gradual reduction of Hawaii's national debt. In 1845 he reported that the government's assets almost equalled its liabilities and that the annual deficit was only $6,491.53. By the spring of 1846 he had balanced the budget and reduced the debt considerably. A windfall appeared in March of that year, when the French returned the $20,000 which Laplace in 1839 had demanded as surety. In 1847 he reported that receipts exceeded expenditures by $12,283.76 and government assets exceeded government liabilities by $24,618.15.[24]

Little glamor attaches to statistics, yet these figures have a glamorous story to tell. Posterity has justly recognized his work in the field of finance as among his most enduring contributions to the welfare of the nation.[25]

15

Minister of Finance

In the spring of 1846 the government underwent a reorganization in accordance with legislation passed in October of the previous year. Wyllie and Ricord retained their former offices as foreign secretary and attorney general; Richards became minister of public instruction; John Young (Keoni Ana), the *kuhina nui*, or premier, took office as minister of the interior, and on April 13 Dr. Judd took office as minister of finance, a post which he held until his retirement from the government in 1853. It was understood that Richards would help Young in the interior department, since Young, a half-white chief, had limited abilities and experience, but Richards, who died in 1847, took little interest in this assignment, and the burden of helping Young fell upon Dr. Judd.[1]

Toward the end of the year the government received a valuable addition in William Little Lee, a brilliant young lawyer from New York State, who had stopped off in Honolulu on his way to the new Oregon Territory. Largely through the efforts of Ricord and Judd, he took office as a judge in the Oahu Court, where he served with the Reverend Lorrin Andrews, a former missionary who had been appointed to the bench the previous June.[2]

The effective government then consisted of Ricord, Wyllie, Lee, and Judd, but it was generally recognized that Judd functioned as the responsible, or prime, minister of the kingdom. Besides being the only one of the four who thoroughly understood the Hawaiian language he had served longer, and his influence with the king and chiefs remained paramount. The king had instructed Wyllie to receive his orders through Judd. At the opening of the legislature in 1845, Dr. Judd marched on the queen's left ahead of Wyllie and Ricord, and when the king read his speech it was Dr. Judd who stood at the king's right hand.[3]

His position naturally subjected him to the calumny which often accompanies political prominence, and his opponents did not hesitate to accuse him of tyranny. General Miller, the British consul, reported in March, 1846, that "Dr. Judd still keeps His Majesty under great restraint, not allowing him to speak scarcely to any body excepting a few about him"—a statement which prompted Lord Palmerston to ask, "Who is the despotic Dr. Judd?" Addington, an undersecretary in the Foreign Office, replied, "He is virtually Prime Minister and conscience-keeper of the King Kamehameha III." Anthony Ten Eyck, Brown's successor as the American Commissioner in Hawaii, stated bluntly, "The king and his native chiefs are mere automatons in the hands of his ministers. . . . I think him [Dr. Judd] a man of ordinary talents, ambitious, fond of power, self-willed and one that allows his personal feelings to control his public acts." Guillaume Patrice Dillon, the French consul, called Judd "a narrow-minded little American from whom no Frenchman could ever obtain justice." Lt. Henry A. Wise, an American naval officer, wrote facetiously,

But Mr. Judd is the Magnus Apollo of the Island. Kamme [Kamehameha III], or the Lonely One—as the word signifies—is his puppet, and most particularly lonely he keeps him! The King is Punch, and Judd is Judy, and the Lonely One is jumped about and thumped, and the wires are pulled unremittingly. Judd is his prime counsellor, his parliament, father confessor and ghostly adviser—his temperance lecturer, purse-bearer, and factotum generally.[4]

Such comments border on satiric overstatement, for, as both Wyllie and Governor Kekuanaoa testified, Judd recognized the constitutional authority of the king and premier, whom he invariably consulted on important government business. Nevertheless, it is clear that he was the most powerful political figure in the Islands, and he is reported (probably correctly) to have declared that nothing could be done in the government without his consent. As he commented jocularly to Henry Peirce in 1845, "You must know that I am at present the King Bingham of the Sandwich Islands."[5]

In time he acquired some outward trappings corresponding to the dignity of his high office. The king presented him with the coat of arms designed in Europe for Haalilio, the only coat of arms bestowed by the Hawaiian monarchy. The heraldry consisted of quarterings representing the four nations which had recognized Hawaii's independence, that is, England, France, Belgium, and the United States. The motto, "*E Hoomaluia*," may be translated, "*It shall be upheld*."[6] He regularly received a salute of seventeen guns.[7] Somewhat later he obtained the state coach which Queen Victoria had presented to Queen Pomare of Tahiti and which Pomare had sold to the Hawaiian royal family after the French seized her kingdom. The coach, gilt-encrusted and lined with yellow brocade, especially delighted the Judd children, who called it the ark.[8]

In the mid-1840s Dr. Judd began to make plans for a splendid new house. After he left the mission he had rented for a time the pleasant stone dwelling of the premier, Kekauluohi (Auhea). This house delighted Mrs. Judd, who wrote, "The high ceiling, large windows, and papered walls afford such a contrast to our little cottage, that I feel like a traveler at a hotel, or on board a finely furnished steamer—a mere lodger for the night."[9] Her words were prophetic, for the premier soon decided to occupy the house herself, and the Judds had to move to another next to the palace. Mrs. Judd commented, "Our new house is not so nice as hers, but in some respects we like it better. The yard is full of rubbish and ruins of adobe walls and pig-sties, and we shall have the pleasure for the *fourth time* of pulling up thistles and planting roses." In many ways this house proved unsatisfactory. Mrs. Judd complained particularly that the children needed more privacy. "I must have a more retired home for them. So much anxiety and so much company unfit me for maternal duty." By the summer of 1846 it became common knowledge in Honolulu that the Judds were planning to build their own home in Nuuanu Valley.[10]

This edifice, known as "Sweet Home" after the popular song (1823) of John Howard Payne, consumed much of his time and strained his finances to the limit. "The rooms," Mrs. Judd wrote in 1847,

are smaller and less elegant than those we have occupied the last four years, but there is an air of home comfort and convenience that pleases me. The house has a chimney and a kitchen within, which is an anomaly in Hawaiian architecture. We had been collecting the materials for two years, a little here and a little there, as we could command the means of payment. The doors, floors, and gates were made in Copenhagen and sent out for sale, and my husband purchased them at auction for much less than we could get them made. The windows, glazed, and blinds already painted were sent out from Boston. . . . I never felt poorer, even when a missionary, for we were obliged to borrow money to pay carpenters and masons who built our house, and give a mortgage on it for security.

Sweet Home was luxurious in its appointments. It had the added distinction of being the first house in the Islands with a lightning rod.[11]

To finance the house he sold some cattle to the government, raised $1,000 on a mortgage from the treasury, and borrowed $5,500 from his colleague Wyllie.[12] The privy council on February 18, 1847, gave him a fee-simple title to the homesite, amounting to 7.61 acres, for $50.00, a figure which the chiefs named, and the family moved into Sweet Home the following month.[13]

At that time the house was far from finished. Entries in the diary of his son Charles reveal that as late as the summer of 1848 he was buying lumber at auction for the veranda. Late in August he bought a scythe and with it mowed the lawn. Shortly thereafter he bought two granite posts for $40.00.[14]

In many ways his social position was ambiguous. As a political leader he gravitated naturally to worldly groups composed of politicians, diplomatists, and businessmen—groups which his former brethren in the mission tended to condemn as sinful. At first, in deference to puritan principles, he refused to countenance dancing, and thus offended a number of foreign residents, but when he began to attend balls he gave even greater offense to the mission, as he did when he called an emergency political conference on a Sunday. Estrella Mott noted with considerable insight, "Dr. Judd's family seemed to be in an intermediate state between the missionaries and the other set. . . . His three daughters, Libbie, Nellie, and Laura, girls about our ages, though not allowed to dance, visited among the society people." Ultimately he yielded to the pressure of the times and let them dance, and in so doing estranged himself still further from his former missionary associates.[15] But, to the end, he retained his teetotal principles. His deep-seated aversion to alcohol and his refusal to grant land to aliens evoked continuing hostility on the part of his new associates in the world of commerce and politics. It is probably true—as Levi Chamberlain observed in 1845—that much of the opposition which in the past had centered on the mission now transferred itself to the Hawaiian government.[16] Not a little of this hostility focused on Dr. Judd as the government's chief officer.

Although his social status was uncertain, his political position at this period remained unassailable. Secure in the good will of the chiefs, and with subordinate officials who dared not challenge his authority, he bore down heavily on the opposition. Selflessly and with more energy than tact he met headlong the recurrent crises which arose to torment him.

His state papers are unusually clear, and, to say the least, forceful. To Ladd & Co. he wrote in July, 1845, "As you expected an answer, within one week, to yours of the 12th instant, I have the pleasure of meeting those expectations herewith, and to demand that you will cease to annoy me with matters with which, as an officer of His Majesty, I have nothing to do. . . . My time is too much occupied to allow me to bear such unnecessary burdens." A week later he began another letter to Ladd & Co. with the words, "Yours of this date, which is of course all Greek to me, I have passed over to Mr. Ricord."[17]

The same abruptness of expression appears in annotations which he made on a memorandum received from General Miller during a dispute over the latter's rent in 1847: "False. Wait until you are ordered off before you refuse to go. Advice not needed. I defy you to prove it. I'll send you a bill of damages for cutting down 2 shade trees."[18]

In 1852 he wrote an official letter to the Roman Catholic missionary, Robert A. Walsh, of which the following is the entire text: "In reply to your note just received, I beg you will not construe my letter of yesterday to mean any thing more than it says, and I refer you to that letter for an answer to your proposal that I fix upon a day and hour for the settlement of the question."[19]

In part, the bluntness of his manner arose from the same stubbornness which his father had shown in Paris Hill twenty years before. In part it was because he overworked himself to the point of exhaustion. He fell ill in the spring of 1847 and in the fall of 1848, and more than once he talked of resigning.[20] On one occasion, upon reflection, he apologized graciously for "any apparent harshness of manner."[21]

In part also he reflected the unsettled temper of the times. The Islands simmered with resentments and rivalries, as single-minded men representing diverse interests battled for control of the sovereignty, wealth, and souls of the bewildered native population. American residents and commissioners tried repeatedly to overthrow the American-dominated government. Wyllie, a Scott, quarreled bitterly with General Miller, the British consul, who in turn had a prolonged feud with the Hudson's Bay Company. French Catholic missionaries infuriated the American mission, and French imperialist threats terrified responsible government officials. The individualism, even eccentricity, of the men in the various interests, brought about a continuous reshifting of alliances and loyalties. Dr. Judd and others in the government deplored but could not curb the chaos. "No one can regret more than I do," he wrote in 1845, "the local feuds which are apt to excite the community of Honolulu." A member of the British Foreign Office complained, "Few things perplex me more than the squabbles in the Sandwich Islands." And to emphasize the need for order, the American commissioner, Ten Eyck, sent to Washington in 1846 a tin case containing 208 feet of manuscript, representing a summary of claims brought against the Hawaiian government by foreign agents in the past four years.[22]

Under such circumstances, dissension naturally broke out within the government itself. Friction arose between Judd and the turbulent attorney general, John Ricord, who, as Mrs. Judd commented, "often pains his best friends by his eccentricities and impulsive temper." It is clear that although outwardly loyal he was jealous of Judd, whom he regarded as inferior to himself in abilities.[23] Both men, of course, were proud and uncompromising, and it pained Ricord beyond measure when Judd repeatedly refused to honor his official drafts at the treasury. The situation received a further ironic twist when, in 1846, he fell in love with Judd's oldest daughter, Elizabeth, then aged only 15, who refused his proposal of marriage. As she later reported, "He tried to enforce his demands and not succeeding poured forth a torrent of abuse, left the Islands and so ended all our kind feelings toward him."[24]

Ricord sent in his resignation on October 29, 1846, and formally left office on May 17, 1847, incidentally, with a $2,000 loan from the government. But while still in office he accused Dr. Judd of making $23,000 for himself out of the government, and proposed an audit of all ministerial accounts. (The audit, presented after Ricord's departure, showed that Judd was overdrawn by about $700, mainly because of his failure to collect his wharf rents from Ladd & Co.)[25] Ricord left the Islands on August 21 for California, where he gave General William T. Sherman, who called him "quite a character," an exaggerated account to the effect that either he or Judd had to leave the government. In later years, as he moved restlessly from Tahiti and Siam to Africa and France, he began to drink heavily—he had been a teetotaler when he first came to Hawaii—and as late as 1857 he still fancied himself betrothed to his beloved Elizabeth. He even wrote a sentimental poem about her.[26]

About three weeks before Ricord's departure, James Jackson Jarves, editor of the government newspaper, the *Polynesian*, sent in his resignation, ostensibly for reasons of ill health. On February 4, 1848, he left the Islands. In letters written to Wyllie after his return to Boston, he made clear his belief that Dr. Judd was incompetent in finance and had treated him in a generally unfriendly manner. Five years later Wyllie summarized the specific reasons for Jarves' resignation. These included Judd's refusal to pay one of his checks and to settle his accounts. According to Wyllie, who was a biased but generally accurate observer, Jarves also condemned Judd for having accepted a fee from Wilkes in 1841 and the wharf rents from the government in 1843, and for trying to get a fee of $1,000 in 1847 as a reward for ending the Ladd & Co. arbitration.[27]

This last episode, which took place during Jarves' final months in the Islands, marks the opening of Wyllie's long and dramatic quarrel with Judd. Wyllie enjoyed extremely friendly relations with both Jarves and Ricord, and their departure from the government in part resulted from their having sided with him in the preliminary stages of the rift. The matter came to a head on October 23, when in the privy council the chiefs voted to Judd a fee of $1,000 for his services in the Ladd & Co. lawsuit. Judd believed that the settlement was due to his efforts, but Wyllie felt that at least part of the credit belonged to Ricord, who should share in the reward. Accordingly, with Judge Lee's support, he objected to the fee on the ground that it should be preceded by a formal report. When Judd read his report on November 9, Wyllie moved for a committee to study the matter, and Judd withdrew his claim.[28] He could not help feeling that Wyllie was depriving him of just recompense for valuable services, while Wyllie on his part honestly believed that he had prevented an injustice to Ricord.

A week later Wyllie wrote Judd a long and hostile letter in support of Ricord's services to the state. On November 26 he had angry words with Judd at a privy council meeting, to the effect that Judd would not properly translate Hawaiian proceedings for him and that Judd would not be his master. He was in fact challenging Judd's position as a responsible minister of state. Although they settled the dispute in a meeting with Judge Lee, who remained ominously silent throughout, both men left the conference with injured feelings. Their relationship did not improve when Wyllie sharply criticized his annual financial report on the ground that it did not contain a properly drawn budget.[29]

In the summer of 1848 Judd's brother-in-law, Asher B. Bates, newly arrived in the Islands, was appointed government attorney. The opposition alleged spitefully that Judd had intrigued against Ricord in order to make a place for Bates.[30] His appointment created a new balance of power in the government, with Judd and Bates forming an interest opposed to Wyllie, who found increasing support from Judge Lee. The appointment in June of the Reverend Richard Armstrong as minister of public instruction did not materially affect the situation. As a former missionary Armstrong tended to be sympathetic to Judd, but in fact he carried little weight with his colleagues.

About this time the already inflamed political situation received a new irritant in the person of the French consul, Guillaume Patrice Dillon, a French-born Irishman with few scruples and a genius for intrigue, who arrived in Honolulu on February 1, 1848. Dillon replaced Wyllie's friend, Jules Dudoit, and sought to promote French interests in the Islands by undermining the unity of the Hawaiian government. He made flattering overtures to both Wyllie and Judd, particularly the latter, to whom, in a letter dated August 11, he proposed the expulsion of Wyllie from office. As might be expected, this letter caused a furious political ruckus. Judd kept Wyllie informed of Dillon's maneuvers and did his best to keep the government intact. In April, 1849, the privy council requested Dillon's recall by the French government, which, in due course but too late to avert another crisis, sent Dillon a reprimand for his conduct.[31]

In the fall of 1848 Dr. Judd faced attack from another quarter. On October 11, George M. Robertson, who was then a clerk in the interior department and who later became a judge of Hawaii's supreme court, filed 16 impeachment charges against him with 175 specifications. The charges, which were loosely drawn, stated that he had usurped the duties of the minister of the interior, embezzled funds, broken laws, and lost the confidence of responsible citizens. The king appointed a commission to hear the evidence, but after Judge Lee resigned from it he appointed a second commission consisting of Wyllie, Armstrong, and Charles Gordon Hopkins (secretary), along with three chiefs, Governor Kekuanaoa, John Ii, and Abner Paki. The next day Judd received an official order to appear before it on December 2.[32]

At this moment of crisis, with impeachment proceedings against him just about to open, Judd took a step which chagrined many of his staunchest supporters. For some time he had smarted under the attacks directed at him and at the government generally in the opposition newspaper, the *Sandwich Islands News*. He particularly wished to find out who was writing the various inflammatory articles, for he suspected both Wyllie and Dillon. With this object in mind he asked William F. Rogers of the customs office to obtain manuscript evidence of the authorship from the newspaper's files. Wyllie, for one, believed that Bates advised this drastic step. In compliance with Judd's request, Rogers approached James Peacock, one of the printers, and on payment of a $300 bribe which Judd supplied, Peacock turned over on November 30 a number of manuscripts from which copy had been set. One of these, for a particularly noxious article signed Artaxerxes in the November 16 issue, was in the handwriting of no less a person than the American commissioner, Anthony Ten Eyck.[33]

The disclosure stirred Honolulu's foreign colony to its depths. Elijah A. Rockwell, editor and publisher of the *Sandwich Islands News*, demanded the return of the manuscripts and tried to institute legal proceedings against Judd. Judge Lee took a neutral position, but Bates advised that Judd was not liable to prosecution, and the matter dropped.[34]

Ten Eyck, in the unenviable position of a diplomatic representative caught in the act of writing articles hostile to the government to which he was accredited, denied authorship and argued weakly that he had merely copied the already printed text. He denounced Judd's use of bribery, but the evidence against him was overwhelming. His hostility to the government was notorious. He had acted as counsel for Ladd & Co. in the arbitration, for which he had received a reprimand from the United States government. In short order, the king directed all departments of the Hawaiian government to cease official relations with him.[35]

A number of businessmen cursed Dr. Judd and muttered about ousting him even at the cost of revolution. Charles E. Hitchcock, Jarves' successor as editor of the government paper, the *Polynesian*, resigned his post. Armstrong expressed grave doubts as to the propriety of Judd's conduct. But the government stood behind him, and ordered the $300, which he had used for the bribe, to be carried on the treasury books as an official expense. Judd justified his use of bribery on the ground of political necessity, that is, to thwart a conspiracy on the part of foreign residents to overthrow the government. He added (so J. G. Munn testified) that sometimes a hunter had to dirty himself when he tracked a fox into its hole.[36]

Meanwhile his impeachment proceeded. Robertson made an eloquent speech in support of the charges, to which Dr. Judd made a long written reply. He explained that the $1,000 credited to his account the previous February did not represent embezzlement but was merely the rent of his wharf lot for the year ending October 31, 1847. John Young testified that Judd's interference in interior department matters in no sense represented a usurpation of power. Under cross-examination he made it clear that Judd's interference had been with his full knowledge and consent. Toward the end of the proceedings Judge Lee gave a legal opinion that, in any event, only six of the sixteen charges were impeachable.[37]

Wyllie's conduct throughout the trial was to a large degree hostile. He testified at some length that Judd had had strained relations with such persons as Jarves and Ricord. When Judd asked if he must reply to irrelevant testimony, such as hearsay, Wyllie answered in the name of the commission, of which he was the dominant member, that to grant the request might result in a pre-judgment. Armstrong, he added significantly, dissented from this opinion.[38]

In later years Wyllie insisted that he had received a message from the king stating that he and the chiefs believed Judd to be guilty and asking for a speedy conviction instead of a sham acquittal. Wyllie insisted further that as a man of honor he could not obey the royal order, and that instead he had delayed the proceedings until the king changed his mind. He thus explained that his apparent hostility at the trial resulted from his ardent wish to be impartial. Wyllie's explanation came in 1860 after a long illness and at a time when he was trying to make a reconciliation with Judd. It is ingenious and uncorroborated, and may be the result of wishful thinking. Judd refused to accept the explanation.

I must think that the real sentiments of his late majesty, upon all subjects were better known by Mr. Young, John Ii, and the Governor [Kekuanaoa] than by any foreigner in his service. For many years I had the king's confidence so far at least, as to know that if he had any design hostile to me or in any way he chose to interfere in the matter of the arbitration, he would have addressed himself first to the native members of the commission.[39]

On the other hand, Wyllie was a man of integrity, and it is hard to believe that he would have told a deliberate lie. Upon occasion, the king was annoyed with Dr. Judd.[40] At the time of the impeachment, the king had broken his temperance pledge and was drinking heavily. Besides, the Hawaiian temperament is volatile and impulsive. It is possible that in a moment of pique or intoxication the king may have sent Wyllie the message and then repented of it.

At any event, the commission met 45 times, heard a mass of testimony, and on April 23, 1849, gave a verdict of not guilty. A few days later the king wrote Dr. Judd a friendly letter urging him to carry on "fearlessly" as before.[41]

The Crisis of 1849

Less than a month after his acquittal Dr. Judd faced another ugly political dispute. For several years the king had been drinking to excess. Wine regularly appeared at his public dinners, and, as Mrs. Judd commented, "it gives us much uneasiness."[1] On Sunday evening, May 20, 1849, the Reverend Richard Armstrong, at that time minister of public instruction, preached a well-meaning but tactless sermon before the king in which he reproached the king for leading a sinful life. The sermon gave great offense to the sensitive monarch, who complained wrathfully to the privy council the next day of Armstrong's conduct.

The privy council agreed generally that Armstrong had been indiscreet, and Armstrong admitted that he had been guilty of an error of judgment. But Dr. Judd insisted that the king was equally at fault. In the course of the discussion Judd revealed that he had made an agreement with the king to serve in the government only so long as the king led a respectable life, and that as early as 1846 he had threatened to resign if the king did not keep sober. He also revealed that he had recently repeated his threat to resign unless the king reformed. He proposed that the privy council, in con-

156

demning Armstrong's indiscretion, also take official notice of the king's misconduct. Wyllie, as might be expected, disagreed on the worldly ground that almost all kings drink and that he had never heard of ministers passing judgment upon their sovereign because he took a glass of wine.

On May 22 the privy council received a message from the king that he would abdicate if Armstrong remained in office. At this meeting John Ii stated that the king was at fault, and Paki agreed to dismiss Armstrong on condition that the king mend his ways. While these two chiefs supported Judd's position, Wyllie once again dissented on the ground that many kings led irregular private lives, "but they were good sovereigns for all that." On the same day, Armstrong sent by Judd a written apology to the king, who at first remained adamant and then reluctantly decided to let Armstrong keep his post.[2]

Dr. Judd did not relax his vigilance. On June 11, when he left Honolulu with the king for a trip to the island of Hawaii, to lay out a road across the island, he made sure that strict teetotalism prevailed on board ship. Robert Elwes, who made the voyage with them, has described the prayers held on deck each morning and the long grace in Hawaiian which Judd delivered before each meal. He also left an unforgettable description of Judd lying in his berth, chewing tobacco and spitting it into a calabash by his side. "I do not smoke," Judd told him, "but I chew a good deal." He had used tobacco as a youth, given it up just before his appointment by the American Board in 1827, and then returned to it in the Islands. That he chewed tobacco was common knowledge in the Honolulu community.

The ship reached Kailua on the island of Hawaii on the 14th. There, a cannon firing a 21-gun salute to the king mangled a man's hand, which Dr. Judd amputated with borrowed surgical instruments. Elwes thought he took a long time about it, since he had not performed an operation for a number of years.[3]

Meanwhile, in Honolulu a political emergency as serious as the Paulet episode of 1843 was rising to a swift and nasty climax. The French consul Dillon continued his spiteful course of vituperation and intrigue, for which he later received a rebuke from his own government. In particular, Dillon made four demands: that Catholics and Protestants have rigorously equal privileges, especially in the schools; that the import duty of $5 per gallon on French brandy be reduced; that French whaleships be permitted to import duty free $200 worth of liquor apiece; and that the French language be used in all official dealings with French nationals. The Hawaiian government refused all four demands, and in April, 1849, not only asked France to recall Dillon but appointed Jarves as a special commissioner to go to Paris and settle the dispute. Dillon then behaved exactly as Alexander Simpson had in 1842. He sent word to the French naval command in the Pacific asking for armed assistance. In response to his request, Rear Admiral Legoarant de Tromelin, commander in chief of the French naval forces in the Pacific, arrived in Honolulu in mid-August with two frigates, *La Poursuivante* and *Le Gassendi*. Mrs. Judd noted correctly, "The political atmosphere portends a storm."[4]

Judd and the king returned to Honolulu, and on August 22 received from De Tromelin an ultimatum based on Dillon's four demands. The ultimatum, reminiscent of Paulet's in 1843, stated that unless satisfaction were given in three days the French would "employ the means at their disposal" to obtain redress for their grievances.

The Hawaiian government protested, wrote appeals to England and the United States to interpose their good offices in the dispute, and rejected the ultimatum mainly on the ground that the questions had already been referred directly to the French government for settlement. Once again a diplomatic maneuver, which had succeeded with the French Captain Mallet in 1842, now failed, as it had failed with Paulet in 1843. On the 25th, at the expiration of the ultimatum's time limit, De Tromelin sent troops ashore, who seized the fort, customs house, and government offices. Mrs. Judd wrote,

All the guns were thrown from the walls of the fort or spiked. The magazine was opened and the powder poured into the sea. All the old muskets, swords, and bayonets that could be found were broken to pieces, and every article on the premises destroyed, not sparing the old clock on the walls of the governor's house. Two large camphor-wood trunks, containing kahili feathers and various articles belonging to Kinau, were carried on board the French ships, and even the calabashes were smashed and thrown into the well. . . . The ground is covered with

158

broken muskets, cartridge boxes, bayonets, and swords. Every window and door of the governor's house is broken and battered, and the walls are covered with charcoal sketches. Every box, barrel, and calabash is crushed to atoms.[5]

The Hawaiian government gave orders that no resistance should be made. The king is reported to have said, "If they fight, let them fight forts and guns but not my men."[6]

On August 27, while the French demolitions were still continuing, the king appointed Dr. Judd and Judge Lee as commissioners to confer with De Tromelin. They were received on board the *Gassendi* the following day. No settlement could be reached. De Tromelin insisted on reduction of the brandy duty as an essential condition for further negotiation. Dillon complained heatedly of Jarves' appointment as envoy to France, because of what Jarves had written about the French in his history of Hawaii. Meanwhile, Mrs. Dillon called on Mrs. Judd and blamed the trouble on Wyllie.

In a final effort to break the deadlock, the Hawaiian government proposed on the 29th, "That all pending difficulties be referred to the decision of the Government of France in concert with the King's special plenipotentiary; and, in case of a non-agreement upon any point, to the final award of any friendly Power, to be named by France herself." But De Tromelin rejected this proposal. He confiscated the royal yacht *Kamehameha* by way of further reprisal, and sailed away with Dillon on September 5. The French government later disavowed certain of his acts, but the royal yacht was never returned.

Mrs. Judd commented with understandable indignation, "In order to appreciate the necessity of this manifestation of French prowess, one must know the magnitude of French interests in these islands. Aside from the priests and their missions, there are twelve French subjects, one of whom is a merchant, who transacts about one-thousandth part of the commercial business of the place."[7]

The same day that the French departed the Hawaiian privy council met. The king recommended that Dr. Judd undertake a diplomatic journey to settle the pending dispute. Judd replied that he had no wish to go but would comply if the government looked after his family. The privy council then approved the royal proposal, and Judd received formal appointment as "His Majesty's Special Commissioner and Plenipotentiary Extraordinary to the Governments of France, England, and the United States." It was decided also that he would co-operate with Jarves, who was reaccredited, and that they would claim $100,000 damages from the French government. Wyllie, who was not present at the meeting of September 5, believed that Judd had recommended himself for the assignment, a belief shared by the American merchant Stephen Reynolds.[8]

In addition to his formal commission, Dr. Judd received secret instructions, dated September 7 and signed by the king, premier, and Wyllie, which empowered him, subject to ratification, to dispose of the sovereignty of the Islands and the private lands of the king and chiefs:

In case our independence be not fully recognized, be endangered by the acts of any other government, or our sovereignty in peril or rendered of no value, our royal domain being exposed to further hostile attacks without just and good reasons, or from any other cause you may find these instructions necessary. These are to command and empower you, on our behalf to treat and negotiate with any king, president or government or agent thereof for the purpose of placing our islands under foreign protection and rule.

And you are hereby further commanded and empowered to treat and negotiate for the sale of and to sell our sovereignty of the Hawaiian Islands, if, for reasons above mentioned, or for other good causes you may deem it wise and prudent so to do, reserving in all cases unto us the ratification of any treaty or convention you may sign on our behalf.

And you are hereby further empowered to bargain for and sell all our private lands, and those of our chiefs, subject to our ratification and the free concurrence of our chiefs.[9]

These secret instructions conferred huge power, comparable to that enjoyed by Richards, who had proceeded on his diplomatic mission in 1842 with blank papers bearing the seal and signature of the king. Wyllie has stated that the document was drawn without his knowledge and presented to him for signature only a few hours before Dr. Judd left the Islands. Wyllie added that he objected to the last two clauses and signed only because any act by Judd under the terms of these instructions had to receive ratification by the king and chiefs. Judd later explained that he took the document solely in case of an emergency which he hoped would not arise.[10]

The privy council meeting of September 5 also agreed that Prince Alexander, aged 15 and heir to the throne, and his elder brother, Prince Lot, who was 18, should accompany Dr. Judd on the diplomatic journey. Wyllie disapproved of their going, and it is clear that their inclusion in the mission was Judd's idea. Both of the princes were restive and subject to moral lapses.[11] Judd believed that a trip abroad would be a salutary educational experience for them. It is logical to assume also, since the princes spoke excellent English and had polite manners, that he wished to use them as living examples of the state of civilization achieved in the Islands, so that diplomatists in the United States and Europe would take seriously the diplomatic pretensions of the Hawaiian Kingdom.

His leave-taking was solemn. During family prayers, which he led on Sunday morning, September 9, his children wept when he exhorted them to "remember our Creator in the days of our youth," and to bear in mind that "life is short." His daughter Elizabeth, for one, believed that he would be gone a year, and she feared that he might not return. She added, "Mother appears calm and composed, but I know by her sighs that her heart is heavy."[12]

At three o'clock on the afternoon of September 11, Dr. Judd and the two princes boarded the schooner *Honolulu*. At four o'clock the ship sailed for San Francisco. Mrs. Judd wrote: "The king, queen, chiefs, and a large concourse of natives and foreigners accompanied them to the ship. The welkin rang with cheers for their success and a speedy return; and all the ships manned their yards to do them honor. But," she added forlornly, "what consolation does it all afford to wife and children quite away from this demonstration in their own distant dwelling, weeping and watching the little craft that bears from them the joy of their hearts, the light of their home, their stay and staff?"[13]

It requires little imagination to picture the schooner riding the swells beyond Waikiki's breakers and heading slowly eastward around Diamond Head. Ordinarily the sea is deep blue there, broken with white wavelets that sparkle in the sunlight. The trade winds hiss through the rigging, and ships creak loudly as they rise and fall in the heaving water. As he stood on deck, watching the receding wharf where the crowds still waved, Dr. Judd could see Kawaiahao Church towering over the cocoanut groves on the Waikiki

Dr. and Mrs. Judd in 1849

plain. He could see also the white beaches and hear the shrill cries of circling birds. In the hours before the schooner passed through the Molokai Channel into the open sea, he had ample time to remember his first sight of the Islands, on a March day twenty-one years before, and to remember also the days and nights of effort which he had given to his adopted nation. Now, on the first stage of a critical venture, he knew how much depended on his judgment. At one stroke of the pen he could cede the Islands to a foreign power, for ratification by the king and chiefs was little more than a formality. Faced with an accomplished fact, they could hardly withhold their consent. It is certain that the responsibility weighed heavily upon him. It is equally certain that he asked God for help.

Meanwhile, in Honolulu Wyllie nursed a monstrous grudge. He felt slighted that as foreign secretary he had not been consulted in planning the diplomatic journey. For the moment he forgot conveniently that Dr. Judd was in fact the head of the government, and he smarted that as foreign secretary he had no control over one of the Kingdom's diplomatic agents. Also, his pride was hurt that he had not been chosen to undertake the mission, for he felt himself vastly superior to Dr. Judd in matters of statecraft and diplomacy. In this morose frame of mind he determined upon a rash and malicious act. Within two weeks after Dr. Judd's departure he went to the British consul, William Miller, and gave him a full and concise account of the secret powers which Dr. Judd carried.[14]

The effectiveness of the instructions depended in large measure on their secrecy, in that they provided a brilliant trump card for a diplomatic emergency. In Honolulu the secret was generally well kept. The American commissioner, Ten Eyck, heard only vague rumors of the extraordinary powers.[15] They did not appear in the first (1880) edition of Mrs. Judd's memoirs, and were not printed until 1894.

But Miller naturally sent a full report to London, so that in the negotiations to follow Lord Palmerston already knew what Dr. Judd most wished to conceal. Wyllie's disclosure, therefore, undermined the Hawaiian diplomatic position, and in a real sense foredoomed the mission to failure even before Dr. Judd and the princes arrived in San Francisco on the first leg of their journey.

Diplomatic Journey, I

Dr. Judd and the two princes reached San Francisco on October 3, 1849. At that time the gold rush was at its height, and they found the place overcrowded and ruinously expensive. The fog and wet weather depressed Judd, and he noted indignantly that they had to pay six dollars a day apiece for poor lodgings without a fire. The streets, so he wrote in a letter home, were "knee deep in mud, and thronged with fierce-looking men. . . . Dead bodies are found almost every morning—perished from hunger, cold, and disease."[1]

Upon arrival he was disappointed to learn that the steamer for Panama, with Dillon aboard, had left two days before. But he was delighted that Charles Eames, Ten Eyck's successor as United States commissioner to Hawaii, was in town with full powers to negotiate a treaty. He called on Eames, a Harvard graduate with a distinguished career as diplomatist, journalist, and jurist, who received him cordially and suggested that they begin negotiations on the spot. Dr. Judd agreed with enthusiasm. By making the United States treaty in San Francisco, he might bypass Washington and reach Paris in time to counter Dillon's representations.[2] Even before he left Honolulu he had hoped to go directly to Europe.

The two men exchanged credentials on October 5. They found that they agreed generally about terms, and they signed the treaty on October 22. In some respects Dr. Judd was not satisfied with the document, which he found "too wordy."[3] He had hoped to obtain a declaration guaranteeing Hawaii's independence, but Eames believed that he lacked authority to make such a statement, and it was omitted. Nonetheless, the Hawaiian government later approved the document, although Wyllie was careful to point out that it had a number of defects from the Hawaiian standpoint.

The Judd-Eames treaty, which never became law, reached Washington on December 8. Meanwhile, Jarves had negotiated a separate treaty there, signed on December 6, which was more favorable to the Hawaiian government. The United States Department of State, then, had two duly negotiated treaties to choose between. After further negotiations, Jarves signed a third treaty on December 20, in some ways less favorable than his previous one; this treaty, when ratified, formed the basis of relations with the United States until Hawaii's annexation in 1898.[4]

In San Francisco Dr. Judd did not neglect his two royal charges. During the week, they acted as his secretaries and copied official documents. On Sundays he was careful to take them to church. On the 14th they attended Presbyterian services in the morning. In the afternoon Alexander (Lot was ill) heard a sermon by Wyllie's friend, the Reverend Timothy Dwight Hunt, a former missionary to Hawaii, who later published a book attacking Judd's political career. On the 21st they went to the Episcopal Church, where Alexander slept through the sermon.[5]

On one unhappy occasion, on board the U.S.S. *Savannah*, the princes were so indiscreet as to drink some ale. Dr. Judd reproved them sharply. He made them promise in writing neither to drink liquor nor to play cards, and to be in bed every night by 11 o'clock. The ale incident may be the basis for the hilarious anecdote which Mark Twain later heard, that when some wags in Sacramento tried to get them drunk the princes calmly drank their hosts under the table.[6]

After sending home daguerreotypes, Dr. Judd and the boys left San Francisco on November 1 on the steamer *California*. Judd was sick all the next week, during which the vessel put in at Monterey and San Diego. After stops at Acapulco, which was uncomfortably hot, and Mazatlan, where he cashed a draft for $96.00 on board a British warship, they reached Panama on the 22nd, which Alexander described as "an uncomfortable and dirty hole."[7]

The next leg of their journey lay across the fever-ridden Isthmus. Three hundred years before, hundreds of slaves, carrying the gold of Peru from Panama on its way to the treasure rooms of Spain, had died in the hideous jungles. Now a frenzied stream of latter-day argonauts fought their way through the same jungles in the opposite direction toward the gold fields of California. Dr. Judd and the two princes rode mules along the muddy trail in a drenching rain some twenty miles from Panama to the Chagres River. Here Alexander was thrown from his mount and nearly fell into the murky water. They spent the night in the halfway house, where they had to sleep on the floor, and next day took a native bungo boat some forty-five miles downstream to the Caribbean. The air teemed with fever-carrying insects. Alligators swarmed in the yellow water. On either side of the river they saw steaming forests, the breeding ground of pumas, lizards, scorpions, and poisonous snakes. At Chagres they left their muddy clothes to be washed, and boarded the *Crescent City*, which sailed on the 28th before they had time to retrieve their laundry.[8]

Two days later they stopped briefly at Kingston, Jamaica, which Dr. Judd characterized as "an old, moss-grown English town." They went ashore for a few hours to buy oranges and see the sights. Afterwards, Dr. Judd wrote sternly in Lot's journal, "Can't you describe Kingston? Why did we go about the town except to see it? If you have seen it you should describe it in your journal."[9] Unquestionably the princes had reason to conclude, as others in similar circumstances have concluded before and since, that escorted travel has its disadvantages.

After a passage which Dr. Judd described as both "agreeable" and "delightful" they reached New York City at noon on December 7. The travel time from Honolulu by way of Panama came to fifty-eight days. In 1828 it had taken three months longer to reach the Islands by way of Cape Horn.

In New York, despite the cold weather, which seemed doubly piercing after Panama and Jamaica, they made themselves com-

166

fortable in the old Irving House. It soon became apparent that they were celebrities. "Our parlor," Dr. Judd wrote home, "is thronged with company, and our table covered with cards left when we are out." The mayor, James Kelly, made a formal call, and the common council escorted them to the city hall and the arsenal. They also received calls from Schuyler Livingston, a distinguished merchant who was the Hawaiian agent in the city, and Charles Samuel Stewart, the former missionary who bade the Judds farewell when the *Parthian* sailed from Boston twenty-two years before. Dr. Judd also saw his uncle, Thomas Hastings, the hymn writer; Charles Wilkes, now a commander, formerly of the United States exploring expedition; and Alfred Grenville Benson, a shipping magnate of Brooklyn with offices in New York, who later figured in Hawaii's commercial development. Meanwhile, they ordered new clothes and found time to visit both a museum and an art gallery.[10]

In New York Dr. Judd conferred with Jarves, who had just signed his first treaty in Washington. The two men decided that, as negotiations with the United States were proceeding smoothly, Dr. Judd should go directly to Europe. Accordingly, he obtained passage on the Cunard steamer *Canada*, which left from Jersey City on the morning of December 12. Dr. Judd wrote to his wife,

We stopped at Halifax two hours, where we had a fine sleigh-ride. It was a bright starlight evening, with the thermometer below zero. The princes enjoyed it, though it was very cold. The passage of twelve days across the Atlantic was rough and boisterous, but the *Canada* ploughed her way at the rate of three hundred miles a day, with dignified indifference to wind and waves. We got into Liverpool on the 24th, and whirled into London on Christmas-day. This was our first ride on the railway, and we were delighted with it.[11]

A garbled version of their arrival appeared in the London *Times* of December 26 as intelligence received from its Paris correspondent. "M. de Riswic, Envoy Extraordinary from the King of the Sandwich Islands, has arrived in Paris. M. de Riswic, who is a native of the Grand Duchy of Baden, has been 12 years in the service of King Kameahmeah [*sic*], and enjoys his confidence. It is said that he has been commissioned by His Majesty to arrange the late misunderstanding with the French authorities." Dr. Judd com-

167

mented wryly, "So you see how clear everything is in France." He added characteristically, "I think it is too bad that I must fight the battle all over again there, where I can not speak a word of the language, nor *pull a string*, but all must be done by main strength."[12]

In London they stayed at the Tavistock Hotel in Covent Garden north of the Strand. On the 26th, the day after their arrival, they received a call from Archibald Barclay, the London representative of the Hawaiian government. After some discussion it was decided that Barclay should arrange an interview with Lord Palmerston, England's forceful and self-willed foreign secretary. England's support would strengthen Judd's position when he presented the Hawaiian case to the French. On January 2 Barclay received word that Palmerston was out of town but would see Dr. Judd upon his return. For the time being, there was nothing to do but wait.[13]

During the next few days they occupied their time in sightseeing. On the evening of December 26 they saw a production of *The Merchant of Venice* at Drury Lane. The next day they went to Madame Toussaud's wax works. In the first week of the new year they visited the House of Commons, Westminster Abbey, the Tower of London, and the Surrey Zoological Gardens (where Alexander was disappointed at the animals), and they attended a concert at Exeter Hall. On one occasion the princes blundered innocently into Piccadilly. Although they insisted that they had no amatory adventures there, they failed to explain their conduct adequately to their stern preceptor, and for some days they languished in disgrace in their hotel room. On January 7 Alexander wrote woefully in his journal, "No prospects of going out today, although the weather is beautiful."[14]

Waiting to see Palmerston made Dr. Judd extremely irritable. He cannot have escaped homesickness when he went to the British Museum on January 9 and saw there the feather cloaks and other articles which Richards had used for the design of the Hawaiian coat of arms. To his wife he complained of the London fog. With conspicuous lack of tact he wrote to Wyllie, who sometimes felt as homesick for London as Judd did for Honolulu, "Of all places in the world London is least to my taste, the people excluded. We see but little day light, which is by no means the thing when sight seeing is all we have to do."[15]

Dr. Judd worried because Alexander could not shake off a cold caught during the sleigh ride at Halifax. Twenty-six years before, the princes' uncle, Kamehameha II, had died of measles on a visit to London, and the responsibility of safeguarding the boys' health weighed heavily upon him. If anything should happen to them he alone would be held accountable, especially since he had insisted, over the objections of others in the government, on bringing them with him. On the 13th his mind was somewhat relieved when Sir James Clark, physician in ordinary to Queen Victoria, paid them a professional visit. By the 24th he could report happily that Alexander had fully recovered.[16] But his anxiety had been genuine and had aggravated his mounting annoyance at Palmerston's procrastination.

On the evening of the 16th, while Alexander was still sick, Judd received a call from his old friend Admiral Thomas, the restorer of Hawaii's independence in 1843. With the concurrence of Thomas and Barclay he wrote a private letter to Palmerston requesting an audience. Thomas promised to use political pressure to expedite matters, and on the 21st Palmerston replied that he would see Dr. Judd at 5:30 P.M. on the 23rd. Meanwhile, Dr. Judd forwarded his credentials to the French foreign minister, General de La Hitte, with a letter stating that he would come to Paris as soon as Prince Alexander recovered.[17]

At the foreign office Palmerston kept him waiting for two hours and then received him "very cordially." The interview lasted about an hour. Dr. Judd outlined the grievances of the Hawaiian government against France, gave him a copy of the new United States treaty just concluded in Washington, and asked his advice whether to open negotiations in England or in France. Palmerston was sympathetic but "exceedingly guarded" in his replies. He advised Dr. Judd to go to Paris, and promised to give him a letter to the Marquess of Normanby, the English ambassador there. When Dr. Judd pressed him for more positive interposition, Palmerston only replied, "We will do all in our power." At one point in the interview Palmerston inquired if Englishmen in Hawaii had the same privileges as Americans. Dr. Judd assured him they did. Palmerston then asked if the natives were intelligent. Again Dr. Judd answered in the affirmative, and added, "The two princes with me are a good specimen. I shall hope to introduce them to your lordship on our return from Paris." Afterwards, he wrote officially to Wyllie that the talk had been satisfactory, but in a private letter he complained, "I am much hurt by the indifference manifested by Lord Palmerston in our affairs. He ought not to have kept me waiting here a whole month, merely to say that he had done nothing, and then put me off with a letter to the British minister in Paris."[18] It may be suggested that Palmerston, like almost all English diplomatists of his generation, thought in European and not in global terms. To him Hawaii seemed remote and therefore inconsequential.

Nonetheless, Palmerston kept his promise. The next day, January 24, he wrote a letter of introduction to Normanby and sent it to Dr. Judd. The letter instructed Normanby to intercede with the French on behalf of the Hawaiian government, but added, "you will limit your interference to the employment of your good offices with a view to bring about an amicable adjustment." On the same day he gave orders for an investigation of the new United States treaty with Hawaii to determine whether the English government should conclude a similar agreement. A week later he acknowledged receipt of Consul Miller's dispatch informing him of Dr. Judd's secret instructions. He told Miller that Judd had not mentioned the instructions in their recent conversation, and he gave orders that Miller should advise the Hawaiian government to weigh well the consequences of giving up its independence. On February 5 he sent a copy of Miller's letter to Normanby in Paris, so that once again information which Judd wished to conceal was in danger of becoming public. Wyllie's rash disclosure had now followed him halfway around the world.[19]

After a stormy crossing from Folkestone to Boulogne, they reached Paris on January 26. They took rooms at the de luxe Hotel Meurice near the Tuileries on the Rue de Rivoli, where some years before Richards and Haalilio had stayed. Here they ate at a long table of some sixty persons and conversed in the Hawaiian language to the obvious mystification of the other diners.[20]

The day after their arrival Dr. Judd delivered Palmerston's letter to the British embassy, and on the 30th he called on Normanby, a seasoned statesman who, before his diplomatic appointment to Paris in 1846, had served as governor of Jamaica, lord lieutenant of

Ireland, and secretary of war. Normanby promised to help arrange an interview with La Hitte, the French minister of foreign affairs. Judd stated that he wanted a disavowal of Dillon's acts, an indemnity for the French damages, and a new treaty. He added that his time was precious and that he hoped to conclude his business within a month. At this point, Normanby "smiled, but looked doubtful and renewed the promise of mentioning me to the French minister."[21]

La Hitte received him courteously at the French foreign office on February 4, listened attentively to the Hawaiian case, took conspicuous notes, gave him a ticket to the National Assembly, and invited him to attend his *soirées* on Tuesday evenings. But when Dr. Judd urged a quick settlement, La Hitte would only promise to reach a decision as soon as possible. Nevertheless, Dr. Judd came away satisfied that the interview had been a success.

Two days later, when he took the princes with him to the foreign office, he had reason to change his mind, for La Hitte remained affable but maddeningly evasive. He invited them to dine with him the next evening, promised to retrieve a box of cigars belonging to Alexander which the customs had seized at Boulogne, and gave them tickets to the artillery museum. Dr. Judd, obviously worried at their expenses of $16 a day, wrote to Wyllie, "I have many doubts whether I shall obtain anything from the minister short of a delay beyond my present means of bearing the expenses of my embassy in Paris."[22]

For the next week they did what they could to ease the tedium of waiting. They dined with La Hitte on the 7th and dutifully attended his *soirée* on the 12th. They went to the Louvre, Bibliothèque Nationale, and opera, and saw two performances of Jean Eugene Robert-Houdin, the juggler. In addition, Dr. Judd arranged for the princes to take daily lessons in French and fencing. As the days passed with no word from La Hitte he became increasingly restless. To make matters worse, on the 13th he suffered from a painful toothache.[23]

Two days later he received word that La Hitte had appointed one of his assistants, the Comte de Cramayel, to hear the Hawaiian argument. At once he went to the foreign office, and the two men had a conversation lasting two and a half hours. Cramayel accused the Hawaiian government of violating the French treaty and repeated Dillon's demands. Dr. Judd remained inflexible, and told him bluntly, "I can yield nothing." The next day, February 16, he sent Cramayel a memorandum summarizing the Hawaiian position, and on the 21st La Hitte withdrew Cramayel from the proceedings.[24] Both sides refused to budge. From the outset, so it appeared, the negotiation had lapsed into stalemate.

In a mood of profound dejection Dr. Judd wrote to Barclay, "There is in my opinion no reason to hope for justice from France without other influences. The British minister [Normanby] is very polite to me but impenetrable. He says *do not speak of indemnity, be satisfied if they do not send back Dillon to your Islands etc.*" To Wyllie he complained of the "great indifference on the part of the British Government. The fact is that the British Government have been transacting in Greece very much after the pattern of the French in our Islands." Shortly thereafter he added, "It is easy to see that the Greek question, in which France is chosen umpire, makes it a delicate matter for England to interfere in our difficulties and coerce the French."[25]

His interpretation of the diplomatic situation was well founded. Palmerston was indeed in no position to intercede vigorously on behalf of the Hawaiian Kingdom, for at that very time, in an action which almost destroyed his political career, he ordered a British naval force to Athens to demand by force the payment of debts owed to an unsavory British subject, Don Pacifico, a Portuguese Jew born in Gibraltar. The British naval action against Greece bore close resemblance to the French naval action against Hawaii. Further, Palmerston resisted French mediation in the Greek dispute. Obviously, therefore, he could not insist on English mediation in the Hawaiian dispute.[26]

Secure from English interference, the French foreign office remained indifferent to Hawaii's grievances. The unstable French Second Republic (1849–1851) did not contemplate a seizure of the Islands,[27] but it was not above bullying the weaker nation in order to obtain economic concessions. And so the diplomatic comedy continued.

After pointless conferences with another representative of the French foreign office, Dr. Judd talked again with La Hitte on

March 1 and 5. La Hitte admitted that possibly the Hawaiian government had not broken the French treaty, and he promised to return the king's yacht, but he insisted that the duty on French brandy was too high. Dr. Judd gave him a copy of the United States treaty and told him that he would like to leave France on March 12, for, as he explained in a letter to Wyllie, "if anything were to happen to our king I would be blamed for keeping the heir so long away." La Hitte assured him that all would be settled within the week. In a letter to Henry Hill Dr. Judd commented, "You can judge as well as I of the value of this assurance."[28]

On March 7 they attended in their court uniforms the reception of Louis Napoleon, president of the short-lived Second Republic and later Emperor Napoleon III. La Hitte made the introductions. Turning to the princes Louis Napoleon inquired, "Is this your first visit to Paris? I hope you like Paris."

Alexander bowed. "We are very much pleased with Paris."

"You have come a very long way," Louis Napoleon said. "I hope you will settle our little quarrels."

"We have great hopes," Dr. Judd replied. "We trust a great deal in the justice and magnanimity of France."

Somewhat later Judd cornered La Hitte and said, "Have you no word of encouragement for me? I am very anxious."

"O yes, very soon. The day after tomorrow. I will appoint Mr. Perrin to negotiate with you."

As a final note to the polite comedy, Dr. Judd added in a letter to his wife, "We were all presented to the Grand Duchess of Baden, aunt of the President, who was covered with diamonds, and almost stout enough for a Hawaiian beauty. She spoke in French, praised our uniforms (which we understood), though it was interpreted as praise of the weather."

Dr. Judd caught cold at the reception and had to stay in bed most of the next week with a sore throat and earache. His tooth was still bothering him. With the princes' help he bled himself.[29]

On the 12th, though still unwell, he called on the Duc de Broglie, a leading statesman of the overthrown July Monarchy, who retained considerable political influence. De Broglie advised him not to make an appeal to the French legislature. The same day he saw Guizot, prime minister in the July Monarchy, then living in retirement. Guizot asked how much French brandy entered the Islands every year, and being told about 5,000 gallons, he said, "Then you have acted up to the spirit and intention of the treaty, but the mischief is done and you will get no indemnity." He advised Dr. Judd to ask for an arbitration with the king of Belgium as umpire.[30]

By this time Dr. Judd was clutching at straws. He believed, as he wrote home, "that six months at least will be required to bring matters to a decision, and then the verdict will be against our claims." He added stubbornly, "They expect me to yield; but the king did not send me on this long journey to grant what he had refused; and for which refusal he had suffered so much." To Wyllie he stated his belief "that no arrangement can be made with a government which in practice utterly denies the sovereignty of the king and the letter and spirit of their own treaties." Nevertheless, he called on the Greek ambassador, who was staying in their hotel, and asked his advice about obtaining a mediation. At the same time he corresponded with Barclay in London about the advisability of presenting the Hawaiian grievances in the public press.[31]

During the next two weeks he had almost daily conferences with Emile Perrin, La Hitte's designated representative. Perrin had orders to uphold, with minor concessions, all of Dillon's demands, and once again the negotiation reached a stalemate. The French foreign office refused to make another treaty based on the new United States treaty and refused to arbitrate the dispute, even though, in accordance with his instructions, Dr. Judd stated that France might choose the umpire.[32]

Despairing of settlement, Dr. Judd made plans to leave on the night of March 28. He wrote to Barclay asking for £50—their money was running short—and he requested that arrangements be made for their baggage to pass the English customs. With forced cheerfulness he added, "The weather is bad. Snow and rain, but we tropical plants are in pretty good condition." That afternoon Perrin called with fresh assurances. Dr. Judd asked him for a loan of 5,000 francs and decided to stay a little longer.[33]

The daily conferences continued. Meanwhile, with the princes he went to Notre Dame, St. Cloud, St. Denis, and Versailles, and he tried to take a hopeful view of the situation. He wrote to Wyllie on April 4, "The turnings, twistings, subterfuges, which are used are amusing enough to me and I trust by a straight forward course to expose them." But on the same day he admitted to Barclay, "I find I have fallen into a hornet's nest and have some fear I may not come out scot free."[34]

On April 5 La Hitte withdrew from the negotiation and declared that henceforth Dr. Judd must deal exclusively with Perrin. If this demand were refused, so Perrin stated, the negotiation must end. La Hitte's withdrawal convinced Dr. Judd that no settlement was possible. On April 6, with "an overpowering sensation of despondency," he rejected the ultimatum and sent to the foreign office a formal reiteration of the Hawaiian claim for damages. His letter to La Hitte announcing his departure was dated April 8.[35]

He and the princes arose at 5:30 A.M. on the 8th, and by 8 A.M. they had left Paris for Calais. To Wyllie he wrote simply, "I took French leave." His feelings at the moment may be inferred from a letter which he wrote home a few weeks before. "Have made the acquaintance of many distinguished people, received much courtesy and many compliments, but *justice* in a *grass hut* would suit me better than all this magnificence without it."[36]

Diplomatic Journey, II

On April 9, the day of his arrival in London, Dr. Judd sent Palmerston an official letter announcing that he had broken off negotiations with France. "Under the circumstances," he added, "nothing remains for the Hawaiian Government but to submit to the physical power of France, or avail themselves of the good offices of some friendly power." Accordingly he requested "that a mediation may speedily be offered by Her Britannic Majesty's Government."[1]

The next day he set out with the princes for Plymouth to visit Admiral Thomas. A waiter in the hotel gave them the wrong time, so that they missed the express and had to take the mail train. The trip of 240 miles lasted ten hours, and they were quite late in arriving. Nonetheless their host received them warmly and gave them an excellent dinner. "It was gratifying to me," Dr. Judd remarked, "to come into contact with a religious family in Europe—and that, too, where mere formality would have been expected by many."[2] His recent experience in France had obviously left a bitter taste in his mouth.

After inspecting the naval dockyard with the port-admiral, Sir William Hall Gage, they returned to the Tavistock Hotel in London on the 11th. The following day Judd wrote Palmerston requesting an early interview. While awaiting a reply they visited the Adelphi Hotel, where Kamehameha II and his queen had died in 1824. "We were received politely," Dr. Judd noted, "and shown the very bed and bedstead on which Liholiho [Kamehameha II] died. The chambermaid remembered Governor Kekuanaoa, and inquired after Madame Boki." On April 13 they went to the East India Company's museum, where an attendant prevented Dr. Judd from playing a piano. They visited the British Museum on the 15th to see the collection of Polynesian idols, and the next evening they went to the opera.[3]

Meanwhile, Dr. Judd received a petulant letter from La Hitte, who complained, "I cannot, Sir, comprehend the motive which induced you to abandon in a manner as unusual as unexpected, the negotiations entered upon." La Hitte also asked if he planned to resume the negotiations at a later period. On the 17th Dr. Judd replied firmly that he had no intention of returning to Paris.[4]

On April 18 he called on Palmerston with the two princes and spent the whole morning reviewing the case. Palmerston admitted that France was in the wrong, but suggested as a compromise that France might give up her demands if the Hawaiian government abandoned the claim for an indemnity. He hinted that possibly Dr. Judd had been unwise to break off the negotiation. He also recommended lowering the duty on brandy. When Judd objected, he explained that he was talking about policy and not rights. Afterwards Judd and the princes had lunch with Admiral Sir George Seymour, who had been commander in chief in the Pacific 1844–1848. Here they met Paulet and Frere, who reminisced in a cordial manner about the cession of 1843.[5]

At 3 P.M. the next day Palmerston presented them to Prince Albert at Buckingham Palace. Queen Victoria did not make an appearance, since at the time she was in seclusion awaiting the birth of her third son (Prince Arthur, born on May 1). At the audience Dr. Judd said,

The King of the Hawaiian Islands sent me to endeavor to obtain justice of France for the injuries he has suffered from French officers, and directed these young Princes to accompany me in order that they may profit by what they would see of foreign countries. I have applied in vain to France and now (pointing to Lord Palmerston) have addressed myself to the greatest diplomatist in Europe.

"I hope," Albert replied, "it is not too late for us to come between you and France."

The situation did not lack irony, for at that moment both Victoria and Albert were enraged at Palmerston's arbitrary conduct of foreign affairs and wished heartily to be rid of him. Dr. Judd noticed that the prince seemed "a little uneasy," and after fifteen minutes of polite conversation about Hawaii the audience ended.

In the antechamber Palmerston asked Dr. Judd to call on the French ambassador the next day. Albert's equerry, Lt. Col. Francis Hugh George Seymour, the eldest son of Admiral Seymour, then took them on a tour of the palace, including the royal stables, and they returned to the hotel at 5 P.M.[6]

In response to Palmerston's request, Dr. Judd spent two and a half hours on April 20 with Edouard Drouyn de Lhuys, the French ambassador, who reproached him with having broken off the negotiation and suggested that mutual concessions might lead to an agreement. But Dr. Judd was in no mood to compromise. He saw Palmerston that evening, and, as he later wrote to Wyllie, "announced that I have no intention of returning to France or of resuming the negotiation with France. I said it is quite useless to waste words with them, but if England will interpose, and send out to the Islands a man who has a good head and a good heart to investigate the affairs there is a hope that France, in the presence of such a noble witness would do us justice."[7]

Two days later Palmerston and Drouyn conferred about the matter. Palmerston suggested as a compromise that the Hawaiian government should give up the indemnity claim and lower the tax on brandy, while France should withdraw her demand that the French language be used in Hawaii's official correspondence. He also expressed his apprehension that Dr. Judd, as an American, might take his complaints to Washington—a move which could lead to Hawaii's annexation by the United States. Drouyn adroitly pointed out the similarity of Hawaii's grievances to the still un-settled Greek question, and in his report of the conversation he suggested to La Hitte that it might be awkward if the Hawaiian affair became too conspicuous.[8]

On the 21st, the day after his talk with Drouyn, Judd and the princes went to Windsor with Bridges Taylor, a clerk in the foreign office whom Prince Albert had designated as their escort so long as they remained in England. They saw the castle and outbuildings, including the kennels and royal dairy. Dr. Judd, so Alexander noted, was particularly interested in the royal pigs. On the 23rd the princes went to the Bank of England and to the Parliament buildings, and on the 24th Taylor took them to Woolwich to see the arsenal. That evening, so Dr. Judd reported sadly, the princes returned somewhat the worse for liquor, and as punishment he cancelled the order for gold watches which he had planned to buy for them. A few days later they saw Bedlam, Newgate prison, Greenwich Hospital, and the London docks.[9]

Dr. Judd had decided to leave London on the 25th, but at Palmerston's request he postponed his departure for a week. He saw Palmerston for a few minutes on the 24th, and the two men had lengthy talks on the 25th and 26th. Judd said that the Hawaiian king wished to protect the Islands from attack by the French or by "hordes of unprincipled men" from California. He rejected as "altogether unjust and unreasonable" Palmerston's proposal to compromise with France. Instead, he asked for English mediation in the French dispute and for England to sign a treaty with Hawaii based on the recent treaty with the United States. Palmerston hesitated about mediation but assured him that the United States treaty was under study, as indeed it was. The conversations left Judd in a despondent mood. "Four months have passed away in Europe," he wrote to Wyllie on April 25, "without my being able to effect any thing conclusive, and I am quite discouraged."[10]

On Saturday, April 27, Dr. Judd and the princes attended a large formal dinner at Palmerston's residence. "In the course of the evening," Judd reported, "a gentleman inquired how long these young men had been in England; and on being told only a few weeks, remarked that they appeared as familiar with society as the best-bred people in England! A lady inquired how they learned to speak English. I told her they were educated in English."

"And where did they acquire court manners?"

"We have a little court of our own," Dr. Judd replied proudly. The conversation became a family anecdote.

Dr. Judd continued in a letter home, "The next day we dined at Brompton Park, with Earl Talbot and lady. Sir George Seymour and Lord Sheffield, with many other distinguished guests, were present. Went with Lady Sanford to Almack's, where we saw all the aristocracy of rank, beauty, wealth, and fashion."[11]

On May 1 he wrote formally to Palmerston requesting England's mediation, and the next day Palmerston replied that "Her Majesty's Government will with great pleasure employ their good offices with a view to effecting an amiable and satisfactory settlement" of the dispute with France. Although Palmerston's promise of "good offices" fell short of the formal "mediation" which had been requested, Dr. Judd replied on the 4th, "These assurances are most satisfactory and will prove encouraging to my Government."[12]

He left England in a buoyant frame of mind. The British government paid their hotel bills and transatlantic passage, amounting to about £200, and their escort, Bridges Taylor, went with them from London to Liverpool. "I am now fully convinced," he wrote to Wyllie, "that the British government have taken up the case with perfect sincerity, and will do all in their power to aid us in our present difficulties." But to the end he remained somewhat wary. From Bridges Taylor he learned a diplomatic maxim, which he recorded in his private journal and in a letter home, "Never tell a lie—and strictly avoid the truth."[13]

They reached Boston on May 17 on board the steamer *Hibernia* after "a cold passage" of thirteen days. The ship encountered icebergs off Halifax, where they stopped on the 16th, and they saw much field ice the next day. In Boston they stayed at the Revere House in rooms prepared for the Swedish singer, Jenny Lind. Once again they found that they were celebrities. Boston's mayor, John P. Bigelow, an ardent temperance man, escorted them to the Navy Yard on the 21st, where Commodore John Downes gave them two 17-gun salutes. The princes made a good impression. Bigelow eulogized them as "among the first and most beautiful fruits of the plantings of missionary labors in Polynesian regions."[14]

That afternoon, at Rufus Anderson's invitation, Dr. Judd and the princes met the American Board's prudential committee in the old Missionary Rooms. While the princes received pocket Bibles Dr. Judd had occasion to recall his last visits to the Rooms, twenty-three years before, when he dedicated himself to serve the heathen and thought longingly of preaching the word of God. But he could not quite forget the strained relations which he had had with the Board when he left the mission in 1842. His letter accepting Anderson's invitation seems cold and stilted. Part of it reads, "Although for many years I have ceased to hold any connection with the American Board, or with the Sandwich Islands Mission, I entertain the highest respect for the institution to which I owe my introduction into those Islands, and fully appreciate the disinterestedness and importance of their labors for the Hawaiian Nation." Nevertheless, the meeting proceeded in an atmosphere of cordiality, and he later pasted into his official letter book a newspaper clipping about it: "Those who have opportunity to see the princes [Alexander] Rihoriho and [Lot] Kamehameha, will need only to reflect a little on the state of the Sandwich Islands in the year 1820, to see abundant cause for exclaiming, 'What hath God wrought!' "[15]

During their stay they visited the Seamen's Hospital in Chelsea, the Massachusetts General Hospital, the Bunker Hill monument, and the public schools. They also met Jarves' aunt, Mrs. Lydia Bacon of Chelsea, who had befriended Mrs. Judd many years before in Sackett's Harbor. Mrs. Bacon commented,

The princes were tired with being "lions," and sighed for their own dear island home. They were truly elegant young men, dignified yet social. . . . Dr. Judd I think an interesting man. It was very gratifying to me to see L[aura]'s *husband*. He spoke in the highest terms of his wife, saying that she had been every thing to him, not only relieving him from domestic cares, but accomplishing much beside by her example.[16]

On the 22nd they had tea with Anderson. That same afternoon they called on Henry Hill, the American Board's treasurer, and in the evening they attended a large party. The next day they had daguerreotypes taken, and on the 24th the princes went to the opera with Mr. and Mrs. Jarves. Dr. Judd stayed in the hotel. He had letters to write and government business to transact, such as the purchase of cannon. On Saturday, May 25, he had a long and apparently unsatisfactory conference with Hiram Bingham about the latter's returning to the Islands. In the afternoon the party boarded a train for New York.[17]

After two days at the Irving House, Judd, Jarves, and the two princes reached Washington, D.C., on May 28, and took rooms at the old National Hotel on the corner of Sixth Street and Pennsylvania Avenue. They found the city seething with political crisis. The controversial and much-abused Clayton-Bulwer treaty, which limited the territorial expansion of both England and the United States in Central America, had been signed but was not yet ratified. The great debate over the extension of slavery into the territories—leading to the famous compromise legislation of September—was proceeding in an atmosphere of mounting tension. Henry Clay, William H. Seward, Daniel Webster, and a host of lesser men hurled verbal thunderbolts at one another, and nerves were frayed in Washington's sultry summer heat. By way of magnificent understatement, Prince Alexander wrote, "Henry Clay was making a good deal of fuss about a compromise between northern and southern states, about the slavery question."[18]

On the 29th they heard debates in both the House and Senate, and met Seward, who introduced them to Clay, Samuel Houston, then a senator from Texas, Senator A. P. Butler of South Carolina, Senator W. C. Dawson of Georgia, Senator Truman Smith of Connecticut, and Representative J. S. Green of Missouri. After calling on his old friend, Commander Wilkes, Dr. Judd took Jarves and the princes with him to the Department of State.[19]

Here he had a long talk with Secretary of State John Middleton Clayton, a Yale graduate with a brilliant record as a senator and judge. Clayton proved warmly sympathetic to Hawaii's diplomatic difficulties. The substance of his attitude appears in the entry in Dr. Judd's private journal dated June 4:

Mr. Clayton said that he should notify France and England that his Govt. will not look with indifference upon any act of oppression committed or any attempt to take the Islands. . . . The U.S. do not want the Islands but will not permit any other nation to have them. I asked if the U.S. would go to war on our account. He replied yes—that is they would send a force and retake the Islands for the King and if that made a war they would carry it out.[20]

The next day at 11:30 A.M. William Hunter, one of Clayton's assistants, presented them to President Zachary Taylor. Prince Alexander received a distinctly unfavorable impression of the White House. "The servant that opened the door," he wrote, "looked more like a street beggar than a porter to the President of the United States. He showed us into a neat little parlor, but the furniture was not magnificent." Taylor greeted them courteously with the words, "Gentlemen, I am at your service," but his manner was distant. As Alexander put it in the callow idiom of youth, "the old fellow's mind seemed to be on other subjects, besides receiving visitors." Taylor was in fact distraught with the slavery crisis, and, by nature a hospitable person, he dissipated his energies by receiving hundreds of callers. At the moment he was on the brink of physical exhaustion and only five weeks from his grave. It is possible also that as a slave-owning southerner he was somewhat disconcerted by the appearance of two brown-skinned Hawaiian youths. Nonetheless, he remained affable. He assured Dr. Judd that the United States would intervene in the French dispute, and he promised to make a three-way pact with England and France to arbitrate any future difficulties. (Only the first promise was kept.) Toward the end of the interview, which lasted only 15 minutes, the conversation languished, and, as his callers left, the President told Judd to settle the details with Clayton.[21]

Accordingly, Dr. Judd and Jarves sent a formal note to Clayton stating that England had promised to intercede with France and asking for similar action on the part of the United States. Clayton replied on June 3 that the United States would do everything possible to settle the dispute. Dr. Judd jubilantly sent copies of the correspondence to Palmerston. A month later Clayton instructed William C. Rives, the United States ambassador in Paris, to try to arrange an accomodation with the French government.[22]

At Clayton's invitation they attended on May 31 the funeral of Franklin Harper Elmore, Calhoun's successor as senator from South Carolina. Wilkes advised them to wear court dress, complete with swords and cocked hats, as was customary in the Islands on such occasions. But the rest of the diplomatic corps dressed informally, and their "superb court suits," as a newspaper noted, made them

Dr. Judd with Prince Lot and Prince Alexander

conspicuous among the mourners. President Taylor was present and spoke to them briefly.[23]

In the evening they went to a reception at the White House, where Taylor appeared "in a plain citizen's dress." Here they met Dillon, the author of the French spoilations, who had followed them from New York. Dillon introduced them to the French ambassador, and tried vainly to persuade Dr. Judd to reopen the negotiation. Prince Alexander took especial pains to snub him.[24]

On the morning of June 1 Dr. Judd and the princes went with Wilkes to the Patent Office and Smithsonian Museum. Thomas Ewbank, the inventor, at that time commissioner of patents, gave Judd some books and seeds for the Islands, and at the museum he located the lava cake which Judd had taken from the Kilauea crater nine years before.[25]

The same day, he and Jarves called on Sir Henry Bulwer, the British ambassador in Washington. In his report to Palmerston, Bulwer enclosed a copy of Jarves' treaty with the United States and stated:

The doctor is anxious that the two Governments of France and Great Britain should enter into similar Treaties, and that the three Governments should agree that whenever any difference may arise between either of them and the Hawaiian Government, the other two Governments should decide such difference. I understand that if France persist in her claims, there is an intention on the part of the Sandwich Islands to endeavour to place himself under the protection of this government [the United States], but I have not ascertained that this government has made any promise to afford such protection should it be asked.[26]

The conversation has more than routine interest. For the first time on his diplomatic mission Dr. Judd took advantage of his secret instructions and intimated that the Islands might seek annexation by the United States.

For the most part their stay in Washington passed pleasantly. Bulwer invited them to dinner. Wilkes gave a party for them. They called on Daniel Webster, and found him, in Dr. Judd's words, "more formal, cold, and stiff than any lord in Europe." The princes made a consistently good impression. Frederick Seward commented, "They were educated, erect, graceful, and were royal princes. Washington society was disposed to adore their rank, but balked at their complexion. It was feared they might be 'black.' "[27]

The princes' dark coloring led to a singularly ugly episode on the morning of June 4, as they boarded a train for Baltimore. While Dr. Judd was checking the baggage, a conductor "uncerimoniously" ordered Alexander out of the railway car. In his journal Alexander wrote that the conductor had "probably taken me for somebody's servant, just because I had a darker skin than he had. Confounded fool." Alexander protested indignantly until Dr. Judd hurried into the car and made the necessary explanations. Somewhat later, on a Hudson River boat, the princes were refused admittance to the dining salon. In later years, when he had come to favor Hawaii's annexation by the United States, Dr. Judd did his best to make light of both episodes. He insisted that the railway car was reserved for women and that the princes were excluded from the steamboat salon merely because they were too late for the first sitting. But Alexander, in particular, attributed the incidents to American color prejudice. As early as 1845 he had heard from William Richards that Haalilio had been mistaken for a negro in the United States and refused a seat on a boat. After having been cordially received in both England and France the princes developed a violent anti-American prejudice. "I must state," Alexander wrote in his journal, "that I am di[s]appointed at the Americans." In consequence, when he came to the throne in 1854 he was strongly pro-British, and he opposed strenuously proposals to annex the Islands to the United States.[28]

Soon enough the story passed into the realm of myth. One version stated that the princes were actually turned out of the railway carriage. According to another account, an Irish waiter insulted them on a steamboat ascending the Connecticut River. A third had it that they were reviled as "niggers" on an omnibus in New York. A fourth related that the rudeness of his countrymen so grieved Dr. Judd that he burst into tears. Because of its dramatic quality and political import the story received wide currency for many years to come.[29]

At Baltimore they boarded the steamer *George Washington* for Philadelphia. To their great annoyance, Dillon took the same ship and followed them all the way to New York. Here Thomas Hastings and Dr. Judd conferred at length about bringing Dr. Judd's mother, widowed since 1845 and now in her late sixties, back from the Michigan frontier to Clinton.[30]

The high point in their stay in New York came on June 10, when with Jarves they attended as guests of honor the splendid *fête champetre* given by Mr. and Mrs. Charles G. Carleton at Clifton, their estate on Staten Island. Well over a thousand guests were invited. When the company had assembled, Mrs. Carleton, wearing a white satin gown overlaid with lace, made a dramatic entrance with Prince Alexander, who wore the Hawaiian royal uniform of dark blue cloth ornamented in gold with a taro-leaf design. After a salute of twenty-one guns the band began to play for dancing. "A fairy scene!" Dr. Judd commented. "A galaxy of beauty!" But he added soberly, "The lady of the mansion, the star of the evening, fairly led one of the princes captive by her charms. I did not enjoy it. Sword and cocked hat, worn on the occasion by particular request, precluded every idea of comfort." They spent the night in a cottage on the estate grounds beside a miniature lake. The next morning they ate an elegant *déjeuner à la fourchette* in a party of sixteen, to the accompaniment of more music from the dance orchestra.[31]

That same day they had a boat ride up the Hudson River. At Albany early the next morning they took "the cars" (the train) to Buffalo. After a side trip to Niagara Falls, they boarded a lake steamer and on the evening of June 14 reached Detroit, at that time a fast-growing frontier town with a population of 21,000. Dr. Judd's brother, the Reverend William Pitt Judd, a Methodist minister, met them at the wharf. Early on the morning of the 15th they took "the cars" from Detroit to nearby Royal Oak and there hired a lumber wagon. In this conveyance they rode about ten miles, to the farm of Dr. Judd's other brother, Henry Augustus, just outside the village of Troy. Here Dr. Judd saw his mother after a separation of 23 years. Alexander wept at the scene. "Mr. J.," he noted, "was in tears most of the afternoon."

During the next week Dr. Judd made the most of the family reunion. The small farmhouse echoed with the shrill cries of the children, and the animated conversation of the adults was punctuated with laughter and tears. On Sunday the 16th, the day after

Betsey Hastings Judd in later years

their arrival, they went to church both morning and afternoon. On Monday the princes were taken on a hunting trip to nearby Rochester, and the next day they had a picnic at Orchard Lake. Dr. Judd spent long hours talking with his mother, his sister Harriet, his two brothers, and his Uncle Charles Hastings. By the end of the week his mother and Harriet had agreed to leave Michigan for the Islands in the fall.

As the weekend approached, the family group proceeded by lumber wagon and "the cars" to Detroit. Sunday afternoon they attended worship at William Pitt Judd's church. Alexander noted candidly, "He appeared very well, though I thought his voice rather weak." The next day, June 24, Dr. Judd and the princes made their farewells and boarded the lake steamer for the trip back to New York.

They stopped briefly in Buffalo, where they sat for daguerreotypes and saw Dr. Judd's uncle, Orlando Hastings. From Buffalo they proceeded to Sackett's Harbor, where Dr. Judd called on his sister-in-law, Sybil Fish Tracy, and from there to Watertown and by stage coach to Rome. They reached Utica on Saturday morning, June 29, and went directly to Clinton to the home of Dr. Judd's uncle, Dr. Seth Hastings, Jr. Here, friends and family clustered around them, and with mounting emotions Dr. Judd renewed friendships from the days of his youth. Certainly he was moved when he went to Paris Hill to see the white frame house of his birth still standing, as it does today, on the Sauquoit Road facing the village green.[32]

In Clinton arrangements were made for him to receive from Hamilton College an honorary degree of Master of Arts, awarded to him *in absentia* at the commencement exercises on July 24.[33]

He also dined with his old friend, the Reverend James Robert Boyd, chaplain of the college. Dr. Boyd's daughter Agnes, who later became Judd's daughter-in-law, was present as a child of six and has preserved an anecdote of the occasion which has been often repeated. By mistake the princes received children's bibs instead of napkins at the table—a situation which cause much merriment until Mrs. Boyd told Peter, "the waiter man," to replace them. "I well remember these young princes," the account continues, "how well they appeared, how nicely they spoke, how happy they seemed to be in our delightful home next to the college—and seemed to feel at home in our family. They were dark complexioned—but had charming manners. We little childern just loved them, and felt sorry when the time came for them to say goodbye."[34]

On their return to New York City they stayed again at the Irving House. A few days after their arrival they received word that the municipal authorities of Brooklyn wished to offer them the hospitality of the city. Accordingly, on July 11 they received a public welcome by Mayor Samuel Smith. Afterwards they visited Greenwood Cemetery, and in company with the city officials proceeded to Coney Island for a swim. The princes responded eagerly to the salt water. One of them, according to a newspaper account, "swam like a fish." Afterwards they sat down to a banquet at the Ocean House. After a speech by his cousin, Samuel George Arnold, Dr. Judd spoke at length about the Islands, "concluding with the remark that he knew of no similar example of progress in the history of the world."[35]

Four days later they were at sea, heading south on board the steamer *Georgia*, with their passage paid by the steamship line. After stopping at Havana, where Dr. Judd learned that slaves cost $500 apiece, they landed at Chagres on the Isthmus and reached Panama on July 29.[36]

At Panama he met Emile Perrin, who had arrived the day before from France. Perrin told him flatly that France had refused England's offer of good offices, that Palmerston condemned the Hawaiian cause, and that within six weeks he (Perrin) would board a French warship for the Islands, to settle the dispute by armed force.

As it happened, Perrin was bluffing, in the belief (as he reported in an official dispatch) that he might obtain concessions from the Hawaiian government by threats and intimidation. He had, in fact, positive orders not to take coercive action without further instructions from the French foreign office. A few months later La Hitte so informed Normanby, and added significantly that "it was not necessary Mr. Judd should know this positively, as it might make him more difficult as to accepting a reasonable accomodation." La Hitte also assured the United States ambassador that France had no intention of menacing Hawaii's independence. Satisfied that France would not seize the Islands, Palmerston adopted a neutral attitude and gave orders that neither the Hawaiian government nor the British consul in Honolulu be informed of France's real intentions.

Dr. Judd, of course, knew nothing of Perrin's instructions nor of the French policy from which they proceeded, and Perrin's blustering attitude threw him into a panic. He told Perrin defiantly that if France used force, another flag, obviously that of the United States, would fly over the Hawaiian Islands—a statement in keeping with his suggestion to Bulwer in Washington two months before.[37]

After he left Perrin he wondered momentarily if he should not return to Washington, but thought better of it. Instead, he wrote four agitated letters: to Palmerston, Clayton, Jarves, and Rufus Anderson, asking for their help in obtaining British and American naval forces to defend Hawaii from the anticipated French invasion.[38]

After an absence of two days less than a year, he reached Honolulu by way of San Francisco on September 9[39] with the sad realization that his diplomatic mission had been in part a failure. He had signed a treaty with the United States which contributed to the definitive treaty which Jarves negotiated, and from Secretary Clayton he had the promise of the good offices of the United States in the French dispute. With Palmerston he had had preliminary talks about negotiating a new treaty with England, and Palmerston had promised to use England's good offices with France. But he had not been able to reach an understanding with the French government, and after talking with Perrin he had grave doubts that an armed conflict could be avoided.

Above all, he was gradually coming to the conclusion that France had malevolent designs on the Islands, that England would do little to help, and that Hawaii's true destiny lay in annexation by the United States.

Three Troubled Years

Judd's homecoming after a year's absence evoked profound emotion in the family circle. Mrs. Judd, especially, had worried about him. On a Sunday morning in March, when a ship had approached the harbor with the flag at half mast, she had become, Mrs. Bates reported, "greatly excited, fearing some sad news." Now, safe and in good health, he returned to Sweet Home. "There he sat," his daughter Nellie wrote in her journal, "the family around him crying and laughing. He looks the same as ever, more fleshy perhaps, wears glasses . . ." He had in fact gained about twenty pounds, as he had gained weight as a young man on the *Parthian* on his first voyage to the Islands.[1]

During his absence, as he soon discovered, some annoying changes had taken place. On July 10, 1850, a law proposed by Judge Lee was passed permitting aliens to hold land in fee simple.[2] This legislation represented a reversal of Dr. Judd's cherished land policy. Also there was a noticeable relaxation in Hawaii's temperance movement. With Wyllie's approval, the king openly served wine at the palace. "It would not have been so," Nellie Judd wrote sadly in her journal, "if father had been here; it will most break his heart." But on the whole Dr. Judd could conclude that the political situation remained much as before.[3]

He had no reason to suspect Wyllie's intentions. In a private letter to Wyllie written shortly after his departure he had signed himself "Your affectionate friend," and while he was away Wyllie had maintained cordial social relations with the Judd family. On October 8 Judd dined at Wyllie's house. Four days later, in a friendly letter, he acknowledged receipt of Wyllie's report on his diplomatic mission, which he promised to read with care. He was totally unprepared for the blow which he was about to receive. On October 14, after he had read the report, he wrote Wyllie an agitated note containing only two sentences. "I return the report in order that you may *bring it forward today* as I consider it a matter of *urgency*. You can have no idea how anxious I am to have the accounts passed so that they may be entered on the books."[4]

Wyllie attacked the mission abroad as a failure. He admitted that possibly no one else could have succeeded with the French and that Perrin's conduct left much to be desired, but he reproached Judd for not demanding interest on the $20,000 impounded by Laplace in 1839, for having dealt with subordinates in the French foreign office, and for having abruptly broken off the negotiation. He added that under the circumstances Judd was not entitled to a vote of thanks by the cabinet. The vindictive spirit in which the report was conceived shows clearly in Wyllie's notes.

Mr. Judd recommended himself for the mission, attached princes of the kingdom to it . . . was ordered to begin his negotiations in Washington, and end them in Paris, but began them in Paris and ended them in Washington, received abundant supplies of money, and expended it just as it pleased himself . . . bolted right off from Paris just as he had commenced negotiations in due form . . . bolted off from London without waiting to give facts to Lord Palmerston in aid of British mediation. . . . My report applauds his zeal in undertaking the mission, and places in a prominent point of view the sacrifices that he made in abandoning his family to undertake it, but I have yet to learn that he deserves praise for anything else.[5]

In private correspondence Wyllie stated, "Nothing was achieved by the mission to Europe. Mr. Judd, not knowing diplomatic usages, did not observe them. . . . I think with more temper, patronage, and courtesy, Mr. Judd might have settled all in Paris, but he bolted off with an abruptness, and omission of diplomatic courtesy, which I much regret."[6]

On October 17 the report came before the cabinet council, consisting of Judd, Wyllie, Richard Armstrong, and John Young, with the government law officers, Judge Lee and Bates, present by request. At the meeting Dr. Judd, who was capable of terrible anger upon occasion, could barely control his emotions. With tears of rage he accused Wyllie of drawing the report in a spirit of hostility, and added, "The fact is, I cannot do business with one towards whom I have lost confidence. I shall therefore retire." Wyllie, on his part, complained that Dr. Judd "upbraids me as a returning envoy never upbraided a minister of foreign relations before." At a meeting of the same group the next day both men stood their ground. Judd insisted with equal vigor that he must submit his report to the king.[7]

Few further details are available. The pages in the journal of Judd's daughter Elizabeth are significantly missing for the entries between October 18 and 22, presumably confiscated by some member of the family in a gesture of pious censorship. But it is certain that the rupture between the two men was explosive. It had the result of weakening Dr. Judd's position in the government, for Judge Lee, a man of first abilities, sided with Wyllie in the dispute.

Unfortunately there exists a breach in our cabinet. The slumbering fires of the old discord broke out afresh on Judd's return. . . . While abroad he got a foolish notion into his head, that he could displace W[yllie] and get the king to call on him to form a new cabinet à l'Anglaise. I told him . . . that any step of the kind would be wrong, and end in his own ruin. Nevertheless, he gave my advice no heed, and told the cabinet he or Mr. Wyllie must resign. The result is, that he has put himself in a fix. He will not resign, and can hardly stay where he is with honor. Just now, all is quiet between them, but the wound will never be healed. Judd is decidedly in the wrong, and I have told him so, but cannot make him see his error.[8]

Meanwhile, Dr. Judd attended to a number of personal matters. On September 30 he obtained an alodial title to the twenty-two acres of land in Pawaa on the Waikiki plain, which he had received some ten years before in recognition of his medical services. The same day he instituted proceedings to buy about six hundred acres of land at Hana, Maui, at $1.00 an acre for sugar land and fifty cents an acre for pasture. On November 20, for $1,300, he bought from the government 622 acres at Kualoa on the windward side of Oahu. In succeeding years he devoted considerable attention to the Kualoa farm. Even before the end of 1850 his daughter Elizabeth observed that both her parents were "enchanted" with it.[9] Dr. Judd's purchases of land gave rise to a number of vicious rumors. According to one account, which is little short of a polemic, he was reputed to have bought 17,000 acres for only fifty cents.[10]

He also took time to grow Hawaii's first royal palm (*oreodoxa regia*) from a seed which he had obtained in Kingston, Jamaica. Family tradition has it that his wife found the seed in his coat pocket after his return. He planted it in the yard of his brother-in-law Bates on Nuuanu Avenue, now the site of the Sacred Hearts Convent. Fourteen years later the American naturalist, Horace Mann, inspected the tree, which he described as large, and took a flower from it.[11]

From Havana Dr. Judd brought to the Islands the water lily, which received much praise when his wife entered it in the exhibition of the Royal Hawaiian Agricultural Society in 1853. This organization, founded during his absence in the summer of 1850, received his enthusiastic support. In 1852, at its annual exhibition, he won prizes (reminiscent of his father's prize for potatoes many years before in western New York) for the best mare, ducks, and asparagus on Oahu.[12] That same year he planted a large number of fruit trees from Oregon.[13]

But, for the most part, the pressure of public business occupied his attention. On December 13 Perrin arrived in Honolulu on the French warship *La Serieuse*. The Hawaiian government awaited him with dread. As Armstrong expressed it, "Dr. Judd had no success, and we may expect another armed negotiation. In God is our trust. . . ."[14] In the conversations which followed, Perrin adopted a threatening attitude and spoke ominously of being "obliged to resort to the extraordinary powers," which in fact he did not possess. On February 1, 1851, he presented ten demands substantially the

Sweet Home, built in 1847, at the corner of Judd and Nuuanu, Honolulu

same as those of Dillon and De Tromelin in 1849, and his blustering manner, along with the presence of a French man-of-war, created a near panic in the Hawaiian government.

At a special meeting on March 10 the privy council resolved to ask the British consul, William Miller, if he could pledge the protection of his government in the event of hostilities with France. Miller, who lacked specific instructions in the matter, evaded the question and declared, on the basis of a talk with Perrin, that France's intentions were not hostile. At the same time, with an oblique reference to American color prejudice, he warned the king against annexation to the United States.

Miller's assurances failed to dispel the panic on the part of the Hawaiian authorities. On March 11 the king, chiefs, and ministers, in a mood of despondency, prepared a document putting the Islands under the protection of the United States. The next day Dr. Judd and John Young called on Luther Severance, the new United States commissioner, showed him the document, and left it with him in a sealed envelope bearing the request that the document be acted upon "in case the flag of the United States is raised above the Hawaiian." Severance assured them unofficially that if the United States flag were raised it would be defended.

Perrin soon learned that the Hawaiian government had taken drastic steps to protect itself, and, in a more conciliatory frame of mind, he signed on March 25 a declaration settling part of the French demands. Thereafter, the French threat diminished, in large measure because of continuing British and American diplomatic pressure, but a final settlement was not reached until 1859. The signature of a treaty with England on July 10, 1851, based on the United States treaty of 1849, further strengthened the Hawaiian position.

But in March, 1851, the Hawaiian authorities had no way of forecasting the turn of future events, and the panic continued. On March 28, after a cabinet meeting, the king ordered Wyllie to draw up with Severance a permanent plan for the protection of the Islands. This plan, signed three days later, called for a protectorate jointly by France, England, and the United States, or by England and the United States, or by the United States alone. Failing a protectorate, the plan offered to cede the Islands to the United States.

The king made no secret of the fact that he found his sovereignty burdensome, and he talked repeatedly of abdicating. Severance strongly urged annexation. "We must not *take* the Islands," he wrote, "in virtue of the 'manifest destiny' principle, but can we not accept their voluntary offer? Who has a right to forbid the banns?"

Dr. Judd also favored annexation. "Will the United States," he wrote, "in these circumstances refuse the offer about to be made them? If they do the responsibility for the consequences must rest upon them, and they must not blame the Islands." He feared besides that the diplomatic agents of England and France, bound by the agreement of 1843 to respect Hawaii's independence, might thwart annexation by conspiring to bring about a seizure by Russia.[15]

The proposals of the Hawaiian government were taken to Washington by the American consul, Elisha H. Allen. But Daniel Webster, secretary of state in Fillmore's administration, was opposed to further territorial expansion. Accordingly, he rejected the Hawaiian proposals and instructed Severance to return the emergency cession statement of the previous March. Webster promised, however, as Clayton had promised the year before, to support the independence of the Islands, if necessary with armed force.[16]

Throughout the tortuous diplomatic proceedings, Dr. Judd managed to maintain a dominant position in the administration, in some measure because of his control of government finances, even though, as Miller observed, the fact that aliens could now buy land in fee simple had diminished his patronage. His quarrel with Wyllie, temporarily set aside during the French troubles, continued to smolder under the surface. Judge Lee, while professing impartiality, still favored Wyllie. In October, 1851, he wrote,

Judd has a great advantage in his knowledge of the native language, and is bold and cunning, but in mind and heart, in all that is generous, liberal, and manly, Wyllie is far his superior. I take sides with neither, though I like Wyllie best. . . . Ever since Judd came home he has been uneasy and dissatisfied. His arbitrary temper, his wounded pride, his hate of all rivals, his solicitude to promote his relatives, and his ambition to preside over the department of the interior, all conspire to render his position grievous to himself and his friends.[17]

Further trouble with Wyllie developed in the fall of 1851, when the king appointed Dr. Judd to the commission to draft a new constitution. Both Wyllie and Lee believed that the king had at first named Wyllie as commissioner, and that Judd had used his influence with the king to have Wyllie displaced. The draft of the new constitution, mainly the work of Lee, contained a paragraph which Wyllie suggested, excluding clergymen from the House of Representatives.[18] In the spring of 1852 Judd and Armstrong managed to defeat this proposal. Significantly, Prince Alexander supported Wyllie against Judd in the dispute.[19]

At this time Dr. Judd became involved in a long series of personality clashes. Prominent among his opponents was Dr. George A. Lathrop, a physician and druggist who had come to Honolulu in the late 1840s. In the fall of 1851 Lathrop operated a sugar plantation at Kaneohe, on windward Oahu, on taro lands leased from Paki, a leading chief. A misunderstanding about the lease arose, and in a lawsuit, in which Dr. Judd and two others acted as judges, Lathrop lost the land. Armstrong, who testified against him, believed that Lathrop was guilty of fraud. A few months later Lathrop was refused a loan of $3,000 by the privy council, even though (as he was well aware) only a week before a loan in the same amount was granted to Aaron B. Howe, who was then courting Nellie Judd. In October, 1852, Lathrop requested permission to import some liquor for medicinal purposes at a nominal tariff. Dr. Judd refused the request on the ground that Lathrop made a practise of serving liquor to customers in his drug store. Lathrop became so incensed that he brought the matter before the House of Representatives in May, 1853, in a petition stating that Dr. Judd had acted from personal motives. After investigation the House decided in Judd's favor.[20]

An equally complex and protracted dispute arose in October, 1851, when Dr. Judd dismissed his clerk, William Jarrett, for drunkenness. He later accused Jarrett of having embezzled over $2,000, but at the trial Wyllie, Charles G. Hopkins, and George M. Robertson testified on Jarrett's behalf, and the verdict was not guilty. The whole affair was vexatious to an extreme. The House of Representatives in May and June, 1852, conducted a detailed investigation of the finance department report. Dr. Judd, as minister of finance, was held responsible for a deficiency of $2,930.44 on the treasury books, and he was not released from the obligation until 1859. At the investigation Jarrett accused him of fraud. It was stated also that in August, 1851, in connivance with John Young, minister of the interior, Dr. Judd bought up the government horses on Kauai at a nominal figure and resold them at a substantial personal profit. Wyllie, who made much of the affair, believed that Judd realized upwards of $3,000 on the transaction. It is a matter of record that Judd bought the horses and that his son Charles sold them at auction, but no evidence has appeared to substantiate Wyllie's accusation of venality. Nonetheless, feeling rose high. Dr. Judd incurred further bitter criticism when he proposed his son Charles as auditor of the public accounts to fill the vacancy created by Jarrett's dismissal.[21]

In the spring of 1852 he engaged in a paper war with George M. Robertson, at that time speaker of the House of Representatives, and with Godfrey Rhodes, an Englishman with violent anti-American feelings, at that time chairman of the House's committee on accounts. The dispute centered around Dr. Judd's refusal to pay from the treasury a draft of the committee on accounts. The correspondence on both sides was terse and unconciliatory.[22]

About a year later his long-standing quarrel with Wyllie erupted again over his refusal to honor an item of $9.06 in Wyllie's official account. In a stinging letter Wyllie reproached him with "incivility" and "great official rudeness." Wyllie added, "Whatever defects I may have, and they are too many, I have not that of taking a narrow, technical or illiberal view of things, nor even, under provocation, of conducting intercourse with my colleagues or others, on the system of *snip, snub,* and *snarl.*"[23]

In June, 1853, he had an even more violent altercation with Dr. Wesley Newcomb, who stormed into the finance office and accused him of having put Dr. William Hillebrand (Newcomb's son-in-law) under arrest in the fort. The charge, as it turned out, was correct only in part. Some constables had detained Hillebrand for a minor infraction, but he was not in the fort. Nonetheless, Newcomb became so abusive that Dr. Judd ordered him out of the office. As Newcomb left he threatened Judd with physical violence of an undignified nature the next time they should meet.[24]

On two occasions after his return from Europe Dr. Judd faced mob violence. On the night of October 22, 1851, a group of native prisoners escaped from the fort, took the battery and magazine on Punch Bowl Hill, which commanded the town, and tried to turn the cannon on two churches and Sweet Home. According to William Miller, they threatened to hang both Armstrong and Judd.[25] On the night of November 10, 1852, after a riot in which a sailor was killed by the police, about fifty drunken crew members from the whaling fleet marched up Nuuanu Valley to do violence to Dr. Judd. According to the account of William Cooper Parke, Hawaii's marshal at the time, "the road was long and dark, turning out to be longer than they thought, and some dropped out, so that by the time they reached their destination there were not many left. Dr. Judd had received word that the sailors were on their way; his family went to one of the neighbors for safety, while the Doctor and a few others remained on the verandah; the sailors came as far as the gate, and after making threats as to what they would do, finally went away."[26]

It is apparent that Dr. Judd was fast approaching physical and psychic exhaustion. The turbulence in the political atmosphere made him irritable, and he dealt so brusquely with his various opponents that he created for himself considerable ill will. In the end his adversaries joined forces to drive him from office.

Retirement from Office

In the spring of 1853 smallpox came to Honolulu. The disease struck with epidemic force and in a matter of months decimated the native population. Mrs. Judd wrote,

It is sickening to recall those days, when a little patch of yellow calico, waving on a pole, indicated pestilence and suffering within. The Board of Health and undertakers were busy men. Physicians and the visiting committee bowed down and became at times utterly prostrate in their untiring efforts by night and by day to dispense medicine, food, and comfort. The Pale Horse and his rider strode on, counting the vanquished by thousands, in spite of human effort, till the destroying angel had finished his work.[1]

In this atmosphere of devastation Honolulu's simmering resentments boiled over. In the end, and after a titanic struggle, Judd was forced to resign from the government.

The first case of smallpox appeared in February on the American clipper ship *Charles Mallory*, which stopped at Honolulu en route from San Francisco to China. At once the privy council took drastic action. On the 14th Dr. Judd was instructed to confer with the resident physicians in Honolulu and to report recommendations to check the spread of the disease. Wyllie (who had a medical education) and most of the resident physicians proposed inoculation with virus taken from a smallpox sufferer, while Dr. Judd, following the procedure devised by Charles Jenner which is now universally adopted, recommended vaccination with cowpox. At that time a controversy existed in medical circles over the proper treatment. Because of variations and inadequacies in the material used, vaccination was not uniformly successful, and many doctors then preferred inoculation. The Honolulu physicians offered to inoculate all the natives on Oahu at ten cents apiece, to be paid by the government, but Dr. Judd refused the offer. On the 15th, after the report had been read, the privy council instructed Armstrong to superintend vaccination throughout the Islands, and Dr. Judd received orders to make plans for a quarantine station.[2]

At the same time Dr. Judd, although obviously lacking in previous experience, did what he could to produce vaccine. He wrote to Dr. Baldwin on the 24th,

I am ashamed to own that I have vaccinated a cow and kept her tied up to a tree through the late storm and found at the end of ten days no effect. I say I am ashamed, 1st because I find by reference to books, lately written that passing V. virus through the cow weakens it, but that after a time by repeated changes from one human system to another it will be restored to its pristine vigor. 2d because we have in Honolulu the very best of vaccine matter taken from babies with white skins. Brother Lowell Smith and Dr. Newcomb and ?? [sic] to the contrary notwithstanding.[3]

The *Charles Mallory* meanwhile lay under a strict quarantine for fourteen days, and for a time it appeared that the danger had passed. But in May, apparently from another source—possibly infected clothes sold to natives at auction—the contagion recurred. On the 16th Dr. Judd, Dr. Rooke, and Marshall Parke were appointed health commissioners to fight the epidemic. Their efforts, while valiant, proved ineffective. Crude hospitals were improvised, and the natives for the most part refused to co-operate. "My father worked day and night," Elizabeth Judd wrote, "until he became a mere shadow. The Hawaiians were just superstitious and ignorant enough to be unmanageable. Hundreds lost their lives because they bathed in the sea or sat in the wind to cool their fever."[4]

On Monday evening, July 18, a number of merchants and others, fearful that the smallpox might do irreparable damage to the economy of the Islands, especially if it were not checked before the arrival of the fall whaling fleet, called a public meeting at the courthouse to consider further measures to fight the disease. Judd, Armstrong, Lee, Bates, and a number of others made speeches. The meeting appointed a committee of twelve, with all the physicians members ex officio, to frame further recommendations. On Tuesday evening the committee proposed and the meeting passed seven resolutions on such matters as hospitals, vaccination, and burial methods. Dr. Lathrop then stood up and read resolutions directly attacking Armstrong and Judd.

The political implications in Lathrop's remarks were all too evident, and the meeting immediately adjourned. Lathrop's act appalled Judge Lee, who stated, "I cannot but think this political movement a most indiscreet and ill-timed one. It is the general feeling, that it is no time to light the flames of discord when our people are dying on every side, and the utmost harmony and union of action is necessary to save them."[5]

But the flames of discord, once lighted, could not be extinguished. The next day, July 20, a notice was posted calling a third meeting at the courthouse at 7:30 that evening, to discuss Lathrop's resolutions. Dr. Newcomb presided. After much oratory the meeting voted that Armstrong and Judd "most wickedly" neglected to protect the Islands from the epidemic, especially because of the refusal to authorize the resident physicians to immunize the natives at government expense. A committee of thirteen was chosen to get signatures to a petition asking the king to dismiss Armstrong and Judd from the government. The petition accused them of "inefficiency and misdeeds . . . selfish cupidity, political imbecility, and malfeasance in office." It stated further that thousands of people had died because of their "criminal parsimony and neglect."[6]

When presented, this petition had the signatures of more than two hundred white residents and more than twelve thousand natives. Some of the residents, including William Ladd (of the former firm of Ladd & Co.), Dr. Lathrop, and Dr. Newcomb, had personal reasons to seek revenge on Dr. Judd. Others in the commercial interest, such as Stephen Reynolds, objected to the strict religious and equally strict temperance principles of both Armstrong and Judd, whom they identified with the still strong missionary group. Armstrong stated, "the most of them, I think, are actuated by a dislike to missionary influence in the government." Luther Severance, the American commissioner, reported:

The active leaders in this movement at this time are two or three physicians and their personal friends who have personal grudges to be revenged, backed up by several persons who have been disappointed applicants for offices or favors—none of them influenced much by any public considerations, but finding it easy to rally the old anti-missionary opposition, and equally easy to obtain the signatures of the brandy drinkers. . . . This is the ruling motive with two-thirds the foreign resident signers. . . . The native names are mostly spurious or obtained by fraud.

In a later letter Severance added:

Two thirds of the white men who have signed the petition for removal, know no more of the facts they allege, or how the ministers have performed their duties, than they do about the parlor furniture of the Seventh Heaven of Mahomet. They are governed more by a desire to get cheaper liquor than any elevated political considerations.

Nonetheless, some men of character and reputation in the community, such as John Mott Smith, later the minister of finance under Kamehameha V, signed the document. It would be unrealistic to dismiss the signatories as representing entirely a disreputable and disgruntled element.[7]

On July 25 another public meeting was held in the Kawaiahao Church. John Ii presided and Governor Kekuanaoa acted as secretary. This meeting adopted resolutions in favor of Armstrong and Judd, and drew up a petition, eventually signed by a thousand persons, to retain them in office. Notice was taken of a rumor that Armstrong and Judd had accepted bribes to introduce the epidemic to the Islands. As political emotionalism reached its climax, both men were in physical danger. There was even talk of casting Dr. Judd adrift at midnight in an open boat without oars, water, or food.[8]

Both petitions came before the cabinet on August 3, with Bates, Lee, and Prince Alexander present by request. Wyllie suggested, and John Young agreed, that, since the matter concerned all the cabinet members, the ministers should not be judges in their own cause. Bates, as Dr. Judd's brother-in-law, disqualified himself. Accordingly, the cabinet adjourned and referred the petitions to the privy council (that is, Judge Lee, the king, and chiefs), which resolved to consider the charges on August 8 with the cabinet members present. On the 8th, after some discussion, the privy council appointed a committee of five, consisting of Prince Lot, Governor Kekuanaoa, Lorrin Andrews, John Ii, and J. Piikoi, to examine the petitions. On August 15 the committee reported that, in the petition against Armstrong and Judd, not more than one-twentieth of the native signatures were genuine and that of the 238 white residents who signed only 65 were naturalized citizens. The committee reported further that the charges were unsubstantiated and that no reason existed to dismiss the two ministers.[9]

That evening the opponents of Armstrong and Judd held a mass meeting, at which a resolution was passed demanding their removal from the government. Bates attended and made an impassioned speech in defense of the accused. Wyllie, who was not present, believed at the time and for some years thereafter that this speech united the opposition, which was already becoming discordant. He stated further that Judd could have stood his ground had it not been for Bates's "excessive indiscretion" on this crucial occasion.[10]

At a meeting of the privy council on August 17, John Young, the premier, announced that the king concurred in the findings of the investigating committee. Judd, Armstrong, and Wyllie departed. The king then asked Bates and the council's secretary, Lorrin Andrews, to leave, so that the chiefs might consult among themselves. There remained in the council chamber the king, Prince Alexander, seven chiefs, and Charles Gordon Hopkins, a naturalized citizen of English descent and an honorary member of the privy council, whom the king asked to keep the minutes. One by one, at the king's request, each of the chiefs gave his opinion whether or not the two ministers should be asked to resign.

Kanaina favored the resignation of Judd but not Armstrong.

Haalelea agreed. Prince Alexander proposed that both men should resign in order to forestall future trouble. John Young, one of Dr. Judd's most faithful supporters, thought that the accused were guiltless of the charges in the opposition petition, but added that he himself would resign if even fewer people had petitioned against him. On the other hand Paki, John Ii, and Kaeo opposed granting the petition for dismissal, and Piikoi said that he agreed partly with Paki and partly with Kanaina. The king then announced that he supported Prince Alexander's view, and left the meeting. At this point Prince Alexander put the question whether it was proper to ask the two ministers to resign. Of the eight natives present, four voted on each side of the question. Hopkins then claimed his right to vote, and voted against the ministers.

After the vote Hopkins read the minutes, which were approved and handed to Lorrin Andrews, the regular secretary, to be entered in the council's minute book. But at the next meeting on August 22, when Wyllie called for them, Kekuanaoa and others told him that the king "had ordered the secretary not to record the minutes that were taken while several of the members were absent from the council at his request, as it then was not properly a council." It was found that the minutes as taken by Hopkins, recording the vote against Armstrong and Judd, had been neatly cut from the minute book. Many years later they were found among Andrews' papers, with the endorsement, signed by Andrews and dated August 18, 1853, "This day His Majesty through Prince [Alexander] Lihiliho ordered me not to cut the foregoing minutes from the book." The British consul, William Miller, who gave Wyllie, Prince Alexander, and Hopkins as his informants, reported that after the meeting of August 17 Dr. Judd went to the palace in the evening and saw the king. Miller added his belief that the king was prevailed upon to accept responsibility for removing the minutes.[11]

The available evidence leaves many questions unanswered, but this much appears clear: according to Andrews' notation, the king gave orders on the 18th *not* to cut out the minutes, but by the 22nd he had reversed his position, and the minutes had disappeared. It is certain that the king was wavering. Probably Dr. Judd, as Miller suggested, persuaded him to change his mind.[12]

Meanwhile, as the epidemic still raged, civil disorder increased.

Filibusters in the group opposed to Armstrong and Judd began agitating to overthrow the government with a view, so Severance reported, to seizing the Islands and selling them to the United States. It has been suggested that this element wished to remove the two ministers in order to weaken the government and thus facilitate the scheme of annexation. Part of the agitation consisted of parades and spirited demonstrations, which caused much alarm among responsible government officials.[13]

In order to counter the threat, nineteen respectable residents, including merchants, planters, and representatives of the missionary bloc, petitioned the king for immediate and peaceful annexation to the United States, in order to preserve prosperity and political quiet in the Islands. Signers of the memorial included Charles R. Bishop, Samuel N. Castle, Amos Starr Cooke, Stephen Reynolds, and William H. Rice.[14]

The memorial came before the cabinet on August 22 and was presented to the king in a special meeting of that body at 11 A.M. on the 24th. After the document was read, Dr. Judd announced that he had submitted to the king a proposal received the previous August from Alfred G. Benson of New York to buy the Islands for five million dollars, the sale to take the form of a mortgage which would be foreclosed for nonpayment. The transaction, it was understood, would lead to annexation by the United States. Wyllie, who later represented Dr. Judd's conduct as dishonorable, added that he also had received a communication from Benson on the same subject but had suppressed it because it contained grave personal inculpations against Dr. Judd.[15]

Benson, a shipping magnate, had conferred with Dr. Judd when he and the princes were in the United States three years before. On his return, Judd helped Benson obtain a franchise to build a drydock and marine railway in Honolulu, and he also promoted Benson's project (which was never realized) for a steamship line between Honolulu and San Francisco.[16] In 1852 Judd was named president of the Sandwich Island Steam Company, an interisland shipping project that did not materialize. Available evidence suggests a direct speculative connection between the formation of such steamship companies and the annexation movement.[17] Speculators such as Benson obviously anticipated large profits from their marine franchises, and Judd as a confirmed annexationist was naturally sympathetic to their ventures.

Aside from his correspondence with Benson, Judd had written to Senator William H. Seward, later United States secretary of state, whom he had met in Washington in 1850, to urge the sale of Hawaii's sovereignty to the United States. He also wrote to the editor of San Francisco's *Alta California*, asking that newspaper's help in promoting the annexation scheme. In addition, his brother-in-law Bates had written a letter in favor of annexation, which was published in the New York *Tribune* of June 4.[18] Judd, it may be noted, found support for his views in a number of quarters. Many American newspapers argued hotly for annexation, and in 1852–1853 the annexation question was twice raised in the United States Congress.[19] But his opponents were quick to point out, with varying degrees of acrimony, that his annexation proposal contrasted strangely with his previous agitation for Hawaiian independence.[20]

In particular, Prince Alexander, heir to the throne, threw his whole weight against Dr. Judd and the annexation movement.[21] His experience with color prejudice in the United States had made him rabidly anti-American. Besides, he was ambitious to enjoy the honors and perquisites of kingship. As Mrs. Judd remarked, "He had not yet tasted the sweets of supreme power, nor felt the thorns in the royal crown."[22] Further, he had rebelled against the repressive puritanism of the missionaries, including Judd, who had directed his education. Some years later Judd commented that the prince, "educated by the mission, most of all things dislikes the mission. Having been compelled to be good when a boy, he is determined not to be good as a man. Driven out to morning prayer meeting, Wednesday evening meeting, monthly concert, Sabbath school, long sermons, and daily exhortations, his heart is hardened to a degree unknown to the heathen."[23] For a combination of reasons, therefore, Prince Alexander—and Prince Lot also—urged the king to dismiss Judd from office. In retrospect, Judd attributed his political downfall to their efforts.[24]

Some of the chiefs opposed annexation with equal vigor, and, in consequence, turned against Dr. Judd. The king, in discussing Judd's removal from office, hinted to Armstrong that "the Dr.'s annexation schemes had excited suspicion." Influential chiefs, such as Paki and John Ii, who had been outspoken in his defense at the privy council meeting of August 17, now argued heatedly against his annexation proposals.[25]

Meanwhile the king wavered. In the past he had chafed occasionally under Dr. Judd's regimen of Calvinist morality, but for the most part his attitude remained one of implicit trust bolstered by warm-hearted sentiments of gratitude. At one time he had even proposed that the two princes should marry Judd's daughters, Elizabeth and Helen.[26] But in 1853 he was drinking to excess, as he had been for some years before. One observer described him as "besotted," and the British consul reported that he was seldom fit to be seen.[27] He was obviously in no condition to take a firm stand in a time of uproar and crisis, particularly in view of continuing pressure from the princes and some of the chiefs to dismiss Judd.

On August 24, after the annexation memorial was presented to the privy council, "wearied with turmoil, and overcome with strong drink," as Mrs. Judd put it, he sent Prince Alexander to demand Dr. Judd's resignation. According to Miller's account, "The doctor came to the palace as desired, but did not bring his commission. He promised, however, to do so the next morning; but the alarm having blown over [the promise was not complied with." Mrs. Judd's version in part corroborates Miller's report. "As the royal wish was about to be complied with on the following morning, persons of rank and influence requested him [Dr. Judd] to wait a little, as other counsels were likely to prevail with the king."[28]

For a week the matter hung fire. The opposition kept up an unremitting pressure for the dismissal of the two ministers, while Dr. Judd, so Miller reported, did everything in his power to persuade the king to open a negotiation for annexation.[29]

At a meeting of the privy council on Thursday, September 1, Miller and Perrin protested strongly to the king against annexation as a breach of existing treaties and a violation of international law. Their action threw into the scale the full diplomatic weight of England and France. On Wyllie's motion, the privy council ordered the protest to be printed in the *Polynesian*, and then adjourned until Monday.[30] At this point Dr. Judd's political career was hanging by a thread.

Judge Lee, who had just returned from the island of Hawaii, added his voice to the opposition clamor and advised Dr. Judd's dismissal.[31] At the king's request, Lee recommended Elisha H. Allen (whose term as American consul had just expired) as Judd's successor.[32]

The king, supported by Prince Alexander, then intimated that the entire cabinet should resign. One by the one the ministers sent in their commissions, and Dr. Judd resigned on Saturday, September 3. Two days later all the ministers except Judd were reappointed, and Allen "most reluctantly" became the new minister of finance.[33]

Wyllie asserted positively that he "had no hand whatever" in Judd's resignation, that he first learned of it on Sunday, September 4, and that Judge Lee was the prime mover in bringing it about. However, Wyllie was not above applying indirect pressure. In a letter to Ricord of October 12, 1853 (which does not agree entirely with other reports), he stated that he sent his commission to the king on August 30 with "a strong letter," and that this action "brought things to a crisis."[34] Presumably he intended, or at least hoped, that it should. On September 3 he wrote an official letter to Severance, the United States commissioner, reminding him significantly that Secretary of State Webster had opposed annexation. A few days later he sent a message to the British foreign office in one of Miller's dispatches, arguing, on the basis of early claims, that England would have cause for war if Hawaii were annexed to the United States.[35] It is clear, in spite of his assertions, that Wyllie took positive steps to displace Judd and to frustrate his annexation plans. Wyllie's maneuvering may not have been direct, but it was persistent and, as it happened, effective.

In retrospect, it appears that a number of forces interoperated to bring about Dr. Judd's downfall. His strict missionary principles, especially with respect to liquor, alienated a large segment of the commercial interest. His advocacy of annexation arrayed against him the two princes, many chiefs, and the resident nationals of England and France. Wyllie, and to a lesser extent Judge Lee, had long sought to undermine his position in the cabinet. In addition, the smallpox epidemic created an atmosphere of political hysteria which the king, sunk in alcoholism, could not withstand.

Each of these forces deserves due weight and consideration, but none appears to have been decisive. Armstrong, an equally stern advocate of missionary principles, was retained in the new administration. Bates, who shared Judd's belief in annexation, continued in office, and Elisha H. Allen, the new minister of finance, was an annexationist also. Further, political hysteria, the hostility of Wyllie and Lee, and the alcoholism of the king were recurrent phenomena in the Hawaiian political scene.

In the final analysis, the decisive factor appears to have been psychological. By temperament Dr. Judd was strong-willed, stubborn, and implacably hostile to all who disagreed with him—characteristics which he inherited from his father and which he transmitted to a number of his descendants. Upon occasion, especially in times of crisis when he drove himself to exhaustion, his manner was abrupt and unconciliatory. At such moments, often with the best of intentions, he goaded his opponents to fury.

His bluntness did not escape the notice of contemporary observers. In an official dispatch Severance commented,

The English interest which has been laboring to get out the two American ministers would not have succeeded at all, I think, had it not been for the bitter personal hostility of certain Americans to Dr. Judd. . . . He has been faithful to the king, and has made some enemies by inflexible discharge of duty, more perhaps by doing a right thing in an offensive manner. He lacks the habitual courtesy and amenity of manners, which distinguishes his successor.

Armstrong noted in his journal that Dr. Judd "has been for many years the butt of a fierce opposition in Honolulu; and although faulty in his manner of doing things, and often gives offense unnecessarily, yet injustice is often done him." In a letter to the American Board, Armstrong added, "For years he had been growing more and more unpopular more owing to an offensive way of doing things, than any wrong doing." [36]

Straightaway and, Armstrong felt, with bad taste, the opposition celebrated Dr. Judd's departure from the government. On the 8th the committee of thirteen held a public meeting which, in one of its resolutions, spoke of "the relief of a people from bondage and a malignant tyranny." On the evening of the 10th, Mrs. Judd noted, "a torchlight procession with music and banners paraded the town, and called at the house of the new incumbent, with speeches and hurrahs."[37]

At the same time, the new cabinet called for an immediate investigation of the treasury accounts. Wyllie, for one, believed that the entire fiscal system, which Dr. Judd had devised, was "suicidal" in structure. But on September 24 the investigating committee reported that its members were "agreeably surprised" to find the government finances in sound condition.[38]

Dr. Judd suffered untold anguish at the turn of political events. Wyllie reported that his dismissal came as "a terrible blow" to him, and Judge Lee wrote, "Judd felt the stroke severely, and his family were more deeply wounded than he."[39] Judd believed that the opposition had used dishonorable methods to dislodge him, but his conscience was clear. He later observed to a friend, "that he thought few generals ever came off from so long a campaign with fewer scars or less injury to their uniforms."[40]

Medicine, Guano, and Sugar

A week or so after his departure from office, Dr. Judd went for
a few days to his farm at Kualoa on windward Oahu, where he
engaged in such bucolic chores as burning grassland and taking
an inventory of his livestock.[1] After the political Armageddon
through which he had just passed, the sunny windswept landscape
must have seemed unbelievably peaceful. It provided a welcome
opportunity to take deep breaths of clean country air, to feel the
comforting heat of the sun, to watch the endless procession of
puffy clouds merge with mist on the mountain peaks, perhaps to
bathe in the clear water of the Pacific, and above all to refresh his
body and mind with long nights of unbroken sleep.

When he returned to Honolulu, his most immediate problem
was financial. His salary as minister of finance had risen to $3,000
in 1848 and to $4,000 in 1852.[2] That, of course, ended when he
left office. Aside from the annuity of $1,000 from his wharf rents
he had no additional income to support a wife and eight children.

On October 1, the *Polynesian* published an announcement of his
return to medical practice. Within three weeks he bought Dr. Ford's
drugstore on Kaahumanu Street and advertised that he had for

sale medicines, drugs, patent medicines, and perfumes. The drugstore, the advertisement added, also had a prescription department and a soda fountain. "Dr. Judd has taken hold of his pill box and lancet," commented the Reverend William P. Alexander, "and commenced practising again as physician." By the end of the year, Charles R. Bishop observed, "Doct. Judd is doing a fair business in his profession."[3]

Among his first patients was Donna Maria, the wife of Captain James Ellis Bennett of the whaler *Massachusetts*. The ship had lost a mast in a storm and was delayed in reaching the Islands. On October 27 Mrs. Bennett bore twin sons at sea some forty miles from Honolulu. When the *Massachusetts* reached port the next day, Captain Bennett sent ashore for medical help. Dr. Judd did what he could, but Mrs. Bennett died of puerperal fever on November 2. Dr. Judd offered to care for the twins while Captain Bennett returned to the northern whaling grounds. The babies remained in his household until the fall of 1854, when their father took them back to New England.

The incident has a charming sequel. In the spring of 1855 Captain Bennett married Donna Maria's older sister, who made him promise to give up the sea. The family moved west to Iowa. One of their sons was named Gerrit Judd Bennett in honor of the physician in Honolulu who had sheltered the twins. Many years later one of Judd's grandsons met Dr. and Mrs. Gerrit Judd Bennett in Waterloo, Iowa, and from them heard a story of tragedy, charity, and gratitude which otherwise might have slipped into oblivion.[4]

Meanwhile, Dr. Judd sought desperately to supplement his income. Early in 1852, through Henry Hill of the American Board, he had taken out $9,000 worth of life insurance from the New England Mutual Life Insurance Company of Boston. In June of that year he became that company's representative in Honolulu, and he is believed to have been the first life insurance agent in the Islands.[5] Presumably the venture had limited success, for in the months immediately following his retirement from office he embarked on a variety of other financial enterprises.

Early in 1854 he tried, without success, to obtain a franchise to supply the town and shipping of Honolulu with water.[6] About the same time he made repeated efforts to buy from the queen her

Family cooking stoves, California and Island oats ;
  Jeffries' strong ale, in jugs; octaves Dennis Maurice cognac
  brandy ; sauterne wine, in casks;
      brandy, in cases ; Hollands gin, Port and Madeira
      wines, cherry cordials and liquors, in cases.

Sperm Oil and Whale Oil. 66-tf

DOCTOR'S SHOP.

G. P. JUDD, AT THE CORNER OF FORT
and Merchant Streets, reminds the public that he continues
to devote himself to the treatment of DISEASES of all kinds, having for sale a great variety of DRUGS and MEDICINES of the best
quality. He sells also

Poisons.
  Arsenic, strichnine, veratrine, corrosive sublimate,
  Oxalic acid, St. Ignasius beans, nux vomica. opium,
  Prussic acid, alcohol.

Perfumery.
  Musk, extract musk, cologne, lavender water,
  Windsor, honey and other soaps.

Miscellaneous.
  Sago, pearl barley, oat meal, gum shellac,
  Writing and marking ink, Sands sarsaparilla,
  Soda water, and other articles too numerous to mention.
  ☞ Easily found when wanted.   6-tf.

HONOLULU SOAP WORKS,

BY

W. J. RAWLINS & CO.,

ARE THANKFUL FOR PAST FAVORS,
and are prepared, with their present improvements, to
supply merchants and families with hard and soft soap ; also,
neats foot oil.

  ☞ And always ready to buy or trade for tallow, slush, and
all kinds of kitchen grease.   53-1y

CABINET-MAKING.

THE UNDERSIGNED HAVING ENGAG-
ed the services of an experienced Upholsterer, is now prepared to make to order Spring Beds, Hair, Pulu and Hay Mat-

Advertisement in the Pacific Commercial Advertiser, March 4, 1858

claim to the Waikahalulu reef, which, when filled, might produce extremely valuable waterfront property. According to one report, he felt extremely sensitive about his meager financial resources, and determined to use his influence with the chiefs to make a remunerative speculation.[7]

Although out of office, he still retained much of his former influence with the king and leading chiefs. Only four days after his resignation he so informed Luther Severance, the United States commissioner, and he took pains to tell Severance's successor, David L. Gregg, who arrived in December, 1853, that he could persuade the native rulers to follow almost any course he recommended. Others in Honolulu came to much the same conclusion.[8]

In full knowledge of his continuing influence at court, he sent to the king in council on January 9, 1854, a petition, signed by fifty-six residents, urging annexation to the United States. He was one of the signers. His signature also appeared, along with that of Thomas Spencer, an American merchant, on the formal covering letter which accompanied the petition.[9]

Dr. Judd knew that the king and many chiefs favored annexation. His own views on the subject had not changed since his retirement from office, and throughout 1854 he made strenuous efforts to achieve his objective. His plan included, so Gregg reported, the removal of Wyllie, for, among other considerations, Wyllie remained a steadfast and vociferous advocate of Hawaiian independence. Although the available evidence is far from conclusive, it seems possible that at this time Judd contemplated a return to public life. According to a newspaper rumor in New York, duly reprinted in the Honolulu press, after annexation Dr. Judd and Elisha Allen would be sent to Washington as the two senators of the newly admitted state of Hawaii.[10]

The annexation petition precipitated a bitter political battle. All the latent animosities which had caused Dr. Judd's retirement the previous September erupted anew in an atmosphere of frantic backbiting. The committee of thirteen petitioned the king on January 14 to remove Bates from office.[11] At that time the committee recommended annexation, but a few weeks later it reversed its stand and spoke darkly of overthrowing the government and establishing a republic. Meanwhile, in the United States pressure for annexation continued in Congress and in the press.

The crisis came to a head on February 6, when the king ordered Wyllie to open annexation negotiations with Commissioner Gregg. In the great debate which followed, Dr. Judd took a vigorous part, and evoked furious hostility from his opponents. Early in March, according to Miller's report, John Ii became so enraged that he ordered Judd out of the house. Later that month, at a large meeting in Kawaiahao Church, Dr. Judd spoke eloquently for annexation, but was "hissed into silence," while Ii and Prince Alexander, who urged Hawaiian independence, were "much applauded" by the native audience.[12]

On July 4, while the negotiations proceeded, Gregg made a persuasive speech in favor of annexation, and a number of American residents staged an annexation parade. As Mrs. Judd described it,

A car, decorated with evergreens, in which were seated thirty-two girls of American parentage, dressed in white, wreathed in flowers, each bearing the name of a State on her sash, in large gold letters, was drawn by a power unseen. Next followed "Young America," a company of very young men in uniform, with another triumphal chariot, on which was placed a beautiful boy, the very personification of health, strength, and beauty. "Young Hawaii" was in tow, and represented by a boat gaily trimmed, in which were eight young native lads, fancifully dressed, and carelessly eating sugar cane.[13]

Meanwhile, Dr. Judd repeatedly saw the king, who was impatient to bring the negotiation to a successful conclusion. At one time the king urged Judd to charter a schooner and go with him to Washington, where they could settle the matter on the spot.[14] On August 19 Gregg and Wyllie finished the draft of the annexation treaty, but continuing pressure, particularly from Prince Alexander and the British authorities, prevented its signature.

The matter remained in tense deadlock until mid-November. At that time Gregg told Wyllie of an impending insurrection, and urged for the safety of the Islands that Dr. Judd and two others should immediately persuade the king to sign the treaty.[15] Wyllie believed that Gregg was trying to coerce him, the cabinet stood firm, and the crisis passed. On December 15 the king died, and with the accession to the throne of the pro-British Prince Alexander all hope of annexation disappeared.

For Dr. Judd the affair ended in disappointment and chagrin.

He could expect no political preferment in the new reign, and his various financial speculations had come to nothing. Consequently, since he had a large family to support, he did everything he could to build up and maintain his medical practice.

Early in 1854 he made a post-mortem examination incident to a lawsuit. About the same time he treated Sophie Emerson for an injured hip. In September, 1855, he was in attendance when Dr. Seth Porter Ford removed the entire left breast of Lucy G. Thurston, who had a cancer. The operation lasted almost ninety minutes and was performed without chloroform, since the doctors believed that an anaesthetic would be harmful in view of her former paralysis. Mrs. Thurston, aged sixty at the time, survived the gruesome ordeal and lived another twenty years. In 1859 Dr. Judd used chloroform successfully to deliver his first grandchild, William Chauncey ("Willie") Wilder.[16]

On May 19, 1856, he and nine other physicians signed a petition to incorporate the Hawaiian Medical Socitey, which received its charter on July 19 of the same year.[17] He thus became a charter member, as his father had been a charter member of the Oneida Medical Society in western New York fifty years before.

Gradually his practice increased. By the end of 1855 he could report that he had "a great many" patients, but three years later he voiced a complaint familiar in the medical profession. "Have had a pretty good sum of practice but not many bills paid." At one time he made overtures to Joel Turrill, a former United States consul in Honolulu, for help in receiving an appointment to a projected American hospital, but nothing conclusive seems to have resulted. In the spring of 1856 he tried to raise money by selling some of his land in Nuuanu adjoining the cemetery.[18]

For a time he experimented with diversified farming at Kualoa. As early as 1851 he had sent green corn to market, and two years later he tried, with limited success, to raise melons, sweet potatoes, pineapples, peanuts, rice, grapes, and figs. Nonetheless, his interest in farming continued. At the 1854 meeting of the Royal Hawaiian Agricultural Society he won prizes for the best watermelons and mangoes. The next year he received an award for the best arrowroot. His wife won frequent praise for the flowers which she exhibited, but their gardening skills produced little income, and in 1856 Dr.

Judd leased Kualoa to local Hawaiians. When next he visited it in December, 1857, the natives had neglected the place. "Desolation runs riot," he wrote sadly. "Not much left of its former glory."[19]

During the next five years Dr. Judd engaged actively in the guano trade. Guano consists of the droppings and dead bodies of sea birds which accumulate on islands and coastlines where there is little rainfall. Rich in phosphoric acid and nitrogen compounds, it is extremely valuable as a fertilizer. In the 1840s Peru began to export guano in quantity and in the next decade took steps to exclude foreigners from her guano grounds. At that time, the market price for high quality guano stood at $45.00 a ton.[20] Alfred G. Benson of Brooklyn, formerly interested in shipping concessions in Honolulu, had exported guano from Peru's Lobos (or seal) Islands.[21] When the United States State Department upheld Peru's monopoly, he sought other sources of the valuable commodity. On September 1, 1855, the American Guano Company, of which he was half owner, was organized in New York. A year later this company filed bonded claims, under the terms of the Act of Congress of August 18, 1856, to two uninhabited guano islands: Baker (0-13N, 176-31W), about 1,900 miles southwest of Honolulu, and Jarvis (0-22S, 160-03W), about 1,300 miles due south of Honolulu.[22] In view of their former association, it is not surprising that Dr. Judd soon became involved in Benson's new enterprise as Honolulu agent of the American Guano Company.

On Christmas day, 1856, Dr. Judd's son Charles and Benson's son Arthur left Honolulu in the schooner *Liholiho*. They reached Jarvis on January 15, 1857. The next day they landed and took formal possession of the island on behalf of Alfred G. Benson and his associates. Sailing westward about 1,100 miles they reached Howland (0-48N, 176-38W) on February 5 and nearby Baker on February 10. After taking formal possession of these two islands they returned to Honolulu on March 7 with considerable guano aboard.[23]

Despite a long continuing and much publicized dispute over the quality of guano from Baker, Howland, and Jarvis, Dr. Judd threw himself into the venture with characteristic enthusiasm. He was particularly excited to learn that the samples of the guano which his son Charles had taken on Howland, at one time believed to be worthless, had an extremely high phosphorus content.[24] On Febru-

GUANO!

 ## Ships of Good Capacity

CAN OBTAIN

Return Cargoes, or Advantageous

CHARTERS,

TO LOAD WITH

GUANO AT JARVIS ISLAND

AND PROCEED DIRECT

TO NEW YORK OR ANY OTHER PORT in the United States, that may be agreed on. Moorings to be provided, and the Guano brought within reach of ships' tackles by the Agent on the Island.

For further particulars, freight or charter, apply to the undersigned, at his Office, corner of Fort and Merchant streets, Honolulu. **G. P. JUDD,**
Agent of the AMERICAN GUANO COMPANY.
Honolulu, March 1, 1858. 88–tf

SCHOONER FOR SALE.
THE WELL KNOWN
 ## Schooner Kekauluohi,

Suitable for a Tender to a Whaleship, or for coasting between the Islands. Inquire of **J. W. AUSTIN,**
88–tf Over the Post Office.

NOTICE.

THE UNDERSIGNED INTENDS SOON TO leave this Kingdom, and requests all persons having de-

Advertisement in the Pacific Commercial Advertiser, March 4, 1858

ary 27, 1858, he sent Charles to Jarvis with twenty-one natives and two Chinese in the *John Marshall*, a ship chartered by the American Guano Company. On March 4, in his capacity as agent, he advertised in the Honolulu press that the company would charter ships to take guano from Jarvis to the United States. About the same time he urged his son-in-law, Samuel Gardner Wilder, whose home was in California, to charter a ship to take guano direct from Jarvis to New York. He estimated that the voyage would yield a net profit of $15,000. When the *John Marshall* returned to Honolulu Dr. Judd sent Wilder a glowing account of the guano aboard and once again urged him to charter a ship for New York.[25]

Wilder accepted the offer. He signed a contract with Dr. Judd on July 5, and the next day, accompanied by his wife, he left Honolulu in the chartered clipper ship *White Swallow*. The vessel reached New York after a passage of only 82 days from Jarvis by way of Cape Horn with 1,200 tons of guano aboard, the first large shipment of mid-Pacific guano to arrive in that port. Wilder sold his interest in the cargo for $10,000. In New York a contract was signed to import 100,000 additional tons from Jarvis alone.[26]

On November 29, 1858, Dr. Judd left Honolulu for the guano islands on board the *Josephine*, a brig of 258 tons.[27] During the voyage he had ample opportunity to savor the challenge and hardships of the guano trade. Both Baker and Howland are sandspit strips less than a mile in area and rising only about twenty feet above the high-tide mark. Jarvis, the largest island of the three, has just over two square miles of land surface. The islands are almost barren of vegetation. The equatorial sun beats upon the bleached sand from a cloudless sky so fiercely that the frequent light showers in the area often split, so that no water falls on the parched land. The islands are places of monotony and madness, where the fair weather is as unvarying as the trade winds. The guano diggers, once the supply ship departed, had no means of communication with the outside world, on which they depended not only for their food but also for the precious drinking water brought ashore in hogsheads. Howland, in particular, had the added discomfort of rats from a shipwreck. On Howland it was not unusual for the workers to kill three thousand rats in a single day.[28] When the *Josephine* returned to Honolulu with a full cargo of guano, Dr.

Judd knew from direct experience the meaning of a sentence which he had written some months before, characterizing living conditions on Jarvis as a compound of "heat, dust, loneliness, and bother."[29]

In characteristic puritan fashion, Dr. Judd remained undaunted. If anything, the hardships in the guano adventure stimulated him to new enthusiasm, as puritans sometimes welcome a difficult task simply because its challenge offers them renewed opportunity to test their faith and resourcefulness. "You have your troubles, I have mine," he wrote in a vein of encouragement to his son-in-law Wilder, "but it is a pleasure to overcome, to conquer." With buoyant enthusiasm he added, "All Honolulu is guano crazy."[30]

About this time the press reported that forty-eight separate claims to the guano islands had been filed with the United States State Department—a figure which ultimately rose to fifty-seven. Charles Judd made regular bimonthly trips south for guano in the *Josephine*, mainly to Jarvis and Howland, and in the fall of 1859 the American Guano Company sent a chemist to make extensive tests of the guano deposits on Howland. In Honolulu it was reported that the Judd family, and the Wilders also, were prospering from their connection with the guano trade.[31]

In 1859 Dr. Judd made another trip south on the *Josephine*, which left Honolulu on August 25. A week later he landed at Washington Island (4-43N, 160-24W) and took formal possession on behalf of the American Guano Company. The *Josephine* reached Jarvis, where Wilder was in residence, on September 8, touched Baker on the 19th, and reached nearby Howland on October 7. Twelve days later, on the voyage homeward, Dr. Judd, accompanied by his son Charles, put in at Palmyra (5-52N, 162-06W), a U-shaped atoll of 53 islets about 960 miles due south of Honolulu. In contrast to the other islands in the area, Palmyra is rain-soaked and lushly verdant, with little if any accessible guano. Nonetheless, on October 20 Dr. Judd took formal possession of the atoll on behalf of the American Guano Company. The *Josephine* returned to Honolulu on the last day of the month. Three years later a Hawaiian commission found on Palmyra an American flag and a notice asserting the claim, signed by Dr. Judd.

Nothing came of the claims to Washington and Palmyra. Washington is now British. Palmyra, claimed by a rival guano company in the United States in 1860 and claimed by the Hawaiian Kingdom in 1862, became part of the Territory of Hawaii, after Hawaii's annexation to the United States.[32]

The rival claims to Palmyra were by no means an isolated phenomenon, for ruthless competition characterized the mid-Pacific guano trade almost from its inception. Alfred G. Benson left the American Guano Company early in 1858 and in the fall of that year helped organize the United States Guano Company, of which he subsequently became president. His new company filed a claim with the United States State Department for Howland Island, and after a long investigation the State Department not only validated the claim but issued an order forbidding the older company to work the Howland guano deposits. In the ensuing struggle between the two companies, an abortive effort was made to eject the American Guano Company from Baker and Jarvis as well, on the ground that it had exported guano to other than United States ports in violation of the Act of Congress of August 18, 1856.[33]

Other factors contributed to depress the operation. The continuing hardship of digging guano in surroundings of numbing isolation made Wilder extremely irritable, particularly when Dr. Judd refused to let his daughter Elizabeth (who had married Wilder in 1857) join her husband on the guano grounds, and when in a stubborn reaffirmation of temperance principles he insisted that no liquor be brought there. Wilder complained bitterly of both prohibitions.[34]

More effectively, the coming of the United States Civil War and the resultant blockade of the Southern ports restricted the guano market. In the summer of 1861 Dr. Judd instructed Wilder to curtail the guano digging. He added that already he was looking for another business. "Don't think of leaving the Sandwich Islands," he added in a tone of unmistakable urgency. "I want all my children with their families settled around me."[35]

Dr. Judd retained his connection with the guano venture for several years more, but, in the meantime, he turned to other pursuits. After the Civil War, Chilean nitrates and phosphates gradually replaced guano as a commercial fertilizer, and one by one the mid-Pacific guano islands were abandoned. It was not until 1936 that the United States repossessed Baker, Howland, and Jarvis as weather stations and emergency landing fields. By that time little remained, save parts of a wharf and roofless coral walls on Baker, to recall the existence of a once prosperous commercial venture.[36]

As the guano trade waned, Dr. Judd turned to what was to become Hawaii's leading industry—sugar. Here, indeed, was a splendid opportunity to recoup previous losses and achieve financial ease.

In the 1840s sugar was only one of many Islands products, widely grown in an experimental and somewhat haphazard manner. It remained so until the California gold rush of 1849–1850 and the resultant sharp increase in population on the United States west coast created an unexpected and huge new market. For a year or so Hawaiian sugar enjoyed a boom, followed by a depression in 1851–1852. Throughout the rest of the 1850s the sugar industry grew slowly, hampered by a shortage of both labor and capital for speculative investment. But the United States Civil War, with its blockade of Confederate sugar, once again created a boom. Prices rose, and Hawaii's sugar exports increased sevenfold between 1861 and 1866. By the end of the Civil War, sugar had replaced whaling as the main support of Hawaii's economy.[37]

As early as 1840, while still in the mission, Dr. Judd had acted as Governor Kekuanaoa's agent for a sugar plantation near Honolulu, and in 1845 as minister of the interior he had given due weight to sugar in framing recommendations for the future development of Hawaii's agriculture. Eight years later, at its annual meeting, the Royal Hawaiian Agricultural Society took notice of an excellent sample of sugar which he had produced at Kualoa.[38] His previous experience with sugar, the all too obvious island-wide prospects for the industry, and diminishing returns from guano led him to undertake sugar production on a large scale. His decision is symbolic of a broad change taking place in the Islands—the emergence in the 1850s and thereafter of resident planters of missionary origin, who, in time, along with their descendants, came to dominate a large share of Hawaii's economic life. The entrance into agriculture and trade of former missionaries and their sons put an end to much of the hostility which had existed between the mission and the commercial interest in the previous generation, and ultimately created an atmosphere of harmony in contrast to the ugly strife of bygone days.[39]

In 1860 Dr. Judd sold Kualoa to his son Charles and his son-in-law Wilder for $3,000, and three years later, when sugar was midway in the Civil War boom, he bought back a one-third interest for $4,000. The lands at that time totalled 3,081.8 acres, and included not only the original Kualoa property but also nearby tracts at Kaaawa and Hakipuu. At the same time, he formed with Charles and Wilder the ill-starred partnership of Judd, Wilder, and Judd. In 1863 the partnership bought for $27,500 the Brewer or Union plantation, consisting of 2,184 acres on East Maui—properties at one time owned by an American merchant, Stephen Reynolds.[40] Part of the capital investment came from an unrecorded mortgage on Sweet Home to Charles R. Bishop in the amount of $3,000.[41]

The Maui venture, on which the family set high hopes, ended abruptly in disaster. One night in August, 1864, the mill caught fire and burned to the ground along with sixteen tons of sugar in the packing house all ready for export. The loss was estimated at about $7,000. In short order the partnership sold out to Captain T. H. Hobron, and Wilder moved to the other properties at Kualoa.[42]

Within a few months Charles and Dr. Judd sold their shares to Wilder, who made a gallant and heartbreaking effort to win back his losses.[43] Evidence exists of ill feeling between Wilder and Dr. Judd at this time, and the friction between the two men may have prompted Dr. Judd to abandon the venture. In an ominous tone of disapproval he wrote to Anderson of the American Board, "My son Charles and myself have sold the sugar plantation to Mr. Wilder, who takes no interest in church matters, so that none of the family or of the 70 or 80 employees attend church upon the Sabbath."[44] At the same time, Dr. Judd set himself with characteristic energy to promoting Hawaii's sugar industry as a whole. Toward the end of 1866 he collected a comprehensive set of sugar statistics and arranged for their publication.[45]

Ultimately the plantation at Kualoa failed. Dr. Judd's daughter Elizabeth summarized its fate in a few succinct sentences.

A mill was built on the extreme point, Wilder and John [Wilder] with their own hands, after three unsuccessful attempts, erecting the stone chimney. Fields were fenced and ploughed for the cane, small flumes were put up, Chinese coolies imported as laborers, and it rapidly assumed a very plantationlike aspect. . . . Wilder worked dreadfully hard against most disheartening odds—poor soil, poor irrigation, poor laborers, and poor cane. The Chinamen were fresh from their native land, an uncivilized troop. . . . In 1867 Mr. Wilder rented Puunui, Judd Street, for me, and I moved up for good. The plantation had proved a failure. One cannot squeeze water from a stone, or grow cane in poor soil.[46]

The slump in the sugar market after the end of the United States Civil War certainly contributed to Kualoa's decline.[47] In 1868 a tragedy on the plantation added a further disheartening blow. The Wilders' eldest son—Dr. Judd's eldest grandson—William Chauncey (Willie), fell into a pan of boiling sugar syrup and died on the morning of August 21. He was just over nine years old.[48] At the time Dr. Judd was in California with his wife on a four-month trip for their health. The news of the child's death affected them deeply. There was no tree that year at the Christmas festivities at Sweet Home.[49]

Two years later Wilder gave up the plantation, which Dr. Judd bought back as the only bidder at a public sale for the amount of his mortgage with interest due, $15,041.66, plus one dollar. The last stick of cane was cut and ground on July 21, 1871.[50]

The collapse of the sugar enterprise, along with the slow extinction of the guano trade, left Dr. Judd in a precarious financial situation. Even before the mill burned on the Maui plantation he wrote to the Wilders, "I am hard up for money, never was more so. . . . I am discouraged about money. Don't know where to get it, but keep trying. . . . Not a cent do I spend that can be avoided, and so must we all for we live upon borrowed money. And I don't know where I can borrow any more."[51]

All in all, in spite of well-laid plans and a lavish expenditure of time and energy, where others found success he tasted instead the bitter fruit of failure. There is nothing to indicate what his reactions were, but in view of his sensitive temperament and puritan religious values, it is more than possible that he had periods of despair tinged with nagging remorse. As one business failure followed another he may well have suspected that God was displeased with him for having left the mission. Else why was he denied the prosperity which Calvinists traditionally interpret as the outward sign of inner grace?

Dr. Judd's Last Years

In the summer of 1864 Dr. Judd wrote to his daughter Elizabeth, "There is nothing on earth I care for except to make my children and grandchildren happy and useful, except to see the cause of religion and civilization extend throughout the Islands."[1] This sentence, written when he was sixty-one years old, sums up the high-flung moral standards to which he had geared his life. Religion, of course, forms the central theme, but hand in hand with religion went "civilization," which may be interpreted to mean such New England virtues as integrity, industry, and frugality. The emphasis on his descendants looks at first like a departure, the expressed wish of an idealist in his declining years for someone in the family to carry forward his unfinished work. But on closer inspection it is in no wise inconsistent with the pattern of his past conduct and aspirations, for devotion to family was a typical New England folkway, part of the "civilization" which moral-minded Yankees brought with them to the Hawaiian frontier. Throughout his life Dr. Judd lived to a great degree in and for his family. In periods of adversity, especially in the lean years after he left politics, the family circle served as a source of comfort and strength.

He depended heavily on his wife for encouragement and counsel. They were inseparable companions, except for his diplomatic mission, 1849–1850, brief periods when he took trips to windward Oahu or to one of the other islands, and a fourteen-month period, 1855–1856, when she took three of their children, Charles, Helen, and Elizabeth, to the United States. The party left Honolulu on September 4, 1855, for New York City by way of San Francisco and Panama. Their itinerary included Norfolk, Washington, Philadelphia, Brooklyn, Buffalo, Geneva, where they stayed with the Boyd family, and New Haven, where they attended the Yale commencement and had a reunion with the Binghams.[2]

After their return to the Islands Mrs. Judd received in the spring of 1858 a sewing machine as a tribute from 273 of her Brooklyn admirers, including Alfred G. and Arthur Benson, and the Reverend Lyman Beecher, then in his eighty-third year. Beecher's signature in a shakey hand appears in the accompanying autograph book and no doubt served to recall vividly the days of their youth, when he led the prayer as the Third Company prepared to go aboard the *Parthian* in Boston harbor thirty-one years before.[3]

In 1852 Dr. Judd joyfully welcomed his aged mother to the Islands. Betsey Judd arrived in Honolulu harbor on Sunday morning, March 28, on the schooner *Esther May*, after an extremely rough passage of a hundred and thirty days around Cape Horn, and, in repudiation of the strict Sabbath restrictions of the immediate past, came ashore the same day.[4] Straightaway she joined the rest of the family at Sweet Home. In time "old grandmother Judd" became a familiar figure in Honolulu society. Commissioner Gregg particularly enjoyed her company and commented that her conversation was "very pleasant and quite intelligent." Despite a protracted illness in the late 1860s, she lived to celebrate her ninetieth birthday on August 28, 1872, at a party including twenty-seven grandmothers and three great-grandmothers. She outlived her son by almost four years.[5]

Dr. Judd's sister, Harriet Breck (Hattie), accompanied her mother to the Islands. For a time she also lived at Sweet Home, but in a spirit of Yankee independence she took a position as companion to six girls in a nearby German family. "For a year and a quarter," she wrote in 1869, "I was in Gerret's [*sic*] family, taking care of

Dr. Judd in middle years

mother, during a long and tedious sickness, being her constant nurse day and night, but as soon as she was better, and able to spare me, I felt that I must push off and support myself. . . . I have my own horse, saddle and bridle here, and ride over every day on horseback to see mother while the girls are in school. You can imagine that this is a pleasant arrangement for me. . . ." Harriet never married. She died in San Francisco in her seventieth year.[6]

Dr. Judd's other sister, Elisabeth Gertrude, the wife of Asher B. Bates, came to Honolulu with her husband in the summer of 1848. Bates, who accepted a subordinate post in the Hawaiian government, remained in office long after Dr. Judd's retirement from politics, but in 1864 he moved with his family to San Francisco. The parting gave Dr. Judd considerable grief. "The Bateses have just sailed," he wrote to Wilder. "A sad business for me, for I have greatly depended on Bates."[7]

Three of Dr. Judd's four sons grew to manhood, the oldest, Gerrit Jr., having died in 1839. His second son, Charles Hastings, had taken part with him in the guano adventure, and had shared briefly the family disaster in sugar. Thereafter, he took up ranching at Waimanalo on windward Oahu, where he raised horses, cattle, and a few sheep. From 1878–1886 he was chamberlain to King Kalakaua and accompanied the king on his celebrated round-the-world tour in 1881.[8] The third son, Albert Francis, graduated from Yale in 1862 and took a law degree from Harvard two years later. From 1881 until his death in 1900 he was chief justice of Hawaii's supreme court. Following a family tradition with its roots in the seventeenth century, he was a deacon of Honolulu's Fort Street Congregational Church. Dr. Judd had high hopes for him. In 1861 he wrote to Rufus Anderson of the American Board, "It is my wish to settle all my children in these Islands. If you see Master Frank, who is now in Yale College, give him a kind word for my sake. I hope he will return a pious lawyer to benefit the Islands."[9] The fourth son, Allan Wilkes, named for Dr. Judd's old friend in the United States exploring expedition, died unmarried at Pawaa, Honolulu, in 1875 in his thirty-fourth year.[10]

Four of Dr. Judd's five daughters lived to womanhood. The oldest, Elizabeth Kinau, married in 1857 Samuel Gardner Wilder, who was intimately associated with Dr. Judd in the guano and sugar ventures. Dr. Judd's solicitude for his son-in-law's financial welfare, at least in the early days of their association, stands clearly revealed in the way he arranged for Wilder to charter a ship in 1858 to take a cargo of guano to New York. The circumstances of the voyage, in which Wilder had little to lose and a substantial profit in expectation, leave no doubt of Dr. Judd's good intentions. After the Kualoa plantation failed, Wilder made a trip to China to recruit Chinese coolies for the growing sugar industry of the Islands, and he later had a prominent part in developing Hawaii's interisland navigation.[11] The second daughter, Helen Seymour (Nellie), remained a spinster. At the age of nineteen she became engaged to Aaron B. Howe, a young man whom Judge Lee described as "unprincipled." It is known that Howe drank to excess, and Wyllie, for one, suspected that he was involved in smuggling liquor. On November 9, 1852, the privy council refused to grant him a government lumber contract, the details of which remain obscure, and four days later, possibly because of the refusal, he committed suicide. Despite scandal about him, which is still repeated in the Islands, Nellie remained faithful to his memory. He was buried in the Judd plot in Nuuanu Cemetery, and many years later, in a union denied them in life, she was buried beside him.[12] Laura Fish, the third daughter, married Joshua Gill Dickson, a lumber merchant in the firm of Lewers and Dickson, the forerunner of the present firm of Lewers and Cooke, Ltd., in Honolulu.[13] The fourth daughter, Sybil Augusta, became the wife of Henry Alpheus Peirce Carter, a businessman of American parentage, who strongly advocated the annexation of the Islands by the United States.[14] Each of the three daughters who married had her wedding at Sweet Home.[15] Imbued with the same Yankee reverence for useful work that motivated their Aunt Hattie, both Nellie and Laura for a time conducted a small school.[16] The youngest of Dr. Judd's children, Juliet Isabella, whom Mrs. Judd described as "the pet of the whole family circle," died at Sweet Home on June 27, 1857, in her twelfth year, after an illness of only four days. Dr. Judd diagnosed her illness as "a bowel complaint."[17] Probably she died of appendicitis, the same malady, then dimly understood, which had taken Gerrit Jr. almost eighteen years before.

As head of a large family, Dr. Judd found himself the central figure in a continuously unfolding drama. The family's life flowed around him like a broad river, with full measure of perplexities, hopes, frustrations, and fulfillments. At Sweet Home the family announced engagements, celebrated weddings, and anxiously a-waited the birth of babies. The house was seldom silent, save during the rare and somber visitations of sickness and death. In 1868, thirty-two members of the family sat down to Christmas dinner, some at the table which Betsey Judd had brought with her from the United States sixteen years before.[18] On less festive occasions Dr. Judd presided over a smaller number gathered at the same table in the evening to talk over the pressing problems of the day. In the private world of the family, Dr. Judd found satisfactions rarely to be encountered in the larger world without. His daughter Elizabeth recalled,

Sweet Home was my golden age. There we played or busied ourselves with household tasks, or entertained our numerous friends. If the after-noon was fine, we sat on the lawn under the cool shade of the low-boughed trees, or, if one of the numerous valley-showers came, we gathered on the broad verandas to watch over the bright flower-pots the rain as it hurried to the town. Ours was a happy family. In the evening we gathered around the shaded lamp and studied our lessons, or listened with bated breaths while mother read some romantic adventure aloud.
. . . .
My parents were genuinely religious, and gave to our spiritual welfare the greatest possible care. We learned long passages from the Scriptures and recited them with much emphasis. On Sundays we were allowed no playthings, and walked to church, so as to give the horses a day of rest.[19]

The satisfactions of family life and the consolations of religion eased the many disappointments which Dr. Judd encountered in the outside world. As time passed he realized increasingly that the anti-American policy of Kamehameha IV (1854–1863) and Kame-hameha V (1863–1872) effectively barred him from a return to high political office. Nonetheless, he made two further excursions into politics, only to meet with rebuff and humiliation on each occasion.

In the spring of 1858, less than five years after his retirement from the government, he was elected to the House of Representa-tives as member for Koolaupoko, the district on windward Oahu which included his Kualoa property. During the June session he attended daily and took active part in the proceedings, but from the first he had a secondary role. When the session opened he was proposed as speaker but lost the election by a vote of fourteen to nine in favor of George M. Robertson, who had instigated his impeachment ten years before. During the opening weeks of the winter session he was absent from the kingdom on a trip south to the guano islands. He resumed his seat on January 4, 1859, and last attended on the 19th. The next day the House accepted his resignation.[20] At that time his involvement in the guano trade was reaching its climax. Perhaps holding a subordinate post in the government of which he was once chief officer put him in an anomalous position. At best the situation was awkward. At worst it served as a cruel reminder of the irretrievable past. Probably only his puritan sense of duty induced him to run for the legislature in the first place and, once elected, to retain his seat as long as he did.

Early in 1864 Kamehameha V, with the support of the cabinet, including Wyllie, called a constitutional convention. The government's intention was to weaken the democratic elements in the constitution of 1852 and to strengthen the prerogatives of the king and cabinet. When the convention met on July 7, Dr. Judd was one of the 26 elected delegates. Assisted by his sons Charles and Albert Francis, along with others of liberal political principles, he headed the opposition. After five stormy weeks of debate the convention ended in deadlock, and in mid-August Kamehameha V dissolved it. Later the same month, by executive action, he issued a new constitution which abolished the office of premier, restricted the power of the privy council, provided for a unicameral legislature, and established property qualifications for representatives and voters. Despite protest, the new constitution became the fundamental law of the kingdom for the next 23 years. Once again Dr. Judd found himself on the losing side.[21]

The constitutional convention represents the final clash between Judd and his antagonist of long standing, Wyllie, who died in October of the following year. After Judd's retirement from office Wyllie's attitude toward him mellowed. In the summer of 1859, when Wyllie fell gravely ill and expected to die, Mrs. Judd visited him at Rosebank. The next winter, possibly from stirrings of conscience, he made elaborately casual overtures for a reconciliation. After several notes to Dr. and Mrs. Judd on carefully chosen pretexts, he wrote to Judd on February 7, 1860, a verbose and ingratiating letter, which stated in part, "It is no flattery to you to say that no history of this kingdom can be true and just that ignores your most valuable services, while, I may say, the universal minister of the late king . . . You have been no zero. . . ." Ten days later Dr. Judd replied in an equally long *apologia* for his entire political career. Here the matter might have rested in amity, but in further correspondence, Wyllie insisted that Kamehameha III had in fact intended to dismiss Dr. Judd during the impeachment proceedings of 1848. Wyllie's unearthing of a sensitive and long dormant issue brought the reconciliation effort to an abrupt close.[22] The conflict between the two men, rooted as it was in fundamental differences of temperament and values, proved irreconcilable.

Naturally, in view of his rebuffs in 1858 and 1864, and possibly also because of some aspects of the abortive reconciliation with Wyllie, Dr. Judd found little to his liking in the political scene under Kamehameha IV and V. In 1861 he wrote to Rufus Anderson, "Times look dark. . . . A new decade is ushered in by the death of the old king and the accession of Kamehameha IV. Pursuing the system devised by me, he has appointed to office men of a lower standard of morals, although not lower perhaps than that of rulers of most governments in the world. The religious element is fast leaving the throne."[23]

Six years later in a letter to William H. Seward he was even more outspoken in his condemnation of the existing regime.

Kamehameha IV by introducing a bishop, clergy, schoolmasters and sisters of charity from England, prepared the way for an union of church and state and the general diffusion among the wealthier classes [of] certain high toned monarchial principles in opposition to those of the American missionaries. Kamehameha V, the present king, while adopting the policy of his brother has gone further, by arbitrarily setting aside our liberal constitution. . . . The labors of the American missionaries are ignored and the men to whom the king, the chiefs and the people owe their education and their independence are set aside and forgotten. The school system is being changed so that education instead of being generally diffused is to be confined to a few and the masses suffered to grow up in ignorance. . . . Teachers are to be anti-American as far as possible. . . . Many [of] our planters are embarrassed with debt. At present nine-tenths of them are desirous of falling into the hands of the United States. . . . The native population are fast fading away. Of the vast numbers one hundred years ago only 58,765 remain . . . for a group of Islands capable of sustaining from 3,000,000 to 5,000,000. . . . The Islands are now ruled by a king whose health is not good, and by a number of persons of foreign birth who are the real rulers, not one of whom is American at heart. The chiefs or true aristocracy are almost extinct, and were the king suddenly to decease, there is reason to fear there would follow a period of anarchy and confusion . . . perhaps bloodshed.[24]

Dr. Judd particularly objected to the coming of the Church of England to Hawaii in 1862—a project, incidentally, which Wyllie had long promoted. Along with other Americans, Dr. Judd regarded the Anglicans as intruders, and their presence in the Islands served to reaffirm his loyalty to the American Board. In the 1860s he corresponded at length about church matters with American Board officials, and when Dr. and Mrs. Rufus Anderson visited the Islands in 1863 he gave them a farewell party.[25] When, in 1854, the Hawaiian Evangelical Association was formed to assume gradually the American Board's activities, he not only became a member but gave the new body his enthusiastic support. In 1872 he sold to the Association for $3,000 a building lot in Honolulu for its new theological seminary. He valued the property at $4,000, but he reduced the price, as he told the Reverend John Davis Paris, in order to make an indirect charitable contribution.[26]

To the end of his life he maintained a strong interest in community affairs. The Fort Street Congregational Church, of which his son Albert Francis later became a deacon, occupied much of his attention. In 1856 he was elected treasurer of the Hawaiian Theater Company, and the next year he was among the subscribers to the Honolulu Rifles, a volunteer military unit.[27] In 1870, following a grant by the Hawaiian legislature, he organized a small medical school. Starting on November 9 he delivered a series of "plain" medical lectures to ten carefully chosen Hawaiian students, who supplemented their formal course of instruction with practical work in the dispensary. It was understood that after two years the students would go to remote districts in the Islands to counteract the still surviving superstitious practises of native healers.[28]

As an elder statesman in semiretirement he remained a prominent, if controversial, figure in Honolulu society. Mark Twain, who spent four months in Honolulu in 1866, praised his state papers and wrote a glowing account of his political judgment. Sophia Cracroft, on the other hand, followed the view prevalent in government circles and characterized his political career as tyrannical. She also noted disapprovingly in her journal that at a hypnotism demonstration Dr. Judd went up on stage, defied the performer to hypnotize him, and argued heatedly that hypnotism was impossible unless the subject co-operated. Naturally enough the hypnotist demurred, and the incident gave occasion for much tongue wagging. "Just like the Doctor," people commented. Some meant the remark to be kindly, but others were abusive.[29]

Dr. Judd, it is clear, never quite lost the knack of goading his opponents to fury. On at least one occasion he wrote a sharply worded letter to the editor of the *Polynesian*, who printed the letter along with a cutting rebuttal on the same page. Commissioner Gregg, for one, firmly believed that Dr. Judd made a regular practice of vilifying his enemies in the public press.[30]

On October 2, 1872, Mrs. Judd died. Toward the end of her life she had been afflicted with paralysis. Dr. Judd, so Elisha Allen reported, "was deeply affected. He said, she had not been a great sufferer in bodily pain. Her son, Frank, told me that she had suffered more, mentally, to feel that her powers were failing." The extent of Dr. Judd's grief shows plainly in the last letter which he wrote to the American Board. "You will notice on page 1 of this sheet the death of Mrs. Judd. I would have written before, but for an attack of apoplexy which befell me on the 2d November, which has laid me up until now. I am still weak and without my usual buoyancy of mind and body."[31]

On December 18 he made his will, beginning with the traditional phrase, "In the name of God, amen."[32] First he divided his real estate among his seven surviving children. He left his acreage on windward Oahu to Charles, his property in downtown Honolulu at Fort and Merchant Streets to Albert Francis, and his pasture land at Pawaa to Allan. Sweet Home and an adjoining building

Dr. Judd in old age

lot went to Helen, and each of his three other daughters received land in Nuuanu Valley. Second, he established a trust fund consisting of his life insurance policy of $9,000, his annuity (which expired in 1876) of $1,000 from the Hawaiian government, and various other securities, to support his mother, his sister Hattie, his unmarried daughter Helen, and his foster daughter Hattie Ellis.[33] After the trust ended, the final cash distribution in 1881 amounted to $16,752.47. His total assets, including the real estate, which had appreciated considerably over the years, amounted to about $50,000—a substantial legacy, and one which should have set his mind at rest, but this was only a fraction of the fortune he might have left had he accepted the whole of Manoa Valley when Auhea offered it to him in 1843.

Shortly after the accession of King Lunalilo in January, 1873, Dr. Judd had the satisfaction of seeing two of his sons take responsible office in the Hawaiian government. On January 13 Albert Francis became attorney general with a seat in the cabinet, and exactly two weeks later Charles was appointed to the king's personal staff with the rank of colonel. On February 18 Charles became adjutant general of the Hawaiian armed forces.[34]

On April 23 Dr. Judd celebrated his seventieth birthday. A newspaper account stated that his health had been poor, and that he had suffered "a severe attack" only three days before, from which, the account added cheerfully, he had "measurably recovered." In later life he had several bouts of sickness. In 1860 his eye trouble recurred, and for a time he was unable to read or write. He fell ill again in 1863; five years later he took a summer trip to California for his health.[35]

Charles Nordhoff noted Dr. Judd's frailness in the months immediately preceding his death. "It was to me a most touching sight," Nordoff wrote, "to see, on a Sunday after church, Mrs. Thurston, his senior by many years but still alert and vigorous, taking hold of his hand and tenderly helping him out of the church and to his carriage."[36] Another account of Dr. Judd in extreme old age, that of Julius Palmer, characterized him as mild and benevolent: "The last picture I see of him is that of a kind old teacher instructing one of his Chinese servants how to read English."[37]

He died suddenly of a paralytic stroke[38] on Saturday evening,

July 12, 1873. The fullest account of his death appears in the journal of his daughter-in-law Agnes, who had married Albert Francis in April of the previous year.

Our father sleeps in Jesus. Just after the Owens left last night, father's nurse came for Frank in great haste, and Frank said, "I fear it is the last of father." The horse flew up the street. Mrs. Joe Carter came in a moment—then I locked up the house, after picking up some things for the night, and trudged up to S[weet] H[ome]. When I entered the room all was over. A handkerchief held up his chin. I threw my arms around my darling's neck. Mr. Thompson had taken dinner with him and he seemed in his usual health. At 7 he went upstairs. Nellie and Hattie were at Cousins Society at Mr. Joe Cooke's. He read his Testament, shut it up, laid it on the table, took off his glasses, put them down, took his watch out of his vest pocket, shut his eyes and leaned his head back. Halakai spoke to him, but he answered not a word. She put him on the floor—rubbed him, then on the bed—called Aunt N. and Gina. They put mustard on, etc. Sent for Frank who arrived just as his life ebbed away. He never spoke again.[39]

The funeral was held at five o'clock the next afternoon. After a sermon by the Reverend Frank Thompson, temporary incumbent of the Fort Street Congregational Church, and a prayer by the Reverend Samuel C. Damon of the eighth missionary company, Dr. Judd's casket, carried to the grave in Nuuanu Cemetery by eight natives reared in his family, was preceded by ten of his seventeen grandchildren. The pallbearers were Henry A. Peirce, U.S. minister to Hawaii; Charles R. Bishop, minister of foreign affairs; Edwin O. Hall, minister of the interior; Governor Paul Kanoa; A. P. Brickwood; Samuel N. Castle; Captain Charles W. Gelett; and Lowell Smith. A large crowd, including the king, attended. In Honolulu all flags flew at half mast, and the following day the supreme court was adjourned in his honor.[40]

His grave, beside that of his wife, has a headstone of classic New England simplicity. At the bottom are words adapted from Second Samuel 1:23, "They were lovely and pleasant in their lives, and in their death they were not divided." Directly above is an often-quoted line from one of Walter Savage Landor's epigrams, "I am ready to depart." Toward the center of the stone, and just underneath the date of his death, is a phrase carved in capital letters, "Hawaii's Friend."

References

Bibliographical Note

Dr. Judd's correspondence and other papers are scattered in public and private collections from London westward to Honolulu. Of his correspondence, 952 letters, including drafts, copies, and extracts, have been located. Of these, 182 are in print.

Six unpublished letters to Charles Grandison Finney 1827–1837 are in the Oberlin College Library.

Dr. Judd's correspondence with the American Board, now in the Houghton Library at Harvard, totals 64 letters, plus a copy of a letter (May 26, 1843) the original of which is in the Hawaiian Mission Children's Society Library in Honolulu. A much paraphrased version of this letter appears in L. F. Judd, *Honolulu* (pp. 86–87). Of the 64 letters in the American Board Papers, 56 (along with an enclosure incorrectly designated as a letter) were privately printed in somewhat garbled form in *Fragments II* (see p. 246). The Hunnewell Papers at Harvard (a split collection) contain two of Dr. Judd's letters, one in the Houghton Library and one in the Baker Library.

The HMCS Library has 117 of Dr. Judd's letters (1828–1860) of which four have been printed: one in George P. Cooke, *Moolelo o Molokai* (pp. 154–155), one in Francis J. Halford, *9 Doctors & God* (p. 219), and two in Mary A. Richards, *Chiefs' Children's School* (pp. 178–179, 181–182). The Samuel Gardner Wilder Papers on deposit in the HMCS Library contain an additional 141 letters (1832–1870), all unpublished.

His wife's memoirs (L. F. Judd, *Honolulu*) contain 16 letters not elsewhere available, often in extract form. His daughter's memoirs (Elizabeth L. Wight, *Memoirs of E. K. Wilder*, pp. 83–84) give one letter, and an extract from another letter appears in *Report to the Stockholders of the United States Guano Company* (p. 29). A copy of this extract is in Miscellaneous Letters relating to Guano Islands (III, 148), U.S. Archives.

Of Dr. Judd's political correspondence, 104 letters (including extracts) are in print. Two of these (October 18, 1842, and February 27, 1843) appear in the British compilation, *Correspondence Relative to the Sandwich Islands* (pp. 161, 258). The former is also in the British Public Record Office (FO 58/18). The latter is also in the Archives of Hawaii and printed in extract form in L.F. Judd, *Honolulu* (pp. 95–96). Two letters (May 11, 1843, and May 30, 1850) appear in official United States publications: *Foreign Relations of the United States, 1894* (appendix 2, p. 56) and *Senate Ex. Docs.*, 52 Congr., 2 Sess., No. 77 (p. 82). The former is also in the Archives of Hawaii and printed in the *Missionary Herald*, XL (January, 1844), 21–22. The latter also exists in two copies in the Archives of Hawaii (FO Letter Book No. 16 and Misc. Foreign File). At least 90 of Dr. Judd's public letters have been printed, sometimes in extract form, in official publications of the Hawaiian Kingdom: *Correspondence . . . in the Case of John Wiley, Correspondence . . . on . . . Charlton's Claim to Land, Ladd and Co. Arbitration* (an extensive collection), *Official Correspondence with . . . Dillon, Official Correspondence* [with Admiral de Tromelin, Honolulu, 1849], *Report of the Case of C. Brewer and Co. vs. John R. von Pfister, Report of the Case of . . . Brinsmade . . . versus . . . Jarves* (Honolulu, 1946), and in the government newspaper, the *Polynesian.* The *Report of the Minister of Foreign Relations* for 1851 (appendix, pp. 26–27) prints an extract from one of Dr. Judd's letters (February 17, 1844) a full copy of which is in the Archives of Hawaii. At least seven of Dr. Judd's public letters appear in other journals: one each in the *Friend* (March 25, 1844) and *Ka Elele* (July 29, 1845), and five in the opposition newspaper, the *Sandwich Islands News* (October 7, 1846, and May 12, 1847). Three of Dr. Judd's letters have been found in pamphlets, one in A. H. Markland, *Conspiracy* (p. 11), and two in Alexander Simpson, *Sandwich Islands* (pp. 55, 60).

By far the greatest part of Dr. Judd's political correspondence is in the Archives of Hawaii, along with his other state papers. The Archives contain over 500 of his letters (1837–1860), of which 486 are unpublished. Some of the correspondence is in Hawaiian. Nine additional political letters, unavailable elsewhere, are in the U.S. Archives in Washington, D.C., and five more letters, also unavailable elsewhere, are in the University of Hawaii Library, four of them in the William Hooper Papers. Part of his diplomatic correspondence is in the British Public Record Office (mainly in the FO 58 file), but copies of all these letters have been found in other places, either in print or in manuscript.

Entries by Dr. Judd as a young man in Paris Hill appear in the record book of two debating clubs, the Ciceronian and Philosophronic Societies, now in the museum of the Sauquoit Valley Central School, Sauquoit, New York.

His journal on the *Parthian* (1827–1828) was privately printed in *Fragments III*. In addition, he made several entries in his wife's journal of the voyage, now in the possession of Mrs. Mary Marks of Old Forge, New York. His journal 1830–1831 was privately printed in *Fragments IV*. Brief mention of his "Journal of a Tour of Oahu in 1834" appears in Harold W. Bradley, *American Frontier in Hawaii* (p. 338). His autobiographic statement, written in 1830 with a continuation in 1846, was privately printed in *Fragments I*.

A page from his treatment book, written in Hawaiian in the 1830s, is reproduced in *Annals of Medical History*, n.s., VII, No. 2 (March, 1935), 158. His medical essay, "Remarks on the Climate of the Sandwich Islands . . .," was published in the *Hawaiian Spectator*, I, No. 2 (April, 1838), 18–27. *Anatomia*, his textbook on anatomy in the Hawaiian language, was published by the mission press at Lahainaluna in 1838.

Extracts from his diaries 1839–1842 appear in Ethel M. Damon, *Stone Church at Kawaiahao* (pp. 52–54). His annual reports for 1839 and 1840 along with some of his miscellaneous papers, which are mainly financial in character, are in the HMCS Library. Extracts from his diary in the summer of 1841 are printed in Mary C. Alexander and Charlotte P. Dodge, *Punahou* (pp. 63, 67). His journal, May 4–25, 1843, is in the Archives of Hawaii.

Dr. Judd kept a private journal in four volumes during his diplomatic journey to the United States and Europe, 1849–1850. Of the original, the first and fourth volumes and part of the third are said to have been lost, but certified extracts, as well as Wyllie's copious notes from the entire journal, are in the Archives of Hawaii. An entry from the journal is printed in Ralph S. Kuykendall, *Hawaiian Kingdom 1778–1854* (p. 398; see also p. 381). Dr. Judd made a pencil note in Prince Lot's journal (November [30], 1849), now in the Bishop Museum in Honolulu.

The Kualoa journal 1852–1859, which contains entries by Dr. Judd, was privately printed in *Fragments V*. His journal of a voyage to the guano islands in 1859 was privately printed in *Fragments VI*, which mentions (p. 3) the existence of a diary on a similar voyage in 1858.

I have only to add my regret that because of circumstances beyond my control I was unable to use the family papers now in the possession of Mrs. Albert Francis Judd 2nd of Honolulu.

Notes

In the following Notes, frequent mention is made of *Fragments I–VI*, privately printed collections of Judd family papers, as follows:

Fragments I: Family Record, House of Judd (Honolulu, 1903). The contents of a large volume bound in red leather with a brass plate on the cover engraved, "Gerrit P. Judd from Charles G. Finney."

Fragments II, H. M. Ballou, ed., *The Letters of Dr. Gerrit P. Judd 1827–1872 Preserved in the Archives of the A.B.C.F.M. Boston* (Honolulu, 1911).

Fragments III, A. F. Judd II, ed., *Pages from the Diary of G. P. Judd on the Voyage around Cape Horn in the Ship "Parthian" 1827–1828 and Pages from a Book of Letters from Friends in Oneida County, New York State 1828 in the possession of A. F. Judd 2nd 1928* (Honolulu, 1928).

Fragments IV, A. F. Judd II, ed., *Pages from the Journals of Gerrit Parmele Judd and Laura Fish Judd 1830–1832 in the possession of A. F. Judd 2nd 1928* (Honolulu, 1928).

Fragments V, Julie Judd Swanzy, ed., *Pages from the Diary of Charles Hastings Judd 1848–1850 and the Kualoa Journal of the Judd Family 1852–1859 also Letters from Charles Hastings Judd written from Jarvis Island 1858, and from Baker's Island, 1859, 1861, in the possession of Julie Judd Swanzy 1930* (Honolulu, 1930).

Fragments VI, A. F. Judd II, ed., *The Guano Islands. Diary of A. Francis Judd's Voyage to Jarvis Island, 1858. Memorandum Journal of G. P. Judd, Voyage to Jarvis, Baker and Howland Islands, 1859. Letter of C. H. Judd to J. O. Carter, Dec. 7, 1859 Written from Baker* (Honolulu, 1935).

246

Abbreviations:

ABCFM: American Board of Commissioners for Foreign Missions
AH: Public Archives of Hawaii
BPRO: British Public Record Office
FO: Foreign Office
FO & EX.:Foreign Office and Executive file
HHC: Hawaiian Historical Commission
HHS: Hawaiian Historical Society
HMCS: Hawaiian Mission Children's Society
UH: University of Hawaii

Notes: The Judd Family in North America (pages 1–11)

1. "The Ancestry of Dr. Gerrit Parmele Judd," typescript dated February 10, 1955, HMCS Library. His direct line of descent was: (1) Thomas (d. 1688); (2) William (*ca.* 1635–1690); (3) Thomas (*ca.* 1662–1747); (4) William (1689–1772); (5) Elnathan (1724–1777); (6) Elnathan (1773–1845).

2. Sylvester Judd, *Thomas Judd and his Descendants* (Northampton, 1856), p. 9. Unless otherwise stated, all genealogical material in this chapter is taken from this reliable work. See also Charles E. Banks, *Topographical Dictionary of 2885 English Emigrants to New England, 1620–1650* (Philadelphia, 1937), p. 45.

3. See Henry Bronson, *The History of Waterbury, Connecticut* (Waterbury, 1858), *passim;* Franklin B. Dexter, *Biographical Sketches of the Graduates of Yale College* (New York and New Haven, 1885–1912), I, 579–580, 677–678, III, 25–27; Mabel S. Hurlburt, *Farmington Town Clerks and their Times* (Hartford, 1943), pp. 90–91; Caroline J. McDowell, *Philip Judd and his Descendants* (Grinnel, Iowa, 1923), pp. 14–23.

4. James H. Trumbull and C. J. Hoadly, eds., *The Public Records of the Colony of Connecticut* (Hartford, 1850–1890), XIII, 385–387; information from Helen L. Wallace, clerk of the Court of Probate, District of Woodbury, Connecticut.

5. David M. Ellis, "The Yankee Invasion of New York, 1783–1850," *New York History*, XXXII (1951), 3–17; Dixon R. Fox, *Yankees and Yorkers* (New York, 1940), pp. 18, 182; Richard J. Purcell, *Connecticut in Transition, 1775–1818* (Washington, 1918), pp. 139–158; Lois K. Mathews Rosenberry, *The Expansion of New England* (Boston, 1909), especially pp. 153–164.

6. Moses M. Bagg, *The Founders of the Oneida County Medical Society* (Utica, 1881), p. 17.

7. A land transfer deed, relative to Meriam Judd and her children, dated February 7, 1795, describes Meriam, Elnathan, and Sarah Judd, along with Joseph and Dotha (Judd) Cutler as "of Paris Hill, N.Y." The same deed describes Smith and Erea (Judd) Arnold, Samuel and Millicent (Judd) Prentice, and Richards S. Judd as variously located in western New York. Clarinda Judd alone appears as "of Watertown, Conn." A deed of February 1, 1791, describes Elnathan and Meriam Judd as "of Watertown, Conn." Church records in Watertown do not give the date of their formal dismissal from the First Congregational Church (Watertown Land Records, VI, 483, and VII, 69, information from the Reverend John H. Westbrook of Watertown, Connecticut).

8. Royden W. Vosburgh, ed., "Records of the Paris Religious Society (A Congregational Church) in the Town of Paris, Oneida County, N.Y.," typescript in the New York Historical Society Library, New York City; verified in the original records at Paris Hill).

9. Henry Adams, *History of the United States from 1801–1817* (New York, 1889–1891), I, 3; Daniel E. Wager, *Our County and Its People: A Descriptive Work on Oneida County* (Boston, 1896), pp. 90, 144.

10. James Fenimore Cooper, *The Pioneers* (1823), chaps. 21, 28, 38; Fox, *Yankees and Yorkers*, p. 182; Pomroy Jones, *Annals and Recollections of Oneida County* (Rome, N.Y., 1851), p. 695; Henry C. Rogers, *History of the Town of Paris and the Valley of the Sauquoit* (Utica, 1881), p. 106; Wager, *Oneida County*, pp. 65, 79, 165.

11. *Ibid.*, pp. 491–495, 503; Samuel W. and P. A. Durant, *History of Oneida County* (Philadelphia, 1878), pp. 495, 500; *Centennial of the Paris Congregational Church 1791–1891* (Utica, [1891]), p. 23; Vosburgh, ed., "Records of the Paris Religious Society," p. 36.

12. The treasurer's records of the college show that he paid his quarterly tuition at the academy of $15 per quarter for the four terms ending December 26, 1797, March 27, June 26, and September 4, 1798 (information from Wyllis E. Wright, librarian of Williams College).

13. [Samuel W. Durant and H. B. Pierce], *History of Oakland County, Michigan* (Philadelphia, 1877), p. 296, where the account, based on information from Elnathan's son, Henry A. Judd, states that he entered the college but did not graduate.

14. Bagg, *Founders of the Oneida County Medical Society*, p. 17.

15. R. Carlyle Buley and Madge E. Pickard, *The Midwest Pioneer: His Ills, Cures, and Doctors* (New York, 1946), pp. 119–120.

16. Durant, *History of Oneida County*, pp. 500–501. The accounts in Rogers (*History of Paris*, p. 39) and Bagg (*Founders of the Oneida County Medical Society*, p. 17) give different dates for the transaction with Dr. Sampson. See also Thomas C. O'Donnell, *Tip of the Hill: An Informal History of the Fairfield Academy and the Fairfield Medical College* (Boonville, N.Y., 1953), pp. 127–128, where it is stated in error that Elnathan died in 1839.

17. Buley and Pickard, *The Midwest Pioneer*, pp. 99–100; Frederick C. Waite, "Medical Education of Dr. Whitman," *Oregon Historical Quarterly*, XXXVII (1936), 207–210.

18. Bagg, *Founders of the Oneida County Medical Society*, pp. 17–19.

19. Elnathan bought the property by deed dated June 10, 1801, and sold it to Dr. Larrabee by deed recorded October 22, 1834. In 1954 the house was in the possession of Frank Palmer (information from Clifford W. Wells, Mid-State Abstract Corporation, Utica).

20. Durant, *History of Oneida County*, p. 247.

21. Fox, *Yankees and Yorkers*, pp. 209–210; Kenneth S. Latourette, *A History of the Expansion of Christianity* (New York, 1937–1945), IV, 43, 45, 65, 77, 204–205, 431; Rosenberry, *Expansion of New England*, pp. 163–164.

22. Dexter, *Biographical Sketches of the Graduates of Yale College*, III, 84–85; Jones, *Annals and Recollections*, pp. 289–291.

23. *Centennial of the Paris Congregational Church*, pp. 28–30; Records of the Paris Hill Church (hereafter cited as Paris Church MSS), in the Utica Public Library, June 7, 1820.

24. William B. Sprague, *Annals of the American Pulpit* (New York, 1859–1873), IV, 473–474. Weeks was author of *The Pilgrim's Progress in the Nineteenth Century* (New York, 1826), a collection of religious essays; he also wrote *The Missionary Arithmetic* (Utica, 1822). For his opposition to Finney see Frank G. Beardsley, *A Mighty Winner of Souls, Charles G. Finney* (New York, [1937]), p. 69.

25. *Centennial of the Paris Congregational Church*, p. 31; Vosburgh, ed., "Records of the Paris Religious Society," p. 96; Paris Church MSS, June 26 and July 3, 1821; Philemon H. Fowler, *Historical Sketch of Presbyterianism within the Bounds of the Synod of Central New York* (Utica, 1877), pp. 172–173.

26. Paris Church MSS, Records . . . Begun, February, 1823; Bagg, *Founders of the Oneida County Medical Society*, pp. 19–20; Vosburgh, ed., "Records of the Paris Religious Society," p. 60; New Hartford Presbyterian Church Records (information from the Reverend George H. Smith of Sauquoit, N.Y.). After Weeks left in 1831, Elnathan rented a pew in the Paris Hill Church 1832–1835 (Paris Church MSS), and it is likely that he attended worship there.

27. Bagg, *Founders of the Oneida County Medical Society*, p. 20; Rogers, *History of Paris*, p. 39; Clinton Congregational Church Records (information from David L.

Johnston of Clinton, N.Y.). The church became Presbyterian in 1864. Their letters of dismissal to the Troy Presbyterian Church are dated April 23, 1837 (*ibid.*). See also, Thomas J. Drake, "History of Oakland County," *Michigan Historical Collections*, XXII (1894), 426; Thaddeus De Witt Seeley, *History of Oakland County, Michigan* (Chicago and New York, 1912), I, 487–488.

28. In 1859 his daughter Elisabeth visited Troy. She found the farm "dreary" and she wept over the "poverty" of her brother Henry, who still lived in the family homestead. By that time Elnathan's gravestone had fallen into disrepair, and she made arrangements to have it fixed (Elisabeth Gertrude Judd [Mrs. Asher B.] Bates, Journal, in the possession of Norwood B. Smith of Menlo Park, California, August 29–31, 1859, pp. 60–62).

29. Oakland County Probate Court Records in Pontiac, Michigan. His trusteeship of the Oneida Institute (later the Whitestown Academy) is mentioned in George W. Gale's, "Autobiography" (typescript in the Collection of Regional History, Cornell University), III, 48.

30. Sylvester Judd, *Thomas Judd and his Descendants*, pp. 25–26.

31. *Memoirs of Rev. Charles G. Finney* (New York, 1876), p. 180.

32. Information from Mrs. Georgia Judd Carpenter of Royal Oak, Michigan. The words on the tombstone are now illegible.

33. Bagg, *Founders of the Oneida County Medical Society*, p. 14; Francis H. Hastings, *Family Record of Dr. Seth Hastings, Senior of Clinton, Oneida County, New York* (Cincinnati, 1899), pp. 11–24. H. H. Kellogg, "The Hastings Family," *The Hamilton Literary Monthly*, XVII (1882), 25–27. Oil paintings of Dr. and Mrs. Hastings are in the possession of Mr. and Mrs. Francis Hastings Gott of Pittsford, New York.

Notes: *Boyhood on the New York Frontier (pages 12–21)*

1. Paris Church MSS; also Vosburgh, ed., "Records of the Paris Religious Society," p. 12.

2. Wager, *Oneida County*, p. 556; Jones, *Annals and Recollections*, pp. 17–18, 295, 300.

3. Purcell, *Connecticut in Transition*, p. 153; Wager, *Oneida County*, pp. 266–269. Dr. Backus is noticed in the *Dictionary of American Biography*, I, 467–468; short lives of the others are in Dexter, *Biographical Sketches of the Graduates of Yale College*, IV, 684–686; V, 160, 303; and VI, 183–184.

4. Adams, *History of the United States*, I, 55; Cooper, *The Pioneers* (1823), chap. 1; Rosenberry, *The Expansion of New England*, p. 159.

5. *Centennial of the Paris Congregational Church 1791–1891*, p. 25; Durant, *History of Oneida County*, pp. 500, 502; A. D. Gridley, *History of the Town of Kirkland, New York* (New York, 1874), p. 196.

6. Sylvester Judd, *Thomas Judd and his Descendants*, pp. 25–26; Paris Church Records (information from Mrs. W. A. Pine of Sauquoit, New York).

7. *Fragments I*, pp. 5–6.

8. Gridley, *History of Kirkland*, p. 132; Wager, *Oneida County*, pp. 266–272. In Hastings, *Family Record of Dr. Seth Hastings*, pp. 98–99, it is stated incorrectly that Gerrit graduated from Hamilton College. His name does not appear in the records of the college or of the Hamilton Oneida Academy, but the latter records are incomplete, and it is possible that he studied briefly at the Academy (information from Edwin Tolan, reference librarian, Hamilton College).

9. Dexter, *Biographical Sketches of the Graduates of Yale College*, VI, 233, 530.

10. *Fragments I*, p. 6.

11. Dexter, *Biographical Sketches of the Graduates of Yale College*, VI, 247–249; Benjamin

W. Dwight, *The History of the Descendants of John Dwight, of Dedham, Mass.* (New York, 1874), pp. 754–755; Antoinette Withington, *The Golden Cloak* (Honolulu, 1953), pp. 84–89. Dwight was minister of the Congregational Church in Richmond, Massachusetts, from 1819 to 1837.

12. *Fragments I*, p. 6.

13. Moses M. Bagg, *The Pioneers of Utica* (Utica, 1877), pp. 446–447; Hastings, *Family Record of Dr. Seth Hastings*, p. 129.

14. *Fragments I*, p. 7. He was 17, not 18, in 1820.

15. Clifford M. Drury, *Marcus Whitman, M.D., Pioneer and Martyr* (Caldwell, Idaho, 1937), pp. 42–46, 52–53; O. Larsell, "Fairfield Medical School and Some Early Oregon Physicians," and Frederick C. Waite, "Medical Education of Dr. Whitman," *Oregon Historical Quarterly*, XXXVII (1936), 102–110 and 198–202; O'Donnell, *Tip of the Hill*, especially pp. 49, 71–75, 101–139; Lucien B. Wells, "Fairfield Medical College," *Transactions of the Oneida Historical Society*, V (1889–1892), 68–71.

16. *Dictionary of American Biography*, II, 116–117.

17. Bagg, *Founders of the Oneida County Medical Society*, p. 18; Levi Beardsley, *Reminiscences* (New York, 1852), p. 425.

18. "He has attended three full courses of medical lectures at Fairfield, N.Y., and one private course at Auburn." (Dr. Bishop to Evarts, February 10, 1827, American Board MSS, XXXVII, No. 26, Houghton Library, Harvard University.) Since Dr. Judd forwarded Bishop's letter to the Board without comment—he commented on Dr. White's —the presumption is that Bishop's statement is correct. For the medical school at Auburn see Elliot G. Storke, *History of Cayuga County, New York* (Syracuse, 1879,) p. 87.

19. The Record Book of the Philosophronic and Ciceronian Societies, in the Sauquoit Valley Central School Museum.

20. R. Carlyle Buley, *The Old Northwest* (Bloomington, 1951), I, 343.

21. *Sentinel and Gazette* (Utica), November 1, 1825.

22. Jones, *Annals and Recollections*, pp. 31–34.

Notes: Appointment as Missionary Physician (pages 22–31)

1. *Dictionary of American Biography*, VI, 394–396; Whitney R. Cross, *The Burned-over District: The Social and Intellectual History of Enthusiastic Religion in Western New York, 1800–1850* (Ithaca, 1950), *passim;* Latourette, *A History of the Expansion of Christianity*, IV, 35, 44, 51, 195, 204–205, 348, 392–393, 431–432; *A Narrative of the Revival of Religion in the County of Oneida, particularly in the Bounds of the Presbytery of Oneida, in the Year 1826* (Utica, 1826), pp. 23–24.

2. *Fragments I*, pp. 7–8. Judd's Bible (in HMCS Library) is dated on the flyleaf April 11, 1826.

3. Charles Beecher, ed., *Autobiography, Correspondence, etc., of Lyman Beecher* (New York, 1864), II, 310–312; *A Narrative of the Revival of Religion*, p. 24; Finney, *Memoirs*, pp. 181–182. The printed text of the *Memoirs* (p. 180) mentions the conversion of "Dr. Garnet Judd," but in the manuscript, which is not in Finney's hand, there is an ink blot over "Garnet," possibly an attempt on Finney's part to correct the spelling (information from Mary C. Venn, Oberlin College Library). It was probably about this time that Finney gave him the family book in which he wrote his autobiographical statement (in *Fragments I*).

4. *Fragments I*, p. 6.

5. *Ibid.*, p. 8.

6. Information from the Reverend George H. Smith, historian of the New Hartford Presbyterian Church. Nothing in the extant records indicates that Dr. Judd ever joined

the church at Paris Hill, and technically New Hartford may claim him as its first missioner.

7. *Fragments I*, pp. 8–9.

8. Hastings, *Family Record of Dr. Seth Hastings*, pp. 189–195; also in Elizabeth L. Wight, ed., *The Memoirs of Elizabeth Kinau Wilder* (Honolulu: privately printed, 1909), pp. 1–6. For Arnold see *National Cyclopaedia of American Biography* (New York, 1907), IX, 226–227, and Sylvester Judd, *Thomas Judd and his Descendants*, p. 18.

9. Oliver W. Elsbree, *The Rise of the Missionary Spirit in America, 1790–1815* (Williamsburg, Pa., 1928), pp. 102–104.

10. Rufus Anderson, *Memorial Volume of the First Fifty Years of the American Board of Commissioners for Foreign Missions* (4th ed., Boston, 1861), pp. 41, 269, 405; William E. Strong, *The Story of the American Board* (New York, 1910), especially pp. 7, 17, 80, 108, 124.

11. *Dictionary of American Biography*, VI, 215.

12. E. Judson [G. P. Judd] to Evarts, September 6, 1826, American Board MSS, XXXVII, No. 34.

13. Judd to Evarts, February 15, 1827, *ibid.*, XXXVII, No. 22; for Davis see *Dictionary of American Biography*, V, 116–117; for Nash see Cross, *Burned-over District*, pp. 160–161.

14. Greene and Evarts to E. Judson [G. P. Judd], January 9, 1827, American Board MSS, Letters 1826–1827; also printed in Wight, *Memoirs of E. K. Wilder*, pp. 28–29.

15. American Board MSS, XXXVII, Nos. 23–33.

16. Aikin, a graduate of Middlebury and Andover, served in Utica until 1835; Brace, a graduate of Hamilton College and Andover, resigned in 1828 (Bagg, *Pioneers of Utica*, pp. 458, 598).

17. Coe, a graduate of Yale and Andover, was minister of the New Hartford Church 1814–1835 (Dexter, *Biographical Sketches of the Graduates of Yale College*, VI, 183–184).

18. American Board MSS, XXXVII, No. 22.

19. American Board MSS, Letters 1827–1828.

20. Judd to Evarts, June 6, 1827, American Board MSS, XXXVII, No. 19.

21. Evarts to Judd, June 11, 1827, American Board MSS, Letters 1827–1828.

22. American Board MSS, XXXVII, No. 18.

23. *Ibid.*, XXXI, Pt. 2, No. 99.

24. "I offered myself to the American Board, and after some correspondence and a little personal acquaintance with the Prudential Committee, was appointed, August 3, 1827, to the work of physician to the Sandwich Island Mission." (*Fragments I*, p. 9); Evarts to Judd, August 10, 1827, in Wight, *Memoirs of E. K. Wilder*, pp. 29–30.

N o t e s :   *Marriage and Farewell (pages 32–41)*

1. Anderson, *Memorial Volume*, p. 272.

2. Lester W. Fish, *The Fish Family in England and America* (Rutland, Vt., [1948]), pp. 252–259.

3. *Fragments I*, pp. 22–25. For an account of her life in Sacketts Harbor see *Biography of Mrs. Lydia B. Bacon* (Boston, 1856), pp. 220–223, 346–348.

4. Laura Fish Judd, *Honolulu: Sketches of the Life, Social, Political and Religious, in the Hawaiian Islands from 1828 to 1861* (Honolulu, 1928), p. 25. Miss Elizabeth Simpson of Littlewood, N.Y., identifies this building as the eastern schoolhouse at the junction of Main Street (or Oswego Road), Pulaski Road, and Maple View Road, the present site of the Park Hotel.

5. Elizabeth M. Simpson, *Mexico, Mother of Towns* [Buffalo, 1949], p. 429; also information from Miss Simpson.

6. "Recollections of Agnes H. B. Judd" (typescript in the possession of Mrs. George P. Cooke of Molokai, Hawaii), February 7, 1924. Agnes Judd was Laura's daughter-in-law.

7. *Fragments I*, p. 26. David Raymond Dixon was minister of the Presbyterian Church in Mexico 1815–1835 (Dexter, *Biographical Sketches of the Graduates of Yale College*, VI, 105–106). She joined his church on April 22, 1821, just after her 17th (not 19th) birthday (Session Book of the First Presbyterian Church, Mexico, N.Y., [in the Archives of the Presbyterian Historical Society, Philadelphia], I, 32–33).

8. *Fragments I*, pp. 26–27. Her letter of dismissal was granted December 7, 1825 (*ibid.*, I, 116); she was admitted to the Clinton church on January 1, 1826 (information from David L. Johnston of Clinton, N.Y.). The printed version of her Memoir gives the date of her arrival in Clinton as 1823 and gives her employer as Miss "Boyce." Miss Royce is mentioned in Laura's letter to Mrs. Finney, written from the Clinton Female Seminary, August 6, [1826] (Finney Papers, Oberlin College Library). The Royces were among the earliest settlers in the area (Wager, *Oneida County*, p. 492).

9. *Fragments I*, p. 26.

10. Arnold's poem in Hastings, *Family Record of Dr. Seth Hastings*, pp. 190–195, and in Wight, *Memoirs of E. K. Wilder*, pp. 1–6.

11. *Fragments I*, p. 28.

12. American Board MSS, XXXVII, No. 104.

13. American Board MSS, Letters 1827–1828, gives a summary of this letter.

14. Finney Papers.

15. Judd to Evarts, September 25, 1827, American Board MSS, XXXVII, No. 17; *Western Recorder*, IV, No. 39 (September 25, 1827), p. 154.

16. Francis J. Halford, *9 Doctors & God* (Honolulu, 1954), *passim;* Buley, *Old Northwest*, I, 328.

17. Finney Papers. The Reverend Hiram Huntington Kellogg signed Mrs. Judd's Book of Farewells (HMCS Library) on October 10, 1827.

18. Dr. Judd's copy of Andrew Fuller, *The Gospel its own Witness* (New York, 1800), inscribed to him by Seth Hastings on October 12, 1827, is in HMCS Library.

19. L. F. Judd, Book of Farewells.

20. Judd to the Sandwich Island Mission, May 26, 1843, HMCS Library; also in American Board MSS, CXXXIV, No. 32. Part of this letter, much paraphrased, is in L. F. Judd, *Honolulu*, pp. 86–87.

21. *Fragments I*, p. 9. They were in Troy on Wednesday, October 17, (L. F. Judd, Book of Farewells), and they had reached Boston by Monday, October 22 (*Fragments IV*, p. 59, L. F. Judd, Journal, October 22, 1832).

22. *Fragments I*, p. 9. Henry Homes lived at Bowdoin Place (see *The Boston Directory* [Boston, 1827], p. 142. His wife Dorcas wrote a poem in Mrs. Judd's Book of Farewells on November 2, 1827. Their son Henry Augustus was a missionary to Turkey (*Dictionary of American Biography*, IX, 191).

23. "I commenced this letter last evening, and after filling one sheet, went to Mr. John Tappan's where the missionaries and a large party of friends were assembled." (Elisha Loomis to the Sandwich Islands missionaries, October 30, 1827, HMCS Library).

24. *Missionary Herald*, XXIII, (1827), 386; Hiram A. Bingham, *A Residence of Twenty-one Years in the Sandwich Islands* (3d ed., Canandaigua, N.Y., 1855), p. 60.

25. Lorrin Andrews, Diary; Theodosia Arnold (Mrs. J. S.) Green, journal-letter; Maria Patton Chamberlain, Journal, all under date of November 3, 1827, HMCS Library.

26. Stewart to Judd, February 22, 1828, *Fragments III*, p. 91.

27. Evarts to Judd, November 2, 1827, Wight, *Memoirs of E. K. Wilder*, p. 31.

28. *Fragments III*, p. 5; Beecher, *Autobiography*, II, 312.

29. Finney Papers. The quotation (slightly paraphrased) at the end of the letter is from Byron's "Fare Thee Well" (1816):

"Fare thee well! and if for ever,
Still for ever, fare *thee well.*"

Margaret (Mrs. Gordon) Hall served in the Maharatta Mission (Anderson, *Memorial Volume*, p. 419). Mr. Ibbetson is doubtless N. N. Ibbetson who wrote a poem in Mrs. Judd's Book of Farewells on October 2. Mrs. Judd's statement that the *Parthian* spread her sails at 9 A.M. may refer to a maneuver preliminary to the actual sailing.

Notes: Around Cape Horn to Hawaii (pages 42–53)

1. Boston ship registers (information from Charles R. Copeland, Peabody Museum, Salem, Massachusetts). Dr. Judd's Journal of the voyage describes her as 337 tons, 105 feet long, 30 feet beam (*Fragments III*, p. 9.)
2. *Missionary Herald*, XXIII (December, 1827), 386, and XXV (January, 1829), 28. For Taylor see George V. Blue, "Green's Missionary Report on Oregon, 1829," *Oregon Historical Quarterly*, XXX (1929), 261–264; for Marshall see Samuel E. Morison, "Boston Traders in Hawaii, 1789–1823," Massachusetts Historical Society *Proceedings*, LIV (1920), 43, reprinted without notes in his *By Land and By Sea* (New York, 1954).
3. Maria Patton Chamberlain, Journal, and Lorrin Andrews, Diary, November 3, 1827.
4. *Fragments III*, p. 9; Samuel E. Morison, *The Maritime History of Massachusetts* (Cambridge, Mass., 1941), pp. 97, 256.
5. *Fragments III*, pp. 6–7.
6. Lorrin Andrews, Diary, November 7, 1827.
7. Laura Fish Judd, Journal of 1827–1828, in the possession of Mrs. Mary H. Marks of Old Forge, N.Y. (hereafter cited as Marks MS). Unless otherwise stated, this Journal and Dr. Judd's (*Fragments III*) are the authority for all incidents in this chapter.
8. Judd to Evarts, December 4, 1827, American Board MSS, XXXII, No. 254; also in *Fragments II*, pp. 5–6. This correspondence as printed contains omissions and inaccuracies; quotations from it have been corrected by reference to the original letters in the American Board MSS.
9. Joint letter to Evarts, May, 1828, American Board MSS, XXXII, No. 255; also in *Fragments II*, p. 13.
10. *Missionary Herald*, XXV (January, 1829), 27–31.
11. L. F. Judd, *Honolulu*, p. 1.
12. Richard Henry Dana, *Two Years before the Mast* (1840), chap. 4 (Everyman ed., pp. 16–17).
13. Frederick W. Beechey, *Narrative of a Voyage to the Pacific and Beering's Straits* (London, 1831), I, 9, and II, 629–632.
14. Judd to Evarts, December 4, 1827, to March 22, 1828, American Board MSS, XXXII, No. 254; also in *Fragments II*, p. 10; Halford, *9 Doctors & God*, p. 93.
15. Morison, *Maritime History of Massachusetts*, p. 53; Felix Riesenberg, *Cape Horn* (New York, 1939), pp. 237, 272, 280, 435–436.
16. Lorrin Andrews, Diary, January 25, 1828; Ephraim W. Clark, Journal, January 25, 1828; Theodosia A. Green, journal-letter, January 28, 1828, HMCS Library.
17. Cf. Louis B. Wright and Mary I. Fry, *Puritans in the South Seas* (New York, 1936), pp. 302–303.
18. Judd to Evarts, December 4, 1827, to March 22, 1828, American Board MSS, XXXII, No. 254; also in *Fragments II*, p. 9. At sea, Sunday was traditionally a day of rest (Dana, *Two Years before the Mast*, p. 16).

19. Jones to Marshall, June 15, 1828, Josiah Marshall MSS, (Houghton Library, Harvard University); for Jones see Morison, *By Land and By Sea*, pp. 76–77, 97.

20. *Fragments III*, pp. 90–96.

21. Judd to Evarts, December 4, 1827, to March 22, 1828, American Board MSS, XXXII, No. 254, also in *Fragments II*, pp. 9–10.

22. Theodosia A. Green, journal-letter, February 25, 1828, HMCS Library.

23. L. F. Judd, *Honolulu*, p. 1. Mrs. Judd's Journal (Marks MS) gives a brief and almost illegible account of the last two days of the voyage.

24. Joint letter to the American Board, April 27, 1828, *Missionary Herald*, XXV (January, 1829), 21.

25. L. F. Judd, *Honolulu*, pp. 4–5.

26. G. P. Judd, Journal, April 1, 1828, *Fragments III*, p. 85.

27. L. F. Judd, *Honolulu*, p. 5. Theodosia A. Green, journal-letter, March 31, 1828; Maria Patton Chamberlain, Journal, March 31, 1828; the hymn may be found in *Hymns for Social Worship* (New York, 1840), p. 450.

28. L. F. Judd, *Honolulu*, pp. 5, 7.

Notes: Hawaiian Islands in 1828 *(pages 54–63)*

1. L. F. Judd, *Honolulu*, p. 2.

2. Francis Warriner, *Cruise of the U.S. Frigate Potomac* (New York, 1835), p. 220.

3. Sereno E. Bishop, *Reminiscences of Old Hawaii* (Honolulu, 1916), pp. 34–35. See also Frederick D. Bennett, *Narrative of a Whaling Voyage Round the Globe from the Year 1833 to 1836* (London, 1840), I, 196; Titus M. Coan, *Life in Hawaii: An Autobiographical Sketch* (New York, 1882), pp. 239–240; George M. Colvocoresses, *Four Years in a Government Exploring Expedition* (New York, 1852), p. 183; John Diell, "Sketch of Honolulu, Oahu," *Hawaiian Spectator*, I, No. 2 (1838), 83; Henry M. Lyman, *Hawaiian Yesterdays* (Chicago, 1906), p. 133.

4. L. F. Judd, Journal (Marks MS), March 31, 1828; G. P. Judd, Journal, March 30, 1828, *Fragments III*, p. 83; Mary C. Alexander, *William Patterson Alexander in Kentucky, the Marquesas, Hawaii* (Honolulu: privately printed, 1934), p. 71; Mary D. Frear, *Lowell and Abigail: A Realistic Idyll* (New Haven: privately printed, 1934), p. 61; Edward T. Perkins, *Na Motu: or Reef-Rovings in the South Seas* (New York, 1854), p. 121; Frederick Walpole, *Four Years in the Pacific in Her Majesty's Ship Collingwood from 1844 to 1848* (London, 1849), II, 247; Theodore Morgan, *Hawaii, a Century of Economic Change 1778-1876* (Cambridge, 1948), pp. 112–113.

5. L. F. Judd, Journal, September 9, 1830, *Fragments IV*, p. 47; see also Charles S. Stewart, *Journal of a Residence in the Sandwich Islands during the Years 1823, 1824, and 1825* (2d ed., New York, 1828), pp. 112–113.

6. James Jackson Jarves, *Why and What Am I?* (London, 1857), quoted in Francis Steegmuller, *The Two Lives of James Jackson Jarves* (New Haven, 1951), p. 18.

7. Ralph S. Kuykendall, *The Hawaiian Kingdom 1778–1854: Foundation and Transformation* (Honolulu, 1938), pp. 1–20; Andrew W. Lind, *An Island Community* (Chicago, 1938), pp. 1–5, 26; Morgan, *Hawaii*, pp. 3–7, 11–13; Joseph C. Furnas, *Anatomy of Paradise: Hawaii and the Islands of the South Seas* (New York, [1948]), pp. 32, 37.

8. Harold W. Bradley, *The American Frontier in Hawaii: The Pioneers, 1789–1843* (Stanford, 1942), pp. 79–82, 214–218; Jean I. Brookes, *International Rivalry in the Pacific Islands 1800–1875* (Berkeley and Los Angeles, 1941), p. 15; John S. Furnivall, *Colonial Policy and Practice* (New York, 1956), pp. 3–4; Kuykendall, *Hawaiian Kingdom 1778-1854*, pp. 21–27, 82–93.

9. *Ibid.*, pp. 101, 336; Bradley, *American Frontier in Hawaii*, pp. 41, 82; Brookes, *International Rivalry in the Pacific Islands*, p. 19; Morgan, *Hawaii*, p. 114.

10. Latourette, *History of the Expansion of Christianity*, V, 200, 219, 226, 261.

11. Lee to Turrill, October 11, 1851 (typescript, HMCS Library); an extract from this letter is in Meiric K. Dutton, *William L. Lee* (Honolulu, 1953), an unpaginated work. See also Furnas, *Anatomy of Paradise*, pp. 119–124; Morgan, *Hawaii*, p. 115; Bradford Smith, *Yankees in Paradise* (Philadelphia, 1956), pp. 87–88, 287.

12. Alfred L. Kroeber, *Anthropology* (New York, 1948), pp. 403–405; Latourette, *History of the Expansion of Christianity*, IV, 198–199.

13. Jacques Arago, *Narrative of a Voyage Round the World* (London, 1823), Pt. 2, pp. 89–90.

14. Latourette, *History of the Expansion of Christianity*, IV, 44, 47–48, 52, 75, and V, 201, 319. For Hastings see *Dictionary of American Biography*, VIII, 387–388.

15. Kuykendall, *Hawaiian Kingdom 1778–1854*, p. 101; Bradley, *American Frontier in Hawaii*, p. 124.

16. Bingham, *Residence*, p. 81; Bradley, *American Frontier in Hawaii*, pp. 129, 386–387.

17. Stewart, *Journal*, p. 103.

18. Jarves, *Why and What Am I?*, quoted in Steegmuller, *James Jackson Jarves*, p. 22.

19. Chester S. Lyman, *Around the Horn to the Sandwich Islands and California, 1845–1850*, Frederick J. Teggart, ed., (New Haven, 1924), pp. 151, 178–179; Mrs. Emerson's Journal' March 1, 1833, in Oliver P. Emerson, *Pioneer Days in Hawaii* (New York, 1928), p. 68.

20. Sereno Bishop, *Reminiscences*, p. 20; Mrs. Jarves to her parents, November 15, 1840, in Steegmuller, *James Jackson Jarves*, p. 51; Mrs. Thurston to Mrs. Homes, October 28, 1835, in *Life and Times of Mrs. Lucy G. Thurston, wife of Rev. Asa Thurston, pioneer missionary to the Sandwich Islands* (2d ed., Ann Arbor, Michigan, 1921), p. 128.

21. Henry A. Wise, *Los Gringos* (New York, 1849), p. 363.

22. Joseph G. Clark, *Lights and Shadows of Sailor Life* (Boston, 1847), p. 172.

23. Sereno Bishop, *Reminiscences*, p. 30; see also Samuel L. Clemens [Mark Twain], *Roughing It* (Hartford, 1884), p. 484.

24. Mrs. Jarves to her parents, October, 1839, in Steegmuller, *James Jackson Jarves*, p. 38.

25. Kroeber, *Anthropology*, p. 403; Latourette, *History of the Expansion of Christianity*, IV, 14, 20, 45, and V, 247, 259–260, 374.

26. Kuykendall, *Hawaiian Kingdom 1778–1854*, pp. 102, 114–117; Bradley, *American Frontier in Hawaii*, pp. 155, 166, 174; Furnas, *Anatomy of Paradise*, pp. 129–133; Wright and Fry, *Puritans in the South Seas*, p. 303; Foster R. Dulles, *America in the Pacific: A Century of Expansion* (Boston and New York, 1938), p. 142.

27. Latourette, *History of the Expansion of Christianity*, IV, 430, and V, 199, 361, 376; Harry R. Rudin, *Germans in the Cameroons 1884–1914: A Case Study in Modern Imperialism* (London, 1938), pp. 218, 221, 381.

28. Brookes, *International Rivalry in the Pacific Islands*, pp. 51, 81, 124.

29. Jones to Marshall and Wildes, March 9, 1823, in Morison, *By Land and By Sea*, p. 97.

30. Bradley, *American Frontier in Hawaii*, p. 175; Sheldon Dibble, *A History of the Sandwich Islands* (Honolulu, 1909), pp. 190–196; Rev. and Mrs. Orramel Gulick, *The Pilgrims of Hawaii* (New York, 1918), p. 112; Samuel Williston, *William Richards* (Cambridge: privately printed, 1938), pp. 36–38.

31. Judd to Evarts, September 26, 1831, American Board MSS, LXVIII, No. 128, partly printed in Kuykendall, *Hawaiian Kingdom 1778–1854*, p. 131.

32. Latourette, *History of the Expansion of Christianity*, V, 205, 213.

33. Bingham, *Residence*, p. 326.

34. Halford, *9 Doctors & God*, p. 90.

35. G. P. Judd, Journal, April 1, 1828, *Fragments III*, pp. 85–86; L. F. Judd, *Honolulu*, p. 9.

36. *Ibid.*, p. 3.

1. L. F. Judd, *Honolulu,* pp. 25–26.
2. Sereno Bishop, *Reminiscences,* p. 16; Emerson, *Pioneer Days in Hawaii,* p. 62 n.; Arthur D. Baldwin, *A Memoir of Henry Perrine Baldwin 1842 to 1911* (Cleveland: privately printed, 1915), p. 24; Coan, *Life in Hawaii,* p. 111.
3. L. F. Judd, Journal, July, 1830, *Fragments IV,* p. 36; Stephen Reynolds, Journal, May 20, 1828, cited in Bradley, *American Frontier in Hawaii,* p. 86.
4. *Instructions of the Prudential Committee of the American Board of Commissioners for Foreign Missions to the Sandwich Islands Mission* (Lahainaluna, 1838), pp. 13–14, 24.
5. L. F. Judd, *Honolulu,* pp. 57, 81, 85; Joseph Tracy, *History of the American Board of Commissioners for Foreign Missions* (2d ed., New York, 1842), pp. 54–55.
6. L. F. Judd, *Honolulu,* pp. 16, 19; L. F. Judd, Journal, October 5, 1830, *Fragments IV,* p. 54.
7. [George Washington Bates], *Sandwich Island Notes* (New York, 1854), p. 252; Coan, *Life in Hawaii,* pp. 111–112; Sereno Bishop, *Reminiscences,* p. 31; James J. Jarves, *Scenes and Scenery in the Sandwich Islands* (Boston, 1843), pp. 90–94; Mrs. Cooke to her sister, April 23, 1842, in Mary A. Richards, *The Chiefs' Children's School: A Record Compiled from the Diary and Letters of Amos Starr Cooke and Juliette Montague Cooke* (Honolulu: privately printed, 1937), p. 135.
8. Judd to Chamberlain, November 6, 1830, in George P. Cooke, *Moolelo o Molokai, A Ranch Story of Molokai* (Honolulu, 1949), pp. 154–155; G. P. Judd, Journal, November 6, 1830, *Fragments IV,* pp. 7–8.
9. Dr. Judd's autobiographical statement, *Fragments I,* p. 13; L. F. Judd, *Honolulu,* p. 34.
10. Judd to Chamberlain, October 24, 1834, HMCS Library; Wight, *Memoirs of E. K. Wilder,* pp. 13–14; G. P. Judd, Jr., to Elizabeth Bingham, July 11, 1837, in L. F. Judd, Book of Farewells, No. 46, HMCS Library.
11. G. P. Judd, Journal, October 25, 1830, *Fragments IV,* p. 6.
12. L. F. Judd, Journal, November 5, 1832, *Fragments IV,* p. 66.
13. G. P. Judd, Journal, April 26, 1831, *Fragments IV,* pp. 22–23; Kuykendall, *Hawaiian Kingdom 1778–1854,* p. 128.
14. Clark, *Lights and Shadows of Sailor Life,* p. 180; Frear, *Lowell and Abigail,* p. 152; Charles Wilkes, *Narrative of the United States Exploring Expedition, 1838–1842* (Philadelphia, 1845), IV, 30.
15. G. P. Judd, Journal, February 6, March 1 and 11, 1831, *Fragments IV,* pp. 16–18; Judd to Chamberlain, March 13, 1832, HMCS Library.
16. G. P. Judd, Journal, March 30, 1828, *Fragments III,* p. 84; Judd to Evarts, October 13, 1828, American Board MSS, XXXII, No. 182, partly printed in *Fragments II,* p. 19.
17. Judd to Finney, December 3, 1828, Finney Papers.
18. *Missionary Herald,* XXVI (1830), 6; *Instructions of the Prudential Committee . . . to the Sandwich Islands Mission,* p. 13.
19. Gulick, *Pilgrims of Hawaii,* p. 115; Halford, *9 Doctors & God,* pp. 123, 159.
20. *Missionary Herald,* XXV (1829), 26; and XXVI (1830), 280; see also *Extracts from the Letters and Journals of Daniel Wheeler* (Philadelphia, 1840), p. 167.
21. Sereno Bishop, *Reminiscences,* p. 36; Judd to Chamberlain, October 4, 1834, HMCS Library; Bennett, *Narrative of a Whaling Voyage,* I, 218.
22. Judd to Thomas Hastings, May 20, [1832], S. G. Wilder Papers, on deposit, HMCS Library; Thurston to Judd, March 1, 1834, HMCS Library; also "Answers by the Sandwich Islands Missionaries to the Questions in the Circular of March 15, 1833" (typescript (from MS), HMCS Library), pp. 111–114; Prince Lot Kamehameha, Journal, April 17, 1850, Bishop Museum, Honolulu.
23. G. P. Judd, Journal, January 16 and May 1, 1831, *Fragments IV,* pp. 14, 24;

Alonzo Chapin, Journal, June 3, 1832, Honolulu Academy of Arts; Levi Chamberlain, Journal, August 22 and October 17, 1830, March 6, May 8 and 22, 1831, June 3 and 16, 1833, HMCS Library, typescript in Yale Library.

24. G. P. Judd, Journal, June 19 and 26, also November 14, 1831, *Fragments IV*, pp. 28–29, 34.

25. L. F. Judd, *Honolulu*, pp. 8, 32; Bingham, *Residence*, p. 345.

26. Charles S. Stewart, *A Visit to the South Seas, in the U.S.S. Vincennes* (London, 1832), II, 256–262.

27. Judd to Chamberlain, December 3, 1839, HMCS Library.

28. Judd to Finney, April 28, 1837, Finney Papers.

29. Bradley, *American Frontier in Hawaii*, p. 209; Dibble, *History of the Sandwich Islands*, pp. 341–342; Kuykendall, *Hawaiian Kingdom 1778–1854*, pp. 140–143, 163–165, 168; *Extracts from the Letters and Journals of Daniel Wheeler*, pp. 167–168, 232; L. F. Judd, *Honolulu*, pp. 59–60.

30. Judd to Hunnewell, October 29, 1832, Hunnewell Papers, Houghton Library, Harvard University; G. P. Judd, Journal of a Tour of Oahu, March 27–28, 1834, cited in Bradley, *American Frontier in Hawaii*, p. 338; Stephen Reynolds, Journal, January 25–26, February 3, 1833, Peabody Museum, Salem, Massachusetts; William S. Ruschenberger, *A Voyage Round the World* (Philadelphia, 1838), p. 455.

31. L. F. Judd, *Honolulu*, p. 41; Mrs. Emerson's Journal, March 1, 1833, in Emerson, *Pioneer Days in Hawaii*, p. 68; Kuykendall, *Hawaiian Kingdom 1778–1854*, p. 134.

32. L. F. Judd, *Honolulu*, pp. 41–42, 46, 191; L. F. Judd, Journal, July 29, 1830, *Fragments IV*, p. 37; Bradley, *American Frontier in Hawaii*, p. 276.

33. Kuykendall, *Hawaiian Kingdom 1778–1854*, pp. 114–116, 136.

34. Judd to Evarts, August 5, 1829, American Board MSS, XXXII, No. 183, also in *Fragments II*, p. 21.

35. G. P. Judd, Journal, July 5, 1831, *Fragments IV*, p. 29.

36. Judd to Greene, October 20, 1835, American Board MSS, LXVIII, No. 135, also in *Fragments II*, p. 101.

37. *Friend* (April, 1928), p. 77; L. F. Judd, *Honolulu*, p. 100; Wight, *Memoirs of E. K. Wilder*, p. 11; Judd to Ruggles, April 18, 1835, HMCS Library.

38. Mrs. Cooke to her aunt, May 25, 1837, in "Letters of Juliette M. Cooke and Amos Starr Cooke 1836–1849" (typescript in the possession of George P. Cooke of Molokai, Hawaii); Fitch W. Taylor, *The Flag Ship: or a Voyage around the World, in the United States Frigate Columbia* (New York, 1840), II, 290.

39. L. F. Judd, Journal, October 22, 1832, *Fragments IV*, p. 59.

Notes: Life in the Mission, II (pages 74–83)

1. Bradley, *American Frontier in Hawaii*, pp. 115–116, 168; Brookes, *International Rivalry in the Pacific Islands*, p. 18; Smith, *Yankees in Paradise*, pp. 55, 330.

2. Addison Gulick, *Evolutionist and Missionary John Thomas Gulick* (Chicago, 1932), p. 10; see also William R. Castle, Jr., *Hawaii Past and Present* (new ed., New York, 1926), p. 41.

3. Gulick, *Pilgrims of Hawaii*, p. 161; see also Coan, *Life in Hawaii*, pp. 254–255; Rudin, *Germans in the Cameroons*, pp. 221, 380.

4. *Instructions of the Prudential Committee . . . to the Sandwich Islands Mission*, p. 43.

5. Bradley, *American Frontier in Hawaii*, pp. 149, 339; Kuykendall, *Hawaiian Kingdom 1778–1854*, pp. 104–106, 111–112; Benjamin O. Wist, *A Century of Public Education in Hawaii* (Honolulu, 1940), p. 23; Williston, *William Richards*, p. 25.

6. Judd to Ruggles, August 28, 1830, and to Chamberlain, October 4, 1834, HMCS Library; L. F. Judd, Journal, August 16, 25, and 26, 1830, *Fragments IV*, pp. 41, 43–44; G. P. Judd, Journal, January 19, 1831, *Fragments IV*, pp. 14–15.

7. Mrs. Judd to Mrs. Finney, December 10, 1832, Finney Papers; Judd to Anderson, October 23, 1833, and October 8, 1835, American Board MSS, LXVIII, Nos. 130 and 134, also in *Fragments II*, pp. 56, 92–93.

8. Judd to Anderson, October 23, 1833 (cited in note 7, above); L. F. Judd, *Honolulu*, pp. 55–56.

9. Judd to Anderson, October 8, 1835 (cited in note 7, above); Furnas, *Anatomy of Paradise*, p. 158.

10. Cooke to Anderson, July 27, 1840, in Richards, *Chiefs' Children's School*, p. 69, also pp. 25–26, 113, 178–183; L. F. Judd, *Honolulu*, pp. 60, 73.

11. *Ibid.*, p. 53.

12. *Ibid.*, p. 74; Mary C. Alexander and Charlotte P. Dodge, *Punahou 1841–1941* (Berkeley, 1941), pp. 53–60; Judd to Anderson, July 2, 1840, American Board MSS, CXXXVII, No. 79, also in *Fragments II*, pp. 114–119.

13. Alexander and Dodge, *Puanhou*, pp. 63, 67; Judd to Chamberlain, July 3 and 12, 1841, HMCS Library. Dr. Judd's salary at the time was $680 a year.

14. Ethel M. Damon, *The Stone Church at Kawaiahao* (Honolulu, 1945), pp. 1, 48, 52–54; Wilkes, *United States Exploring Expedition*, IV, 52; L. F. Judd, *Honolulu*, p. 49; see also Judd's Annual Report for 1840 and 1841, American Board MSS, CXXXVII, No. 91, also in *Fragments II*, p. 126; Judd to Anderson, April 19, 1842, American Board MSS, CXXXVII, No. 84; the paragraph containing the sentence quoted is not in *Fragments II*, pp. 134–137.

15. Testimony of Kekuanaoa, January 31, 1849, Privy Council Record, V, 329, AH; Jean Hobbs, *Hawaii: A Pageant of the Soil* (Stanford University Press, 1935), pp. 171–172; Judd's Annual Report for 1840 and 1841 (cited in note above).

16. Herman Melville, *Typee* (1846), appendix (Everyman ed., p. 286); Robert Louis Stevenson, *In the South Seas*, p. 275, *et seq.*, cited in Furnas, *Anatomy of Paradise*, p. 337.

17. Judd to Finney, April 28, 1837, Finney Papers; G. P. Judd, Journal, January 15, also April 1 and 6, 1831, *Fragments IV*, pp. 14, 19–21; Judd to Evarts, September 26, 1831, American Board MSS, LXVIII, No. 128; Kuykendall, *Hawaiian Kingdom 1778–1854*, pp. 130–131.

18. Miller's memorandum of September 25, 1831, and Judd to Hunnewell, October 29, 1832 (Hunnewell Papers, Houghton Library, Harvard University), quoted in Bradley, *American Frontier in Hawaii*, pp. 200, 202; G. P. Judd, Journal, November 10, 1831, *Fragments IV*, p. 32.

19. Judd to Wyllie, February 17, 1860, L. F. Judd, *Honolulu*, p. 191; see also Mrs. Emerson's Journal, April 7, 1834, in Emerson, *Pioneer Days in Hawaii*, p. 94.

20. L. F. Judd, *Honolulu*, pp. 83, 89; Baldwin's letter of July 18, 1842, in Gulick, *Pilgrims of Hawaii*, p. 205; Kuykendall, *Hawaiian Kingdom 1778–1854*, p. 162. The cold-water procession took place on October 27, 1842 (Mrs. Gorham Nye, Journal, AH).

21. L. F. Judd, *Honolulu*, pp. 99, 122, 131; Wight, *Memoirs of E. K. Wilder*, p. 74.

22. Judd to Greene, August 20, 1844, American Board MSS, CCXXXV, No. 127; the last sentence does not appear in the letter as printed in *Fragments II*, p. 165.

23. *Friend*, August 1, 1845; "Reminiscences of Henry L. Sheldon," I, 16 (typescript, AH); Steen Bille, "Report on the Corvette Galathea's Circumnavigation 1845, 1846. and 1847" (typescript translation of the 1851 Dutch edition, HMCS Library), pp. 50, 150,

24. Meiric K. Dutton, *His Swedish Majesty's Frigate Eugenie at Honolulu* (Honolulu, 1954), an unpaginated translation from vol. I of C. Skogman's account.

25. "Reminiscences of Henry L. Sheldon," I, 30, AH.

26. Printed minutes of the annual meetings of the mission, 1832–1842, HMCS Library; Judd to Anderson, January 7, 1834, American Board MSS, LXVIII, No. 131, also in *Fragments II*, pp. 69–70; G. P. Judd, Journal, March 22, 1831, *Fragments IV*, p. 19.

27. Mrs. Judd to Mrs. Finney, December 10, 1832, Finney Papers.

28. Judd to Anderson, October 23, 1833, American Board MSS, LXVIII, No. 130, also in *Fragments II*, pp. 67–68; Halford, *9 Doctors & God*, p. 145.

29. *The Revised Minutes of the Delegate Meeting of the Sandwich Islands Mission, June 4th to 20th, 1838* (Honolulu, 1839), p. 9; Judd to Anderson, August 27 and October 7, 1838, American Board MSS, CXXXVII, Nos. 75 and 77, also in *Fragments II*, pp. 106, 111; Judd's Annual Report for 1839, HMCS Library; Kuykendall, *Hawaiian Kingdom 1778–1854*, pp. 105, 158.

30. T. C. Rooke in *Hawaiian Spectator*, I, No. 2 (1838), 27–28; G. P. Judd, "Remarks on the Climate of the Sandwich Islands . . ." *ibid.*, I, No. 2 (1838), 18–27; Francis A. Olmsted, *Incidents of a Whaling Voyage* (New York, 1841), p. 258; Kuykendall, *Hawaiian Kingdom 1778–1854*, p. 105; Steegmuller, *James Jackson Jarves*, p. 37.

31. Warriner, *Cruise of the Potomac*, p. 224; Wilkes, *United States Exploring Expedition*, IV, 115; Charles Nordhoff, *Northern California, Oregon, and the Sandwich Islands* (New York, 1874), pp. 22–23; see also, Gulick, *Pilgrims of Hawaii*, p. 210; Smith, *Yankees in Paradise*, pp. 163, 298.

32. Bingham to Judd, October 26, 1835, HMCS Library.

Notes: Medical Practice (pages 84–95)

1. Judd to Ruggles, August 28, 1830, and to Chamberlain, March 13, 1832, HMCS Library; *Extracts from the Minutes of a General Meeting of the Sandwich Islands Mission, Held at Honolulu, June, 1832* (Oahu, 1832), p. 25; "Answers . . . to the questions . . . of March 15, 1833," HMCS Library.

2. Judd to Anderson, October 15, 1832, American Board MSS, LXVIII, No. 129, also in *Fragments II*, pp. 51–52.

3. Judd to Greene, October 20, 1835, American Board MSS, LXVIII, No. 135, also in *Fragments II*, pp. 97, 99; Judd to Ruggles (in Boston), April 18, 1835, HMCS Library.

4. Judd to Evarts, August 5, 1829, American Board MSS, CXXXII, No. 183, also in *Fragments II*, pp. 21–25; Judd's autobiographical statement, *Fragments I*, p. 13; Levi Chamberlain, Journal, May 18 and June 22, 1829; G. P. Judd, Journal, July 31, 1831, *Fragments IV*, p. 29.

5. Judd to Greene, October 20, 1835 (cited in note 3, above); L. F. Judd, *Honolulu*, p. 16; Amos S. Cooke, Journal, October 23 and December 18, 1841, in Richards, *Chiefs' Children's School*, pp. 120, 124; Judd to Ruggles, October 16, 1831, HMCS Library.

6. Richards' letter of October 16, 1832, in Williston, *William Richards*, pp. 29–30; Alonzo Chapin, Journal, November 22, 1832.

7. Judd to Evarts, August 19, 1830, American Board MSS, LXVIII, No. 127, also in *Fragments II*, pp. 26–42 and partly printed in Gulick, *Pilgrims of Hawaii*, pp. 128–132; L. F. Judd, *Honolulu*, pp. 34–37; Judd's autobiographical statement, *Fragments I*, pp. 13–15; Judd to Chamberlain, December 20, 1829, March 20, April 12, and May 21, 1830, HMCS Library.

8. Judd's Report for 1839, and Judd to Chamberlain, April 25, 1829, HMCS Library; extract from the mission report, October 16, 1829, *Missionary Herald*, XXVI (1830), 280.

9. G. P. Judd, Journal, March 11 and April 17, 1831, *Fragments IV*, pp. 18, 22.

10. G. P. Judd, Journal, May 18, 1831, *Fragments IV*, p. 25.

11. G. P. Judd, Journal, January 8, 1831, and L. F. Judd, Journal, September 11, [1830], *Fragments IV*, pp. 12, 50; Mrs. Emerson's Journal, April 8, 1833, in Emerson,

Pioneer Days in Hawaii, p. 71; L. F. Judd, *Honolulu*, pp. 138–139; Wight, *Memoirs of E. K. Wilder*, p. 105; S. S. Hill, *Travels in the Sandwich and Society Islands* (London, 1856), p. 113.

12. Judd to Greene, October 20, 1835, American Board MSS, LXVIII, No. 135, also in *Fragments II*, p. 100; see also Judd's article in the *Hawaiian Spectator*, I, No. 2 (1838), 22.

13. Wight, *Memoirs of E. K. Wilder*, p. 11; L. F. Judd, *Honolulu*, p. 60; Martha Ann Chamberlain, "Memories of the Past, linked to Scenes of the Present," in the "History of Kawaiahao Seminary, 1889" (typescript, HMCS Library), p. 3.

14. Levi Chamberlain, Journal, Thursday, August 26, 1830; see also L. F. Judd, Journal, Saturday, [August 28, 1830], *Fragments IV*, p. 45.

15. G. P. Judd, Journal, November 18 and December 24, 1830, *ibid.*, p. 9; Francis J. Halford, "Gerrit Parmelee Judd, M.D., Surgeon and Diplomatist of the Sandwich Islands (1828–1873)," *Annals of Medical History*, n.s., VII, (March, 1935), 159. Leprosy was in Hawaii in the 1830s but was not officially acknowledged until 1863 (Ralph S. Kuykendall, *The Hawaiian Kingdom 1854–1874* [Honolulu, 1953], p. 73).

16. Dr. and Mrs. Alonzo Chapin, Journal, May 20, 1832, Honolulu Academy of Arts; L. F. Judd, *Honolulu*, pp. 38–39.

17. Wight, *Memoirs of E. K. Wilder*, p. 56; see also Withington, *Golden Cloak*, pp. 157–165; L. F. Judd, *Honolulu*, p. 77; Levi Chamberlain, Journal, March 23, 1841; Amos S. Cooke, Journal, March 22, 1841, *et seq.*, in Richards, *Chiefs' Children's School*, pp. 99–100.

18. Judd's Annual Report for 1840 and 1841, American Board MSS, CXXXVII, No. 91, also in *Fragments II*, pp. 122–123.

19. *Ibid.*; Judd's Report for 1839, HMCS Library; G. P. Judd, Journal, March 22, 1831, *Fragments IV*, p. 19; L. F. Judd, *Honolulu*, p. 67; Unpublished Minutes of the Prudential Meetings of the Mission, May 3, 1828 (typescript from MS, HMCS Library); also the general letter of the mission, June 12, 1828, *Missionary Herald*, XXV (1829), 26.

20. Judd's Report for 1839, HMCS Library; Judd's Annual Report for 1840 and 1841 (cited in note 18 above,); Halford, *9 Doctors & God*, p. 98.

21. Judd to Anderson, December 15, 1834, American Board MSS, LXVIII, No. 132, also in *Fragments II*, pp. 71–79; Halford in *Annals of Medical History*, n.s., VII (March, 1935), 158, where a page of the treatment book is reproduced; Mrs. Emerson's Journal, September 16, 1832, in Emerson, *Pioneer Days in Hawaii*, p. 63; L. F. Judd, *Honolulu*, p. 139.

22. Printed minutes of the mission meetings for 1835 (p. 18) and for 1838 (p. 19), HMCS Library; Halford in *Annals of Medical History*, n.s., VII (March, 1935), 160.

23. Judd to Anderson, September 1, 1838, American Board MSS, CXXXVII, No. 76, also in *Fragments II*, pp. 106–107. The famous engraving of the kneeling skeleton appears in Smith's *Anatomy* (10th ed., 1848, p. 48), not for reasons of religious symbolism, but, as Smith stated, "merely because a larger sized drawing could thus be given in a little space." Nathan van Patten, "Early Native Engravers of Hawaii," *Papers of the Bibliographical Society of America*, XX (1926), 91–94; Robert W. Andrews, "Lorrin Andrews and his Relation to Copper-plate Engraving," *Friend*, LXXIII (July, 1906), 13; H. M. Luquiens, "Engraving at Lahainaluna," *ibid.*, CIII (February, 1933), 35–39.

24. Sereno Bishop, *Reminiscences*, p. 38; *Sandwich Island Gazette*, June 23 and November 10, 1838; printed minutes of the mission meeting for 1839 (p. 21); also Judd to Chamberlain, December 17, 1839, HMCS Library.

25. Judd's Annual Account for 1834–1835, HMCS Library; Wight, *Memoirs of E. K. Wilder*, p. 21.

26. L. F. Judd, *Honolulu*, p. 81.

27. Judd to Anderson, October 15, 1832, American Board MSS, LXVIII, No. 129, also in *Fragments II*, p. 52.

28. Halford, *9 Doctors & God*, pp. 104–105; Levi Chamberlain, Journal, November

10, 13, and 15, 1839; Wight, *Memoirs of E. K. Wilder*, pp. 25–26; Mrs. Judd's autobiographical statement, *Fragments I*, p. 30; Frances G. Jewett, *Luther Halsey Gulick* (Boston, 1895), pp. 22–23; L. F. Judd, *Honolulu*, pp. 67–68; his body was later removed to the family plot in Nuuanu Cemetery.

29. Judd's Report for 1840, HMCS Library; Taylor, *The Flag Ship*, II, 290; L. F. Judd, *Honolulu*, p. 68; Levi Chamberlain, Journal, November 17, 1839.

30. Judd's Report for 1840, HMCS Library; L. F. Judd, *Honolulu*, pp. 69–71; Halford, *9 Doctors & God*, p. 107; Dibble, *History of the Sandwich Islands*, p. 284; printed minutes of the mission meeting for 1840, p. 7, HMCS Library.

31. *Friend* (April, 1928), p. 77.

Notes: Adviser to the Chiefs (pages 95–103)

1. Kuykendall, *Hawaiian Kingdom 1778–1854*, pp. 102–106; George F. M. Nellist, *The Story of Hawaii* (Honolulu, 1925), p. 136, where it is stated incorrectly that Judd also translated a life of Abraham Lincoln.

2. L. F. Judd, *Honolulu*, p. 21; Loomis to Chamberlain, November 1, 1827, HMCS Library; Lorrin Andrews, Diary, November 10, 1827, February 12 and March 5, 1828, *ibid.*; also Theodosia A. Green, journal-letter, February 1 and 16, 1828, *ibid.*; L. F. Judd, Journal, April 1, 1828, *ibid.*; G. P. Judd, Journal, February 20, 1828, *Fragments III*, pp. 65–66; see also Mrs. Judd's autobiographical statement, *Fragments I*, p. 29.

3. Elisabeth Gertrude Judd (Mrs. Asher B.) Bates, Journal, Monday, [March 4, 1850], p. 12, where Mrs. Judd's "Hawaiian eloquence" is mentioned.

4. Warriner, *Cruise of the Potomac*, p. 228; *Extracts from the Letters and Journals of Daniel Wheeler*, pp. 167–168; see also Frear, *Lowell and Abigail*, p. 57.

5. L. F. Judd, *Honolulu*, pp. 63–64, also Judd to Wyllie, February 17, 1860, *ibid.*, pp. 191–192; Judd's Report for 1839, HMCS Library.

6. Judd to Chamberlain, July 26, 1837, HMCS Library.

7. Kuykendall, *Hawaiian Kingdom 1778–1854*, pp. 148–151.

8. Judd to Chamberlain, July 11, 1837, HMCS Library.

9. AH, FO & Ex.

10. Kuykendall, *Hawaiian Kingdom 1778–1854*, pp. 165–166; L. F. Judd, *Honolulu*, pp. 65–66; Judd to Anderson, July 12, 1839, American Board MSS, CXXXVII, No. 78, also in *Fragments II*, p. 113.

11. Jarves, *Scenes and Scenery in the Sandwich Islands*, quoted in Steegmuller, *James Jackson Jarves*, p. 66.

12. Arthur M. Schlesinger, *Paths to the Present* (New York, 1949), p. 11.

13. *Dictionary of American Biography*, XX, 216–218. Wilkes is best known for seizing two Confederate agents from the British ship *Trent* in 1861, an act which almost caused war between Britain and the United States.

14. Judd's printed circular letter, September 20, 1839, HMCS Library.

15. Wilkes, *United States Exploring Expedition*, IV, 112, 235; Clark, *Lights and Shadows of Sailor Life*, pp. 180–181; Judd's Annual Report for 1840 and 1841, American Board MSS, CXXXVII, No. 91, also in *Fragments II*, p. 128; L. F. Judd, *Honolulu*, pp. 78–79.

16. Judd's Annual Report for 1840 and 1841 (cited in note above).

17. Judd's autobiographical statement, *Fragments I*, p. 17.

18. Wilkes, *United States Exploring Expedition*, IV, 169–174, 181; see also Clark, *Lights and Shadows of Sailor Life*, p. 204; Lyman, *Hawaiian Yesterdays*, p. 53.

19. L. F. Judd, *Honolulu*, p. 81; Charles Wilkes, Autobiography, VI, 1293, Library of Congress; Smith to Anderson, June 8, 1842, American Board MSS, CXXXVII, No. 36; *Sandwich Islands News*, October 14, 1846.

20. Armstrong to Baldwin, December 2, [1840], HMCS Library.
21. Chamberlain to Judd, May 4 and 6, 1841, HMCS Library.
22. Judd to Chamberlain, May 5, 1841, HMCS Library; Judd's Annual Report for 1840 and 1841 (cited in note 15, above); Judd to the Sandwich Islands Mission, May 26, 1843, HMCS Library, copy in American Board MSS, CXXXIV, No. 32, an extract of which, much paraphrased, is in L.F. Judd, *Honolulu*, p. 86; L. F. Judd to Anderson, August, [1841], American Board MSS, CCXXXV, No. 126.
23. Anderson to Judd, April 28, 1842, *ibid.*, Foreign Letter Book, XI, 9–11; Judd to the Sandwich Islands Mission, May 26, 1843 (cited in note 22, above); also May 18, 1843, in HMCS Library; Chamberlain (for the mission) to Judd, May 27, 1843, HMCS Library, copy in American Board MSS, CXXXIV, No. 32.

Notes: Translator and Recorder *(pages 104–113)*

1. Furnas, *Anatomy of Paradise*, p. 153; Wright and Fry, *Puritans in the South Seas*, p. 311; *Instructions of the Prudential Committee . . . to the Sandwich Islands Mission*, p. 41; Kuykendall, *Hawaiian Kingdom 1778–1854*, pp. 154–155.
2. *Ibid.*, pp. 156, 159–161, 167–169, 189–191.
3. Brookes, *International Rivalry in the Pacific Islands*, pp. 127–128; Judd to Richards, August 8, 1842, incompletely given in *Report of the Proceedings and Evidence in the Arbitration between the King and Government of the Hawaiian Islands and Messrs. Ladd and Co.* (Honolulu, 1846), (hereafter cited as *Ladd and Co. Arbitration*), appendix, pp. 112–113. A short extract of this letter, much paraphrased, appears in L. F. Judd, *Honolulu*, p. 88.
4. Bradley, *American Frontier in Hawaii*, p. 158; Furnas *Anatomy of Paradise*, pp. 146–147; Ruschenberger, *Voyage Round the World*, p. 475; Smith ,*Yankees in Paradise*, p. 218.
5. Simpson to Pelly, March 10, 1842, *American Historical Review*, XIV (1908), 90–92; Sir George Simpson, *Narrative of a Journey Round the World, During the Years 1841 and 1842* (London, 1847), II, 165; Brookes, *International Rivalry in the Pacific Islands*, p. 125; Kuykendall, *Hawaiian Kingdom 1778–1854*, p. 301.
6. *Ibid.*, p. 192.
7. Judd to Alexander Simpson, May 21, 1842, in Alexander Simpson, *The Sandwich Islands* (London, 1843), p. 55. That Sir George recommended Judd is stated in [A. H. Markland], *A Conspiracy on the Part of Garrett P. Judd and others, advisers of the King of Hawaii, to deprive Ladd and Co. of Legal Rights* [Honolulu, 1846], pp. 5, 16; while this work is a polemic, it offers confirmation of sorts to what is almost a foregone conclusion. Sir George's high regard for Judd appears in his *Narrative of a Journey*, II, 96.
8. *Ibid.*, II, 173–174; Simpson to Ross, March 12, 1842, in Donald Ross Collection, Provincial Archives, Victoria, British Columbia.
9. Judd to the Sandwich Islands Mission, May 26, 1843, HMCS Library, copy in American Board MSS, CXXXIV, No. 32. This statement, much paraphrased, appears in an extract of the letter in L. F. Judd, *Honolulu*, p. 86.
10. Judd to Anderson, April 19, June 11, and September 26, 1842, also March 20, 1843, American Board MSS, CXXXVII, Nos. 84, 85, 86, and 88, also in *Fragments II*, pp. 134–144, 147–161; Judd to Mrs. Judd (extract), April 27, 1842, and Judd to Wyllie, February 17, 1860, in L. F. Judd, *Honolulu*, pp. 84, 193; Mrs. Cooke to her sister, April 23, 1842, in Richards, *Chiefs' Children's School*, pp. 134–136.
11. Kuykendall, *Hawaiian Kingdom 1778–1854*, pp. 231–232; L. F. Judd, *Honolulu*, pp. 84–85; Judd to Anderson, September 26, 1842 (cited in note 10, above).
12. Judd to Anderson, June 11, 1842 (cited in note 10, above). His commission of July 18 is printed in L. F. Judd, *Honolulu*, p. 86, and in *Ladd and Co. Arbitration*, appendix, p. 107; the original is in AH.

13. Judd to Anderson, April 19, 1842, and March 20, 1843 (cited in note 10, above); Judd's autobiographical statement, *Fragments I*, pp. 18–19.

14. Judd to Simpson, July 3, 1844, in *Correspondence . . . on the Subject of Richard Charlton's Claim to Land* (Honolulu, 1845), p. 180.

15. Simpson, *Sandwich Islands*, pp. 32, 57, 72; Stephen Reynolds, Journal, October 12, 1843, and August 3, 1844; Reynolds to Larkin, July 31, 1842, in George P. Hammond, ed., *The Larkin Papers* (Berkeley and Los Angeles, 1951), I, 256; see also Gustavus Hines, *Oregon* (Buffalo, 1851), p. 222.

16. Herman Melville, *Typee*, appendix (Everyman ed., p. 281). Melville left Honolulu on August 17, 1843, after about six months in the Islands. For part of the time he was a clerk to Isaac Montgomery, an Englishman. This circumstance may explain part of his hostility, as Judd was at the time opposed to the provisional English government (see Charles R. Anderson, *Melville in the South Seas* [New York, 1939], pp. 330–345).

17. Printed minutes of the mission meeting for 1842 (pp. 30–32), HMCS Library, partly given in Halford, *9 Doctors & God*, p. 112, and in James J. Jarves, *History of the Hawaiian Islands* (3d ed., Honolulu, 1847), p. 174.

18. Armstrong to Anderson, September 14, 1842, American Board MSS, CXXXVI, No. 87; Judd to Anderson, March 20, 1843 (cited in note 10 above).

19. Smith to Anderson, June 8, 1842, American Board MSS, CXXXVII, No. 26; Judd to Anderson, April 19, 1842 (cited in note 10, above).

20. Armstrong to Anderson, June 8, 1842, American Board MSS, CXXXVI, No. 86, and Chamberlain to Anderson, July 8, 1842, *ibid.*, CXXXV, No. 149; see also Bradley, *American Frontier in Hawaii*, pp. 415–416.

21. Anderson to the Sandwich Islands Mission, October 28, 1842, and to Judd, October 31, 1842, American Board MSS, Foreign Letter Book, XI, pp. 425–451, 464–465.

22. Judd to Anderson, March 20, 1843 (cited in note 10, above).

23. Armstrong to Anderson, February 14 and March 2–6, 1843, American Board MSS, CXXXVI, Nos. 95, 96; Lowell Smith to Anderson, March 10 and November 15, 1843; *ibid.*, CXXXVII, Nos. 28, 29; Greene to Judd, November 11, 1843 (two letters), *ibid.*, Foreign Letter Book, XIII, pp. 252–255.

24. "Mr. Judd made some long explanation showing how he had come into an agreement with the King to do whatever he could in His Majesty's service, if the King, on his part, did what he could, that is to say, lived a respectable life. For some time things went well. Afterwards a bad change took place. He wrote to the King in 1846, saying that if he did not keep sober, he (Mr. Judd) could not serve him." (Privy Council Record, IIIa, 280, May 21, 1849, AH.) L. F. Judd, *Honolulu*, pp. 102–103.

25. Judd to Evarts, September 26, 1831, American Board MSS, LXVIII, No. 128; Judd to Wyllie, February 17, 1860, L. F. Judd, *Honolulu*, p. 194; Kuykendall, *Hawaiian Kingdom 1778–1854*, pp. 210–211, 349–350; Bradley, *American Frontier in Hawaii*, p. 420.

26. Judd to Richards, October 27, 1842, American Board MSS, CXXXVII, No. 87, also in *Fragments II*, p. 146; Judd to Wyllie, February 17, 1860, L. F. Judd, *Honolulu*, p. 194; depositions by Dr. Judd on September 20, 1842, by William Baker and J. F. B. Marshall on February 14, 1843, and by William Paty on March 9, 1843, AH, FO & Ex.

27. Simpson, *Sandwich Islands*, pp. 60–61; Kuykendall, *Hawaiian Kingdom 1778–1854*, pp. 211–212; Bradley, *American Frontier in Hawaii*, pp. 422–423.

28. *Report of the Minister of Finance* (Honolulu, 1851), p. 12.

29. "Report of the Minister of the Interior . . . May 21, 1845," in the *Polynesian*, May 31, 1845; Judd to Richards, September 16, 1842, and Judd to Haalilio, November 12, 1842, AH, FO & Ex.

30. Kuykendall, *Hawaiian Kingdom 1778–1854*, p. 232.

31. For example, Judd to Haalilio and Mi Kamelani [Chamberlain], May 17, 1842 (in Hawaiian), endorsed by Kamehameha III, an order to pay Chamberlain on account of Mr. Cooke, AH, FO & Ex.

32. Bradley, *American Frontier in Hawaii*, p. 417; L. F. Judd, *Honolulu*, p. 90; Stephen

Reynolds, Journal, June 4, 1842; Judd to Haalilio, November 12, 1842, AH, FO & Ex.

33. "Report of the Minister of Finance . . . August 1, 1846," in the *Polynesian*, August 8, 1846; Judd to Richards, August 2, 1842, in *Ladd and Co. Arbitration*, appendix, p. 114.

34. Simpson, *Sandwich Islands*, p. 72; Stephen Reynolds, Journal, August 8, 1842; see also Timothy D. Hunt, *The Past and Present of the Sandwich Islands* (San Francisco, 1853), p. 149.

35. Judd to Wyllie, February 17, 1860, L. F. Judd, *Honolulu*, p. 193; Judd to Haalilio, November 12, 1842 and Judd's memorandum of receipts and expenditures from May, 1842, to February 28, 1843, AH, FO & Ex. and Finance Dept.; Bradley, *American Frontier in Hawaii*, p. 418.

36. Judd to Richards, October 27, 1842 (cited in note 26, above).

Notes: The Paulet Episode (*pages 114–125*)

1. For the Paulet episode see Kuykendall, *Hawaiian Kingdom 1778–1854*, pp. 186, 206–226; Bradley, *American Frontier in Hawaii*, pp. 428–434. For Paulet see Frederic Boase, *Modern English Biography* (Truro, 1892–1901), II, 1396–1397; Lyman, *Hawaiian Yesterdays*, p. 105.

2. Klaus E. Knorr, *British Colonial Theories 1570–1850* (Toronto, 1944), pp. 372–375, 410–412; Latourette, *History of the Expansion of Christianity*, V, 234.

3. Official correspondence arising from the cession is printed in a number of places, such as: *British and Foreign State Papers* (London, 1858), XXXI, 1023–1029; *Foreign Relations of the United States, 1894* (Washington, 1895), appendix 2, pp. 45–60; *Senate Ex. Docs.*, 52 Cong., 2 Sess., No. 77 (1893), pp. 43–54.

4. Judd to the Commissioners in Europe, February 27, 1843, AH, British Commission Documents; also printed in *Correspondence Relative to the Sandwich Islands, 1824–1843* [London, 1843], p. 258.

5. *Ibid.*; also Judd to Wyllie, February 17, 1860, L. F. Judd, *Honolulu*, pp. 194–195.

6. Judd to the Commissioners in Europe, February 27, 1843 (cited in note 4, above); also Paulet to Secretary of the Admiralty, March 9, 1843, BPRO, Admiralty, 1/5531.

7. Judd to the Commissioners in Europe, February 27, 1843 (cited in note 4, above).

8. L. F. Judd, *Honolulu*, pp. 94–95. "Isle of Beauty" was written by Thomas Haynes Bayly (1797–1839). It contains the familiar line, "Absence makes the heart grow fonder."

9. L. F. Judd, *Honolulu*, p. 93; J. F. B. Marshall, "An Unpublished Chapter of Hawaiian History,"*Harper's Magazine*, LXVII (1883), 512; William Paty, Journal, February 25, 1843, AH; long extracts from this journal appear in *Hawaiian Almanac and Annual* (1905), pp. 80–102; Sylvester K. Stevens, *American Expansion in Hawaii 1842–1898* (Harrisburg, 1945), pp. 16–17.

10. Paulet to Secretary of the Admiralty, March 9, 1843 (cited in note 6, above); Brookes, *International Rivalry in the Pacific Islands*, p. 133; S. N. Castle in the *Hawaiian Star*, June 13, 1893.

11. Armstrong to Baldwin, February [*sic*] 9, 1843, HMCS Library; Chamberlain to Elkanah Walker, April 4, 1843, Western Americana Collection, Yale Library; Chamberlain to Anderson, May 3, 1843, American Board MSS, CXXXV, No. 161.

12. Judd to Anderson, March 20, 1843, American Board MSS, CXXXVII, No. 88, also in *Fragments II*, pp. 156–158. Mackay's letter of resignation is in AH. A short notice of Frere, who later became a captain, is in Burke's *Landed Gentry* (1952), p. 930.

13. Judd to the Commissioners in Europe, February 27, 1843 (cited in note 4, above); also Judd to Paulet, February 27, 1843, AH, British Commission Documents. The

proclamation of Judd's appointment, dated February 27, 1843, is printed in *Ladd and Co. Arbitration,* appendix, p. 107.

14. Armstrong to Anderson, March 2–6, 1843, American Board MSS, CXXXVI, No. 96; also Levi Chamberlain, Journal, February 25, 1843.

15. For Marshall's mission see his account in *Harper's Magazine,* LXVII (1883), 511–520, and a second account in *Friend* (1879), p. 98; L. F. Judd, *Honolulu,* p. 95; Kekuanaoa's testimony, November 25, 1846, *Ladd and Co. Arbitration,* pp. 294–295. For Marshall see *Dictionary of American Biography,* XII, 312–313.

16. The best account of the old royal tomb, which was razed in 1865, is in Albert P. Taylor, *The Rulers of Hawaii* (Honolulu, 1927), pp. 14–19; see also Andrew Farrell, *The Story of Iolani Palace* (Honolulu, 1936), p. 47; Steen Bille, Report, pp. 46–47, HMCS Library.

17. Judd to Richards, March 13, 1843 (extract), *Ladd and Co. Arbitration,* appendix, p. 115; Pelly to Aberdeen, March 12, 1843, BPRO, FO 58/19; George Traill Allan, "Reminiscences" (typescript in Provincial Archives, Victoria, British Columbia).

18. Cooke to Anderson, April 8, 1843, Richards, *Chiefs' Children's School,* p. 172; Levi Chamberlain, Journal, April 4, 1843; Evert Duyckinck, Diary, July 11, 1847, quoted in Jay Leyda, *The Melville Log, A Documentary Life of Herman Melville 1819–1891* (New York, 1951), I, 250; Journal of the House of Nobles 1841–1845 (original and translation), pp. 35–50, AH.

19. Testimony of Kekuanaoa, January 31, 1849, Privy Council Record, V, 323–324, AH. A garbled version of the offer appears in Wight, *Memoirs of E. K. Wilder,* p. 107.

20. Warriner, *Cruise of the Potomac,* p. 223; Ethel M. Damon, "From Manoa to Punahou," HHS, *Forty-Ninth Annual Report for the Year 1940,* pp. 5–8; Ephraim W. Clark, Journal, May 13, 1828; Dr. and Mrs. Alonzo Chapin, Journal, May 22, 1832; also quotations from it in Halford, *9 Doctors & God,* p. 138; Levi Chamberlain, Journal, August 17 and 19, 1832.

21. Privy Council Record, V, 277–278, 320–326, 332–336, 355, AH; *Sandwich Islands News,* May 12 and 19, 1847; *Motion . . . made by R. C. Wyllie . . . to release John Ricord . . . from a debt* (Honolulu, [1853]), p. 26.

22. G. P. Judd, Journal, May 4–25, 1843, AH, British Commission Documents; Judd to Richards, May 8 and 11, 1843, *ibid.,* also an extract in *Ladd and Co. Arbitration,* appendix, p. 113.

23. Chamberlain to Judd, May 13, 1843, AH, British Commission Documents.

24. Judd to Baldwin, Saturday, P.M. [?May 27, 1843], HMCS Library; Henry Sea (secretary of the commission) to Kamehameha III, May 15, 1843, and John Ii to Judd, June 6, 1843, AH, British Commission Documents.

25. Kamehameha III to Paulet, May 17, 1843 (in Hawaiian) AH, British Commission Documents; Sea to Kamehameha III, May 22, 1843, *ibid.*; Kamehameha III to Judd, June 12, 1843, *ibid.*; Stephen Reynolds, Journal, May 29, 1843.

26. Kamehameha III to Judd, June 12 and 18, 1843, AH, British Commission Documents; Judd to the Commissioners, June 14, 1843, *ibid.*; Judd's memorandum, June 20, 1843, *ibid.*; Judd to the Commissioners, June 20, 1843, *ibid.*; Sea to Judd, June 20, 1843, *ibid.* (the last two letters also in BPRO, Admiralty, 1/5529); also Judd to Richards, July 4, and 13, 1843 (extracts), *Ladd and Co. Arbitration,* appendix, pp. 115–116.

27. Judd's autobiographical statement, *Fragments I,* p. 20; see also L. F. Judd, *Honolulu,* p. 96; Wight, *Memoirs of E. K. Wilder,* pp. 60–61.

28. Sea to Judd (at the Treasury), July 21 and 25, 1843, AH, British Commission Documents; Judd (at the Treasury) to the Commissioners, July 21 and 23, 1843, *ibid.*; Judd to Chamberlain, July 3, 1843, HMCS Library.

29. L. F. Judd, *Honolulu,* p. 96.

30. Judd to Richards, August 1, 1843, AH, British Commission Documents; Judd to Wyllie, February 17, 1860, L. F. Judd, *Honolulu,* p. 195.

31. Judd to Richards, August 1, 1843 (cited in note above).

32. L. F. Judd, *Honolulu*, pp. 96–97; for other accounts see Herman Melville, *Typee*, appendix; Adm. Richard Thomas, Journal, July 31, 1843, BPRO, Admiralty, 50/229.

33. Lowell Smith, Journal, July 31, 1843, in Frear, *Lowell and Abigail*, p. 167; correspondence in Gulick, *Pilgrims of Hawaii*, p. 217. Since Judd probably wrote or inspired the king's speech, he may be the original author of Hawaii's motto, which has a Biblical flavor in keeping with his background (information from Dr. Thomas D. Murphy of the University of Hawaii).

34. Wight, *Memoirs of E. K. Wilder*, p. 64.

35. Kuykendall, *Hawaiian Kingdom 1778–1854*, pp. 195–196; Bradley, *American Frontier in Hawaii*, pp. 444–445, 463.

Notes: Minister of Foreign Affairs (pages 126–135)

1. Judd to Anderson, October 5, 1843, American Board MSS, CXXXVII, No. 90, also in *Fragments II*, pp. 162–163.

2. Judd to Richards, November 4 and December 16, 1843 (extracts), *Ladd and Co. Arbitration*, appendix, pp. 116–117. The commission, signed by the king and premier, is in *ibid.*, appendix, p. 108. Another version of the December 16 letter (in extracted form) is in L. F. Judd, *Honolulu*, p. 101. Brown's dispatch, November 4, 1843 (extract), in Ralph S. Kuykendall, ed., *Hawaiian Diplomatic Correspondence in . . . the Department of State* (Publications of the Historical Commission of the Territory of Hawaii, I, No. 3, Honolulu, 1926), p. 12.

3. Judd to Anderson, December 16, 1846, American Board MSS, CLXXIII, No. 103; also in *Fragments II*, pp. 174–182; political creed, June 19, 1845, signed by Judd, Ricord, and Wyllie, AH, FO & Ex.; Kuykendall, *Hawaiian Kingdom 1778–1854*, pp. 238, 260–261; L. F. Judd, *Honolulu*, p. 115.

4. Judd to Richards, October 5, 1843 (extract), *Ladd and Co. Arbitration*, appendix, pp. 113–114; Judd to Simpson, July 3, 1844, *Correspondence . . . on . . . Charlton's Claim to Land*, p. 182; Kuykendall, *Hawaiian Kingdom 1778–1854*, pp. 236–237.

5. *Ibid.*; Andrew F. Muir, "John Ricord," *Southwestern Historical Quarterly*, LII (July, 1948), 49–59; Lyman, *Hawaiian Yesterdays*, p. 138; Judd's declaration enclosed in Wyllie to U.S. Secretary of State, September 1, 1845, AH, FO & Ex.; L. F. Judd, *Honolulu*, p. 100; Judd to Wyllie, February 17, 1860, *ibid.*, p. 195.

6. *Ibid.*, p. 100.

7. Brown to Calhoun, September 10, 1844, HHC, *Publications* (1926), I, No. 3, p. 12; Reynolds to Larkin, November 4 and December 1, 1844, *Larkin Papers*, II, 276, 301; Jones to Thompson, January 31, 1845, in D. Mackenzie Brown, *China Trade Days in California, Selected Letters from the Thompson Papers, 1832–1863* (Berkeley and Los Angeles, 1947), p. 44; see also Armstrong to Chapman, November 19, 1844, Richard Armstrong Papers, Library of Congress.

8. Kuykendall, *Hawaiian Kingdom 1778–1854*, p. 249. In the *Hawaiian Kingdom 1854–1874* (p. 290, n. 33) Professor Kuykendall lists biographical materials on Wyllie.

9. Miller's memorandum relative to Mr. Wyllie, August 11, 1845, BPRO, FO 58/36.

10. Kuykendall, *Hawaiian Kingdom 1778–1854*, p. 238, n. 54; L. F. Judd, *Honolulu*, p. 112.

11. Judd to Wyllie, February 17, 1860, *ibid.*, p. 195; Naturalization Book C, 1844–1846, AH.

12. Judd to Dillon, May 18, 1848, AH, Finance Department Letter Book 1848–1859.

13. Judd to Secretaries A.B.C.F.M., September 5, 1844, American Board MSS, CCXXXV, No. 127 1/2, also in *Fragments II*, pp. 167–170; Kuykendall, *Hawaiian*

Kingdom 1778–1854, p. 239; Chamberlain to Elkanah Walker, May 30, 1845, Western Americana Collection, Yale Library.

14. Bishop to Judd, December 31, 1844, AH, FO & Ex.; for a list of naturalized missionaries see *Friend* (July, 1934), 350.

15. L. F. Judd, *Honolulu*, p. 117; Kuykendall, *Hawaiian Kingdom 1778–1854*, pp. 279–280, 295.

16. Marshall to Hunnewell, September 4, 1845, Hunnewell Papers; L. F. Judd, *Honolulu*, pp. 136–137.

17. *Ibid.*, pp. 108, 111–112, 121–122; C. S. Lyman, Journal, January 10 and 17, 1847, in Lyman, *Around the Horn to the Sandwich Islands*, pp. 163, 165; Wise, *Los Gringos*, p. 370.

18. Kuykendall, *Hawaiian Kingdom 1778–1854*, pp. 240–241; Hill, *Travels in the Sandwich and Society Islands*, p. 105.

19. C. S. Lyman, Journal, January 8, 1847, HMCS Library; this passage does not appear in the printed edition of Lyman, *Around the Horn to the Sandwich Islands*, which is a selective compilation. Wise, *Los Gringos*, pp. 371–372.

20. See for example Edward Lucatt, *Rovings in the Pacific from 1837 to 1849* (London, 1851), II, 270.

21. Letter from a distinguished traveler (not further identified), May 26, 1845, L. F. Judd, *Honolulu*, pp. 120–121; see also Kuykendall, *Hawaiian Kingdom 1778–1854*, pp. 257–258.

22. *Ibid.*, pp. 234–235; Judd to Aberdeen, February 17, 1844, AH, FO & Ex., partly printed in *Report of the Minister of Foreign Relations, 1851* [Honolulu, 1851], appendix, pp. 26–27.

23. Kuykendall, *Hawaiian Kingdom 1778–1854*, pp. 208–209, 223, 245–246; Miller to Kamehameha III, June 1, 1844, *Correspondence . . . on . . . Charlton's Claim to Land*, p. 67.

24. Judd to Miller, April 2, 1844, *ibid.*, p. 52; see also Bradley, *American Frontier in Hawaii*, p. 415; Judd to Greene, January 25, 1845, American Board MSS, CCXXXV, No. 128; also in *Fragments II*, p. 172.

25. Judd to Richards and Haalilio or Sir George Simpson, May 4, 1844, *Correspondence . . . on . . . Charlton's Claim to Land*, pp. 174–175.

26. Judd's autobiographical statement, *Fragments I*, p. 21; Judd to Greene, August 20, 1844, and January 25, 1845, American Board MSS, CCXXXV, Nos. 127 and 128; also in *Fragments II*, pp. 165, 173; Judd to his parents, March 31, 1845 (extract), L. F. Judd, *Honolulu*, p. 124.

27. Mrs. Judd to Mrs. Bingham, March 24, 1845, L. F. Judd, *Honolulu*, p. 107; Reynolds to Larkin, April 19, 1845, *Larkin Papers*, III, 139; *Report of the Minister of Foreign Relations, 1851*, p. 3; Dr. Judd's commission, dated March 30, 1845, is printed in *Ladd and Co. Arbitration*, appendix, pp. 108–109.

Notes: Minister of the Interior (pages 136–143)

1. *Correspondence . . . in the Case of John Wiley . . .* (Honolulu, 1844); *Table of Consular Grievances, 1843–1846* [Honolulu, 1862], pp. 7–8; *Senate Ex. Docs.*, 52 Congr., 2 Sess., No. 77 (1893), pp. 62–63; Kuykendall, *Hawaiian Kingdom 1778–1854*, pp. 247–251.

2. *Report of the Case of James Gray . . .* (Honolulu, 1845).

3. Testimony of F. G. Blume, March 24, 1845, Depositions at the Palace, AH, FO & Ex.

4. Testimony of J. J. Jarves, March 14, 1845, Judd to Henry A. Pearce [Peirce],

January 1, 1845, Wyllie's memorandum, March 7–26, 1845, AH, FO & Ex.; *Table of Consular Grievances, 1843–1846*, p. 11.

5. Brown to Calhoun (No. 26), March 17, and (No. 27), April 4, 1845, U.S. Archives.

6. Testimony of Jarves, March 14, 1845 (cited in note 4, above); Brewer to Hunnewell, March 12, 1845, Hunnewell Papers, Houghton Library, Harvard University.

7. Mrs. A. S. Cooke to her mother, March 11, 1845, in Mary A. Richards, *Amos Starr Cooke and Juliette Montague Cooke* (Honolulu, privately printed, 1941), p. 291; Depositions at the Palace, March 14–25, 1845, AH, FO & Ex.; *Table of Consular Grievances, 1843–1846*, p. 11; *Report of the Case of C. Brewer and Co. vs. John R. von Pfister . . .* (Honolulu, 1845).

8. Kuykendall, *Hawaiian Kingdom 1778–1854*, pp. 258–260; Journal of the House of Nobles 1845–1847, June 25, 1845, p. 20, AH.

9. L. F. Judd, *Honolulu*, p. 116, also pp. 107, 109; Judd to Wyllie, February 17, 1860, *ibid.*, p. 196.

10. Kuykendall, *Hawaiian Kingdom 1778–1854*, pp. 252–255.

11. Judd to Wyllie, February 17, 1860, L. F. Judd, *Honolulu*, p. 196; Judd to Anderson, December 16, 1846, American Board MSS, CLXXIII, No. 103, also in *Fragments II*, p. 180; Privy Council Record, IV, 152–153 (November 9, 1847), AH; Wyllie's memorandum, October 28, 1847, AH, FO & Ex.

12. Judd to Fiennes, May 14, June 7, and June 16, 1845, *Ladd and Co. Arbitration*, appendix, pp. 95–97; Judd to Baldwin, June 7, 1845, HMCS Library; Brown to Calhoun (No. 26), March 17, 1845, U.S. Archives; Fiennes to Judd, June 4, 1848 [?1845], in Arthur C. Alexander, *Koloa Plantation 1835–1935* (Honolulu, 1937), pp. 192–204.

13. L. F. Judd, *Honolulu*, p. 132; *Ladd and Co. Arbitration*, especially Judd to Williams and Marshall, May 29, 1847, appendix, p. 548.

14. "Reminiscences of Henry L. Sheldon," I, 7–8, AH; Lee's address, July 5, 1852, in Dutton, *William L. Lee*, [p. 8]; Privy Council Record, II, 314–316 (March 4, 1847), AH.

15. Judd to Wyllie, February 17, 1860, L. F. Judd, *Honolulu*, p. 197; Privy Council Record, II, 44, 58, and V, 327, 333, AH.

16. Judd to Brown, February 2, 1844, AH; Interior Department Letter Book No. 1, April 16, May 2, and June 12, 1845, pp. 17, 19, 29, 74, *ibid.*; Memorandum, February 8, 1849, Finance Department Letter Book 1848–1859, *ibid.*; testimony of Kekuanaoa, January 31, 1849, Privy Council Record, V, 330, *ibid.*

17. *Polynesian*, June 28, 1845; L. F. Judd, *Honolulu*, p. 130; Sereno Bishop, *Reminiscences*, p. 60; Miller to Aberdeen, December 31, 1845, in Montague Paske-Smith, "Early British Consuls in Honolulu," *Mid Pacific Magazine*, XLIX (1936), 255 n.; *Pacific Commercial Advertiser*, September 12, 1861.

18. Privy Council Record, III, 297, AH.; Kuykendall, *Hawaiian Kingdom 1778–1854*, p. 26.

19. *Ibid.*, p. 179; Judd to Anderson, October 7, 1838, and Dr. Judd's Annual Report for 1840 and 1841, American Board MSS, CXXXVII, Nos. 77 and 91, also in *Fragments II*, pp. 110, 126–127; Judd to Brinsmade, November 18, 1834, William Hooper Papers, UH Library; *Polynesian*, May 31, 1845.

20. For Hawaii's land revolution see Kuykendall, *Hawaiian Kingdom 1778–1854*, pp. 269–298; Judd to Wyllie, February 17, 1860, L. F. Judd, *Honolulu*, pp. 196–197.

21. *Report of the Minister of the Interior, 1856* [Honolulu, 1856], pp. 16–17.

22. Kuykendall, *Hawaiian Kingdom 1778–1854*, p. 333; *Polynesian*, May 31, 1845; Judd to Wyllie, February 17, 1860, L. F. Judd, *Honolulu*, pp. 197–198.

23. Bruce Cartwright, "The Money of Hawaii," *Hawaiian Almanac and Annual* (1929), 70–71; *Catalogue of Coins, Tokens, and Medals in the Numismatic Collection of the Mint of the United States at Philadelphia, Pa.* (Washington, 1912), p. 573.

24. Report of the Minister of the Interior, May, 21, 1845, *Polynesian*, May 31, 1845; also Report of the Minister of Finance, August 1, 1846; *ibid.*, August 8, 1846; *Report*

of the Minister of Finance, April 28, 1847 [Honolulu, 1847]; Kuykendall, *Hawaiian Kingdom 1778–1854*, p. 370.

25. See for example *Hawaiian Gazette*, July 16, 1873; *Pacific Commercial Advertiser*, July 19, 1873.

Notes: *Minister of Finance (pages 144–155)*

1. Kuykendall, *Hawaiian Kingdom 1778–1854*, pp. 262–263. Dr. Judd's commission, dated April 13, 1846, is in *Ladd and Co. Arbitration*, appendix, p. 109; his signed oath of office is in AH, Finance Department. See also Young's testimony, January 9, 1849, Privy Council Record, V, 269–270, AH; Judd to Wyllie, February 17, 1860, L. F. Judd, *Honolulu*, p. 197.

2. William C. Parke, *Personal Reminiscences* (Cambridge, 1891), p. 14; Dutton, *William L. Lee, passim; Dictionary of American Biography*, XI, 135; for Andrews' appointment see Kuykendall, *Hawaiian Kingdom 1778–1854*, p. 244.

3. *Ibid.*, p. 265; Kamehameha III to Wyllie, March, 1845, AH, Interior Department Letter Book, I, 7; Journal of the House of Nobles, May 19 and 20, 1845, I, 66–68, and II, 2, AH.

4. Miller's dispatch, March 18, 1846, with annotations by Palmerston and Addington, BPRO, FO 58/44; Ten Eyck's dispatch, July 18, 1846 (extract), in HHC *Publications* (1926), I, No. 3, p. 14; Ten Eyck to Buchanan (No. 4), August 4, 1846, U.S. Archives; Wyllie's pencil note on Wyllie to Dillon, March 18, 1848, AH, FO & Ex.; Wise, *Los Gringos*, p. 369.

5. Testimony of Kekuanaoa, E. H. Boardman, and Wyllie, November 25, December 14 and 15, 1846, in *Ladd and Co. Arbitration*, pp. 290, 456, 465; Judd to Pearce [Peirce], January 1, 1845, AH, FO & Ex.

6. A. P. Taylor in Honolulu *Advertiser*, April 22, 1923, p. 14; Nellist, *Story of Hawaii*, p. 136.

7. See, for example, *Polynesian*, November 16, 1844, p. 107.

8. L. F. Judd, *Honolulu*, pp. 130–131; Wight, *Memoirs of E. K. Wilder*, p. 76; E. K. Wilder, memorandum (undated) in 1866 folder, S. G. Wilder Papers, on deposit, HMCS Library.

9. L. F. Judd, *Honolulu*, p. 100; Judd to Greene, August 20, 1844, American Board MSS, CCXXXV, No. 127, also in *Fragments II*, p. 165. On July 21, 1843, Armstrong wrote to Chapman that he had moved into the Judds' former house in the mission (Richard Armstrong Papers).

10. L. F. Judd, *Honolulu*, pp. 112, 129; Lyman, *Around the Horn to the Sandwich Islands*, p. 162; Reynolds to Larkin, August 16, 1846, *Larkin Papers*, V, 200.

11. L. F. Judd, *Honolulu*, pp. 129, 134; Wight, *Memoirs of E. K. Wilder*, pp. 72–73.

12. Judd to Wyllie, January 15, 1848, and Wyllie to Judd, January 19, 1848, AH, Wyllie Collection; AH, Privy Council Record, II, 104 (December 10, 1846), and 311 (February 18, 1847). The house and lot were estimated at $6,000 (Wyllie to Hall, December 26, 1849, AH, FO Letter Book, XIII).

13. AH, Privy Council Record, II, 312; Hobbs, *Hawaii: A Pageant of the Soil*, p. 171; Mrs. Judd's autobiographic statement, *Fragments I*, p. 31. Sweet Home, which stood on the south side of what is now Nuuanu Cemetery, was demolished in 1911 (Ray J. Baker, *Honolulu in 1853* [Honolulu, 1950], p. 69).

14. Charles H. Judd, Diary, August 19 and 25, September 2 and 19, 1848, in *Fragments V*, pp. 8, 10, 13, 18.

15. Armstrong to Chapman, November, 1843, Richard Armstrong Papers; Steen Bille, Report, pp. 48, 142, HMCS Library; Levi Chamberlain, Journal, April 6, 1844;

Estrella C. Mott, "Honolulu in 1848," (typescript, HHS); E. K. Wilder, Journal, October 8 and 9, 1850, HMCS Library.

16. Chamberlain to Elkanah Walker, May 30, 1845, Western Americana Collection, Yale Library.

17. Judd to Ladd & Co., July 19 and 28, 1845, *Ladd and Co. Arbitration*, appendix, pp. 82, 90.

18. Judd's annotations on Miller's memorandum of April 12, 1847, AH, FO & Ex.

19. Judd to Walsh, November 2, 1852, UH Library.

20. Wyllie to Armstrong, March 12, 1847, AH, FO & Ex.; Charles H. Judd, Diary, September 23 and 24, 1848, *Fragments V*, pp. 18–19; Judd to Greene, January 25, 1845, American Board MSS, CCXXXV, No. 128, also in *Fragments II*, p. 173; Judd to Milo Calkin, August 12, 1845, in Markland, *Conspiracy*, p. 8.

21. Judd to Marshall, July 31, 1846, AH, Privy Council Record, II, 81.

22. Judd to George T. Allan, May 22, 1845, AH, Interior Department Letter Book No. 1, p. 44; minute on Miller to Palmerston, June 10, 1847, and Ten Eyck to Buchanan, December 21, 1846, cited in Brookes, *International Rivalry in the Pacific Islands*, pp. 182, 187.

23. L. F. Judd, *Honolulu*, p. 133; Ricord's testimony (favorable to Judd), October 5, 1846, in *Ladd and Co. Arbitration*, pp. 196–197; Wyllie to Judd, November 18, 1847, in the Honolulu *Times* (Extra), December 27, 1849.

24. Testimony of John R. Jasper, December 8, 1848, AH, Privy Council Record, V, 65, 76; Wyllie to Judd, July 14, 1853, AH, Local Officials File; E. K. Wilder, Journal, January 6, 1850.

25. *Motion . . . made by R. C. Wyllie . . . to release John Ricord . . . from a debt*, pp. 4–5. His naturalization oath was returned to him on May 17, 1847 (AH, Naturalization Book C). His loan was approved June 18 (AH, Privy Council Record, II, 433); Wyllie's memorandum, October 28, 1847, AH, FO & Ex.; Wyllie to Judd, November 18, 1847 (cited in note 23, above).

26. *Memoirs of General William T. Sherman* (New York, 1875), I, 41–42; Armstrong to Baldwin, March 16, 1844, HMCS Library; Wyllie to Ricord, March 3, 1857, AH; Misc. Foreign File; David L. Gregg, Diary, March 5, 1857, UH Library. For the poem, see Muir in *Southwestern Historical Quarterly*, LII (1948), 49–59.

27. Jarves to Kamehameha III, August 3, 1847, AH, FO & Ex., also to Wyllie, August 15 (two letters) and September 11, 1848, *ibid.*; Wyllie to Ricord, March 9, 1853, AH, Misc. Foreign File.

28. Steegmuller, *James Jackson Jarves*, pp. 84–85; AH, Privy Council Record, IV, 97–103, 133–153.

29. Wyllie to Judd, November 18, 1847 (cited in note 23, above); AH, Privy Council Record, IV, 165–177; Wyllie to Judd, December 4, 1847, and April 20, 1848, AH, FO & Ex.; L. F. Judd, *Honolulu*, p. 162.

30. David L. Gregg, Diary, March 5, 1857, UH Library. Bates (1810–1873), a native of Le Roy, New York, married Judd's sister Elisabeth Gertrude. They reached Honolulu on June 28, 1848. He took office on August 19. In the spring of 1864 he moved with his wife to San Francisco (San Francisco *Alta California*, June 2, 1873; Baker, *Honolulu in 1853*, pp. 67–78; *Fragments V*, p. 79).

31. Kuykendall, *Hawaiian Kingdom 1778–1854*, pp. 389–391; Manley Hopkins, *Hawaii* (2d ed., New York, 1869), pp. 318–320; *Official Correspondence with Le Chevalier Dillon* (Honolulu, 1849), especially p. 249; Dillon to Judd, May 17 and August 11, 1848, AH, Finance Department Letter Book 1848–1859; the second letter is also in AH, FO & Ex. and printed in the *Polynesian*, March 23, 1850, and in *Report of the Minister of Foreign Relations, 1851*, appendix, pp. 141–144; Wyllie's private journal (copy), August 11, 1848, AH, FO & Ex.; Wyllie to Thomas, August 29, 1848; Wyllie to Dudoit, November 6 and December 11, 1848, Wyllie Collection; AH, Privy Council Record, V, 373–374 (February 27, 1849).

32. Robertson's memorial, October 11, 1848, AH; royal orders of October 18 and November 29, 1848, *ibid.*; Royal Commission to Judd, November 30, 1848, AH, Privy Council Record, V.

33. Manley Hopkins, *Hawaii*, p. 320; "Reminiscences of Henry L. Sheldon," I, 106, AH; Wyllie to Ricord, November 19, 1853, AH; Misc. Foreign File; Judd to Wyllie, December 4 and 6, 1848, and Judd's declaration to the king at the privy council, December 9, 1848, AH, FO & Ex.; testimony of Peacock and others, AH, Privy Council Record, IIIa, 177–194 (December 27, 1848). Armstrong to Baldwin, December 7, 1848, HMCS Library.

34. Ten Eyck to Wyllie, December 8, 1848, AH, FO & Ex.; Lee to Wyllie, December 9, 1848, *ibid.*; Bates to Lee, December 11, 1848, *ibid.*

35. Armstrong to Baldwin, December 25, 1848, HMCS Library; Wyllie to U.S. Secretary of State, January 8, 1849, AH, FO Letter Book, XIII, 371; Ten Eyck to Wyllie, January 26, 1849, AH, FO & Ex. For Ten Eyck's involvement with Ladd & Co., see Kuykendall, *Hawaiian Kingdom 1778–1854*, p. 255.

36. Mrs. E. M. Wills Parker, *The Sandwich Islands as They Are, Not as They Should Be* (San Francisco, 1852), p. 11; Dominis to Johnson, December 17, 1848, Hunnewell Papers, Houghton Library, Harvard University; Hitchcock's letter of resignation, December 8, 1848, AH, FO & Ex.; Armstrong to Kamehameha III, December 11, 1848, *ibid.*; AH, Privy Council Record, IIIa, 251 (April 24, 1849) and IIIb, 451 (January 30, 1850); Deposition of John G. Munn, December 7, 1848, AH, FO & Ex.

37. Robertson's speech and Judd's written reply, both undated, *ibid.*; testimony of John Young, January 9 and 10, 1849, AH, Privy Council Record, V, 269–270 and 288–289; Lee to Hopkins, March 7, 1849, *ibid.*

38. Testimony of Wyllie, January 10, 1849, AH, Privy Council Record, V, 295; Judd to the Impeachment Board, January 18, 1849; Wyllie to Judd, January 19, 1849, AH, FO & Ex.

39. Wyllie to Prince Lot Kanehaneha, January 13, 1860, to Judd, March 19, 1860; and to Kamehameha IV, March 31, 1860; also Judd to Wyllie, May 20, 1860, AH, Local Officials File.

40. Miller to Addington, April 9, 1846, BPRO, FO 58/44.

41. Report of the Royal Commission, April 23, 1849, and Kamehameha III to Judd, April 28, 1849, AH, FO & Ex.

Notes: *The Crisis of 1849 (pages 156–163)*

1. L. F. Judd, *Honolulu*, p. 136.

2. AH, Privy Council Record, IIIa, 278–291 (May 21 and 22, 1849); Richard Armstrong, Journal, May 20–22, 1849, HMCS Library.

3. G. P. Judd, Journal, November 17, 1827, *Fragments III*, p. 18; Armstrong to Chapman, November, 1843, Richard Armstrong Papers; *Sandwich Islands News*, October 14, 1846; Robert Elwes, *A Sketcher's Tour round the World* (2d ed., London, 1854), pp. 193–197; E. K. Wilder, Journal, June 17 and 24, 1849.

4. For the French crisis of 1849 see Kuykendall, *Hawaiian Kingdom 1778–1854*, pp. 390–395; L. F. Judd, *Honolulu*, p. 144.

5. *Ibid.*, pp. 145, 149.

6. Translation of an address at Waimea by the Reverend Lorenzo Lyons on January 10, 1855 (typescript in the possession of Mrs. Emma Doyle of Honolulu).

7. L. F. Judd, *Honolulu*, pp. 146–148.

8. *Ibid.*; AH, Privy Council Record, IIIa, 347 (September 5, 1849); Wyllie's report

on Judd's mission, read in the cabinet council on October 17–18, 1850, AH, FO & Ex.; Stephen Reynolds, Journal, September 6, 1849.

9. L. F. Judd, *Honolulu*, pp. 178–179 (not in the 1880 edition); also in Julius A. Palmer, Jr., *Memories of Hawaii* (Boston, 1894), pp. 118–119; W. D. Alexander, "A Suppressed Chapter of Hawaiian History by Mrs. Laura F. Judd," HHS *Tenth Annual Report* (1903), pp. 7–12; Wight, *Memoirs of E. K. Wilder* [1909], pp. 81–82.

10. Bradley, *American Frontier in Hawaii*, p. 412; Miller to Palmerston, September 25, 1849, and Miller's memorandum, October 1, 1849, BPRO, FO 58/64; Judd to Wyllie, January 24, 1850, AH, FO & Ex.

11. AH, Privy Council Record, IIIa, 349 (September 5, 1849); Wyllie's report on Dr. Judd's mission (cited in note 8, above); L. F. Judd, *Honolulu*, pp. 138, 141; E. K. Wilder, Journal, August 12 and 30, 1849; Smith, *Yankees in Paradise*, p. 230. There is material in the Archives of Hawaii dealing with an investigation into the princes' conduct about this time.

12. E. K. Wilder, Journal, September 9, 1849,

13. L. F. Judd, *Honolulu*, p. 148; A. S. Cooke, Journal, September 11, 1849, in Richards, *Chiefs' Children's School*, p. 336; *Friend*, September 11, 1849.

14. Wyllie's attitude shows clearly in his report on Dr. Judd's mission (cited in note 8, above); Miller to Palmerston, September 25, 1849 (cited in note 10, above).

15. Ten Eyck to U.S. Secretary of State (No. 56), September 10, 1849, U.S. Archives.

Notes: Diplomatic Journey, I (pages 164–175)

1. Judd's letter, October 4, 1849 (extract), L. F. Judd, *Honolulu*, pp. 152–153; Judd to Mr. and Mrs. Bates, September 28 to October 5, 1849, HMCS Library; C. S. Lyman, Diary, [October] 3, 1849, in Lyman, *Around the Horn to the Sandwich Islands*, p. 300.

2. Miller to Palmerston, September 25, 1849, BPRO, FO 58/64; Prince Alexander Liholiho, Journal, October 8, 1849, HHS (also extracts in Withington, *Golden Cloak*, pp. 188–199); Judd to Wyllie (No. 3), October 4, 1849, AH, FO & Ex. and FO Letter Book No. 16. For Eames see *Dictionary of American Biography*, V, 592–593.

3. Judd's letter (undated extract), L. F. Judd, *Honolulu*, p. 153.

4. Kuykendall, *Hawaiian Kingdom 1778–1854*, pp. 379–380.

5. Hunt, *Sandwich Islands*, pp. 147–152; Gulick, *Pilgrims of Hawaii*, p. 243; Wyllie to Forbes, October 10, 1848, AH, FO & Ex.; Prince Alexander, Journal, October 15 and 29, 1849.

6. *Ibid.*; Prince Lot, Journal, October 15, 1849, Bishop Museum, Honolulu; Judd to Wyllie (No. 5), October 15, 1849, AH, FO & Ex.; Mark Twain's second letter to the New York *Daily Tribune*, dated January 6, and published January 9, 1873, in Walter F. Frear, *Mark Twain and Hawaii* (Chicago, 1947), pp. 496–497.

7. Prince Alexander, Journal, November 3, 8, 12, 14, and 27, and December 7, 1849; E. K. Wilder, Journal, November 10, 1849; Judd to Wyllie (private), November 10, 1849, AH, FO & Ex.

8. John E. Minter, *The Chagres: River of Westward Passage* (New York, 1948), especially pp. 8, 213, 381; Wight, *Memoirs of E. K. Wilder*, p. 83; Prince Alexander, Journal, November 27, 1849; Prince Lot, Journal, November [25] and [30], 1849, and Judd's pencil note.

9. *Ibid.*; Judd's letter, December 11, 1849 (extract), L. F. Judd, *Honolulu*, p. 153.

10. *Ibid.*; Prince Alexander, Journal, December 7 and 11, 1849; Prince Lot, Journal, December 10, 1849; Judd to Wyllie (No. 8), December 10, 1849, AH, FO & Ex. For Livingston, see Walter Barrett [Joseph A. Scoville], *The Old Merchants of New York City*

(2d ser., New York, 1864), pp. 72–75. For Benson see John H. Rollo, *A Genealogical Record of the Descendants of Alexander Rollo* (Wilmington, Del., privately printed, 1896), pp. 13, 45.

11. Judd to Wyllie (No. 8, cited in note above); Prince Lot, Journal, January 6, 1850; Judd's letter (undated extract), L. F. Judd,*Honolulu*, pp. 153–154.

12. *Ibid.*

13. Judd to Wyllie (Nos. 9 and 10), December 27, 1849, and January 11, 1850 (the latter enclosing a copy of Addington to Barclay, January 2, 1850), AH, FO & Ex. Addington's letter, and Barclay's of December 26, are also in the BPRO.

14. Prince Lot, Journal, January 6, 1850; Prince Alexander, Journal, January 3, 5, 7, and 9, 1850.

15. Judd to Wyllie, January 11, 1850, AH, FO & Ex.; Judd's letter (undated extract), L. F. Judd, *Honolulu*, p. 154.

16. Prince Alexander, Journal, January 3, 1849 [*sic*]; Judd to Wyllie (No. 11), January 24, 1850, AH, FO & Ex.; for Clark see *Dictionary of National Biography*, IV, 401–402.

17. Judd to Palmerston (private), January 16, 1850; Palmerston to Judd, January 21, 1850; Judd to La Hitte, January 14, 1850, AH, FO & Ex.; Judd's note in AH, FO Letter Book No. 16, January 14, 1850. The correspondence with Palmerston is also in BPRO, FO 58/69.

18. Judd to Wyllie (No. 11), January 24, 1850, and private letter same date, AH, FO & Ex.; Judd's letter, January 23, 1850 (extract), L. F. Judd, *Honolulu*, p. 154.

19. Palmerston to Normanby (No. 35), January 24, 1850, BPRO, FO 27/861; Palmerston's order, same date, BPRO, FO 58/69; Palmerston to Miller (No. 3), January 31, 1850, BPRO 58/67; Palmerston to Normanby (No. 59), February 5, 1850, BPRO, FO 27/861.

20. Prince Lot, Journal, February 7, 1850; Judd to E. K. Judd, February 12, 1850, also Prince Alexander to E. K. Judd, April 4, 1850, in Wight, *Memoirs of E. K. Wilder*, pp. 84–85, and extracts in L. F. Judd, *Honolulu*, pp. 155–156.

21. Judd's letter, January 30, 1850 (extract), *ibid.*, p. 155; Judd to Wyllie (No. 12), February 7, 1850, AH, FO & Ex. For Normanby, see *Dictionary of National Biography*, XV, 1116–1117; for La Hitte see *La grande encyclopédie* (Paris, 1886–1902), XIV, 1193.

22. Normanby to Palmerston, February 7, 1850, BPRO, FO 27/868; Judd to Wyllie (No. 12, cited in note above).

23. Prince Alexander, Journal, February 7, 12, 13, and 15, 1850.

24. La Hitte to Judd, February 15 and 21, 1850, also Judd's memorandum, AH, FO Letter Book No. 16; Judd to Wyllie (No. 14), February 20, 1850, AH, FO & Ex. For Cramayel see Woelmont de Brumagne, *Notices généalogiques* (Paris, 1931–1935), VIII, 495.

25. Judd to Barclay, February 20, 1850, AH, FO Letter Book No. 16; Judd to Wyllie (No. 14, cited in note above); Judd's letter, May 1, 1850 (extract), L. F. Judd, *Honolulu*, p. 161.

26. *Cambridge History of British Foreign Policy* (Cambridge, 1929–), II, 330–331, 596–599; Herbert C. F. Bell, *Lord Palmerston* (London, 1936), II, 20–27.

27. Instructions to Dillon, July 13 and 14, 1849, quoted in Kuykendall, *Hawaiian Kingdom 1778–1854*, pp. 391–392.

28. Judd to Barclay, February 21 and 22, 1850; Judd to Henry Hill, March 2, 1850; Judd to Wyllie (No. 15), March 7, 1850, AH, FO Letter Book No. 16; G. P. Judd, Journal, March 1, 1850 (extract) and Wyllie's memorandum from it, same date, AH, FO & Ex.

29. Judd to Barclay, March 8, 1850, AH, FO Letter Book 16; Judd's letter, March 7, 1850 (extract), L. F. Judd, *Honolulu*, pp. 156–157; Prince Alexander, Journal, March 8–10, 1850; Prince Lot, Journal, March 9, 10, and 12, 1850.

30. Judd to Barclay, March 14, 1850, AH, FO Letter Book 16; G. P. Judd, Journal, March 12, 1850 (certified extract), AH, FO & Ex.; Judd's letter, March 11 [?], 1850 (extract), L. F. Judd, *Honolulu*, p. 157.

31. *Ibid.*; Judd to Wyllie (No. 16), March 21, 1850, and February 21, 1850 (private), AH, FO & Ex.; Judd to Barclay, February 21 and 27, March 2, 1850, AH, FO Letter Book 16.

32. Kuykendall, *Hawaiian Kingdom 1778–1854*, p. 397; Judd to Barclay, March 23, 1850; La Hitte to Judd, March 25, 1850, AH, FO Letter Book 16; Judd to Palmerston, April 9, 1850, AH, FO & Ex. and BPRO, FO 58/69.

33. Judd to Barclay, March 24 and 28, 1850, AH, FO Letter Book 16.

34. Judd to Barclay, April 4, 1850, *ibid.*; Judd to Wyllie (No. 17), April 4, 1850, AH, FO & Ex.; Prince Alexander, Journal, March 27, 1850; Prince Alexander to Mrs. Bates, April 1, 1850, HMCS Library; Judd's letter (undated extract), L. F. Judd, *Honolulu*, p. 156.

35. Perrin's declaration, April 5, 1850; Judd to Perrin, April 6, 1850 (two letters); Judd to La Hitte, April 6 (two letters), April 8, and April 17, 1850, AH, FO & Ex.

36. Judd to Wyllie (No. 18), April 19, 1850; Wyllie's memoranda from Judd's private journal, April 8, 1850, AH, FO & Ex.; Judd's letter (undated extract), L. F. Judd, *Honolulu*, p. 156.

Notes: Diplomatic Journey, II *(pages 176–191)*

1. Judd to Palmerston (No. 2), April 9, 1850, BPRO, FO 58/69 and AH, FO & Ex.

2. Prince Alexander, Journal, April 13, 1850; Prince Lot, Journal, April 12, 1850; Judd's letter (undated extract), L. F. Judd, *Honolulu*, p. 159.

3. *Ibid.*; Prince Lot, Journal, April 17, 1850; Judd to Palmerston, April 12, 1850, BPRO, FO 58/69 and AH, FO Letter Book 16. For Gage see *Dictionary of National Biography*, VII, 797.

4. La Hitte to Judd, April 12, 1850, and Judd to La Hitte, April 17, 1850, AH, FO Letter Book 16.

5. Wyllie's memoranda from Judd's private journal, April 18, 1850; Judd to Wyllie (No. 18), April 19, 1850, AH, FO & Ex.; Judd's letter (undated extract), L. F. Judd, *Honolulu*, p. 159. For Seymour see *Dictionary of National Biography*, XVII, 1259.

6. Judd's letter (undated extract), L. F. Judd, *Honolulu*, p. 160; Prince Alexander, Journal, April 19, 1850; Prince Lot, Journal, April 20, 1850; Wyllie's memoranda from Judd's private journal, [April 19, 1850], and Judd to Wyllie (No. 19), April 25, 1850, AH, FO & Ex. For Lt. Col. (later General) Seymour, see G. E. Cokayne, *Complete Peerage*, V. Gibbs, *et al*, eds. (London, 1910–), VI, 514–515.

7. Judd to Wyllie (No. 19), April 25, 1850, AH, FO & Ex. For Drouyn de Lhuys see *Nouvelle biographie generale* (Paris, 1853–1866), XIV, 803–806.

8. Drouyn de Lhuys to La Hitte (No. 219), April 22, 1850, Iles Sandwich, VIII, No. 180, Archives du Ministère des Affaires Étrangères, Paris (transcript in UH Library).

9. Prince Alexander, Journal, April 21, 1850; Prince Lot, Journal, April 25 and 29, 1850; Wyllie's memoranda from Judd's private journal, April 25, 1850, AH, FO & Ex. In 1852 Taylor was appointed British consul in Denmark, a post which he held for 20 years (*Gentleman's Magazine* [1853], Pt. I, 83; *Royal Kalendar* 1853–1873).

10. Judd to Wyllie (No. 19), April 25, 1850; Wyllie's memoranda from Judd's private journal, April 26, 1850, AH, FO & Ex.; Judd's letter (undated extract), L. F. Judd, *Honolulu*, pp. 160–162. According to a much later unconfirmed report, said to be based on information from Judd, Palmerston recommended that Hawaii become a protectorate or an integral part of the United States (H. A. Peirce to Hamilton Fish, February 25, 1871, *Senate Ex. Docs.*, 52 Congr., 2 Sess., No. 77 (1873), p. 14).

11. Judd's letter (undated extract), L. F. Judd, *Honolulu*, p. 161; Wight, *Memoirs of*

E. K. *Wilder*, p. 95; Wyllie's memoranda from Judd's private journal, April 27, 1850, AH, FO & Ex.; two newspaper clippings in AH, FO Letter Book 16, pp. 142–143.

12. Judd to Palmerston (Nos. 3 and 4), May 1 and 4, 1850; Palmerston to Judd, May 2, 1850, *ibid.* and BPRO, FO 58/69.

13. Judd to Wyllie (No. 20), May 17, 1850; Wyllie's memoranda from Judd's private journal, May 3 and 4, 1850, AH, FO & Ex.; Judd's letter (undated extract), L. F. Judd, *Honolulu*, p. 161.

14. *Ibid.*, p. 163; Prince Alexander, Journal, [May, 1850]; Wyllie's memoranda from Judd's private journal, May 16, 17, and 21, 1850; Bigelow to Judd, May 24, 1850; newspaper clippings, AH, FO Letter Book 16, pp. 148, 153. For Downes see *Dictionary of American Biography*, V, 415–416.

15. Judd to Anderson, May 20, 1850, American Board MSS, CCXXXV, No. 131, also in *Fragments II*, p. 183; newspaper clippings, AH, FO Letter Book 16, p. 153.

16. *Ibid.*, p. 148; Mrs. Lydia Bacon to Mrs. E. C. B., August 8, 1850, *Biography of Mrs. Lydia B. Bacon*, pp. 274–275; Steegmuller, *James Jackson Jarves*, pp. 41, 96–97; L. F. Judd, *Honolulu*, p. 81.

17. Prince Alexander, Journal, May 29, 1850; Wyllie's memoranda from Judd's private journal, May 23–25, 1850, AH, FO & Ex.

18. Prince Alexander to Mrs. Bates, June 8, 1850, HMCS Library; Holman Hamilton, *Zachary Taylor, Soldier in the White House* (New York, 1951), pp. 357–367, 372–385; Wilhelmus B. Bryan, *A History of the National Capital* (New York, 1916), II, 61.

19. Prince Alexander, Journal, May 29, 1850; Judd's letter (undated extract), L. F. Judd, *Honolulu*, p. 164.

20. *Ibid.*, p. 165; Judd's private journal, June 4, 1850, quoted in Kuykendall, *Hawaiian Kingdom 1778–1854*, p. 398. For Clayton see *Dictionary of American Biography*, IV, 185–186.

21. Wyllie's memoranda from Judd's private journal, May 30, 1850, AH, FO & Ex.; Prince Lot, Journal, May 30, 1850; Prince Alexander, Journal, Thursday, May 29 [30], 1850; Hamilton, *Zachary Taylor*, pp. 352–355. Taylor died on July 9.

22. Judd and Jarves to Clayton, May 30, 1850; Clayton to Judd and Jarves, June 3, 1850; Clayton to Rives, July 5, 1850, *Senate Ex. Docs.*, 52 Congr., 2 Sess., No. 17 (1893), pp. 82–84; Judd to Palmerston (No. 6), June 3, 1850, BPRO, FO 58/69, and AH, FO Letter Book 16.

23. Newspaper clippings, *ibid.*, p. 154; Prince Alexander to Elizabeth K. Judd, [June, 1850], in Wight, *Memoirs of E. K. Wilder*, pp. 85–86, and in L. F. Judd, *Honolulu*, pp. 163–164; Prince Alexander, Journal, May 31, 1850; Prince Lot, Journal, June 1, 1850. For Elmore see *Dictionary of American Biography*, VI, 118–119.

24. Judd to Wyllie (No. 21), June 7, 1850, AH, FO & Ex.; Prince Alexander, Journal, June 1, 1850.

25. Judd's letter (undated extract), L. F. Judd, *Honolulu*, p. 164; Judd to Ewbank, June 3, 1850, AH, FO Letter Book 16; Prince Lot, Journal, June 1, 1850. For Ewbank see *Dictionary of American Biography*, VI, 227–228.

26. Bulwer to Palmerston (No. 105), June 9, 1850, BPRO, FO 5/513; Wyllie's memoranda from Dr. Judd's private journal, June 1, 1850, AH, FO & Ex.; cf. Richard W. Van Alstyne, "Great Britain, the United States, and Hawaiian Independence, 1850–1855," *Pacific Historical Review*, IV (1935), 16. For Bulwer see *Dictionary of National Biography*, III, 263–265.

27. Judd's letter (undated extract), L. F. Judd, *Honolulu*, p. 164; Frederick W. Seward, *Reminiscences of a War-Time Statesman and Diplomat 1830–1915* (New York, 1916), p. 81.

28. Prince Alexander, Journal, June 5, 1850; information from Judd reported in David L. Gregg, Diary, May 21, 1855, UH Library, and in Albert Bigelow Paine, ed., *Mark Twain's Notebook*, [New York, 1935), p. 27; Wight, *Memoirs of E. K. Wilder*, p. 95; Prince Alexander, Journal, 1844–1845, Bishop Museum, Honolulu.

29. B. F. Snow to H. A. Peirce, January 18, 1854, Hunnewell Papers, Houghton Library, Harvard University; Frank Vincent, Jr., *Through and Through the Tropics*

(2d ed., New York, 1875), p. 62; Sophia Cracroft, journal letters, April 22, 1861, in Alfons L. Korn, *The Victorian Visitors* (Honolulu, 1958), p. 30; Miller to Addington (No. 94), March 18, 1851, BPRO, FO 58/70; Gregg to Marcy (No. 7), January 21, 1854, U.S. Archives; Manley Hopkins, *Hawaii*, p. 329; Charles V. C. Varigny, *Quatorze Ans aux Iles Sandwich* (Paris, 1874), p. 78; "Reminiscences of Henry L. Sheldon," I, 186, AH.

30. Prince Lot, Journal, June 5 and 9, 1850; Judd to Wyllie (No. 21), June 7, 1850, AH, FO & Ex.

31. Judd's letter (undated extract), L. F. Judd, *Honolulu*, p. 165; *Two Worlds*, June 22, 1850, of which a long extract is in Steegmuller, *James Jackson Jarves*, pp. 95–96; Prince Alexander, Journal, [June 10, 1850]. Carleton is mentioned briefly in Charles W. Leng and William T. Davis, *Staten Island and Its People* (New York, 1930–1933), II, 874.

32. Prince Alexander, Journal, June 11–29, 1850; newspaper clippings in AH, FO Letter Book 16, p. 168; Wyllie's memoranda from Judd's private journal, June 11–26, 1850, AH, FO & Ex.; George B. Catlin, *The Story of Detroit* (Chicago, 1923), pp. 281, 460.

33. Clinton *Signal*, August 2, 1850; minutes of the meeting of the board of trustees, Hamilton College, July 23, 1850, and MS certificate of the award, same date (information from Edwin K. Tolan, reference librarian, Hamilton College). In the newspaper account and in both college documents his name appears as "Garritt Pitt Judd."

34. "Recollections of Agnes H. B. Judd" (MS in the possession of Mrs. George P. Cooke of Molokai, Hawaii), January 27, 1927; cf. Wight, *Memoirs of E. K. Wilder*, p. 95.

35. Samuel Smith to Judd and the princes, July 9, 1850, also newspaper clippings, AH, FO Letter Book 16, pp. 166–167.

36. Judd to George Law, July 12, 1850; Wyllie's memoranda from Judd's private journal, July 15–29, 1850, AH, FO & Ex.

37. *Ibid.*, August 1, 1850; Perrin to La Hitte, August 9, 1850, Iles Sandwich, VIII, No. 239, Archives du Ministère des Affaires Étrangères, Paris (transcripts in UH Library); Normanby to Palmerston (No. 338), October 17, 1850, and Palmerston to Normanby (No. 513), October 23, 1850, BPRO, FO 27/875 and 27/866; Rives to Webster (Nos. 95 and 97), July 8 and 22, 1851, *Senate Ex. Docs.*, 52 Congr., 2 Sess., No. 77 (1893), pp. 94, 100; also a summary in Kuykendall, *Hawaiian Kingdom 1778–1854*, p. 399.

38. Judd to Palmerston (No. 7), August 1, 1850, BPRO, FO 58/69 and AH, FO & Ex.; Judd to Clayton, August 1, 1850, U.S. Archives and AH, FO & Ex.; Judd to Jarves, August 1, 1850, AH, FO Letter Book 16; Judd to Anderson, August 1, 1850, U.S. Archives and American Board MSS, CCXXXV, No. 132, also in *Fragments II*, pp. 184–186.

39. Wyllie's memoranda from Judd's private journal, August 3–23, 1850, AH, FO & Ex.; "Reminiscences of Henry L. Sheldon," I, 185.

Notes: Three Troubled Years (pages 192–201)

1. Elisabeth Gertrude Judd (Mrs. Asher B.) Bates, Journal, Sunday, March [10], 1850; Helen Seymour ("Nellie") Judd, Journal, September 9, 1850, in Wight, *Memoirs of E. K. Wilder*, p. 93; Prince Alexander to Mrs. Bates, April 1 and June 8, 1850, HMCS Library; G. P. Judd, Journal, November 17, 1827, *Fragments III*, p. 17.

2. Kuykendall, *Hawaiian Kingdom 1778–1854*, pp. 297–298.

3. Helen Seymour Judd, Journal, December 11, 1849, in Wight, *Memoirs of E. K. Wilder*, p. 90; Miller to Addington, November 10, 1849, BPRO, FO 58/64; Ten Eyck to Clayton, December 3, 1849, U.S. Archives; Richard Armstrong, Journal, December 14, 1849.

4. Judd to Wyllie, November 10, 1849, October 12 and October 14, 1850, AH,

FO & Ex.; Elisabeth G. J. Bates, Journal, April 1 and 7, August 7, 1850; E. K. Wilder, Journal, October 8, 1850.

5. Wyllie's report on Dr. Judd's mission, read in the cabinet October 17 and 18, 1850, also Wyllie's notes on the report, AH, FO & Ex.

6. Wyllie to Turrill, November 24, 1850, and Wyllie to Caldclough, November 13, 1850, AH, Misc. Foreign File.

7. Cabinet Council Record, October 17 and 18, 1850, I, 48–50; Wyllie's minutes, October 17, 1850, AH, FO & Ex.; Wyllie's notes, cited in note 5 above.

8. Lee to Turrill, December 29, 1850, HMCS Library.

9. AH, Privy Council Record, September 30 and October 1, 1850, also January 22 and June 27, 1851; Hobbs, *Hawaii: A Pageant of the Soil*, pp. 171–172; *Fragments V*, p. 82; E. K. Wilder, Journal, December 17, 1850.

10. Parker, *Sandwich Islands*, p. 10.

11. Mary Dillingham Frear, *Our Familiar Island Trees* (Boston, 1929), p. 113; Marie C. Neal, *In Honolulu Gardens* (Bishop Museum Special Publication No. 13, Honolulu, 1928), p. 45, also her *In Gardens of Honolulu* (Bishop Museum Special Publication No. 40, Honolulu, 1948), p. 97; *Hawaiian Almanac and Annual*, XXXV (1909), 129; Baker, *Honolulu in 1853*, p. 68; Sereno Bishop, *Reminiscences*, p. 6; Horace Mann, Journal, May 9, [1864], the Clements Library, University of Michigan. Mann was author of *Enumeration of Hawaiian Plants* (Cambridge, 1867).

12. Royal Hawaiian Agricultural Society *Transactions*, I, No. 1 (1850), 18; No. 2 (1851), 17; No. 3 (1852), 19–20, 22; No. 4 (1853), 42, 165; also Kuykendall, *Hawaiian Kingdom 1778–1854*, pp. 327–328.

13. A. F. Judd to W. N. Armstrong, April 10, 1852, Richard Armstrong Papers.

14. Armstrong to Baldwin, September 21, 1850, HMCS Library.

15. Judd to Anderson, March 30, 1851, American Board MSS, CCXXXV, No. 135, also in *Fragments II*, pp. 191–192.

16. Kuykendall, *Hawaiian Kingdom 1778–1854*, pp. 381, 399–407; also his *Hawaiian Kingdom 1854–1874*, pp. 47–54.

17. Lee to Turrill, June 1 and October 11, 1851, HMCS Library; Miller to Addington, May 19, 1851, BPRO, FO 58/71.

18. Chap. 1, Art. 23.

19. Kuykendall, *Hawaiian Kingdom 1778–1854*, pp. 266–268. For the defeat of Wyllie's proposal see Journal of the House of Nobles 1851–1854, April 14, 27, 28, and 29, 1852, pp. 75–82, AH.

20. C. R. Bishop to Turrill, October 9 and December 16, 1851; F. L. Hanks to Turrill, August 14, 1853; Richard Armstrong, Journal, July 20, 1853, HMCS Library; AH, Privy Council Record, 554, 556 (January 5 and 12, 1852); Judd to Lathrop, November 15, 1852, AH, Finance Department Letter Book 1848–1859; Journal of the House of Representatives, May 25 and June 7, 1853, pp. 442, 482, AH; Baker, *Honolulu in 1853*, p. 42.

21. AH, Privy Council Record, VI, 402–404 (July 21, 1851); Journal of the House of Representatives, May 27, 1852, and May 25, 1855; Journal of the House of Nobles, May 31, 1855; Wyllie to Armstrong, August 7, 1851, and Wyllie to Lee, October 18 and November 7, 1851, AH, Local Officials File; Wyllie to Ricord, March 9, 1853, and March 3, 1857, AH, Misc. Foreign File; *Session Laws of 1858–1859*, p. 437; *Polynesian*, January 6, 1853; C. H. Judd to W. N. Armstrong, October 15, 1851, Richard Armstrong Papers. The records of the House of Representatives in the Archives of Hawaii are missing between June 18 and 23, 1852, but the proceedings are reported in the *Polynesian* for June 26, 1852.

22. *Ibid.*, June 19, 1852. For Rhodes, see Kuykendall, *Hawaiian Kingdom 1854–1874*, p. 255.

23. Wyllie to Judd, July 14, 1853, AH, Local Officials File; also Judd to Wyllie, July 1, 7, 9, 11, and 12, 1853, and Wyllie to Judd, July 8, and 9, 1853, AH, Finance Department Letter Book.

24. C. H. Judd to W. N. Armstrong, June 26, 1853, Richard Armstrong Papers. For Newcomb see the *Friend* (March, 1892), p. 17. For Hillebrand see Halford, *9 Doctors & God*, p. 303.

25. Miller's dispatch, October 25, 1851 (extract), quoted in Montague Paske-Smith, "Early British Consuls in Honolulu," *Mid Pacific Magazine*, XLIX (1936), 253; Parker, *Sandwich Islands*, p. 13.

26. Parke, *Personal Reminiscences*, p. 41.

Notes: Retirement from Office (pages 202–213)

1. L. F. Judd, *Honolulu*, p. 175; and for a general summary Kuykendall, *Hawaiian Kingdom 1778–1854*, p. 412.

2. AH, Privy Council Record, VII, 99, 101 (February 14 and 15, 1853); also Judd to Young, February 15, 1853, and Judd's report, February 19, 1853, AH, FO & Ex.; Wyllie to Ricord, October 12, 1853, AH, Misc. Foreign File; Miller's memorandum, September 7, 1853, in Miller to Addington, September 9, 1853, BPRO, FO 58/76, partly printed in Hawaiian Historical Commission *Publications* (1927), I, No. 4, pp. 35–36.

3. Judd to Baldwin, February 24, 1853, HMCS Library, also in Halford, *9 Doctors & God*, p. 219.

4. Wight, *Memoirs of E. K. Wilder*, p. 105; L. F. Judd, *Honolulu*, p. 174; *Polynesian*, May 21, 1853.

5. Lee to Turrill, July 30, 1853, HMCS Library.

6. For the meetings of July 18, 19, and 20, see *Polynesian*, July 23, 1853; [Bates], *Sandwich Island Notes*, pp. 437–443; also a summary in Kuykendall, *Hawaiian Kingdom 1778–1854*, pp. 413–415.

7. Richard Armstrong, Journal, July 20, 1853; Severance to Marcy (No. 88), August 15, 1853, and to Hammond, August 24, 1853, U.S. Archives, and extracts in Hawaiian Historical Commission *Publications* (1927), I, No. 4, pp. 24, 27–29. The petition with signatures is in the *Polynesian*, August 20, 1853.

8. *Ibid.*, July 30, 1853; Alexander's letter, [summer, 1853], in Mary C. Alexander, *William Patterson Alexander*, pp. 327–328; L. F. Judd, *Honolulu*, pp. 175–176.

9. Cabinet Council Record, August 3, 1853, I, 73–81; AH, Privy Council Record, VII, 249, 257–259, 265 (August 3, 8, 15, 1853); the committee's report, August 15, 1853, AH, FO & Ex.; *Polynesian*, August 20, 1853.

10. Wyllie to Turrill, August 10–16, 1853, HMCS Library; Wyllie to Turrill, September 6, 1853; Wyllie to Ricord, November 19, 1853, March 3 and May 30, 1857; Wyllie to Jarves, January 19, 1857, AH, Misc. Foreign File.

11. AH, Privy Council Record, VII, 267–269, 271 (August 17 and 22, 1853), including the missing minutes, which were restored to the Archives by G. R. Carter on April 4, 1922. Miller's memorandum of September 7, 1853 (cited in note 2 above) corroborates the minutes and adds a few details, such as the fact that Hopkins cast the deciding vote. Hopkins was, to say the least, pleasure-loving in his private life, and as such opposed to the puritan moral standards of Armstrong and Judd (Severance to Marcy [No. 93], September 8, 1853, U.S. Archives). Other evidence than Severance's could be cited.

12. This view is given in [Bates], *Sandwich Island Notes*, p. 443.

13. *Ibid.*; Severance to Marcy (Nos. 88 and 89), August 15 and 24, 1853, also Severance to Hammond, August 24, 1853, U.S. Archives and extracts in Hawaiian Historical Commission *Publications* (1927), I, No. 4, pp. 24–29; Nellist, *Story of Hawaii*, p. 136; Kuykendall, *Hawaiian Kingdom 1778–1854*, pp. 416–417.

14. For a list of the signers see *ibid.*, p. 417, n. 178, also *Mid Pacific Magazine*, XLIX, (1936), 256. A copy of the petition was sent as an enclosure in Miller to Clarendon (No. 18), September 3, 1853, BPRO, FO 58/76.

15. Cabinet Council Record, August 22 and 24, 1853, I, 82–88, AH; Hitchcock to Wyllie, March 20, 1853, AH, FO & Ex.; Wyllie to Richard Thomas, July 27, 1854; Wyllie to Ricord, August 30, 1853, July 31 and August 31, 1854; Richard Thomas to Wyllie, January 11, 1854, AH, Misc. Foreign File. In the last letter cited, Admiral Thomas (replying to Wyllie's letter of September 3, 1853) called Judd an "arch traitor." See also Miller's memorandum, September 7, 1853, cited in note 2 above.

16. Aside from the references to Benson in the Archives of Hawaii index, the following items are noteworthy: Benson's bond, January 20, 1853, Finance Department File; Cabinet Council Record, September 16, 1850; Privy Council Record, September 26, October 21 and 31, 1850, October 4, 1852, and August 8, 1853.

17. *Polynesian*, April 10, 1852; Kuykendall, *Hawaiian Kingdom 1778–1854*, p. 424, also his *Hawaiian Kingdom 1854–1874*, pp. 12, 14.

18. Judd to Seward, April 20, 1867, U.S. Archives, which mentions the earlier correspondence; Hooper to Miller, November 14, 1853, BPRO, FO 58/79; Judd's memorandum on annexation, October 20, 1853, AH, Local Officials File. For comment on Bates's letter see Wyllie to Ricord, November 19, 1853, AH, Misc. Foreign File, and Miller's memorandum, September 7, 1853, cited in note 2 above.

19. Kuykendall, *Hawaiian Kingdom 1778–1854*, pp. 407–411.

20. For example, Hooper to Miller, November 14, 1853, cited in note 18 above; Wyllie to Ricord, August 31, 1854, AH, Misc. Foreign File.

21. Miller to Addington, September 9, 1853, BPRO, FO 58/76; Kuykendall, *Hawaiian Kingdom 1778–1854*, pp. 415, 424, 426.

22. L. F. Judd, *Honolulu*, p. 181.

23. Judd to Anderson, May 1, 1861, American Board MSS, CCCV, No. 133, also in *Fragments II*, p. 207.

24. Judd to Seward, April 20, 1867, U.S. Archives.

25. Richard Armstrong, Journal, September 5, 1853; Kuykendall, *Hawaiian Kingdom 1778–1854*, p. 424.

26. Wight, *Memoirs of E. K. Wilder*, p. 72; Nellist, *Story of Hawaii*, p. 136.

27. [Bates], *Sandwich Island Notes*, p. 443; Miller to Clarendon (No. 17), August 13, 1853, BPRO, FO 58/76; Severance to Marcy (No. 93), September 8, 1853, U.S. Archives; Richard Armstrong, Journal, November 15, 1851.

28. L. F. Judd, *Honolulu*, p. 176; Miller's memorandum, September 7, 1853, cited in note 2 above.

29. Miller to Addington, August 30, 1853, BPRO, FO 58/76, also an extract in Hawaiian Historical Commission *Publications*, (1927), I, No. 4, pp. 32–33; Wyllie to Ricord, August 30, 1853, AH, Misc. Foreign File.

30. AH, Privy Council Record, VII, 287 (September 1, 1853); *Polynesian*, September 3, 1853; Miller to Clarendon (No. 18), September 3, 1853, BPRO, FO 58/76.

31. Miller's memorandum, September 7, 1853, cited in note 2 above; Wyllie to Ricord, May 30, 1857, AH, Misc. Foreign File.

32. Lee to Turrill, December 17, 1853, HMCS Library.

33. L. F. Judd, *Honolulu*, p. 176; Severance to Marcy (No. 92), September 5, 1853, U.S. Archives, and Miller to Clarendon (No. 19), September 7, 1853, BPRO, FO 58/76, also extracts in Hawaiian Historical Commission *Publications* (1927), I, No. 4, pp. 29–30, 34; Wyllie to Ricord, October 12, 1853, AH, Misc. Foreign File; Allen to Mary H. Hobbs, September 5, 1853, Elisha H. Allen Papers, Library of Congress; also a summary in Kuykendall, *Hawaiian Kingdom 1778–1854*, p. 415. Other accounts, less well informed appear in Alexander's letter, [?September, 1853], in Mary C. Alexander, *William Patterson Alexander*, p. 328; R. Coady to Hunnewell, September 10, 1853, Hunnewell Papers, Baker Library, Harvard University; W. Chamberlain to Hill, September 10, 1853, Ameri-

can Board MSS, CCXXXIV, No. 64; Crabb to Treadway, September 23, 1853, AH, Parke Collection.

34. Wyllie to Turrill, September 6, 1853; Wyllie to Ricord, October 12, 1853, December 4, 1853, and May 30, 1857; Wyllie to Jarves, January 19, 1857, AH, Misc. Foreign File; see also Wyllie to Kamehameha IV, March 31, 1860, AH, Local Officials File.

35. Wyllie to Severance (No. 8), September 3, 1853, enclosed in Barclay to Clarendon (No. 9), December 7, 1853, also Miller to Addington, September 9, 1853, BPRO, FO 58/78 and 58/76.

36. Severance to Marcy (No. 92), September 5, 1853, cited in note 33 above; Richard Armstrong, Journal, September 5, 1853; Armstrong to Anderson, September 10, 1853, American Board MSS, CCXXXIII, No. 123; see also C. R. Bishop to Turrill, October 7, 1853, HMCS Library.

37. L. F. Judd, *Honolulu*, pp. 176–177; Armstrong to Baldwin, September 9 and 12, 1853, HMCS Library.

38. Cabinet Council Record, September 24, 1853, I, 104–106, AH; Wyllie to Ricord, December 4, 1853, AH, Misc. Foreign File.

39. Wyllie to Ricord, October 12, 1853, AH, Misc. Foreign File; Lee to Turrill, December 17, 1853, HMCS Library.

40. L. F. Judd, *Honolulu*, p. 177; Wight, *Memoirs of E. K. Wilder*, pp. 106–107.

Notes: *Medicine, Guano, and Sugar (pages 214–227)*

1. Kualoa Journal, September 16, 1853, *Fragments V*, pp. 43–44.

2. Journal of the House of Representatives, June 29, 1852, and June 6, 1853, pp. 286, 480, AH; Receipts and Expenditures for the Year ending March 31, 1851, AH, Finance Department; *Motion . . . made by R. C. Wyllie . . . to release John Ricord . . . from a debt*, p. 6.

3. *Polynesian*, October 1 and 22, 1853; Alexander's letter, [?September, 1853], in Mary C. Alexander, *William Patterson Alexander*, p. 328; Bishop to Turrill, December 22, 1853, HMCS Library.

4. Memorandum (typescript) of Lawrence M. Judd, March 3, 1940, in the possession of Mrs. William A. Jackson of Cambridge, Massachusetts. The *Polynesian* of November 5, 1853, mentions the arrival of the *Massachusetts* and the death of Mrs. Bennett.

5. Kenneth W. Barr, "Roots of Old New England," *Hawaiian Almanac and Annual* (1938), pp. 83–85, which quotes Dr. Judd's insurance advertisement in the *Polynesian* of June 12, 1852; photostat of Dr. Judd's insurance application and policy (No. 3630), written by the New England Mutual Life Insurance Co., on January 8, 1852, in the possession of K. W. Barr in the office of the Home Insurance Co., Honolulu.

6. AH, Privy Council Record, VIII, 109 (February 20, 1854), with Wyllie's minute reporting the adverse decision of the cabinet on February 16.

7. David L. Gregg, Diary, January 14 and June 27, 1854, UH Library; Kuykendall, *Hawaiian Kingdom 1854–1874*, pp. 20, 22.

8. Severance to Marcy (No. 93), September 8, 1853, and Gregg to Marcy (Nos. 3 and 5), January 5 and 12, 1854, U.S. Archives; David L. Gregg, Diary, January 4, 1854 (in HHS) and January 11, 1854 (in UH Library); Stephen Reynolds, Journal, March 22, 1854.

9. For the annexation movement of 1854 see Kuykendall, *Hawaiian Kingdom 1778–1854*, pp. 419–427.

10. David L. Gregg, Diary and correspondence, cited in note 8 above; also Gregg, Diary, February 1, 5, 13, and 14, 1854, UH Library; Gregg to Marcy (No. 9), February 6,

1854, U.S. Archives; unsigned letter to the New York *Times*, November 13, 1853, reprinted in the *Friend*, February, 1854, p. 12.

11. The petition is in AH, FO & Ex.

12. Miller to Wodehouse, March 14–23, 1854, BPRO, FO 58/79.

13. L. F. Judd, *Honolulu*, p. 181.

14. *Ibid.*, p. 180; David L. Gregg, Diary, June 29 and July 1, 1854.

15. Dr. Judd's involvement is stated in Wyllie to Kekuanaoa, November 17, 1854, AH, Local Officials File, and in Wyllie to Ricord, December 1, 1854, AH, Misc. Foreign File.

16. *Polynesian*, January 21, 1854; Emerson, *Pioneer Days in Hawaii*, pp. 181–182; *Life and Times of Mrs. Lucy G. Thurston*, pp. 168–175; Judd to Wilder, May 12, 1859, S. G. Wilder Papers, on deposit, HMCS Library.

17. *Polynesian*, August 30, 1856.

18. Kualoa Journal, December 21, 1855, *Fragments V*, p. 53; Judd to Wilder, April 1, 1858, S. G. Wilder Papers; Judd to Turrill, April 6, 1857, HMCS Library; Judd to the Trustees of the Nuuanu Cemetery Association, March 1, 1856, Cartwright Collection, AH.

19. E. K. Wilder, Journal, July 10, 1851; Kualoa Journal, February 4, 1853, and December 16, 1857, *Fragments V*, pp. 41, 64; Royal Hawaiian Agricultural Society *Transactions*, I, No. 2 (1851), 15; II, No. 1 (1854), 88; II, No. 2 (1855), 22.

20. G. H. Collings, *Commercial Fertilizers, their Sources and Use* (4th ed., Philadelphia, 1947), pp. 2, 120–122; *Hunt's Merchants' Magazine*, XXXIV (1856), 431.

21. *Memorial of Alfred G. Benson . . .* [1855], *passim*.

22. Brookes, *International Rivalry in the Pacific Islands*, pp. 224, 226; David N. Leff, *Uncle Sam's Pacific Islets* (Stanford University Press, 1940), pp. 7–8, 44; indenture of the American Guano Company, September 1, 1855, in Miscellaneous Letters relating to Guano Islands, III, 83–101, U.S. Archives; bonded claim of the American Guano Company to Baker Island, October 28, 1856, and to Jarvis Island, November 3–5, 1856, in Bonds, Correspondence with Treasury, Commerce and Labor relating to Guano Islands 1856–1912, *ibid*.

23. Edwin H. Bryan, Jr., *American Polynesia* (Honolulu, 1941), p. 40; affidavit of Charles H. Judd, September 7, 1860, and of Arthur Benson, May 2, 1857, in Miscellaneous Letters relating to Guano Islands, III, 108–110, 139–140, U.S. Archives.

24. Judd to Alfred G. Benson, March 18–19, 1858 (extract), in *ibid.*, III, 148, also in *Report to the Stockholders of the United States Guano Company* (New York, 1859), appendix, p. 29. For the dispute about the quality of the guano see *De Bow's Commercial Review*, XXIII (1857), 85; *Hunt's Merchants' Magazine*, XLI (1859), 477; Gregg, Diary, January 26 and 30, 1858.

25. Honolulu *Advertiser*, March 4, 1858; Judd to Wilder, March 12 and June 1, 1858, S. G. Wilder Papers.

26. Contract between G. P. Judd and S. G. Wilder, July 5, 1858, also Judd to S. G. and E. K. Wilder, October 5, 1858, S. G. Wilder Papers; "Reminiscences of Henry L. Sheldon," II, chap. 58, p. 3, AH; *Pacific Commercial Advertiser*, January 20, 1859.

27. Editor's note in *Fragments VI*, p. 3; Judd to Henry Hill, February 11, 1859, American Board MSS, CCXXXV, No. 141, also in *Fragments II*, pp. 203–204.

28. Leff, *Uncle Sam's Pacific Islets*, pp. 43–45; *American Journal of Science*, XXXIV (November, 1862), 224–243, an article by J. D. Hague, a chemist who lived for several months on Baker, Howland, and Jarvis in 1859–1861; Judd to Wilder, March 17, 1859, S. G. Wilder Papers.

29. *Ibid.*, Judd to S. G. and E. K. Wilder, October 5, 1858.

30. *Ibid.*, Judd to Wilder, April 23, 1859.

31. Leff, *Uncle Sam's Pacific Islets*, p. 8; affidavit of Charles H. Judd, September 7, 1860, Miscellaneous Papers relating to Guano Islands, III, 108–110, U.S. Archives; Wyllie to Ricord, March 2, 1859, and August 27, 1860, AH, Misc. Foreign File.

32. Bryan, *American Polynesia*, pp. 148, 151; Leff, *Uncle Sam's Pacific Islets*, pp. 30–31, where Dr. Judd's claim is printed; Kathleen D. Mellen, *The Gods Depart* (New York, Hastings House, 1956), p. 189, for the Hawaiian claim of 1862; G. P. Judd, Journal, August 25 to October 31, 1859, *Fragments VI*, pp. 69–100; Gregg, Diary, October 31, 1859; claim of the United States Guano Company to Palmyra, February 8, 1860, in Bonds, Correspondence with Treasury, Commerce and Labor relating to Guano Islands 1856–1912, U.S. Archives.

33. Leff, *Uncle Sam's Pacific Islets*, pp. 44–45; *Polynesian*, February 8, 1862; documents in Miscellaneous Letters relating to Guano Islands, III, U.S. Archives; Judd to Wilder, March 12, 1858, S. G. Wilder Papers.

34. Dr. Judd to his children, April 21, 1860, and to Wilder, June 20, 1860, and March 22, 1861 (with Wilder's annotation), also Wilder to C. H. Judd, May 19, 1861, *ibid.*

35. Judd to Wilder, June 3, 1861, *ibid.*; George R. Carter, "The Wilder Letters," (typescript (1922), HMCS Library), p. 21.

36. Leff, *Uncle Sam's Pacific Islets*, pp. 43, 49; S. C. Damon to Mrs. Gregg, December 14, 1864, Gregg Collection, UH Library; Judd to James Hunnewell, September 12, 1865, Hunnewell Papers, Baker Library, Harvard University.

37. Kuykendall, *Hawaiian Kingdom 1778–1854*, pp. 314–316, 323–333, also his *Hawaiian Kingdom 1854–1874*, pp. 140–149.

38. See above, p. 141; Royal Hawaiian Agricultural Society *Transactions*, I, No. 4 (1853), 39.

39. Lind, *An Island Community*, p. 169; Smith, *Yankees in Paradise*, pp. 324–327.

40. Editor's note in *Fragments V*, p. 82; Hobbs, *Hawaii: A Pageant of the Soil*, p. 171; Judd to Anderson, October 2, 1863, American Board MSS, CCCVII, No. 176, also in *Fragments II*, pp. 213–214; Kuykendall, *Hawaiian Kingdom 1778–1854*, p. 325.

41. Mortgage, November 16, 1863, and Judd to Wilder, same date, S. G. Wilder Papers.

42. Wight, *Memoirs of E. K. Wilder*, p. 131; Irwin to Gregg, September 4, 1864, Gregg Collection, UH Library.

43. Charles sold out on December 15, 1864, and Dr. Judd on March 14, 1865, see editor's note in *Fragments V*, p. 82, also Hobbs, *Hawaii: A Pageant of the Soil*, p. 171.

44. Judd to Anderson, April 24, 1865, American Board MSS, CCCVII, No. 179, also in *Fragments II*, p. 227.

45. *Hawaiian Almanac and Annual* (1875), 40.

46. Wight, *Memoirs of E. K. Wilder*, pp. 133, 136, 143.

47. Kuykendall, *Hawaiian Kingdom 1854–1874*, pp. 146–148.

48. Wight, *Memoirs of E. K. Wilder*, p. 144; *Hawaiian Gazette*, August 26, 1868. The attending physician was Dr. Robert McKibben (S. G. Wilder Papers, 1868).

49. Harriet Breck Judd to Sophie Elizabeth Hastings (Mrs. Robert L.) Douglass, January 4, 1869, sent to me by Mrs. Francis Hastings Gott of Pittsford, New York, and now in HMCS Library. The Judds left Honolulu on May 9 and returned August 28 (the *Friend* [June, 1868], 48, and [October, 1868], 88).

50. Editor's note in *Fragments V*, p. 83; George R. Carter, "The Wilder Letters," (typescript (1922) HMCS Library), p. 8.

51. Judd to Wilder, January 18 and 24, 1864; Judd to Mrs. Wilder, June 22, 1864, S. G. Wilder Papers.

1. Judd to Elizabeth Wilder, June 22, 1864, S. G. Wilder Papers.
2. L. F. Judd, *Honolulu*, pp. 184–186; Mrs. Judd's autobiographical statement, *Fragments I*, p. 31; Wight, *Memoirs of E. K. Wilder*, pp. 109–116; Dwight Baldwin, Journal, July 31, 1856, HMCS Library. Dr. Judd did *not* accompany them (Maria N. Ford, Diary, October 3, 1855, Yale Library; David L. Gregg, Diary, November 5, 1855; entry by Judd in the Kualoa Journal, December 21, 1855, *Fragments V*, p. 53).
3. Autograph Book [sent to Mrs. Judd], from her young friends of Brooklyn, N.Y., [1858], HMCS Library; Judd to Wilder, April 1, 1858, S. G. Wilder Papers.
4. Ethel Damon, *Letters from the Life of Abner and Lucy Wilcox* (Honolulu, privately printed, 1950), pp. 338–345; Wyllie to Turrill, March 30, 1852, AH, Misc. Foreign File; Henry Hill of the American Board arranged for their passage (Hill to Judd, September 9, 1851, S. G. Wilder Papers).
5. Gregg, Diary, April 22, 1857, and March 2, 1858; Harriet Breck Judd to Sophie Elizabeth Hastings (Mrs. Robert L.) Douglass, January 4, 1869, HMCS Library; *Life and Times of Mrs. Lucy G. Thurston*, pp. 273–278.
6. References in note 4 above, also her letter to Mrs. Douglass, cited in note 5 above; *Fragments I*, p. 3. Her will was presented for probate in the Supreme Court, Honolulu, on October 7, 1880.
7. See above p. 151; Judd to Wilder, May 28, 1864, S. G. Wilder Papers.
8. Nellist, *Story of Hawaii*, pp. 133–134; Emma Theodora Paty Yates, "Reminiscences of Honolulu" (undated typescript, HHS), pp. 9–10.
9. *Obituary Record of Graduates of Yale University Deceased from June, 1890, to June, 1900* (New Haven, 1900), pp. 705–706; Judd to Anderson, May 1, 1861, American Board MSS, CCCV, No. 133, also in *Fragments II*, p. 211.
10. The *Friend* (April, 1875), 29.
11. Kuykendall, *Hawaiian Kingdom 1854–1874*, pp. 167, 184.
12. Entry by Nellie Judd in the Kualoa Journal, November 20, 1852, *Fragments V*, pp. 36–37; E. K. Wilder, Journal, April 16 and July 6, 1850; also Lee to Turrill, January 15, 1853, HMCS Library; AH, Privy Council Record, November 9, 1852; Wyllie to Ricord, March 9 and November 19, 1853, AH, Misc. Foreign File.
13. *Hawaiian Gazette*, July 14, 1880.
14. Kuykendall, *Hawaiian Kingdom 1854–1874*, pp. 221, 224, 250. Mrs. Carter's biography of Kaahumanu was published in Honolulu in 1893.
15. *Record of the Descendants of Dr. Gerrit P. Judd of Hawaii* (Genealogical Series No. 3, Honolulu; Hawaiian Historical Society, 1922), pp. 3, 4, 6.
16. Yates, "Reminiscences," p. 13.
17. Family Record, also Mrs. Judd's autobiographical statement, *Fragments I*, pp. 4, 31–32; Judd to Hill, June 25, 1857, American Board MSS, CCXXXV, No. 137, also in *Fragments II*, p. 198.
18. H. B. Judd to Mrs. Douglass, January 4, 1869, cited in note 5 above; E. K. Wilder, undated memorandum in 1866 folder, S. G. Wilder Papers.
19. Wight, *Memoirs of E. K. Wilder*, pp. 101–102.
20. Robert C. Lydecker, ed., *Roster Legislatures of Hawaii 1841–1918* (Archives of Hawaii Publication No. 1, Honolulu, 1918), p. 74; Journal of the House of Representatives, June 11–28, 1858, and December 6, 1858 to January 20, 1859, AH; Gregg, Diary, January 20, 1859.
21. Kuykendall, *Hawaiian Kingdom 1854–1874*, pp. 127–134; also day-to-day accounts of the proceedings in the official periodical, the *Convention*, Nos. 1–18, July 14 to August 31, 1864.
22. Wyllie to Ricord, June 21, 1857, AH, Misc. Foreign File; Wyllie to Mrs. Judd, December 10, 1859, and January 13, 1860; Wyllie to Judd, [docketed 1860], January 14,

February 7, and March 19, 1860; Judd to Wyllie, March 13 and May 20, 1860, AH, Misc. Local File; Judd to Wyllie, February 17, 1860, L. F. Judd, *Honolulu*, pp. 190–198.

23. Judd to Anderson, May 1, 1861, American Board MSS, CCCV, No. 133, also in *Fragments II*, pp. 207, 210.

24. Judd to Seward, April 20, 1867, U.S. Archives.

25. Dr. Judd's correspondence 1857–1870 with Anderson, Clark, and Hill, American Board MSS, CCXXXV, CCCV, and CCCVII, also in *Fragments II*, pp. 198–238; Mary E. Anderson, *Scenes in the Hawaiian Islands and California* (New York, 1865), p. 201. For the coming of the Church of England to Hawaii see Kuykendall, *Hawaiian Kingdom 1854–1874*, pp. 84–99.

26. The *Friend* (July, 1873, supplement) and (June, 1926), 138. For the Hawaiian Evangelical Association see Kuykendall, *Hawaiian Kingdom 1854–1874*, pp. 99–101.

27. Frear, *Mark Twain and Hawaii*, p. 25, n. 11; minutes of the meeting of the Hawaiian Theater Company, February 1, 1856, Wyllie Collection, AH; Honolulu Rifles Subscriptions, 1857, Cartwright Collection, AH.

28. *Biennial Report of the President of the Board of Education . . . for 1872* [Honolulu, 1872], pp. 7–8; the *Friend* (July, 1871), 58; Lorenzo Lyons, Journal [?1870], in Emma L. Doyle, *Makua Laiana, the Story of Lorenzo Lyons* (Honolulu: privately printed, 1945), p. 205; Wetmore to Coan, September 4, 1871, HMCS Library.

29. Frear, *Mark Twain and Hawaii*, p. 25; Cracroft, journal-letter, May 21, 1861, Korn, *Victorian Visitors*, pp. 107–108.

30. *Polynesian*, January 12, 1861; Gregg, Diary, January 16, 1862.

31. Wight, *Memoirs of E. K. Wilder*, p. 152; Allen to Mrs. Allen, October 4, 1872, E. H. Allen Papers; Judd to Clark, November 25, 1872, American Board MSS, CCCLXXIV, No. 222, also in *Fragments II*, p. 239.

32. Probate 497, Supreme Court of the Hawaiian Islands.

33. Hattie Ellis (1854–1877) was "one of Hawaii's daughters, brought up as a daughter in the family of Dr. and Mrs. Judd. She ministered to them both in their last days" (HMCS, *26th Annual Report* [1878], p. 23). She died at Sweet Home and was buried in the Judd family plot in Nuuanu Cemetery.

34. *Hawaiian Gazette*, January 15, January 29, and February 19, 1873.

35. *Pacific Commercial Advertiser*, April 26, 1873; Judd to Wilder, July 26, 1860; E. K. to S. G. Wilder, September 9, 1860; Betsey Judd to Wilder, September 12, 1860; Judd to C. H. Judd and S. G. Wilder, February 16, 1863, in S. G. Wilder Papers; Judd to Anderson, May 1, 1861, American Board MSS, vol. CCCV, No. 133, also in *Fragments II*, p. 211.

36. Nordhoff, *Northern California, Oregon, and the Sandwich Islands*, p. 27. Mrs. Thurston was less than eight years older than Dr. Judd.

37. Palmer, *Memories of Hawaii*, pp. 5, 10.

38. Halford in *Annals of Medical History*, n.s., VII, No. 2 (1935), 163.

39. Agnes Hall Boyd Judd, Journal, July 13, 1873 (in the possession of Walter F. Judd of Kaneohe, Oahu).

40. *Ibid.*, July 13 and 14, 1873; *Hawaiian Gazette*, July 16, 1873; *Pacific Commercial Advertiser*, July 19, 1873.

Bibliography

Adams, Henry, *History of the United States from 1801–1817*. New York, 1889–1891.

Alexander, Arthur C., *Koloa Plantation 1835–1935*. Honolulu, 1937.

Alexander, Mary C., *William Patterson Alexander in Kentucky, the Marquesas, Hawaii*. Honolulu, 1934.

Alexander, Mary C., and Charlotte P. Dodge, *Punahou 1841–1941*. Berkeley, 1941.

Anderson, Charles R., *Melville in the South Seas*. [New York, 1939.]

Anderson, Mary E., *Scenes in the Hawaiian Islands and California*. New York, 1865.

Anderson, Rufus, *Memorial Volume of the First Fifty Years of the American Board of Commissioners for Foreign Missions* (4th ed.). Boston, 1861.

Arago, Jacques, *Narrative of a Voyage Round the World*. London, 1823.

Bagg, Moses M., *The Founders of the Oneida County Medical Society*. Utica, 1881.

————, *The Pioneers of Utica*. Utica, 1877.

Baker, Ray J., *Honolulu in 1853*. [Honolulu, 1950.]

Baldwin, Arthur D., *A Memoir of Henry Perrine Baldwin 1842 to 1911*. Cleveland, 1915.

Banks, Charles E., *Topographical Dictionary of 2885 English Emigrants to New England 1620–1650*. Philadelphia, 1937.

Barrett, Walter [Joseph A. Scoville], *The Old Merchants of New York City* (2nd ser.). New York, 1864.

[Bates, George Washington], *Sandwich Island Notes.* New York, 1854.

Beardsley, Frank G., *A Mighty Winner of Souls, Charles G. Finney.* New York, [1937].

Beardsley, Levi, *Reminiscences.* New York, 1852.

Beecher, Charles, ed., *Autobiography, Correspondence, etc., of Lyman Beecher.* New York, 1864.

Beechey, Frederick W., *Narrative of a Voyage to the Pacific and Beering's Straits.* London, 1831.

Bell, Herbert C. F., *Lord Palmerston.* London, 1936.

Bennett, Frederick D., *Narrative of a Whaling Voyage Round the Globe from the Year 1833–1836.* London, 1840.

Bienniel Report of the President of the Board of Education . . . for 1872. [Honolulu, 1872.]

Bingham, Hiram A., *A Residence of Twenty-One Years in the Sandwich Islands* (3rd ed.). Canandaigua, N.Y., 1855.

Biography of Mrs. Lydia B. Bacon. Boston, 1856.

Bishop, Sereno E., *Reminiscences of Old Hawaii.* Honolulu, 1916.

Bradley, Harold W., *The American Frontier in Hawaii. The Pioneers, 1789–1843.* Stanford, 1942.

British and Foreign State Papers. London, 1858.

Bronson, Henry, *The History of Waterbury, Connecticut.* Waterbury, 1858.

Brookes, Jean I., *International Rivalry in the Pacific Islands 1800–1875.* Berkeley and Los Angeles, 1941.

Brown, D. Mackenzie, *China Trade Days in California, Selected Letters from the Thompson Papers, 1832–1863.* Berkeley and Los Angeles, 1947.

Bryan, Edwin H., Jr., *American Polynesia.* Honolulu, 1941.

Bryan, Wilhelmus B., *A History of the National Capital.* New York, 1916.

Buley, R. Carlyle, and Madge E. Pickard, *The Midwest Pioneer: His Ills, Cures, and Doctors.* New York, 1946.

Buley, R. Carlyle, *The Old Northwest.* Bloomington, Ind., 1951.

Burke's Landed Gentry. 1952.

Cambridge History of British Foreign Policy. Cambridge, 1929.

Castle, William R., Jr., *Hawaii Past and Present.* New York, 1926.

Catalogue of Coins, Tokens, and Medals in the Numismatic Collection of the Mint of the United States at Philadelphia, Pa. Washington, D.C., 1912.

Catlin, George B., *The Story of Detroit.* Chicago, 1923.

Centennial of the Paris Congregational Church 1791–1891. Utica, [1891].

Clark, Joseph G., *Lights and Shadows of Sailor Life.* Boston, 1847.

Clemens, Samuel L. [Mark Twain], *Roughing It.* Hartford, 1884.

Coan, Titus M., *Life in Hawaii: An Autobiographical Sketch.* New York, 1882.

Cokayne, G. E., *Complete Peerage*, V. Gibbs *et al*, eds. London, 1910–.

Collings, G. H., *Commercial Fertilizers, their Sources and Use* (4th ed.). Philadelphia, 1947.

Colvocoresses, George M., *Four Years in a Government Exploring Expedition.* New York, 1852.

Cooke, George P., *Moolelo o Molokai: A Ranch Story of Molokai*. Honolulu, 1949.

Cooper, James Fenimore, *The Pioneers*. 1823.

Correspondence . . . in the Case of John Wiley. Honolulu, 1844.

Correspondence . . . on . . . the Subject of Richard Charlton's Claim to Land. Honolulu, 1845.

Correspondence Relative to the Sandwich Islands, 1824–1843. [London, 1843.]

Cross, Whitney R., *The Burned-over District: The Social and Intellectual History of Enthusiastic Religion in Western New York, 1800–1850*. Ithaca, 1950.

Damon, Ethel M., *The Stone Church at Kawaiahao*. Honolulu, 1945.

————, *Letters from the Life of Abner and Lucy Wilcox*. Honolulu, 1950.

Dana, Richard Henry, *Two Years Before the Mast* (Everyman ed.). New York.

Dexter, Franklin B., *Biographical Sketches of the Graduates of Yale College*. New York and New Haven, 1885–1912.

Dibble, Sheldon, *A History of the Sandwich Islands*. Honolulu, 1909.

Doyle, Emma L., *Makua Laiana, The Story of Lorenzo Lyons*. Honolulu, 1945.

Drury, Clifford M., *Marcus Whitman, M.D., Pioneer and Martyr*. Caldwell, Ida., 1937.

Dulles, Foster R., *America in the Pacific: A Century of Expansion*. Boston and New York, 1938.

[Durant, Samuel W., and H. B. Pierce], *History of Oakland County, Michigan*. Philadelphia, 1877.

Durant, Samuel W., and P. A., *History of Oneida County*. Philadelphia, 1878.

Dutton, Meiric K., *William L. Lee*. Honolulu, 1953.

————, *His Swedish Majesty's Frigate Eugenie at Honolulu*. Honolulu, 1954.

Dwight, Benjamin W., *The History of the Descendants of John Dwight, of Dedham, Mass*. New York, 1874.

Elsbree, Oliver W., *The Rise of the Missionary Spirit in America, 1790–1815*. Williamsburg, Pa., 1928.

Elwes, Robert, *A Sketcher's Tour Round the World* (2nd ed.). London, 1854.

Emerson, Oliver P., *Pioneer Days in Hawaii*. New York, 1928.

Extracts from the Letters and Journals of Daniel Wheeler. Philadelphia, 1840.

Extracts from the Minutes of a General Meeting of the Sandwich Islands Mission, Held at Honolulu, June, 1832. Oahu, 1832.

Farrell, Andrew, *The Story of Iolani Palace*. Honolulu, 1936.

Fish, Lester W., *The Fish Family in England and America*. Rutland, Vt., [1948].

Foreign Relations of the United States, 1894. Washington, 1895.

Fowler, Philemon H., *Historical Sketch of Presbyterianism within the Bounds of the Synod of Central New York*. Utica, 1877.

Fox. Dixon R., *Yankees and Yorkers*. New York, 1940.

Frear, Mary D., *Lowell and Abigail: A Realistic Idyll*. New Haven, 1934.

————, *Our Familiar Island Trees*. Boston, 1929.

Frear, Walter F., *Mark Twain and Hawaii*. Chicago, 1947.

Fuller, Andrew, *The Gospel its own Witness*. New York, 1800.

Furnas, Joseph C., *Anatomy of Paradise: Hawaii and the Islands of the South Seas*. New York, [1948].

Furnivall, John S., *Colonial Policy and Practice*. New York, 1956.

Gridley, A. D., *History of the Town of Kirkland, New York*. New York, 1874.

Gulick, Addison, *Evolutionist and Missionary John Thomas Gulick*. Chicago, 1932.

Gulick, Rev., and Mrs. Orramel, *The Pilgrims of Hawaii*. New York, 1918.

Halford, Francis J., *9 Doctors & God*. Honolulu, 1954.

Hamilton, Holman, *Zachary Taylor, Soldier in the White House*. New York, 1951.

Hammond, George P., ed., *The Larkin Papers*. Berkeley and Los Angeles, 1951.

Hastings, Francis H., *Family Record of Dr. Seth Hastings, Senior of Clinton, Oneida County, New York*. Cincinnati, 1889.

Hawaiian Mission Children's Society, *26th Annual Report*. [Honolulu, 1878.]

Hill, S. S., *Travels in the Sandwich and Society Islands*. London, 1856.

Hines, Gustavus, *Oregon*. Buffalo, 1851.

History of Enthusiastic Religion in Western New York, 1800–1850. Ithaca, 1950.

Hobbs, Jean, *Hawaii: A Pageant of the Soil*. Stanford University Press, 1935.

Hopkins, Manley, *Hawaii* (2nd ed.). New York, 1869.

Hunt, Timothy D., *The Past and Present of the Sandwich Islands*. San Francisco, 1853.

Hurlburt, Mabel S., *Farmington Town Clerks and their Times*. Hartford, 1943.

Instructions of the Prudential Committee of the American Board of Commissioners for Foreign Missions to the Sandwich Islands Mission. Lahainaluna, 1838.

Jarves, James J., *History of the Hawaiian Islands* (3rd ed.). Honolulu, 1847.

————, *Scenes and Scenery in the Sandwich Islands*. Boston, 1843.

————, *Why and What Am I?* London, 1857.

Jewett, Frances G., *Luther Halsey Gulick*. Boston, 1895.

Jones, Pomroy, *Annals and Recollections of Oneida County*. Rome, N.Y., 1851.

Judd, Laura Fish, *Honolulu: Sketches of the Life, Social, Political and Religious, in the Hawaiian Islands from 1828 to 1861*. Honolulu, 1928.

Judd, Sylvester, *Thomas Judd and his Descendants*. Northampton, 1856.

Knorr, Klaus E., *British Colonial Theories 1570–1850*. Toronto, 1944.

Korn, Alfons L., *The Victorian Visitors*. Honolulu, 1958.

Kroeber, Alfred L., *Anthropology*. New York, 1948.

Kuykendall, Ralph S., *The Hawaiian Kingdom 1778–1854: Foundation and Transformation*. Honolulu, 1938.

————, *The Hawaiian Kingdom 1854–1874: Twenty Critical Years*. Honolulu, 1953.

————, ed., *Hawaiian Diplomatic Correspondence in . . . the Department of State*. ("Publications of the Historical Commission of the Territory of Hawaii" I, No. 3.) Honolulu, 1926.

Latourette, Kenneth S., *A History of the Expansion of Christianity*. New York, 1937–1945.

Leff, David N., *Uncle Sam's Pacific Islets*. Stanford, 1940.

Leng, Charles W., and William T. Davis, *Staten Island and Its People*. New York, 1930–1933.

Leyda, Jay, *The Melville Log, A Documentary Life of Herman Melville 1819–1891*. New York, 1951.

Lind, Andrew W., *An Island Community*. Chicago, 1938.

Lucatt, Edward, *Rovings in the Pacific from 1837 to 1849*. London, 1851.

Lydecker, Robert C., *Roster Legislatures of Hawaii 1841–1918*. ("Archives of Hawaii Publication" No. 1.) Honolulu, 1918.

Lyman, Chester S., *Around the Horn to the Sandwich Islands and California, 1845–1850* (Frederick J. Teggart, ed.). New Haven, 1924.

Lyman, Henry M., *Hawaiian Yesterdays*. Chicago, 1906.

Mann, Horace, *Enumeration of Hawaiian Plants*. Cambridge, 1867.

[Markland, A. H.], *A Conspiracy on the Part of Garrett P. Judd and others, advisers of the King of Hawaii, to deprive Ladd & Co. of Legal Rights*. [Honolulu, 1846.]

McDowell, Caroline J., *Philip Judd and his Descendants*. Grinnel, Ia., 1923.

Mellen, Kathleen D., *The Gods Depart*. New York, 1956.

Melville, Herman, *Typee* (Everyman ed.). New York.

Memorial of Alfred G. Benson . . . [1855].

Memoirs of Rev. Charles G. Finney. New York, 1876.

Memoirs of General William T. Sherman. New York, 1875.

Minter, John E., *The Chagres: River of Westward Passage*. New York, 1948.

Morgan, Theodore, *Hawaii, a Century of Economic Change 1778–1876*. Cambridge, Mass., 1948.

Morison, Samuel E., *By Land and By Sea*. New York, 1954.

————, *The Maritime History of Massachusetts*. Cambridge, 1941.

Motion . . . made by R. C. Wiley . . . to release John Ricord . . . from a debt. Honolulu, [1853].

A Narrative of the Revival of Religion in the County of Oneida, particularly in the Bounds of the Presbytery of Oneida, in the Year 1826. Utica, 1826.

Neal, Marie C., *In Honolulu Gardens*. ("Bishop Museum Special Publication," No. 13.) Honolulu, 1948.

————, *In Gardens of Honolulu*. ("Bishop Museum Special Publication," No. 40.) Honolulu, 1948.

Nellist, George F., *The Story of Hawaii*. Honolulu, 1925.

Nordoff, Charles, *Northern California, Oregon, and the Sandwich Islands*. New York, 1874.

Obituary Record of Graduates of Yale University Deceased from June, 1890, to June, 1900. New Haven, 1900.

O'Donnell, Thomas C., *Tip of the Hill: An Informal History of the Fairfield Academy and the Fairfield Medical College*. Boonville, N.Y., 1953.

Official Correspondence with Le Chevalier Dillon. Honolulu, 1849.

Olmsted, Francis A., *Incidents of a Whaling Voyage*. New York, 1841.

Paine, Albert Bigelow, ed., *Mark Twain's Notebook* [1866]. New York, 1935.

Palmer, Julius A., Jr., *Memories of Hawaii*. Boston, 1894.

Parke, William C., *Personal Reminiscences*. Cambridge, 1891.

Parker, Mrs. E. M. Wills, *The Sandwich Islands as They Are, Not as They Should Be*. San Francisco, 1852.

Perkins, Edward T., *Na Motu: or Reef-Rovings in the South Seas*. New York, 1854.

Purcell, Richard J., *Connecticut in Transition 1775–1818*. Washington, 1918.

Record of the Descendants of Dr. Gerrit P. Judd of Hawaii. ("Hawaiian Historical Society, Genealogical Series," No. 3.) Honolulu, 1922.

Report of the Case of C. Brewer and Co. vs. John R. von Pfister . . . Honolulu, 1845.

Report of the Case of James Gray . . . Honolulu, 1845.

Report of the Minister of Finance. Honolulu, 1851.

Report of the Minister of Finance, April 28, 1847. [Honolulu, 1847.]

Report of the Minister of Foreign Relations, 1851. [Honolulu, 1851.]

Report of the Minister of the Interior, 1856. [Honolulu, 1856.]

Report of the Proceedings and Evidence in the Arbitration between the King and Government of the Hawaiian Islands and Messrs. Ladd and Co. Honolulu, 1846.

Report to the Stockholders of the United States Guano Company. New York, 1859.

The Revised Minutes of the Delegate Meeting of the Sandwich Islands Mission, June 4th to 20th, 1838. Honolulu, 1939.

Richards, Mary A., *The Chiefs' Children's School: A Record Compiled from the Diary and Letters of Amos Starr Cooke and Juliette Montague Cooke*. Honolulu, 1937.

————, *Amos Starr Cooke and Juliette Montague Cooke*. Honolulu, 1941.

Riesenberg, Felix, *Cape Horn*. New York, 1939.

Rogers, Henry C., *History of the Town of Paris and the Valley of the Sauquoit*. Utica, 1881.

Rollo, John H., *A Genealogical Record of the Descendants of Alexander Rollo*. Wilmington, Del., 1896.

Rosenberry, Lois K. Mathews, *The Expansion of New England*. Boston, 1909.

Royal Hawaiian Agricultural Society, *Transactions*, I, Nos. 1 (1850), 2 (1851), 3 (1852), and 4 (1853).

Rudin, Harry R., *Germans in the Cameroons 1884–1914: A Case Study in Modern Imperialism*. London, 1938.

Ruschenberger, William S., *A Voyage Round the World*. Philadelphia, 1838.

Schlesinger, Arthur M., *Paths to the Present*. New York, 1949.

Seeley, Thaddeus De Witt, *History of Oakland County, Michigan*. Chicago and New York, 1912.

Session Laws of 1858–1859, in *The Civil Code of the Hawaiian Islands*. Honolulu, 1859.

Seward, Frederick W., *Reminiscences of a War-Time Statesman and Diplomat 1830–1915*. New York, 1916.

Simpson, Alexander, *The Sandwich Islands*. London, 1843.

Simpson, Elizabeth M., *Mexico, Mother of Towns*. [Buffalo, 1949.]

Simpson, Sir George, *Narrative of a Journey Round the World, During the Years 1841 and 1842*. London, 1847.

Smith, Bradford, *Yankees in Paradise*. Philadelphia, 1956.

Sprague, William B., *Annals of the American Pulpit*. New York, 1859–1873.

Steegmuller, Francis, *The Two Lives of James Jackson Jarves*. New Haven, 1951.

Stevens, Sylvester K., *American Expansion in Hawaii 1842–1898*. Harrisburg, 1945.

Stewart, Charles S., *Journal of a Residence in the Sandwich Islands during the Years 1823, 1824, and 1825* (2d ed.). New York, 1828.

————, *A Visit to the South Seas, in the U.S.S. Vincennes*. London, 1832.

Storke, Elliot G., *History of Cayuga County, New York*. Syracuse, 1879.

Strong, William E., *The Story of the American Board*. New York, 1910.

Table of Consular Grievances, 1843–1846. [Honolulu, 1862.]

Taylor, Albert P., *The Rulers of Hawaii*. Honolulu, 1927.

Taylor, Fitch W., *The Flag Ship: or a Voyage around the World, in the United States Frigate Columbia*. New York, 1840.

Thurston, Mrs. Lucy (Goodale), *Life and Times of Lucy G. Thurston, Wife of Rev. Asa Thurston, pioneer missionary to the Sandwich Islands* (2d ed.). Ann Arbor, Mich., 1921.

Tracy, Joseph, *History of the American Board of Commissioners for Foreign Missions* (2d ed.). New York, 1842.

Trumbull, James H., and C. J. Hoadly, eds., *The Public Records of the Colony of Connecticut*. Hartford, 1850–1890.

Varigny, Charles V. C., *Quatorze Ans aux Iles Sandwich*. Paris, 1874.

Vincent, Frank, Jr., *Through and Through the Tropics* (2d ed.). New York, 1875.

Wager, Daniel E., *Our County and its People: A Descriptive Work on Oneida County*. Boston, 1896.

Walpole, Frederick, *Four Years in the Pacific in Her Majesty's Ship Collingwood from 1844 to 1848*. London, 1849.

Warriner, Francis, *Cruise of the U.S. Frigate Potomac*. New York, 1835.

Wight, Elizabeth L., ed., *The Memoirs of Elizabeth Kinau Wilder*. Honolulu, 1909.

Wilkes, Charles, *Narrative of the United States Exploring Expedition, 1838–1842*. Philadelphia, 1845.

Williston, Samuel, *William Richards*. Cambridge, Mass. 1938.

Wise, Henry A., *Los Gringos*. New York, 1849.

Wist, Benjamin O., *A Century of Public Education in Hawaii*. Honolulu, 1940.

Withington, Antoinette, *The Golden Cloak*. Honolulu, 1953.

Wright, Louis B., and Mary I. Fry, *Puritans in the South Seas*. New York, 1936.

Index

This book has been set in Monotype Garamond: text in 12 point leaded 1 point, extracts in 11 point leaded 1 point, Bibliography in 10 point leaded 1 point, Bibliographical Note and Notes in 8 point leaded 1 point, and Index in 8 point solid. Display type is Garamond in various sizes. Hand lettering and chapter numbers were designed by Kenneth Kingrey and executed by Kenneth Miyamoto. Reproduction was by letterpress on Warren's Olde Style Wove, substance 60; the end leaves are white Ticonderoga Textbook, substance 70. The cases were manufactured and die-stamped by Russell-Rutter Company, Inc., using Nelson-Whitehead Corporation's Komagami #161 paper on boards and Bancroft Book Cloth Linen Finish 1465 for the spine. Printing and binding were done by the Advertiser Publishing Company, Limited, under the supervision of Thomas W. Shootman, with monotype composition by Robert E. Emerson, make-up by August D. Castro, engraving by Raymond W. Reardon, proof-reading by Blanche Kort, Katherine Hyams, and James Y. Jay, presswork by Reinhold W. Julich, binding by William Nainoa. This book was designed for the University of Hawaii Press by Kenneth Kingrey and produced under the supervision of Aldyth V. Morris.